HOW TO MAKE

White Magic

HOW TO MAKE

White Magic

Working with the forces of nature for personal empowerment and successful spellweaving

CONSULTANT EDITOR:
RAJE AIREY

Contents

INTRODUCTION

Essentially, magic is the art of making things happen by drawing on the powers of the natural world. But even if we are not yet able to influence events, most of us retain a sense of the magical, despite living in an urban, technological society and, for the most part, out of touch with the natural world and its powers.

"Magic" is often the word we instinctively use to describe a stunning sunset, a leafy forest glade, or a wintry landscape transformed by a carpet of snow. It may also be how we refer to an idyllic time, such as a love affair or dream holiday, or to one of life's very special moments, such as the birth of a child or an outstanding achievement. All of these experiences, however diverse, have something in common: they touch us at our deepest core, enchanting, surprising and delighting us.

We may also use the term "magic" to express our sense of wonder and awe at creation and our place in it: the feeling that for this moment at least, all is right with the world. Magic is what can happen when we step outside our everyday reality to connect with something precious and much bigger than our "little selves".

THE OTHERWORLD

Regardless of time or place, magic is based on the understanding that behind the ordinary, everyday world, there exists another dimension, or "otherworld", a spiritual domain that is said to co-exist with the mundane. A realm of deities, spirits and other discarnate beings, it is also a place of knowledge and sacred power, and whenever we experience a "magic" moment, we are tapping into this dimension, albeit accidentally. In this context we can say that the word "magic" describes the inner nature of the beings that make up the universe – the spiritual part of all things that is cosmic and eternal.

The practice of magic involves making contact with this otherworld through special rituals and ceremonies, and because this world is invisible to the naked eye magic is often referred to as "the occult" (literally "concealed" or "hidden" in Latin). Magic then is primarily concerned with a spiritual experience of hidden worlds; this lies at its heart and informs magical practice.

REDEFINING OUR VALUES

In modern western society, with its emphasis on reason, logic and scientific enquiry, a living relationship with the otherworld has largely been lost. Although we are materially wealthy, many people feel dissatisfied with their lives; there is the feeling that something is missing

Sharing rituals and ceremonies with a magical partner can be a source of strength and inspiration.

Using the four Elements in your magic is one of the most obvious magical links to the natural world.

One of the most challenging and rewarding ways to practise magic is to use your mind to access other worlds and dimensions.

but we are not quite sure what. This condition has engendered a search for meaning and a spirituality that makes sense, and it is in this context that interest in magic is steadily growing.

Magic suggests that there is more to our world than can be seen with the naked eye, and that a rational and objective approach is not always the best way. In fact, to establish a relationship with the otherworld, it is necessary to put logic and reason aside, and to engage with the irrational, emotional and intuitive, or the forces of "unreason". Connecting with the world of magic means rediscovering the languages of dreams and visions, imagination and fantasy, myth and story, image and symbol and to be prepared to enter the unknown.

About this Book

The aim of this book is to give the reader enough information and practical techniques to enable them to establish their own unique relationship with the otherworld and learn how to use its powers for self-mastery. While there are many schools of magic, each with its own path and set of disciplines, this book does not adhere to any one particular way, but draws on material from a diversity of magical traditions, including shamanism, wicca and "high magic". An important central theme in the book is that to become a magic-worker involves responsibility – towards yourself and others – and teaches that magic powers should always be used for the greatest good of all.

The book is divided into two parts: the first part covers the basics of magical "theory" and tells you all you need to know before you begin practising magic. The first section of the book starts with important background information on some of the key principles of magic and includes a cultural overview of magical practice throughout the world. This is followed by detailed information on the magic-workers' toolkit, which includes herbs and spices, incenses, crystals and natural objects. It goes on to explain the significance of cosmic powers, such as the sun and moon and the four elements, before concluding with a discussion of how timing can affect your magic. The second section of the book is practical and includes detailed instructions on how to work with specific spells and rituals and create and nurture sacred space. Information on divination, including tarot and astrology, is also given, while a special section shows how to develop intuitive powers.

Hopefully, as you turn the pages of this book, you will discover how to step outside your everyday self and enter into a magical world full of self-discovery and adventure.

A magic circle, whether it is made of candles, a cord, or is one that you conjure up in your mind, will protect you from negative energies.

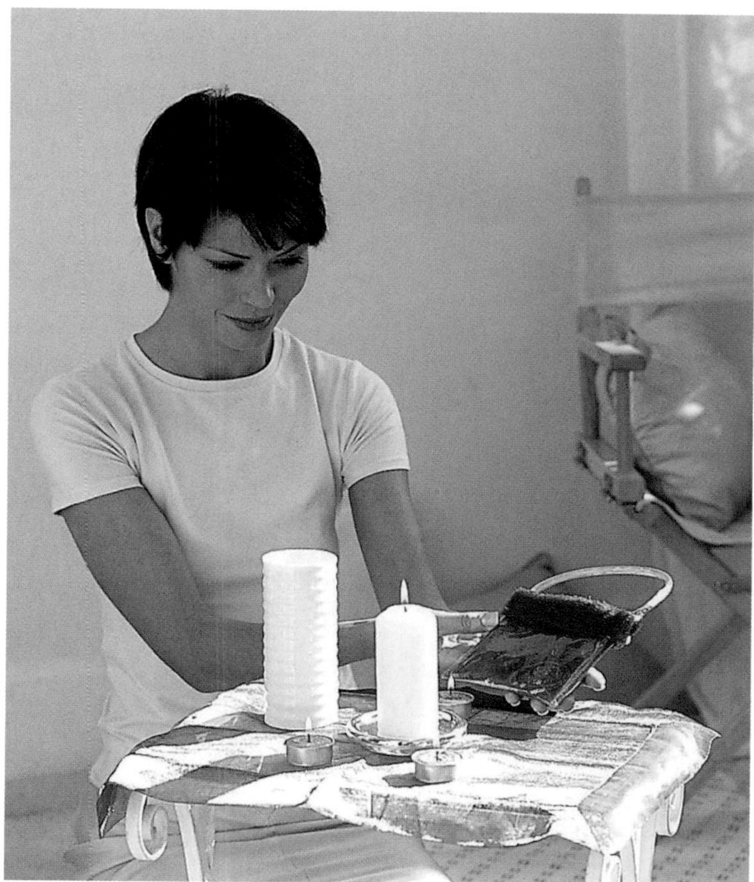

Learning how to choose your tools and ingredients is a key part of gaining magical expertise.

The natural world is full of its own special magic, and this book will help you access it, and become part of it.

APPRENTICED TO MAGIC

In days gone by, a magician might take an apprentice, a young novice as yet lacking in magical skills and knowledge but having the desire and potential to become a great magic-worker. Similarly, wise women passed on their knowledge to the next generation, teaching which herbs were safe and which were poisonous, and how to use "magic" to treat all manner of ills – or else to protect and empower. In this way, knowledge of the occult was passed on, often in secret, and over time a great body of magical knowledge has built up. Today, the written word has largely replaced this oral tradition, and we can rediscover some of this ancient knowledge through books, although of course many teachers of magic still exist. The first part of this book is designed to initiate the reader into the ways of magic. Take time to absorb and digest the information contained in this section – it will stand you in good stead when you come to put your knowledge into practice.

MAGIC AND THE SACRED TRADITION

Since the earliest times, magic has been practised in many different guises throughout the world, despite opposition from orthodox religion and mainstream society at various points along the way. Magic is an ancient art, and far from being something "bad" or "evil", it has played an important part in the psycho-spiritual development of the human race. To many, this may sound preposterous, yet if we look at cultures other than our own we can see evidence of "magical" thinking and how this informs the way people live. For instance, Native American Indians regard the Earth as a living spirit whose voice can be heard in the roaring, sighing or whistling of the wind. Consequently, they believe in treating the land with respect and living in harmony with nature's laws.

In this chapter we shall look at the link between magic and sacred tradition and how magical thinking is embodied in the myths and rituals that have played a central part in shaping human society. We shall look at the differences and similarities between different practitioners of magic – witches, magicians, sorcerers and shamans – and give a brief overview of some of the main schools of magic in existence today. Sacred places, various gods and goddesses, angels, fairies and spirit beings also play a special role in magic, but underlying almost all magical thinking is the idea that the universe is a living and interconnected entity whose energies we can work with once we know how.

The Origins of Magic

A medicine man of the Moquis people of North America performing a snake dance.

Throughout the world, human beings have developed a multitude of beliefs and practices to explain and give meaning to the cosmos. Almost without exception, early cultures evolved with a world view wherein magic and spirituality were inextricably bound, and in some parts of the world this is still true today. In fact, the word "magic" comes from the Greek *mageia*, which derives from *magoi*, an ancient Persian caste of priests who studied astrology and divination. Even before written records were kept, however, cave paintings dating back some 30,000 years indicate that our earliest ancestors practised what we would now call magic in the form of shamanism.

Shamanism

Claimed as the oldest spiritual practice, shamanism is still embraced by many small-scale societies around the world – from Siberia to the Amazonian region to Africa – albeit under increasingly difficult conditions. A shaman takes on the role of mediator between the everyday world and the spiritual dimension. By entering into a trance, he or she "journeys" to the otherworld in an attempt to resolve some difficulty or dilemma in the human domain. Shamanic cosmologies are frequently formed from three regions: a middle world corresponding to our everyday reality on earth; an upper world relating to the sky and celestial realms; and a lower or underworld, which reaches deep down into the earth. These three regions are connected by a central axis, and are often represented by a tree.

Most of the world's sacred traditions have been influenced in one way or another by shamanism. For instance, magic was very important in the Chinese royal-ancestral religion of the Shang and early Chou (16th–8th centuries BC), where the wu was a shaman or sorcerer who sacrificed to and invoked the spirits, and also cured physical and spiritual complaints or maladies by means of medicinal plants and spells.

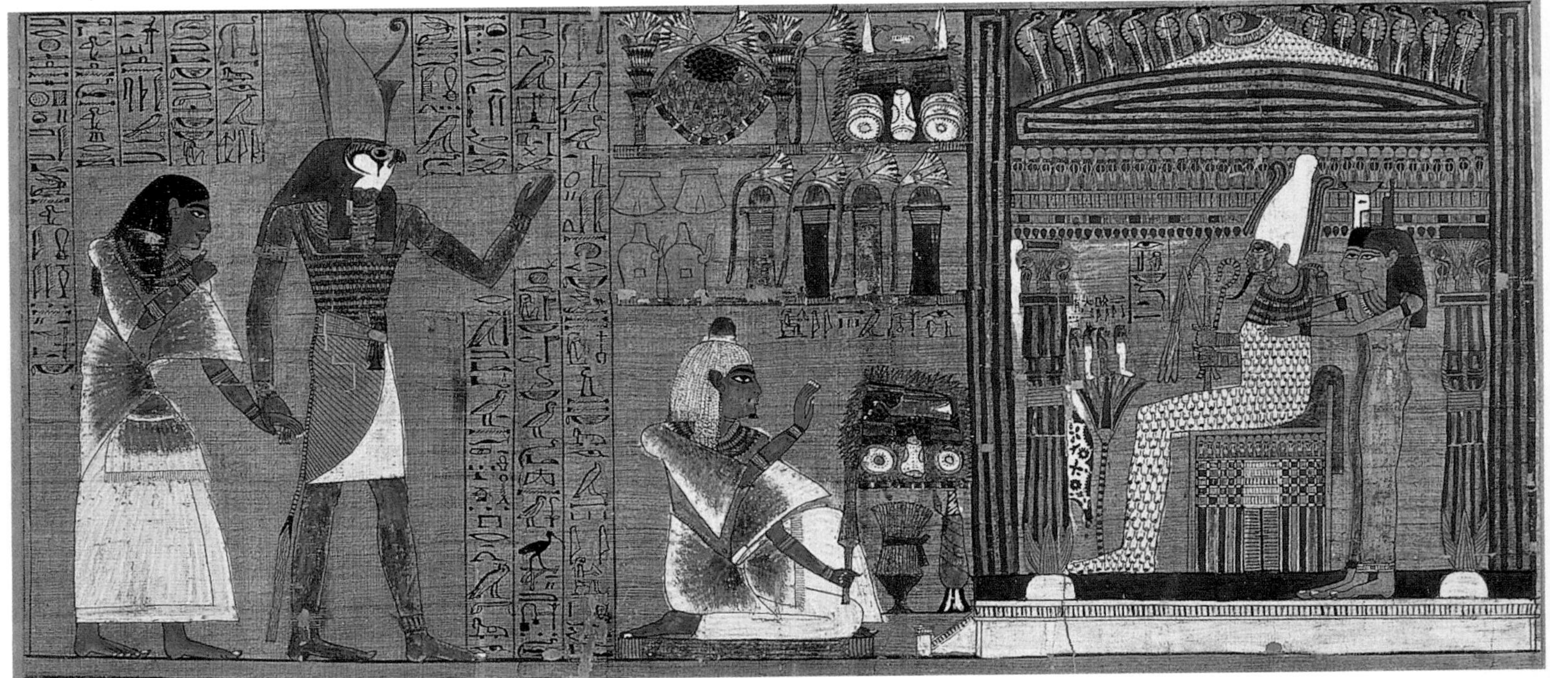
The beliefs of the Ancient Egyptians were expressed in complex creation myths involving the of deeds all-powerful gods and goddesses, and were administered to the people by priests, and later magicians.

Ancient Egyptian Beliefs

The dual development of magic and religious custom and belief became more sophisticated in ancient Egypt. Egyptian magic dates back to a time when the region's pre-dynastic, prehistoric inhabitants believed that the earth, the underworld, the air and the sky were populated by countless supernatural beings, some of whom affirmed life and were friendly while others caused death and destruction. Complex rites and rituals were devised to honour or appease these beings – the vast pantheon of Egyptian gods and goddesses – and temples were constructed in their honour. Priests became the guardians of a secret knowledge revealed by the deities to help humanity, and their books of spells and other magical formulae were safeguarded in temple and palace libraries. In popular tales, they were credited with the power to bring wax animals to life, or roll back the waters of a lake. The priests' role was eventually taken over by magicians (*hekau*), who carried metal or ivory wands as symbols of their authority and ability to summon and control powerful spirits.

Mainly concerned with healing and self-preservation, ancient Egyptian magic permeated every aspect of daily life. Rituals were conducted for all kinds of purposes – to protect the king, to safeguard a woman and her baby during childbirth, or even to help the dead in the afterlife. Egyptians of all classes wore protective amulets inscribed with magical symbols and the names of gods or pharaohs.

Destructive magic was also practised in ancient Egypt. It was believed, for instance, that foreign enemies and Egyptian traitors could be weakened or destroyed by inscribing their names on clay pots and figurines, then smashing, burning or burying these. Enemies of the divine order could be similarly cursed. For example, to counter the influences of Apophis, the chaos serpent, his image would be drawn on papyrus or modelled in wax and then spat on, trampled, stabbed or burnt in temple ceremonies; any remaining pieces were dissolved in buckets of urine.

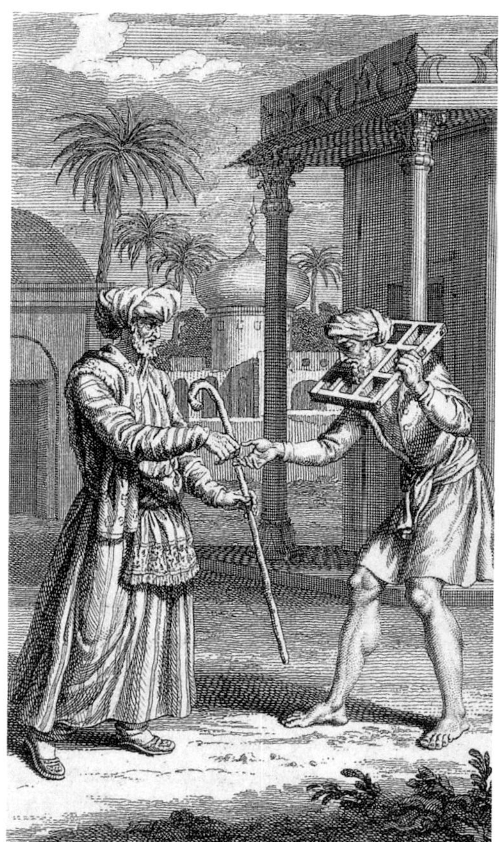

A Hindu Brahmin, wearing an iron collar, raises funds for a hospital.

A Brahmin shows his religious devotion by suspending himself over a fire.

Magic and Ritual in India

In India magical thought was inseparable from the sacred tradition. According to legend, the ancient sacred texts known as the Vedas (meaning "what is known" in Sanskrit) were revealed more than 4,000 years ago to 52 great rishis, or seers, during meditation. The Vedas praise and appease forces of nature and "higher beings", which are depicted as deities. A rich source of magical ideas, they reveal the unity of creation as a mysterious interconnectedness and co-dependence. Each bio-organism, element or species has a purpose within a larger scheme and is sacred, and reality is built up from various networks of affinities or connections, which can be evoked and controlled by human beings.

Magical Rites in the Indian Vedas

The ancient Indian Vedas are divided into smaller books, of which the Atharva-Veda contains a rich collection of spells and magical rites. These are arranged according to those concerned with positive welfare and the pacification of evil influences, and those directed against hostile powers or individuals. The priestly Brahmin caste, or class, performed the rituals, which were to do with restoring equilibrium rather than controlling nature. Their purpose was to keep the life processes of the universe moving and to maintain good relations with the powers of the unseen. They were held on special occasions, such as festivals, and for specific purposes, such as curing disease or exorcizing spirits.

A ritual might include divination and the manipulation of spirits or deities. Sacred sounds, such as a ceremonially uttered word or mantra, were often used in spells and rituals as a way of making contact with the hidden world. Many mantras were believed to hold so much power in awakening the spirit world that they could only be performed under the guidance of a guru. Extensive preparation – such as astrological readings, long recitations and a knowledge of how to regulate breathing – was also necessary before it was considered safe to use them.

Monotheism and Mysticism

Unlike the plural religions of ancient Egypt and India, Judaism and Christianity are monotheistic, holding a belief in one creator God who is separate from humankind. Both traditions officially condemn magic, describing it as evil and seeing it as a way of manipulating supernatural power for human ends. Islam also believes in one God, Allah, who is separate from humans: he has no likeness and is transcendent. He is believed to preside over two worlds: the visible al-Shahada, which is accessible to humans, and the unseen al-Ghaib, which is unknowable, mysterious and only revealed through divine revelation, such as miracles. However, both the Judaeo-Christian tradition and Islam have inspired unorthodox mystical traditions that teach that it is possible to be reunited with or to know God.

A 17th-century Indian painting depicts a mystical conversation between Sufi sheikhs.

The Cabbala

In the Judaeo-Christian tradition, a form of mysticism was developed that sought to reunite human beings with God. Known as the Cabbala (also spelt Kabbalah and Qabalah), this secret doctrine concerns the unexplained "mysteries" in Genesis and is passed on to initiates only. It contains a series of meditations on the 22 letters of the Hebrew alphabet and the four-letter name of God (Yod-Heh-Vav-Heh) and is a collection of the writings of various anonymous learned authors, the most important being the Sepher Yetzirah (Book of Creation), probably produced in Babylonia around 2,000 years ago, and the Sepher Zohar (Book of Splendour) written in 13th-century Spain.

Cabbalists believe that God created the universe in stages, with not one world but four. The "highest" of these is a world of pure light and closest to God, while the lowest is the everyday world we humans inhabit. In each world, creation moves through a series of ten emanations, known as "sephiroth" and symbolized by the Tree of Life, through which the infinite relates with the finite. By meditating on the sephiroth, a person is said to be able to link up with the greater plan of the universe and so become closer to God. Because the Cabbala challenges interpretations based on the scriptures and encourages a direct and unmediated relationship with God, it is regarded as heretical by orthodox Jews and Christians.

A pilgrim meets a messenger of necromancy, standing in a circle of Cabbalistic signs.

Renaissance Christian Cabbalists

During the Renaissance, some Christians interpreted the writings of the Cabbala as a means to bring higher angelic forces down to the ordinary world. Three magicians of this time were particularly influential. A priest and physician, Marsilio Ficino (1433–99), developed a system of "natural magic" that was concerned with drawing down the powers of the cosmos. His theory of magic was based on the guiding of spirit from the stars using the natural sympathies running through nature.

Giovanni Pico Della Mirandola (1463–94) was influenced by Ficino's natural magic but, in an attempt to increase its power, incorporated the mysteries of the Cabbala to tap the higher powers of angels and archangels.

Giordano Bruno (1548–1600) sought to return magic to what he saw as its purer pagan origin in Egypt. Bruno also used the Cabbala, but in contrast to Pico, who wanted to work only with angelic forces, he used it in attempts to unlock demonic forces.

People of the Masai gather underneath a tree at sunset. African traditions are closely linked to the land and its spirits.

Sufism

In Islam there has always been a strong emphasis on the difference between human beings and God, yet Sufism developed as a form of mystical training that aimed to overcome this distinction. Sufism (so called after the suf, or woollen garments, worn by its first practitioners) introduced an inner spirituality into Islam, proposing that the self and God could merge through the purification of consciousness. The idea of attaining union with God is seen by some as blasphemous and is rejected by more orthodox Muslims.

African Traditions

Although African cultures are very diverse, they are similar in the way they connect human beings (both living and deceased) and the natural world with a strong magical power. This power is viewed as a kind of vital force that flows through the universe and permeates all aspects of life. Some societies see it as originating from a creator spirit, and in many places the notion of a named supreme god is well established. The Janjero of Ethiopia, for instance, believe in a supreme being called Hao, while the Nupe of Nigeria say that their deity, Soko, is in the sky.

There is often a hierarchy of spirits in African tradition: from the nature spirits of rivers, rocks, trees and animals, through ancestor spirits, to divinities who derive their power from the creator spirit.

In the Lugbara cult, which is centred on the spirits of the dead, the living are seen to belong to the "outside" world while the dead belong "in the earth". If the dead are neglected, they punish their descendants by inflicting misfortune and sickness on them, and so need to be appeased by the living. Magical power is seen to come either directly from the creator spirit, or through the spirits of the ancestors, or as part of the invisible force of nature in the universe.

Voodoo

Essentially a fusion of African spirit beliefs with Roman Catholic Christianity, voodoo is today a peasant religion practised by 90 per cent of Haitians. The Christian God (known as Bondeye in Haitian Creole) presides over a variety of voodoo rituals, ranging from the lighting of candles to animal sacrifice, and sends down his loa (angels or spirits) in response. Voodoo ceremonies may involve ancestor worship, spirit possession, dance, song and drumming. When the loa takes possession, a new devotee has to be baptized and take holy communion.

Magic in Myth

A myth may be described as a way of explaining humanity's attempts to understand the universe and its place in it; it is a sacred legend or story, shared by a group of people and expressing their most important meanings. In Western cultures, mythology is often equated with fairy stories, the "unreal" or even falsehood, in contrast with history, which is associated with truth. However, myth has played an important part in magic by explaining how the world came to be formed, and by marking out significant relationships with ancestors and other beings. Many myths are celebrated and re-enacted through ritual and ceremony, and are used by magical traditions, both ancient and modern.

The mythology of Atlantis is based almost entirely on the imaginations of writers and artists.

Myth and Culture

It is impossible to separate myth from its cultural context. In ancient Egypt, for instance, all life was said to originate from the waters of the Nile, while Norse cosmology tells us that life was created through the union of fire and ice, with Ymir, the frost-giant, being one of the first creatures. Magic played a central part in early Graeco-Roman culture, too, and was a common theme in literary works, such as Homer's *Iliad* and *Odyssey*. The *Odyssey* in particular was recognized primarily as a book of magical deeds, and Homeric verses were used later as magical formulae.

Sir Galahad personified the chivalric ideal, and being noble in thought, courageous in action and pure in spirit was destined to achieve the Grail.

In early societies myths were often linked to religious ceremony and ritual. For instance, the Greeks practised a form of rites called "Mysteries" (the most famous being the "Eleusinian Mysteries"), which were known only to initiates. After a preparatory purifying stage that led a neophyte to a state of readiness, sacred objects were shown to him. It is likely that the myth of Demeter and Persephone was performed as a form of initiation into the process of life and death. Similarly, the myth of Isis and Osiris played an important role in the religious ceremonials of ancient Egypt, with the death of Osiris and the lamentations of Isis (his half-sister and wife) being re-enacted each year.

The Role of Myth

As well as playing an important role in the enactment of ritual and ceremony, myths also provide a moral and spiritual framework on which magical practice can be based. For instance, modern magicians who follow the Western Mystery Tradition (a form of magical practice based on initiation into secret knowledge) embrace the mythology of King Arthur, while the myth of Atlantis also has a very important position in Western magic.

The Arthurian Legends

Arthur is a Celtic hero, whose birth was made possible by the magical workings of Merlin, the magician. A blend of history has combined with oral traditions and myth, making Arthur and Merlin hybrids – historical people with mythological characteristics.

According to legend, Camelot was Arthur's famous court where he established a knightly order, made up of the greatest and most chivalrous warriors in Europe. Arthur and his knights became known as the Knights of the Round Table, named after a huge round table that was set up by Merlin, with places for 150 knights, all equal in rank and loyal to Arthur. In the Arthurian legends the knights embark on quests, venturing deep into primeval forests, which are metaphors for the soul's journey through uncharted worlds. The quest is an archetypal motif of a spiritual search for the soul. Its goal may be an individual, such as a maiden in distress, or a divine object such as the Holy Grail. The Grail itself is a complex symbol with many meanings. Allegedly the cup from the Last Supper used to collect the blood of Christ, it is a sacred vessel that symbolizes the potentiality of all wisdom, intuition and knowledge. It is also thought to be the source of creativity and inspiration, a magical chalice of transformation, a cauldron of rebirth.

The King Arthur stories offer magicians a range of heroic patterns or archetypes with which to identify in a personal quest for a higher form of consciousness whereby the individual soul is reunited with the cosmic source of all things, or the One.

The Atlantis Myth

According to legend, the "lost continent" of Atlantis occupied most of the area of today's Atlantic Ocean. Destroyed by natural disaster, the civilization was highly sophisticated, a pinnacle of truth and beauty. The Greek philosopher Plato (c.428–347BC) refers to it in his writings as a wonderful empire, pre-eminent in courage and military skill, that was destroyed by earthquakes and floods. He wrote: "and in a single day and night of misfortune all your warlike men in a body sank into the earth, and the island of Atlantis in like manner disappeared in the depths of the sea."

The myth of Atlantis forms an ideal vision of a golden age: a Garden of Eden before the Fall, when humans were in touch with divinity, and peace and harmony reigned. Many magicians share a great interest in the legend, some claiming to be in telepathic communication with the erstwhile inhabitants of Atlantis, and others having past-life memories of previous incarnations spent on the island. Today, the legend's power may be attributed to nostalgia for living in harmony with nature and the longing of the soul for perfection. Many people see magic as a path to reconnect with this ideal state of existence, while at the same time working on their inner, spiritual selves.

Demeter and Persephone

In Greek mythology, Persephone is the beautiful daughter of Demeter, the goddess of corn and the harvest, and Zeus, the mighty king of the Olympians. While picking meadow flowers, the young maiden was abducted by Hades, the ruler of the Underworld, who made her his queen. Consumed by grief and sorrow, Demeter searched for her daughter. The land became barren as crops withered and died and it became perpetual winter.

Zeus intervened, sending Hermes, the messenger god, to bring Persephone back. Persephone had eaten the food of the dead (in the form of pomegranate seeds), however, and so was not able to return to the upper world forever. Instead, she was restored to Demeter for two-thirds of the year only. Her arrival each year is marked by the rebirth of spring, but when she has to return to Hades for one-third of the year, the earth once again becomes barren.

The grief of Demeter is so intense and unremitting that it blights the world with perpetual winter.

MAGIC-WORKERS

Nearly all societies have some concept of witchcraft in which individuals are thought to possess a form of extraordinary power. A belief in witchcraft is part of a magical world view that sees inherent in the universe powers and forces that may be directed by certain people. These "magic-workers" have been called by many different names, most commonly witches, magicians, sorcerers, shamans or witch doctors. Having all manner of special abilities, they are thought to be able to change their shape, fly and sometimes trick and deceive. Often regarded as frightening, they have been the subject of folklore in numerous countries and used as scapegoats for unexplained or unexpected elements of everyday life.

A Zulu witch doctor depicted in an engraving from the early 1900s.

WITCHES

The word "witch" comes from the Old English wician, meaning "to cast a spell", but the meaning of witch and witchcraft changes from society to society and there is no neat and precise definition with which everyone agrees. In general, however, witches are usually female, associated with darkness and night-time, and with the reversal of normal human lives. Roman literature is full of references to a creature called a strix (a word of Greek origin meaning "to screech"), which flew about at night, uttering piercing screams and feeding on the flesh and blood of human beings. The Yoruba of Nigeria believe that witches are generally women who fly about at night and meet in secret places. In European folklore, a witch is frequently depicted as an ugly old hag, or else a beautiful enchantress, who uses her powers to allure and seduce. Witches are also commonly believed to have special spirit animals or familiars that perform services for them; typical examples include black cats, newts and snakes. They also have knowledge of plants and herbs, and they concoct their spells using a giant pot, or cauldron.

This photograph, c.1915, entitled Medicine Man, shows a North American Indian shaman.

Theories about how witches get their power vary. In some parts of the world it is thought that power derives from an association with carnivorous predators; gained through acquired knowledge or skills; or inherited, as in the African society of the Azande. At the time of the witch hunts in Europe (16th–17th centuries), the Christian church was convinced that a witch's power was the reward for making a pact with the Devil.

WISE WOMEN, CUNNING MEN

Alongside the idea of "bad" witches there co-exists the idea of magic-workers who use their powers for the good of the community. In the European tradition these are often referred to as "cunning folk", also known as wizards, wise folk, wise women or white witches. Once found in every village, these magical practitioners were commonly consulted for identifying witches (of the bad kind), fortune-telling, finding lost or stolen goods and naming the thief, as well as for providing remedies for a wide range of

The crime of practising magic

Over the centuries, thousands of men, women and children have been tortured, tried and condemned to death for the "crime" of practising witchcraft. In Europe, witch-hunting was at its peak from 1580 to 1650, a period when the growing strength of the Christian church coincided with the emergence of the modern nation state and new attitudes to science. Zealous Puritan ministers condemned magic, and witch-finders were appointed on behalf of church and state to seek out and try those individuals who were suspected of sorcery. The focus of the witch-hunting process was on finding so-called "Devil's marks" on the accused. In the United Kingdom, witchcraft remained illegal until 1951, when the British Witchcraft Act was repealed. Until then people could be tried and imprisoned; the last such case involved a spirit medium, Helen Duncan, who was sent to jail during World War II.

illnesses. In fact, many illnesses and misfortunes were attributed to the workings of spirits, so that a sick or unlucky person or animal was considered to be "bewitched". It was the job of the cunning worker to lift spells and to provide antidotes to, and protection against, witchcraft.

Shamans

Common in early traditions, and still practised by some societies in Siberia, the Amazonian region and Africa, shamanism is a tradition whereby an individual works magic for the benefit of the social group. Shamans use their power to communicate with the spirit world to protect the group from magical aggression and natural calamities. They also heal sick people, communicate with the spirits of the dead, find lost objects and predict the future. They can do this by entering a trance during which the soul leaves the body and changes, or shape-shifts, into spirit forms, such as various animals. This altered state enables shamans to battle with spirits or forces, or to gain valuable information.

Magical Medicine

The link between magic and medicine exists in many cultures and healers are often referred to as medicine men or women. A medicine may be used for more than healing the body, however. In many traditional African societies, for instance, magical "medicines" may be used to bring or prevent rain, to delay sunset, as an aid in hunting, for success in love affairs or to find stolen property, as well as for treating illnesses.

The medicine man, or diviner, may also use spiritual power in amulets or charms to protect individuals. The magic may also involve rites using medicines made from trees and plants, with the magician telling the medicines what he wants them to do. In most Bantu languages the term used to refer to a medicine man, magician, herbalist or shaman is nganga. The nganga goes into the forest to collect herbs, roots, bark, and plants for the medicine. Some nganga families have a tradition of healing that goes back many generations; the living members receive guidance from their ancestors, who speak to them in dreams, instructing them about which herbs to use and where to find them.

The link between magic and medicine has always been strong, and the image of the witch with her cauldron steaming on an open fire is a part of this.

Sorcery

A sharp distinction between witchcraft and sorcery is impossible to maintain. However, the latter is usually associated with maleficent magic, evil spells and injury, which some claim is purposely intended.

Magic in the Modern World

Today, Western magical practices, including modern witchcraft, offer a kaleidoscope of paths or techniques for attaining alternative forms of consciousness. Many of these, such as Western shamanism, have their roots in ancient practices, while others, such as Wicca, have been developed in more recent times for use in the modern Western world. All see the world in a spiritual way, perpetuating the link between magic and sacred tradition. There is no one right way to practise magic and many modern magic workers use a synthesis of techniques drawn from different traditions.

Ancient woodlands hold much power and mystery for many magical traditions.

Wicca

A far cry from either the type of witchcraft practised in small traditional societies around the world, or the diabolic type that was once so feared by the Christian church, Wicca is a modern form of witchcraft that venerates nature. Created in the 1950s by Gerald Gardner, it uses the structure of Western high magic ritual to worship the powerful forces inherent in nature and personified as various gods and goddesses. It has also reclaimed the word "witch" as meaning the resident "wise woman" or "cunning man" of the old European village.

Wiccans are usually members of a coven, or group, led by a high priestess and high priest. As independent bodies, covens follow their own path, although all have a series of rituals and prayers that are written down in what is sometimes called a Book of Shadows. Essentially, Wicca is a spiritual movement, based on witchcraft, but dealing with modern themes and issues. Many Wiccans, for instance, are ardent environmentalists and campaign in many ways to protect the planet's resources.

By returning to nature and ancient practices, Wicca offers a spiritual path for those searching for meaning in today's materialistic, fast-paced modern world. Wiccans are prevented from using negative magic through their adherence to the Wiccan Rede, or rule: "As thou harm none, do what thou wilt". Their rites and celebrations are centred around their oneness with life and the earth, and the passing of the seasons, and use many ancient magic symbols.

Paganism

Like Wicca, modern paganism is a religion that honours women, the earth, the dark and nature, all of which have been denigrated in Western society.

Gerald Gardner

An English witch, Gerald Gardner (1884–1964) is regarded as the founder of modern-day Wicca. He argued that witchcraft was an ancient, pre-Christian pagan mystery tradition and, after the repeal of the witchcraft laws in 1951, published *Witchcraft Today* (1954), which described witchcraft as practised in his coven. He also rewrote many rituals and charms for his coven's *Book of Shadows*, which he also published.

A pagan ceremony using the ancient magical symbols of the circle and the pentagram.

Summer solstice celebrations at Stonehenge take inspiration from ancient Celtic and druid traditions.

Pagans worship the Great Mother and the Horned, or Solar, God as supreme deities, above lesser gods and goddesses, and their year is defined by a cycle of sacred celebrations. They employ the seasons and tides of the earth, moon and sun to strengthen their spells, and work with the energy of the full moon. Some pagan witches function as individuals, performing their rituals alone. Others are members of a family or tradition, while many are initiated into covens and share meetings and festivals with a group throughout the sacred year.

Ceremonial Magic

The central ethos of ceremonial magic is based on the idea of spiritual evolution – the bringing down of higher angelic or elemental forces into the magician – which process is thought to enable the evolution of the soul. Ceremonial, or ritual, magicians usually follow one of the aspects of the Western Mystery Tradition, which goes back to the time of ancient Egypt. There are several schools. Many magicians follow the Cabbala, of which there are at least three branches – the Jewish, the Christian and the mystical or magical Cabbala. Others work with the Arthurian legends and the Holy Grail, or the Celtic, Greek, Roman or Egyptian traditions. Each school provides a framework of symbols, mythological stories of the deities, magical practices and a great body of inherited wisdom. As we forge our way into the 21st century, many magicians are involved with research, in a quest to develop new magical techniques.

Druidism

The esoteric origins of modern Druidism are located in the Western Mystery Tradition, with links to Atlantis. As catastrophe struck Atlantis, those magicians who had used their powers for selfish ends were engulfed, but those who had used magic to help humanity escaped the destruction due to their greater gifts of foreknowledge. These magicians journeyed eastward and westward, landing on the shores of Ireland and western Britain and the east coast of America respectively, taking their knowledge with them. Modern Druidism encompasses a wide spectrum of beliefs and practices, but a common love of the earth is central and fundamental. Communing with nature means learning to grow, to trust and to hear the response of the earth – nature as deity is drawn down into the ritual circle and is experienced as joy and love.

Western Shamanism

The 1970s saw the emergence of contemporary shamanism, also called neo-shamanism or Western shamanism, as a new form of spirituality emanating from the USA. The central precept of Western shamanism is regeneration and a revitalization of earth-based "ways of knowing". Inspired by the notion that shamanism is humanity's most ancient and authentic form of spirituality, many modern shamanic practitioners turn to what they see as a primordial means of healing and creating connections to nature. Practices include techniques for self-realization and making contact with an otherworldly realm of spirits. Some practitioners emphasize the importance of traditions, such as those practised by Native American Indians, while others place more importance on finding new ways of engaging with the living world.

The web of life

A web holds all kinds of mystical significance, and is often used as a magical metaphor.

Natural magic honours the earth and the physical body rather than a transcendental spirit. The idea that the physical body and all of nature are inherently divine and part of a larger whole is based on the underlying principle that everything in the universe is connected to everything else and that each part has an influence on the whole. In Anglo-Saxon times this magical interconnectedness was known as "the Wyrd", which translates as destiny, power and also prophetic knowledge. It may be visualized as a giant web in which everything links up with everything else along fine pathways or channels of energy. This view is backed up by modern physics, which essentially recognizes that we are living in an energy universe. Magic workers draw on the powers of nature to learn how to tap into this web in order to influence events – and this is what natural magic is all about.

Sacred for thousands of years for the Aborigines of Australia, Uluru is just one part of that culture's conceptualization of the dreamtime.

Connecting with Spirit

Spirit is the essence of creation, the unifying force that is present throughout the universe, the energy possessed by all things. Spirit not only connects us with each other, but also with animals, plants, rocks, water, air, the stars and the space between the stars. It is the skein of being beyond the physical, the otherworld that can be accessed for communication, healing and understanding. Using the symbol of the web, spirit is the first thread from which all other emanations are produced, creating webs within webs, or worlds within worlds, as we interact with our families, friends, workmates, wider social groups and physical environment.

The fundamental link in the web is energy. All of us are aware of energy on an instinctive level. For instance, we may sense the atmosphere or energy vibration in a room after an argument and describe it as thick or heavy. On a more subtle level, there is the instinctive feeling when we are liked or disliked by someone. Energy suffuses all things, but the energy of each part of creation vibrates at its own particular frequency. The extent to which we can be affected by these energetic communications depends upon how receptive we are. Learning about natural magic involves developing sensitivity so that we can attune to vibrations in other parts of creation, be they a rock, a blade of grass, a faraway star or another human being.

The Dreamtime

Aboriginal Australians conceptualize the "web of life" in a unique way. In their view, Australia is covered by a web of "Dreamings". The Dreamtime relates to a state of reality beyond the everyday, an otherworld in which ancestral creators travelled across the land, shaping it as they went. During the Dreamtime an all-encompassing law bound people and the natural world together as one organic whole, and it is through Dreaming affiliations and ritual associations that people remain connected to one another and to the land.

The Human Energy Field

Our first point of contact with the physical world is through the body and its five senses – touch, taste, sight, hearing and smell – and many traditions have seen the body as a microcosm of the macrocosm (the universe). During medieval and Renaissance times it was quite common to link the body's organs with cosmology: the astrological sign of Cancer (ruled by the moon) was associated with the upper chest, the sign of Leo (ruled by the sun) with the heart and solar plexus, and so on. These ideas are more sophisticated in the East, where it is understood that it is spirit, or energy, that suffuses us with life and that it flows through the body along invisible channels known as meridians, or nadis.

The subtle bodies

The aura (energy field) around the human body is said to comprise seven different layers, each layer vibrating at a higher frequency than the preceding one.

1. Etheric body: closest to the physical body
2. Emotional body: seat of the emotions
3. Mental body: mental activity, thoughts, ideas and day-to-day concerns
4. Astral body: "out of body" experiences; dream travel; journeying
5. Causal body: seat of willpower and gateway to higher consciousness
6. Celestial soul body: spiritual essence, the "higher self"
7. Illuminated spiritual body: cosmic unity, the One or the Divine

The chakra system

The chakras (energy centres) of the human body are connected with different colours, organs and levels of experience that encompass all aspects of life – from the mundane to the sacred.

Chakra	Colour	Governs	Concerned with
1st chakra: base of spine	red	skeletal structure, lower body	physical survival; ambition; security
2nd chakra: just below the navel	orange	bladder, circulation	sexuality; creativity; feelings, emotions; pleasure
3rd chakra: just below ribcage	yellow	adrenal glands, stomach	identity; self-confidence; personal power; desires and wishes
4th chakra: centre of the chest	green	immune system, lungs	relationships, compassion; personal development
5th chakra: at the throat	blue/turquoise	lymphatic, immune and neurological systems	self-expression; communication; trust
6th chakra: "third eye" at the centre of the brow	indigo	pituitary gland, central nervous system	understanding; perception; intuition; spiritual knowing; psychic abilities
7th chakra: crown, at the top of the head	violet, also magenta	pineal gland, ancient mammalian gland	openness; connection to higher energies and spiritual realms; self-realization

Subtle Bodies and Chakras

Oriental sensitives have documented the existence of seven subtle bodies (layers of the body's electromagnetic energy field, or aura) and seven energy centres known as "chakras" (from the Sanskrit word for "wheel") to which they are linked. A chakra is like an entry/exit point or gateway for each energy body, with each chakra roughly corresponding to its equivalent in the subtle body. As vortices of energy chakras connect us with the energies of the universe, and in this context the idea of an organ of the body being "linked" to a particular constellation of stars may not seem so far-fetched. Each one vibrates at a particular frequency and is connected with different organs, colours and qualities.

Developing psychic ability and fine-tuning sensitivity to subtle energies is especially connected with the 6th chakra, or "third eye", situated between the brows.

Chakras are wheels of energy in the body that are reflected in the world outside by nature's spirals.

Animism

Magic involves an animistic world view. "Anima" means "the soul", the innermost part or essence of a being and its animating principle. Animism is the belief that the world is profoundly alive and that all of nature – the trees and rocks, animals, insects and fish, and even the weather, as well as human beings, has vital essence. Everything that exists has consciousness. The consciousness of spirits can merge into human consciousness, and the soul of a living human is believed to become spirit when they die, becoming either an ancestor spirit or part of an elemental spirit.

Sacred Places

In natural magic, the earth is regarded as a sacred manifestation of spirit and, like everything else in the universe, it too is made up of invisible energies. Over time, the places where these energies were most powerfully felt became sacred sites, where people gathered to perform rituals and sacrifice offerings in order to give thanks, seek protection from harmful influences, and gain the favour of spiritual powers. In ancient times, rites of earth worship would have been associated with the times of year when the spirits were most active and their help most needed. Modern witches and pagans work with the seasons and the energies of the earth to forge a link with nature and all her powers.

The power and majesty of the pyramids has endured for thousands of years.

Sacred Sites

Many sacred sites around the world have special significance to particular communities: Stonehenge for Druids; Mount Olympus for the ancient Greeks; the San Francisco Mountains for the Native American Zuni tribe; the Black Hills of South Dakota for the plains tribes; the Great Pyramids for the ancient Egyptians; and Uluru (formerly known as Ayers Rock) for the aboriginal tribes of Australia. These sites are usually associated with the ancestors, gods or spirits of a given culture and are important to the community's collective psyche. Acting as gateways to the otherworld, such energy hotspots play an important role in natural magic.

Geomancy

The particular branch of natural magic that involves reading and relating to the subtle energies of the earth is known as geomancy. It is a core part of the relationship that all magical traditions have had with the environment and is intimately woven into the cultural fabric of indigenous people everywhere, be they Celt or Saami, !Kung or Inuit, Aboriginal Australian or Native American. Feng Shui, the Chinese code of geomancy that stems from the imperial culture of China, has become popular in the West and is widely studied.

Standing Stones

The oldest megaliths in the world are at Carnac in Brittany, France, where thousands of large stones are arranged to form avenues, chambers and mounds. Stone circles, the best-known of which is Stonehenge in England, began to be constructed from around 3000 BC. These mighty structures required huge resources of materials and manpower, and their survival demonstrates that those who built them certainly intended them to be permanent structures.

Megaliths may have had astronomical as well as spiritual significance, and it is likely that priests attended them and used them for measuring time, foretelling eclipses and predicting the movement of the stars. A prehistoric burial chamber surrounded by a circle of 12 great stones in Newgrange, Ireland, is an excellent example. At the winter solstice, the rising sun shines directly into the passage to the chamber, while the circle stones, which are carved with magical symbols recording the movements of the sun, moon and planets, are aligned with sunrises and sunsets at the solstices and equinoxes. At a number of sites in North America large, wheel-like circles orientated to the points of the compass have been outlined in stone. Traditionally, people come to them to pray and leave offerings.

Early Christian churches and abbeys in Europe were often built on the site of, or close to, megaliths and stone circles, presumably in recognition of the sacred energies that were present there.

Holy Springs

Water is one of life's essentials, and when it flows underground it carries strong earth energy, which can be detected by dowsing. The point where water forces its way out from the depths of the earth is a powerful focus for energy, and natural springs are often associated with natural magic. Most of us have at some time tossed a coin into a well or pool while making a wish, and in many places local folklore claims that drinking or bathing in the water of a particular spring or well can help promote fertility or cure disease. Every year, thousands of people make their way to Lourdes, France, where the holy water is said to have cured many illnesses. The holy "chalice well" at Glastonbury, England, has also become a focus for pilgrimage.

The Power of Trees

Large trees are also powerful energy centres, and their sheer size reminds us of the enduring presence of nature and can help to put our human life span into perspective. A great mature tree, with roots locked deep in the earth and

It is believed that megalithic monuments such as Stonehenge may have had astronomical as well as spiritual significance. They were usually erected at natural power spots – places where earth energy is particularly strong – and were lined up to connect with the yearly movements of the sun and stars.

branches reaching up into the sky, can also help us to appreciate and celebrate the "connectedness" of creation.

The image of the Tree of Knowledge occurs in the mythologies of many cultures, such as Yggdrasil, the Norse world tree, and the holy trees that grow on the Japanese Mountain of Heaven. In ancient times, sacred groves were sites of worship and divination, while pagan aspects of tree magic lie behind the modern custom of bringing evergreens indoors at Christmas.

In hot and arid lands, where trees indicate the vital presence of water and therefore life, they were often honoured as fertility symbols and associated and involved with fertility rites.

A Personal Sacred Place

Many people find their own personal sacred space, somewhere that inspires a feeling of being part of creation, a place to meditate on the complexity of nature, feel its vitality and reflect on their own part in the immensity of the universe. There is no set formula for finding or nurturing a personal sacred place; each magician or witch has his or her own personal awareness of the land and therefore of the places where they feel particularly attuned to it. Some people are instinctively drawn to a traditional energy hotspot, while others seek a place that is uniquely special to them, such as a beautiful meadow or an ancient fallen tree in a glade. Although it seems more obvious to choose somewhere far from human habitation to connect with the earth's energies, the neglected hearts of cities and towns are just as important and have their own potency. Urban areas can offer healing and a new current of life-giving energy if they are located, cleared out, honoured and acknowledged.

GODS AND GODDESSES

A belief in gods and goddesses often originates from the pagan religions of ancient times, which acknowledge both a male and a female aspect of deity. In many traditions, these are thought of as the Sky Father and the Earth Mother, personifications of the forces and powers of nature – the essential energies of male and female that combine to create life and are present in all aspects of creation. In classical paganism, these two energies were further divided into whole pantheons of gods and goddesses, each with their own powers and specialities. It is possible to work magic with an eclectic mix of deities taken from many pantheons, or to work within one tradition.

Lilith is a complex figure from Judaic mythology who embodies many of the characteristics and contradictions of the Dark Goddess.

ARCHETYPAL PATTERNS

While gods and goddesses occur in various guises in mythology and sacred tradition, they very often share essential characteristics, which gives them an archetypal or primordial quality that transcends time and place. They can be seen as archetypal patterns, a way of expressing the enduring themes of human existence. In the ancient Greek pantheon, for instance, Aphrodite is recognized as the goddess of love, and Hermes is the patron of messages, healing and teaching, yet to the Romans, they are Venus and Mercury respectively. The Anglo-Saxon sky-god Tiw (from whose name we derive Tuesday) can be identified with Tyr in Scandinavia, Tiwaz in northern Europe, Ziu in Germany and Dyaus in ancient India, as well as with the Greek Zeus and the Roman Jove.

SUN AND MOON DEITIES

In many traditions, the sun is a male god of light, and the moon a goddess with three faces. Encountered in several ancient religions, these deities form the foundation upon which much natural magic is based; they can also be thought of in terms of lunar and solar principles, or feminine and masculine energies.

The lunar principle is associated with the earth, fertility, the dark, gestation, growth and decay. Her powers include intuitive, non-linear thinking. Artemis (Greek), Diana (Roman), Isis (Egyptian) and Ceridwen (Celtic) are all names of different aspects of the moon goddess. The solar principle is associated with the heavens, with creativity, light, clarity and truth. His powers are reason and logical, linear thinking, embodying the principle of rational consciousness. Names for the sun god include Apollo (Greek), Re (Egyptian), Odin (Norse), Wotan (Teutonic) and Tawa (Native American).

Diana is the Roman manifestation of the maiden, one of the three aspects of the moon Goddess, and is associated with hunting, wild nature and the protection of women.

THE GODDESS AND THE GOD

In modern witchcraft, the divine is usually represented by two deities – the Goddess and the God – who take different names and forms. The Goddess is usually seen as having three dimensions, which correspond with the waxing, full and waning moon. These are her Maiden, Mother and Crone aspects, a trinity that is linked with the goddesses Diana (or Artemis), Demeter and Hecate respectively. When the Goddess is known as the Great Mother, she is the creatrix whose limitless fertility brings new life. Also identified with Mother

Nature, she can be destructive as part of her regenerative cycle of birth, growth, death and rebirth.

As Queen of Heaven, the Goddess represents the moon as the source of feminine attributes connected to intuition, emotion and psychic ability. Her divine feminine force is manifested in a polarity with the masculine principle, often portrayed as the Horned God, who has two aspects related to the waxing and the waning year. As both her consort and son, these two gods are rivals and in constant competition with each other for her favours. The union of the Goddess and the Horned God is described as a sacred marriage that transcends all difference.

Also known as Cerunnos, Herne, Pan or the Green Man, the Horned God is not to be confused with the Christian Devil, which is a demonization of pagan god forms. Horns were a common attribute of gods in ancient cultures, and those of the Horned God are a symbol of male authority and sexual potency.

The Dark Goddess

In addition to the Great Mother, modern witchcraft venerates many other goddesses. Some of these embody the dark and death as well as more obvious life-giving and nurturing qualities. Typical is Lilith, a hybrid bird-woman who according to legend was Adam's first wife but refused to lie beneath him. Uttering the magical name of God, Lilith flew away to the wilderness where she gave birth to demons. God sent three angels to bring her back to Eden, but she refused to return.

The figure of Lilith is perhaps the source of ideas about strix, or striges, owl-like creatures of classical and European myth, and later the prototype of the diabolical witch stereotype fostered by the Christian church.

Accessing Different Traditions

Perhaps the most accessible of all the pantheons are those of the classical world. This is because the Greeks and Romans had a written tradition, so their mythologies have been handed down to us largely intact. However, the Celtic gods and goddesses are also very popular, even though they come from an oral tradition. The King Arthur legends, the Mabinogion (a Welsh mythological epic) and many modern fantasy cycles inform the Celtic tradition. The pantheon of ancient Egypt is also widely used in magic. These deities took both human and animal form, like Bastet the Cat Goddess. The gods and goddesses of the Northern Tradition (Scandinavian, Germanic and Anglo-Saxon) are easily accessed, too, while most indigenous peoples also have a rich pantheon.

The gift of the goddess

By its very nature, magic depends on the development and use of our psychic and intuitive faculties – the 'gift of the Goddess'. Although the 'gift of the God', which represents the linear, logical and conscious faculties, is also important, the Goddess in particular needs to be reawakened. It has been claimed that the early agricultural societies in Neolithic Europe, which lived in peace with nature and focused on women, were dominated by goddess-worship until they were invaded by warlike Indo-Europeans, whose sky gods supplanted the Goddess. Subsequently, she has been sidelined by the emphasis placed on the God of the monotheistic religions of Judaism, Christianity and Islam.

The Horned God has many manifestations. In Greek mythology his name is Pan, but in all traditions he is associated with male authority and sexual potency.

ANGELS, FAIRIES AND OTHER GUIDES

Ideas about magic are often associated with spirit forms that are believed to inhabit the otherworld. These spiritual entities act as intermediaries between the ordinary everyday world and the enchanted realm, appearing in various guises, but commonly as angels, fairies or guides. Tales of fairies have often become mingled with tales of witches and sorcery, while angels are generally seen as high and pure spiritual energies that act as messengers, protectors and guides to humans. The concept of a guiding spirit appears in many traditions; the guide may be an angel, an ancestral spirit or that of any deceased person, a mythological being or even an animal.

Angelic beings emanate a powerful radiance. They can be called upon for healing and protection.

ANGELS

The concept of angels is familiar in the Judaeo-Christian tradition. Some, such as Gabriel, are mentioned in the Bible, and there are famous stories of individuals claiming to have been saved by angels. Angels predate the biblical period, however, and references to such beings have been found in the earlier cultures of Sumer, Babylon and Ur (modern Iraq). Angelic invocations form the basis of many ancient occult practices and individual angels are traditionally associated with various entities, such as

The attributes of angels

When calling on the power of the angels, use this guide to help you direct your plea to the right being.

Angel	Planet	Influences	Day	Colour	Symbol	Incense
Michael	Sun	Guardian and protector; encourages success with issues involving the maintenance of stamina or physical health	Sunday	Orange/red	Six-pointed star	Olibanum, frankincense
Gabriel	Moon	Protector of women and children; summon for fertility, healing and psychic abilities	Monday	Pale blue	Nine-pointed star	Myrrh, jasmine
Zamael	Mars	Protector and guardian guide to men; summon to protect against violence, to dispel negative opposition and for justice	Tuesday	Red	Five-pointed star	Tobacco, dragon's blood
Raphael	Mercury	Summon to protect during times of change and upheaval; travel; mental stress	Wednesday	Yellow	Eight-pointed star	Galbanum, storax
Sachiel	Jupiter	Summon for justice or to protect finances	Thursday	Purple	Square	Cedar
Anael	Venus	Summon for love, when conflict involves relatives or friends, where emotional harmony is lacking	Friday	Green	Seven-pointed star	Rose, sandalwood
Cassiel	Saturn	Summon for protection of property, land or possessions; to clear obstacles	Saturday	Indigo or black	Straight line	Myrrh

the seven ancient planets, specific days of the week, certain colours, incenses, symbols and powers. When an angelic power is called upon in making magic, it will leave behind a lingering protective energy and some of its special character.

Meeting your guardian angel

Everyone has a personal Holy Guardian Angel. You can try to visualize your own angel in the following way.

1 Light a candle and burn some incense. Sit with your eyes closed and imagine a long ladder reaching up to the sky.

2 Ask to see your angel, and as you do so, imagine one coming down the ladder.

3 Imagine your angel in as much detail as you can. Feel its angelic power flowing all around you. Thank the angel for its visit; it will fade away when it has blessed you.

Fairies

There are many types of fairies, including pixies, elves, lubberkins, goblins, hobgoblins, banshees, sidhes and leprechauns. Ranging in height from the size of a human being down to minute proportions, their appearance varies from extreme beauty to grotesque ugliness. The land of fairies, Faerie, is an enchanted world of captivating beauty, humour, mischief, laughter and love; it is also a world of darkness, ugliness, superficiality, terror and tragedy. It is an otherworld, a place of magical power that can reveal itself to certain people. Many fairies were believed to live inside hollow hills or barrows of the dead, which were thought to be entrances to the otherworld.

In Celtic folklore the fairy king and lord of the underworld is Gwyn ap Nudd, a wild huntsman who rides a demon horse in waste places at night accompanied by a pack of red-eared white hunting dogs. Numerous folk myths are associated with similar chases, usually referred to as "The Wild Hunt", with many different leaders, including the Scandinavian Odin, or Anglo-Saxon Wotan, and England's Herne the Hunter. The goddess Diana, later identified in Shakespeare's play *A Midsummer Night's Dream* as Titania, queen of the fairies, is also sometimes associated with this spectral rout.

Guides

Mythological figures and ancestral spirits are also believed to inhabit the otherworld, and can be called upon to guide and assist you when working magic. Which figures you choose to work with will be up to you and will depend to some extent on the culture or tradition within which you are working. For instance, if you work with the Arthurian legends, King Arthur would represent the master of mysteries, while the knight Gawain would be the defender of all that is right. The Lady of the Lake would be the guardian of the ancient mysteries and secrets, and holder of the Holy Grail; a pagan priestess, this dreamer and all-knowing visionary is mistress of wisdom. As the Arch Mage, Merlin would be the master of magic, ready to teach all who are willing to learn. If you follow Western shamanism your guide figures may appear as animal or totem spirits.

The spirit of a deceased loved one will sometimes appear to guide and direct you through the otherworld, while some people make contact with the powerful spirits of great teachers or magicians who lived long ago.

The land of Faerie is a place of enchantment and a popular subject in myth and legend. Rings of dew on morning grass are known as "fairy rings", a tell-tale sign that the fairies were dancing while humans lay sleeping.

Inner and Outer Worlds

Many people who have become disillusioned with the dogma and rules of organized religion have sought a more individual and less regulated direction. Attracted by the very personal approach to spirituality, many have turned to the old arts of magic. Although these are very old, they are quite simple, and can be mastered by anyone who has a little patience and application. To practise natural magic it is not necessary to belong to any particular group or to follow any particular path. It is about finding a spiritual source or way of working magic that has meaning for you. The best maxim is, "If it works, use it", but always followed by the adage, "So long as it feels right for you and harms none".

The expression "pearls of wisdom" is based on the understanding that wisdom is hidden deep inside us, just like pearls in an oyster shell.

Pathways to Natural Magic

You can choose to work magic within a particular tradition, or adopt a more eclectic approach, adapting myths and symbols that resonate with you at a particular time. Similarly, it does not matter if you see these otherworldly beings, the gods and goddesses, angels, fairies and guides as actual spirit entities or as archetypal forces, as symbolic representations of cosmic powers and energies. All witches and Wiccans are pagan in that they are individuals who venerate nature, but not all pagans are witches or Wiccans. It is possible to be a pagan Druid, a pagan follower of the Norse deities, or a pagan worshipper of the gods of ancient Egypt, Greece, Rome or of many ancient deities of other lands around the globe. If you dislike the idea of labels of any kind, it is also possible to practise natural magic without identifying yourself as a pagan at all – it really is up to the individual.

Meditation is a way of stilling our senses so that we are able to connect with our inner knowing, or intuition – one of the most powerful magical tools we have.

Tuning in to the Inner World

It is easy to assume that the otherworld is somehow "out there" and divorced or separate from us. Paradoxically, however, it is both within and without, for it is only by tuning in to our inner world, the deepest centre of who we are, that we are able to make a connection with the world of spirit, the etheric vibrations of the cosmos that are all around us. This connection thrives not on logic and reason, but on a felt sense, often referred to as our "sixth sense", or intuition. Intuition is our inner knowing; the word is derived from two Latin words that mean "to look" and "in", and it is through this "looking in" that we are able to know things that are "out there" directly, without having to reason or think about them. This is why the disciplines of meditation and creative visualization have always played a key role in the practice of magic. Both of these skills help to put us in touch with our inner world and increase our powers of concentration. It is concentration, or focus of intent, that helps to keep the desire of a spell or ritual in mind, and it is this that makes magic happen.

Meditation

In both the East and the West, meditation is practised as part of many ancient religions and cultures. This art of utter relaxation enables the practitioner to "drop" into that quiet, inner space deep inside. Essentially, it is a way of stilling the conscious mind; it involves letting go of everyday concerns and allowing the deeper, more subtle senses to awake and inform your conscious awareness. You can use meditation to put you in touch with your inner sense of power and creativity, and then with the gods and goddesses, angels and elemental beings – the partners of witches and magicians in their rituals. Unless you can withdraw from the everyday world for a few minutes each day, these archetypal forces will be unable to connect or resonate with you in any meaningful way.

There are literally hundreds of different ways to meditate, so you need to find one that works for you. Most meditation involves sitting quietly and focusing attention on an object, such as a candle flame, or on your breathing. It is also possible to meditate while lying down (provided you don't fall asleep) or even while walking or moving about, as long as you bring conscious awareness to every movement you make. Early morning meditation is generally better than late night sessions, but any time is good as long as it works for you, and you will not be disturbed. Your results will only become reliable if you persist with regular practice, so try to set aside at least 15 minutes each day, six days a week, for a couple of months.

Visualization

To practise natural magic, it is essential to develop your skills in imagining, or visualizing, alongside those of meditation. As children, most of us are able to imagine quite well, but as we get older we tend to lose this ability. Fortunately, as with meditation, practice makes perfect.

The swirling smoke of incense, flickering candle flames and subtle scents are all used in natural magic as aids to meditation and to open up our senses to the otherworld.

There are various exercises you can try to improve your ability to visualize. A good way to start it is to close your eyes and imagine a series of simple objects in your mind's eye. For instance, these could include a ball, an apple, a tree, a flower, or even an animal. It doesn't matter what you pick, the aim is to try and see it in as much detail as possible.

A more complicated exercise is to close your eyes and see yourself travelling a particular route, choose one you are familiar with. See it in as much detail as possible, noticing any colours, signs, or other landmarks. When your attention wanders, come back and start again. Finally, another very useful visualization exercise is the Sphere of Protection described below. Practised regularly, it can help strengthen your aura while improving your ability to meditate.

The sphere of protection

Try combining the following visualization technique with your meditation practice to develop the two skills at the same time. Sit comfortably and close your eyes. Now imagine or mentally create a ball of white fire about arm's length in front of you. See it spinning and glowing strongly. See the ball begin to expand so that it surrounds you, below your feet and above your head, enclosing you in a sphere of brilliant light like a luminous bubble. Continue to imagine yourself seated within this rainbow-hued globe, and notice how it feels. To come out of the visualization, gradually let the image fade away and take a few deep breaths.

MAGICAL TOOLS

When practising natural magic there are a great many tools at the disposal of the witch or magician. Many of these are special objects that hold particular symbolism and magical power, and they are usually associated with the natural world in some way. These objects can be real or imagined, and are a personal expression of the magic worker. As you go along, you will build up your own collection of tools that have meaning for you. It is important to keep them safe and use them solely for magical purposes – in this way they will build up subtle vibrations of power that are uniquely attuned to you.

This chapter covers a wide range of equipment that can help you in your magical practices – from altars, shrines and robes to crystals and stones, and even mundane items such as pens, paper and furniture. It includes information on herbs and spices, trees, fruit and flowers, incenses and oils as well as preparing candles for magic. The symbolism of light and colour, as well as the traditional witch's tools (like the cauldron, broomstick and pentacle), is also discussed, together with information on charms, talismans and animal totems. The chapter finishes with the power of ancient symbols, such as the spiral, cross and circle, all of which are used in magic.

ALTARS AND SHRINES

We're all familiar with altars, and the term probably conjures up some richly decorated object that may be seen in a temple or a church, but of course they don't have to be like that. The earliest kinds of altars were open to the sky, with the smoke of burnt offerings rising towards the gods, and it was only later that they were enclosed in temples erected to honour specific deities. Like the hearth at the centre of the home, the altar was the focal point of sacred activity, where ritual took place. Altars have always played an important role in magic: they serve primarily to focus attention, turning it away from the mundane towards the sacred and the magical.

If you dedicate a permanent space in your home as an altar you can change the items on it to reflect your prayers and wishes. This healing altar enlists the cleansing energy.

A simple altar in which the yellow flowers, candle and burning incense represent the Air element.

WHERE TO PLACE AN ALTAR

If you are going to create a permanent altar in your home the first thing you need to consider is where to place it. In the Judaeo-Christian tradition, altars are positioned in the east of a building, the direction of the Holy Land (from Europe) and the rising sun. Similarly, whenever Muslims pray they face the Ka'aba in Mecca, Islam's holiest shrine, believed to be the site of God's first house on earth. You might want to follow the Wiccan tradition, however, and place your altar in the north, the compass direction associated with the Earth.

The altar should be in proportion with the space it is in, so do not create a huge one in a small room, or make it obstructive in any way. Don't clutter your altar with too many items, and keep it clear of dust and debris.

ALTAR SYMBOLISM

What you place on your altar depends entirely on you. You can choose symbols to represent the four elements of earth, water, fire and air using a stone for earth in the north, a bowl of water to represent water in the west, a lighted candle for fire in the south, and either some scented flowers, a feather, joss sticks or incense for air in the east. Represent the fifth element, ether or spirit, at the centre of the altar; a clear quartz crystal is a good choice. Square altars are said to represent the sky, while circular altars symbolize the earth. Most people have a selection of favourite objects that can be dedicated for use in magical work, such as statues or simple objects of beauty that have a special significance for them. For rituals or specific purposes, other elemental objects can also be added to your altar. These may include a centre lamp, salt for cleansing and purification, and some incense grains burned on charcoal.

A cup of wine or fruit juice and a platter of bread may also be positioned on the altar, to be drunk and eaten as part of the sacred meal during ritual.

Altars are best kept simple, with just a few well-chosen objects that have personal meaning.

Types of Altar

Big, brightly coloured altars are good for large places, and have a greater impact on the subconscious and therefore a greater power. Bright colours also have specific purposes, such as helping to improve creative powers. But small, low-impact altars have their own power and purpose, and a little personal altar, using something like a small table or a flat stone, can be easily placed in your home or garden. An altar does not have to be permanent: you can create small, temporary altars that serve a specific purpose or simply reflect how you are feeling at the time.

Whatever you use, and wherever you place the altar, look after it, keep it clean and give it your attention for a few minutes each day. This will help to focus your awareness and strengthen your spiritual connections.

Creating a Shrine

An altar is set out specifically for each piece of work, but a more permanent display is usually called a shrine. A shrine can be created in a small corner or on a tabletop; it may be indoors or outside (or both). The point is to create something that has meaning for you and helps you connect to the power of natural magic and focus your meditations. The objects you choose to display should be very personal, evoking a special response in you. Typical items that are often selected include a statue of a god or goddess, or a picture of an angel or other sacred symbol. Shrines displaying seasonal symbols, such as flowers, fruit or foliage, are useful to celebrate the festivals of the year; or if you are working with the phases of the moon, you can select different symbols to represent the moon in all her phases. These can be changed as time passes.

An outdoor shrine is sometimes referred to as a grotto. This is generally bigger than a shrine and should contain growing flowers and herbs, larger rocks, pieces of sea-washed wood and other pleasing items that help you connect to the natural world. Many people also like to include a goddess statue to symbolize Mother Nature and all her bounty.

Offerings

An altar or shrine is also a place to leave offerings. Offerings play an important part in magical rituals. When you make an offering you are exchanging energy, as well as giving thanks. It helps to reinforce your connection with the universe; the conscious intent, coupled with the physical action, makes this a powerful ritual. Typical offerings may include tobacco, a sacred herb for Native American Indians and widely used in their ceremonies and rituals, and salt, regarded as sacred by the Celts. You can also leave a small coin to represent material wealth, or natural items like a shell, a pebble, a single flower that you've gathered on a country walk. It doesn't really matter what you offer as long as it has meaning for you and your intent is clear.

An outdoor shrine can be something you maintain in your own garden, or a way of honouring nature on the spur of the moment as you walk through the countryside.

ROBES AND OTHER EQUIPMENT

Since antiquity, those who have worked magic have worn ceremonial robes and used special equipment, and these still form an important part of a magic-worker's tool-kit today. The idea behind them is that such objects will facilitate the psychological transition from everyday life to being a worker of magic. Many of the tools also have a practical purpose and will be needed in rituals and spells. It is important that you set aside your magical clothes and equipment and only use them when making magic. Thus they will absorb the subtle energetic vibrations of your magical work and over time will become imbued with magical power. Keeping your clothing and equipment in a safe and private place, as well as keeping them clean, is also important.

A straight-backed chair, a small table and a box for your materials are important for magic work.

Sleeveless robes work well as magical garments as they leave the arms free.

CEREMONIAL ROBES

A special robe or other ceremonial costume is important to the working of magic. Although many people do just change into clean clothes for rituals, actually wearing a robe specifically dedicated to magic can really help put you in the right mood.

Traditional costumes are simple T-shaped garments, reaching to the ankles and with long sleeves, similar to a kaftan or kimono design. The important thing is that the robe should be loose-fitting so as not to restrict the flow of energy through your body. Ideally costumes are made from natural fibres, such as cotton, silk, linen or wool, as a reminder of your connection to nature.

Some organized groups have a specific colour or design, but for working on your own or with friends, a simple garment in any design will be fine. Some people like to embroider or decorate their robes; some have long sleeves, which may be wide or close-fitting (although the latter are safer when dealing with lit candles and fire); others are sleeveless or short-sleeved: really it is up to you to choose something that you feel comfortable in, but which you also feel is appropriate. Treat your magic-making clothes with respect, keep them clean and crease-free, and hang or fold them carefully when you put them away.

Making a Robe

The most basic robe can be a tube of material, with armholes but no sleeves, and a simple neckline that is big enough to put on over your head. All that is needed is a piece of material that reaches from your neck to your heels, and is wide enough to make two matching pieces for the front and back. Obviously the actual design will depend on how much skill you have at dressmaking, and how much time and effort you spend on decoration. The choice of colour will be important: let your intuition guide you when picking the fabric. If you need design ideas, historical costumes or stage-costume books can be a good source.

Temple or Sanctuary Furniture

As most people do not have the space for a full-time temple or sanctuary area in their homes, your temple furniture may have to serve a dual role. In this case, make sure you clean it before and after using it for magical work. If you do decide to invest in special furniture, it should always be chosen for its practicality. Don't be tempted to pay a lot of money for fancy items that may look good but won't work well in practice, or which are too large to be stored easily.

You will need a table for an altar, a comfortable and supportive chair (ideally one that has arms and is straight-backed) for meditations and inner work, and some kind of cupboard, chest or box in which to keep your equipment when it is not in use. Magical equipment should definitely be kept separate from other household items as this will help to increase its magical significance, and a special box or chest to keep it in is the one item that you should consider buying if you don't already have anything suitable. If you decide to set out a shrine to celebrate the changing seasons or moons, you will need a small area for a few flowers, symbols, statues or pictures to reflect the patterns of your own land and surroundings.

The materials that are needed for spells should be kept together and used only for magical purposes.

Filling a magic casket

Start to build up a store or 'casket' of general magical ingredients and equipment. Your casket can be a cupboard, chest or special box, or a collection of several different sized boxes, perhaps kept inside a cupboard. You can often find something interesting in a second-hand or antique shop, or perhaps you, or someone you know, can make something specially. If you buy something that has been used, make sure you cleanse it thoroughly first to rid it of any unwanted emanations from its previous owners. Ideally your casket should be made of wood or other natural material rather than anything man-made.

The casket will need to contain the following basic elements:

- natural sea salt (for cleansing and purifying)
- a length of white cord for casting circles
- a selection of incenses and essential oils
- candles in various colours
- special crystals, stones and gems of your choice
- a selection of dried herbs
- feathers
- gold and silver pens (to represent the sun and the moon respectively)
- silk and cotton fabrics in a choice of colours
- a variety of coloured threads
- good-quality natural paper (for writing spells)
- a goblet and platter
- a spell bag (a drawstring pouch for keeping spells in)

Symbolic tools

Several tools traditionally associated with magic-workers may seem archaic or stereotypical, but do have a number of functions and have not been bettered. They include the cauldron, wand, broomstick and pentacle, as well as the sword, athame or dagger. Also known as magical weapons, each of these instruments has a number of practical purposes and is richly imbued with symbolic meaning. Understanding this symbolism is essential if you are to work with these tools confidently and effectively, and successfully follow the well-trodden path of ancient magical practice.

The Cauldron

The meeting place of all four elements, cauldrons are used in nearly all traditions of natural magic. The iron pot itself represents the earth, the fluid it contains stands for water, the burning wood or peat below for fire, and the rising steam and aromas are air. In medieval times, most cooking was done in an iron pot hanging over an open fire at the centre of the home. The hearth had to be regularly tended and stoked up with fuel by the woman of the house and her cauldron was usually the focus of household life, providing physical nourishment and inner wisdom. Some women were sensitive to the strange patterns that might be seen in the swirling water, and some could see the future, or events happening far away, in the drifting spirals of smoke. Today, many witches do not have an open fire in their homes, so will light a candle in a cauldron to represent the hearth fire of old. If it is not possible to find a suitable cauldron, you can use a chalice or goblet to symbolize it.

If you have a small cauldron, a candle placed inside can represent Fire.

The Broomstick

Another vital piece of household equipment in days gone by was the besom, or traditional broomstick. It was made up of materials that were easy to come by, and many lands have their own simple versions. In Europe many besoms were made with birch twigs for the bristles, a handle of hazel, and a binding of willow withies. Each of these plants has magical associations: birch being linked to birth and beginnings, hazel to wisdom or far seeing, and willow to the healing power of the old Crone Goddess.

Once you have made a wand you can adapt it to fit your spell-making.

The besom, made of birch twigs, is still used as a magical tool by modern witches.

The whole implement was used domestically for sweeping the floor, and magically for clearing out any invisible disturbances from a place used as a magical circle. In the days when houses had earth floors, a circle would literally be swept into the dust, and this ring would form the limits of magical work. Modern witches sometimes still sweep the area they are about to use for magic, and may place the besom on the edge of the ritual circle to symbolize a doorway through which their companions may enter the sacred ring.

The Wand

Traditionally associated with wizards, wands are still much used by modern magic-workers. The simplest kind is a straight stick from which the bark may have been cut in a spiral or other pattern. Carved or painted, the wand basically is a symbol of the magician's power and authority to command the forces of

Making a wand

While witches mostly use simple wands – such as a plain hazel stick, perhaps carved with a spiral – you might also want to make a more elaborate wand.

you will need:
a willow stick, cut about 1 m (3 ft) long, 1.5 cm (2/3 in) thick
coarse sandpaper
fine sandpaper
PVA (white) glue
ribbons in the seven colours of the rainbow
a quartz crystal
copper wire

1 Strip the bark away from the stick and sand it down with coarse sandpaper. Sand again with fine sandpaper until the wand is completely smooth.

2 Glue strips of ribbon to the wand in order of the rainbow: red, orange, yellow, green, blue, indigo, violet.

3 Attach the quartz crystal to the top of the wand, using copper wire.

You can adapt your wand for different purposes by attaching small symbolic items to it, such as rose quartz for love, seashells for fertility, fresh mint for prosperity or holly and oak leaves for protection.

A pentacle is a five-pointed star. It can be painted on a surface or made from twigs.

The traditional tools of the Wiccan practitioner are the chalice (representing the cauldron), the athame (or knife), the wand and the pentacle.

magic. Sometimes it is used to mark a magical circle, either by physically scratching a line or describing a circle in the air, to create the "place that is between the worlds of time and space" where all natural magic is performed.

The Pentacle

The five-pointed star known as the pentacle has been closely associated with different kinds of magic and religious symbolism for thousands of years. It has been found painted on the walls of the temples of ancient religions, carved on the stones of Christian churches by the masons who built them, and used as a pattern for many stained-glass windows in cathedrals.

The five points of the pentacle are sometimes seen as symbolizing the head, hands and feet of the witch, and it is sometimes also enclosed in a circle, representing wholeness and oneness with the universe. Sometimes witches wear this symbol as a pendant or on a ring, traditionally in silver, the metal of the moon and the pagans' Goddess.

The Sword

Based on the idea that metal is a good conductor of energy, many witches use a sword to draw the magic circle. The use of a sword probably derives from ritual magic and freemasonry. In his Book of Shadows, Gerald Gardner, founder of the modern Wicca movement, refers to an athame, or black-handled knife, as "the true witches' weapon". It is used for drawing pentacles and may also be used for drawing the circle if you do not have a sword. A wand may be used in place of the sword or dagger if you prefer.

Magic symbols

The tools described here differ from those of a ceremonial magician, whose four magical instruments are the pentacle, chalice, sword and wand, chosen to represent the four elements of earth, water, air and fire respectively. These tools also correspond to the four suits of the Minor Arcana in a traditional Tarot deck.

DARKNESS, LIGHT AND COLOUR

According to the wisdom of ancient China, everything in the universe is made up of two opposite but complementary forces. Known as "yin" and "yang", these polarities are seen to represent certain energetic qualities that exist in all things to a greater or lesser extent. Yin is the female or negative polarity, and represents the forces of darkness, while yang is the positive or masculine polarity, and represents the forces of light. Neither yin nor yang is superior to the other and each contains the seeds of its opposite. The universe exists in a state of energetic tension between these two forces, each ready to transform into the other, just as day follows night. Magic is also based on this principle: the forces of darkness are as important as light and understanding these two polarities forms the basis of magical thinking. Colour, which is an important part of the magic-worker's tool kit, is essentially composed of more or less light.

Understanding and implementing the opposite, and complementary, forces of light and darkness will add power and depth to magic work.

THE DARK AND THE LIGHT

In Western culture, we tend to split the world into "good" and "evil", embracing all that is "good" while rejecting all that we see as "evil". In its turn, "evil" is associated with darkness, which has long been feared, for both rational and irrational reasons. Although darkness is negative – it is an absence of light – magic teaches us that it is an essential and profound part of life. The dark is associated with gestation, rest and renewal. Night-time is when we dream and drift into otherworlds that are as valid as the ordinary everyday world we consider reality. In magical thinking, the darkness represents Earth and the moon. It is the unconscious, psychic power, intuition, imagination, emotion, and irrationality; it is soft, yielding and feminine. The light on the other hand is associated with the sun and the Heavenly Sky. It is conscious awareness and represents reason and logic, ambition and the desire to forge ahead in the world. Like an arrow shooting forth, its qualities are focused, disciplined, hard, unyielding and masculine. A magic worker needs this power to have the intent to direct or focus energy.

Colours, when used in magic making, can have great energetic powers.

Nature's cycles of light

At sunrise, the sun low on the horizon is red. As it climbs into the sky, the widening angle with our point on the earth's surface allows more orange and then yellow light to reach the ground. Experiments have shown that red light increases blood pressure, pulse rate and breathing rate, and that these functions increase even more in orange light and reach their peak in yellow light. Our physiological response to light has evolved so that the rising sun stimulates us into activity and alertness.

Other experiments have shown a decrease in blood pressure, pulse rate and breathing rate when people are exposed to green light. As daylight fades the green light is subdued, and changes to the blue of evening, when relaxation increases further and is at its fullest in complete darkness. Night, or no-light, is the natural time of rest and reflection.

Colour chart

As each colour has its own distinct properties and effects, we can also use the vibrations of colour for particular purposes when making magic. Essentially this means we are working with the subtle interplay between the powers of light and darkness, with intense colours such as deep reds, purples and indigo blues having more darkness as well as different qualities from sunny yellows, sharp greens and bright oranges. Different colours are chosen according to the type of magic that is being worked.

Colour	Energy correspondence	Chakra correspondence	Useful for
Red	Stimulating, energizing	1st, or base	Low energy, sexual problems, blood disorders, lack of confidence
Orange	Cheering, enlivening	2nd	Depression, mental disorders, asthma, rheumatism
Yellow	Inspiring, helping mental clarity and detachment	3rd, or solar plexus	Detoxifying, hormonal problems (menopause, menstrual difficulties)
Green	Fresh, vibrant, harmonious	4th, or heart	Antisceptic, balancing, tonic; good for shock and fatigue; soothes headaches
Blue	Soothing, calming, promoting truth and inner reflection	5th, or throat	Insomnia, nervous disorders, throat problems, general healing
Indigo	Transforming, purifying	6th, or third eye	Painkiller, sinus problems, migraine, eczema, inflammation, chest complaints
Violet/ Purple	Regal, dignifying	7th, or crown	Love of self, self-respect, psychological disorders and scalp problems
Magenta	Letting go	7th, or crown	Emotional hurts and upsets, accepting life's problems
Black	Absorbing, secretive; night-time; the occult		Power and control; self-discipline
White	Reflecting, purity, innocence; day-time		Tonic; replaces all colours
Gold	Divine power, purity; the Sun		Depression and low energy; digestive disturbances
Silver	Cosmic intelligence; the Moon		Hormonal and emotional balance, calms the nerves

The Energy of Colours

Colour has always been associated with certain types of energy that are useful in magic. In the Middle Ages, colour was one of the correspondences used in magic along with planets, elements, spirits and angelic beings, metals, herbs, shapes and numbers. However, it was the German philosopher, dramatist, artist and scientist, Goethe (1749–1832) who combined scientific observations with metaphysical concepts, describing colour as an interplay of the polarities of light and dark. He saw colour as an expression of spirituality and a way of expressing the inner nature of humanity. His thinking influenced later theorists, such as Rudolf Steiner, who was influential in forming colour theories in the 20th century.

We know instinctively that colours affect us in different ways. We speak of feeling blue, being green with envy, red with anger, or in the pink when we are feeling especially happy. Each band of energy in the colour spectrum vibrates at a particular frequency that not only influences our mood, but also corresponds to the body's organs and energy systems. What is more, it is not necessary to be able to see to have a sense of these resonances of colour. Many blind people have developed their sensitivity to the subtle vibrations of different colours, so that they are able to identify colours without ever being able to see them.

CANDLES

Traditionally, candles have always played a significant part in magic and sacred ceremony and no altar is complete without them. They embody the positive symbolism of light as spiritual illumination, and a fragile candle flame is a powerful emblem of the individual soul, especially in times of darkness and difficulty. Other lights, such as oil lamps and lanterns, can have a similar reassuring significance, and a perpetual flame on an altar stands for the constant presence of the divine.

Lit candles represent the Fire element, but their colours and shapes can also be used symbolically.

CANDLE RITUALS

The lighting of candles is a simple ceremonial act that initiates and hallows ritual. It acts as an announcement of your intention to work magic, perhaps to revere your chosen spirit beings or gods, or to summon their presence to your work. It is common practice in many sacred traditions to light a candle and leave it to burn out before the shrine of a saint or deity as an act of devotion, symbolizing both prayer and sacrifice. Candles are also used to mark rites of passage, from baptism to funerals. Placed around a coffin, their light is believed to protect the dead from harm during the vulnerable time of transition from this world to the next.

The Christian feast of Candlemas (the lighting of candles) at the beginning of February was grafted on to the pagan fire festival of Imbolc, when all the candles that were to be used in the year ahead were blessed. Candlemas is a time of purification and a good time to clean or re-dedicate your magical tools and equipment. In pagan tradition, the candle flame represents the element of

Snuffing a candle flame, rather than blowing it out, gives greater power to the ritual or spell.

Colours for candles

When using candles in your spells or rituals, make sure their colour reflects the magic you are working.

White: enlightenment, healing, peace, purity; can be a substitute for another colour
Yellow: communication, concentration, movement
Orange: attraction, strength, luck
Gold: confidence, health, prosperity; honours solar deities
Pink: love, harmony, family, affection
Red: sexuality, courage, passion
Violet or purple: spirituality, inner harmony, wisdom
Indigo: cleansing, meditation
Blue: wisdom, inspiration, truth, healing; honours lunar deities
Green: love, nature, renewal, abundance
Brown: home, wealth, stability, family elders
Silver: secrets, psychic power, lunar magic
Black: conclusions; banishes guilt, regret and negativity

fire, associated with life, creative energy and passion. Blowing candles out is said to have the effect of blowing away your intent or desire, so it is best to let the candle burn down completely. If this is not possible, then you can pinch out the flame instead. For the same reason, incense sticks should be waved rather than blown before the altar.

Candle

Casting spells using candles is one form of basic magic that is quite easy to do. A spell is a set of words (sung, chanted, spoken or written) that asks for a specific kind of change to come about. Lighting a candle to signify you are beginning the spell, and then snuffing it out at the end, gives your spell definition and focus.

Another simple form of candle magic involves writing the name of something you wish for on a piece of paper and then burning the paper in the candle flame, so that the wish is carried away in the smoke. In another candle charm, a symbol of the wish is engraved in the wax. As the candle burns down, you may find that the melted wax dripping down its side forms an image to indicate how your wish might come true.

Once you have made up your mind exactly what you intend to achieve, you will need to set out a place to work and find a suitable candle and holder. If the candle is central to the spell, it is generally best to use a new one. You may also want to mentally conjure up your desired wish, or a symbol associated with it, and hold this in your imagination as you work your magic. For instance, if your wish is for a new job, then you might want to visualize your desired working environment and the kind of colleagues you would like to work with.

Burning a spell or blessing in the flame of a candle is one way to complete your magic work.

Preparing a Candle

A candle is often used as the focus for magic, but it needs to be properly prepared. For ritual use, candles can be empowered by "dressing" or anointing them with oil, to clean them of any unwanted energies and to personalize them to your needs. If you prefer, you may use a cotton bud to put the oil on to the candle rather than your fingers, particularly if you have sensitive skin.

1 Choose a new candle and an essential oil that corresponds with the spell. Take a few drops of the oil and "anoint" the candle with it. If the ritual is intended to send energy out, you should wipe the oil along the candle from the middle to the ends. If you are performing a spell that aims to achieve or attract something, wipe the oil from the ends of the candle to the middle.

2 As you concentrate on your aim, wind a length of narrow coloured ribbon around the candle to bind your intention to it. Choose a colour that corresponds with your magic.

You can now use the candle in a ritual to accomplish your will.

Psychic Atmospheres

You can use a lighted candle to see if the psychic atmosphere of an area is clear. Put the candle in a holder and stand it on a table or other surface away from draughts. Light it and notice how it burns. In a well-balanced room, the flame should burn gently with a small golden-yellow flame, flickering only now and then, perhaps in the natural movement of air in the room. If the candle flame splutters, burns blue, behaves erratically, jumps rapidly or sparks, or does anything else unusual and unexpected, it indicates a charged psychic atmosphere that would benefit from a space clearing.

Candles in sacred tradition

In the Catholic church, a prescribed number of candles must be lit before each mass, the number varying according to the solemnity of the service. However, the Christian use of altar candles was adopted from much older traditions. For instance, the ancient Egyptians used candles when practising dream incubation as a way of seeking answers; the questioner would sit in a cave staring at a candle flame until he saw a deity in it, then when he fell asleep, the deity that had been seen would provide an answer.

INCENSE AND AROMATICS

Like candles, incense and aromatics have a long tradition of use in both magic and sacred ceremony. In ancient temples, incense was burned to purify the atmosphere, focus the mind and calm the senses as well as to symbolically carry the prayers and requests of the worshippers to the gods and goddesses above. As it spirals up to the heavens, the fragrant smoke forges a link between earth and the heavenly realms, becoming a flight-path for prayers, spells and incantations to deities and angelic beings. Furthermore, each fragrance has its own unique properties, which can be used in magic to stimulate, relax, rebalance, transform or purify energetic states, as well as to influence possible outcomes. A working knowledge of aromatics is essential in the practice of natural magic.

Fragrant smoke gives atmosphere to magical ritual, and provides a link between worlds.

How Fragrance Works

Our sense of smell is registered in the part of the brain that is connected with memory, emotion and instinctive activities. Fragrance plays a very important part in controlling our feelings and responses: foul or acrid fumes repel us, whereas sweet or fragrant aromas tend to draw us closer to their source. This response is the basis for the choice of the different incenses and oils used in magic: just as they attract or repel us, some scents can be used to attract positive vibrations, and others to drive away negative influences. Similarly, some scents have a refreshing or energizing action, while others promote calm and relaxation; some aromas invoke sexual desire, while others quell it; some are head-clearing and encourage clarity of thought, while others promote dreams and intuition, creativity and inspiration. It is a matter of knowing which scents do what and learning how to use them.

Incense and Essential Oils

Deriving from the Latin *incendere*, meaning to kindle, incense is the term for the fragrant aroma that is produced when certain plant material is burned or vaporized. It is also the term for the actual material – typically resins and barks, herbs and spices, and essential oils. Essential oils are contained to a

Incense in ancient Egypt

The ancient Egyptians regarded fragrant resins as the life-breath of the tree that provided them, and placed them in graves to assist the soul's survival in the next world. Rites and prayers accompanied the creation of incense-burning mixtures and the recipes were recorded in "magic books". One of the most precious mixtures was kyphi, meaning "welcome to the gods", which was used as an aid to sleep and dreaming as well as for treating all manner of complaints. Frankincense and myrrh were two key ingredients of kyphi, while other substances, such as cinnamon, spikenard, sandalwood, coriander, raisins and wine, were added to make fragrant incense pellets.

Resins, such as frankincense and myrrh, produce impressive clouds of fragrant smoke.

greater or lesser extent in all parts of a plant and are believed to represent its "quintessence" or life-blood. These oils have always been imbued with magical, transforming properties. The ancient Chinese, for instance, believed that by extracting a plant's oils they were liberating its soul, and alchemists strove to find the elixir of life in these "magical" essences. It is the essential oil present in all parts of a plant that gives it its distinctive aroma.

Using Aromatics

You can use incense and essential oils in different ways – as ready-made sticks or cones, loose as resins or incense pellets, or by vaporizing one or two drops of an essential oil in a burner. You can also make up recipes to suit your particular needs, or take them from books. If you have the chance to try out single-scented incenses one at a time you will soon learn those that you like and those you don't, and which evoke the kinds of powers you require. You may find that the scents you like tend to fall into the same fragrance group or family. Fragrance families are a way of classifying scents according to their aroma as follows: floral, herbaceous, woody, spicy, earthy, resinous and citrus. Floral scents are sweet and flowery, and include rose and jasmine; herbaceous are the fresh "green" herbal scents such as rosemary or eucalyptus; fresh, uplifting citrus scents include bergamot and grapefruit. Woody, earthy and resinous scents are taken from bark, roots and resins, and include sandalwood, cypress and frankincense. Spicy fragrances include cinnamon and coriander.

A starter kit of magical scents and aromas would include resins and gums, as well as the more familiar incense cones and sticks.

White sage has magical and cleansing properties.

This is an ancient craft, but with a little experience you can create a selection of scents that will conjure up just the right mood and atmosphere for any ritual or celebration. Having a mixture of loose resins and barks, dried herbs and spices, and a range of good-quality essential oils is a good place to start.

Burning Loose Incense

You will need a suitable fireproof container for burning loose incense. A censer is a vessel designed for burning loose incenses and resins: a church thurible is ideal, although incense stoves made of clay and other materials are also available. You will also need the special charcoal blocks that are sold by occult supply houses. Light the charcoal with a match and leave it for a few moments. When the charcoal is hot, sprinkle on a very small amount of the incense mixture. A mere pinch will be enough to discover whether you like the smell and how much smoke it is giving off.

An incense kit

When building up a collection of oils and incenses, try to include as many different types of fragrance as possible.

Loose resins: frankincense, myrrh, copal, dammar, mastic

Wood barks: agarwood (also known as "aloes"), sandalwood, cypress, cedar, pine

Herbs and spices: star anise, cinnamon, cloves, sage, sweetgrass, rosemary, basil

Earthy: patchouli, vetiver

Florals: rose, lavender, jasmine, ylang ylang, geranium, tuberose

Citrus: orange, lemon, bergamot, grapefruit

Solar incense recipe

This multi-purpose loose incense will suit any healing ritual, or you can use it to celebrate a solstice or equinox. To make it, you will need a pestle and mortar.

1 Crush about 5ml/1tsp frankincense resin. Add a little crushed cinnamon quill, some marigold petals and a few drops of honey and orange oil.

2 Mix well until the texture is like breadcrumbs. Leave to blend for a few hours. Burn on hot charcoal.

Herbs and Spices

The use of herbs and spices in natural magic is centuries old. In the past, magic and medicine were inextricably bound, and in some parts of the world this is still the case today; for instance, in the Fipa language (spoken in Tanzania and Malawi) separate words for either concept do not exist. It is not difficult to see why. Plants are the basis on which all other life depends, providing us with life-giving oxygen as well as materials for other essentials such as fuel, food, clothing and shelter, together with healing medicines and mind-altering drugs. Knowledge of plant lore is the foundation on which shamans, medicine men and wise women have based their magic, using herbs and spices in healing potions to treat "dis-ease" and in spells and amulets to ward off "the evil eye", or negative influences.

An illustrated herbal can help you identify which plants are safe to use and which are poisonous.

Plant Medicine

In Western society our idea of a "medicine" is comparatively limited compared to many other areas of the world. In some cultures, medicines are not just substances that possess healing powers, but can also make people fall in love, appease the spirits, gain prosperity or do anything else that is sacred, unusual and imbued with magical power. In this context medicine means using the inherent potency of a plant to maintain, restore, attract or repel energies from a person, place or thing. This is because every plant has special attributes, some of which are helpful and have positive effects, while others may be dangerous.

Collections of dried herbs should be kept in airtight containers and thrown away if they lose their scent.

In days gone by, knowledge of plant lore was passed on from generation to generation, particularly through the female lineage. Today, much of this received wisdom has been lost, so we need to re-educate ourselves in order to learn about herbs. Ideally, you can do this by finding a teacher who can show you how to recognize each plant, where it grows, how to cultivate and harvest it and how to prepare it in the most effective way. Many places now have herb societies that run training courses and there are also some very good correspondence courses available. Alternatively, a family member or friend may be able to pass on information, while a good, well-illustrated reference book can help you begin to learn how to identify what you are dealing with.

Once you know all about a plant and its properties, you will need to learn how to prepare it properly for use in herbal remedies and your magic work.

USING HERBS AND SPICES

There are a number of ways to use herbs and spices to give a spell its potency: they may be ingested in food, or drunk in teas, infusions or decoctions, and even used in bathing or steam inhalations. Knowing which part of a plant to use – leaves, fruits, roots or seeds – is as vital as knowing exactly which plant you are dealing with, especially if you are going to eat or drink it. As a general rule of thumb, any herb that is commonly used in cooking will be safe to use for any other purpose, although you need to learn its special properties before attempting to use it in magic.

DECOCTIONS

Spices are usually derived from a plant's bark, fruit, seeds or root rather than its leaves and flowers, and these tougher plant pieces need to be simmered or "decocted" in boiling water in order to extract their essences and magical properties. Use approximately 10–15g ($^1/_4$–1oz) dried spice to 750ml ($1^1/_4$ pints/3 cups) cold water, reduced to about 475ml (16fl oz/2 cups) after simmering. If you are using fresh herbs or spices, double up the quantity.

TALISMANS

Herbs are used as talismans in magic: St John's wort (*Hypericum*), for example, can be hung over windows and doors on Midsummer's Day to cleanse and protect the house, while cloves of garlic are a traditional protector against psychic disturbances or harmful presences. In folkloric traditions, strings of garlic are hung around windows, doors or even people, for protection.

OFFERINGS

Another use for some kinds of herbs, such as tobacco, is as an offering. Tobacco is seen as a sacred herb by the Native American Indians, and is left as a gift on altars, or burned in a flame as an offering. Salt is used in rituals in the same way, and also as a means of cleansing or grounding. White sage is also used as an offering by the Native American Indians, as the smoke it produces is thought to be specially pure.

Native American sacred herbs

For thousands of years, the indigenous people of North America have maintained a very close relationship with the plant kingdom. They use many herbs for healing, protection and blessings, but their four most sacred herbs for purification and protection are sweetgrass, sage, cedar and tobacco.

Sweetgrass: this is traditionally used for self-blessing, for keeping evil spirits away from the home and to purify tools and equipment, because its sweet smell calls up the good spirits. It is plaited into a braid, then the end is lit and the smoke wafted over magical tools or around the room.

Sage: a powerful cleanser and purifier, and Native American Indians have been known to sit on sage leaves in sweat lodges, thus physically being submerged in its purifying abilities. The leaves can also be used for smudging (burning and waving it where the purifying smoke is needed), either loose or in smudge sticks. The most effective types are white or mountain sage.

Cedar: an evergreen tree also known as the Tree of Life. It is a very powerful psychic and spiritual cleanser. Smudging with cedar is advised when conditions are particuarly difficult or obstructive, as its powers deal with the more problematic energies.

Tobacco: used for offerings to the Great Spirit and to the elemental and natural powers of creation. Tobacco is also cast into the sweat lodge fire as an offering to the fire spirits, and is sometimes given to elders and medicine men as a mark of respect.

Steep a handful of fresh sacred herbs in hot water to release their aroma and cleanse the atmosphere.

Trees, flowers and fruit

Even if urban living makes us feel removed from the natural world, a walk through a leafy forest glade, a summer display of garden flowers, shells and driftwood from a beachcombing trip, or a bowl of autumn fruits, all remind us of our connection with the Earth and can help us appreciate nature's bounty. As powerful emblems of nature, trees, fruit and flowers have their own attributes and symbolism. This symbolism has always played an important role in natural magic: the unique properties of each species are harnessed to create spells and charms and used in ritual and ceremony for a wide variety of magical purposes.

Flowers have symbolic meanings and play an important part in natural magic. A single blossom makes a stunning altar display.

The Beauty of Trees

Possessing a unique natural beauty, trees have a timeless quality. With roots reaching deep down into the earth below and branches rising into the sky above, they are a perfect symbol of our connection with both the underworld and the heavenly realm. Trees were used in the development of one of the first alphabets: the Celtic Ogham alphabet, consisting of horizontal and diagonal strokes, which were inscribed on pieces of wood. Wood rituals have been used for love charms all over the world. By walking through a forest and noticing how each tree is different, you can find something that speaks to your heart and soul and so can be used in creating natural magic. Remember that if you are taking a twig from a tree you must ask permission of the tree's spirit, and give something back in return. Also, bear in mind that wild flowers are protected by law, and must not be picked.

Groves of trees were sacred to the Druids and played an important part in their magic and ritual. Just by standing next to a huge and ancient tree you can feel its power for yourself.

Making a floral essence

Infuse your chosen tree or flower blooms by placing them in cold water and leaving to stand for several hours in sunlight. Strain off the water and add a preservative, such as brandy, vodka or vinegar. Use up to seven flowerheads to 300ml/ $\frac{1}{2}$ pint/1 $\frac{1}{4}$cups of water and 150ml/$\frac{1}{4}$ pint/$\frac{2}{3}$ cup preservative. The essence will keep for several months in a dark glass bottle, and you can use this when you want to call on a particular tree or flower for a spell. Many trees and their fruits are poisonous, so always check on a plant's properties before using its medicine.

Trees in Mythology

The symbolism of trees is to be found in sacred and mythological traditions all over the world. Through the symbolism of the Tree of Life in the Cabbala tradition, for instance, the universe is seen as encompassing different levels of reality at the same time. Northern European cosmology is focused on a world tree, Yggdrasil, the connecting point of nine worlds, each of which is populated by one race or type of being, such as giants, dwarves, elves, deities and humans. In Norse mythology, three sisters known as the Norns sit at the base of Yggdrasil weaving a web of fate called the Wyrd, where past and future are not separate but co-exist, world upon world, with actions in one influencing events in the other.

Flower Symbolism

With a long history as lovers' gifts, a "language" of flowers has evolved wherein we understand a flower in terms of its symbolism. They are a universal symbol of youth and gentleness, and an appreciation of their beauty has helped civilizations to flourish artistically since ancient times. The brief life of a flower encapsulates the cycle of birth, life and return to the earth to nurture the next generation. A single bloom is an expression of natural but fleeting perfection; gazing into one, you can find a peace and serenity that you can take into yourself.

Fruit and Rebirth

A universal symbol of nature's abundance and generosity, fruit represents the harvest, when we reap what has been sown. Each fruit also contains the seeds for the next generation. In this way fruits symbolize completion and endings as well as new beginnings, reminding us of nature's cycle of growth, decay and rebirth.

Magical Essences

It is possible to capture the vibrational pattern of a tree or flower in a magical essence. Such an essence may be used for healing negative emotional and psychological states as well as fostering the development of certain "soul" qualities. Several plant essence systems have been developed by sensitives who have attuned themselves to a plant's auric field (subtle energy field, or aura) and then noticed how this influenced their mood. The most well-known of these systems include the British Bach flowers, the Australian Bush flowers and the Californian flower essences, which are widely available. Alternatively, you can make your own essence.

Magical trees and fruit

- **Apple:** particularly associated with peace and the giving and receiving of love; "poisoned" apples represent seduction, wickedness and false knowledge.
- **Oak:** sacred in many traditions, including Druid, Judaeo-Christian and Norse; it is particularly associated with protection and endurance. Fruit: acorns.
- **Hazel:** tree of knowledge and wisdom. Hazel rods are traditionally used for dowsing, while hazel twigs woven into "wishing caps" were said to grant the wearer's desires. Hazelnuts have long been revered as the food of the gods.
- **Silver birch:** the "Lady of the Woods", a tree of enchantment, especially associated with feminine intuition and wisdom. The twigs were traditionally used to make brooms, with an ash or hazel handle. Fruit: catkins.
- **Willow:** represents forgiveness and acceptance; sitting in a willow grove was said to produce inspiration and visions.
- **Holly:** protection against evil spirits and lightning; used in dream magic.

Fruit is one of Mother Earth's gifts and a symbol of her abundance and generosity. Peaches are particularly associated with love magic.

Fairies and Dryads

If you pay close attention to a tree or plant's physical make-up you may start to notice various qualities or characteristics. Some of these may be visible, observed from the plant's physical structure – its shape, how it moves or how it sounds in the wind – while others may be experienced as a subtle resonance or aura emanating from it. In natural magic, this is attributed to the plant's guardian spirit, usually referred to as a dryad, wood-nymph or fairy. These elementals protect the plant and may also give us counsel when we approach the tree or flower with an open heart and honest intent.

Crystals and Stones

Treasures from the earth, crystals and stones are not only objects of great beauty, but are also storehouses of powerful energies that are of great value in natural magic. Created in the darkness of the earth, sparkling crystals are potent symbols of spiritual illumination, purity and durability. The word "crystal" is derived from the Greek *krustallos*, meaning ice, and to the ancient Greeks, all quartz crystals were believed to be fragments that had fallen from the perfect crystal of truth that resided on Mount Olympus, home to the gods. Gemstones have a long magical tradition, too. For instance, wearing emeralds was said to give protection against poison and negative spirits, while rubies helped those gifted with psychic powers to see into the future.

Choose stones that you feel drawn to when you are building up your own collection.

Magical Properties

As part of the earth's structure, crystals and gemstones are coherent, organized forms of matter. The properties of quartz crystals in particular are derived from their special orderliness and the stability of their atomic structure, which is not upset by outside forces such as heat or pressure, giving them unusual strength. Both crystals and gemstones are able to store, magnify and transform energy, emitting energy waves at natural frequencies that are in harmony with our own biological make-up.

Each type of crystal and stone has a particular vibration, derived in part from its colour but also from its atomic structure, which exerts a specific influence on our subtle energy system at the level of mind, body and soul. This is what gives crystals and stones their magical properties and their long association with ritual and healing.

Choosing Stones

It is very likely that you will be attracted to different stones at different times, depending on your need. The best way of choosing a stone is to let your intuition guide you rather than thinking too much about what it means. Often the stone you are first drawn to is the one for you, and it is better to check its magical correspondences afterwards, although some spells will call for specific stones. You can put your stones on your altar or shrine to lend power to your invocations, or else you can programme them for specific results.

The way crystals absorb and reflect light gives them a unique visual appeal.

Every crystal is unique in shape and size as well as magical potency, and using them will inspire your senses as well as engage your powers.

The colour properties of crystals and gemstones

The colour transmitted by crystals and gemstones is a particularly focused, powerful vibration. Remember that translucent crystals have a more pronounced effect than opaque stones. Use your intuition as well as the guide below to help choose the right stone.

Colour	Useful for	Crystals and gemstones
Red	Warming and energizing	Garnet, ruby, jasper, quartz
Orange	Shock and trauma	Carnelian, orange calcite, topaz
Yellow	Energizes solar plexus, reduces tension and anxiety, promotes confidence	Citrine, yellow fluorite, tiger's eye, amber
Light blue	Communication skills, immunity boosters	Turquoise, aquamarine, blue lace agate, celestite
Dark blue	Inner peace, calming the mind, developing intuition	Lapis lazuli, sodalite, sapphire, kyanite
Violet	Meditation, integration of the self	Amethyst, fluorite, sugilite
White and clear	Clarity, purification and order	Clear quartz, calcite and selenite energize, while moonstone and milky quartz are soothing
Black	Energy imbalances, focus awareness inwards, speed release of unwanted energies	Obsidian, smoky quartz, black tourmaline and haematite
Pink	Releasing emotional tension	Rose quartz, rhodonite and kunzite

Cleansing crystals or stones with incense smoke is especially suitable for magical purposes.

Cleaning Stones

Because crystals and gemstones hold energy, it is important that they are always thoroughly cleansed. Do this whenever you bring a new stone into your home, and keep your stone collection free of psychic dirt at all times. You may be able to detect negative vibrations in a stone by a feeling of heaviness or unpleasantness when you handle it, or you may suddenly feel an impulse to give your stone collection a thorough clean. Stones should always be specially cleansed before using them in a particular piece of magic.

To clean hard stones, place them in a bowl of salt water and leave overnight. Throw away the salt or salt water afterwards. A gentler method is to use pure spring water, or simply to leave the stone in direct sunlight. All hard or soft stones can also be cleansed using the smoke from incense cones or burning resin and smudge sticks.

Programming stones

It is possible to direct your conscious intent into a stone to help you achieve a result. This is called programming, and it is very simple.

- Take a clean stone of your choice and sit with it quietly.
- As you hold the stone, visualize your desire and see it entering the stone. As you do this, "speak it" into the stone.
- If you are working with any gods or angels, you could ask for their assistance to empower the stone, offering it up to their guidance. For instance, if you are working on a sleep problem, you may ask Hypnos, god of sleep and dreams, to empower your stone.
- Spend some time each day with your stone, or wear it throughout the day. Remember to clean it once you have finished using it for a particular issue.

Music and sound

Sound is a form of vibration that is at the root of our existence. It is one of our first experiences of life – the heartbeat is the first sound we hear in the darkness of the womb – and different sounds evoke different responses. For instance, we feel most at ease with naturally occurring sounds, such as waves breaking on a beach, a running stream, birdsong, or rustling leaves. Conversely, discordant noises and high levels of background noise, such as from traffic, or music we don't want to listen to, undermine the sensitivity of our hearing. The vibrations of sound – whether from musical instruments or the human voice – can be used in natural magic to summon spirits, dispel negativity and to cleanse, purify and heal.

Bells and chimes can be used to gently vibrate the energies in a room, and calm discordancy.

Vibrational Fields

Albert Einstein asserted that what appears to be solid matter is actually a dance of atoms in space, and when we look closely at our physical nature, this is indeed the case. All matter vibrates, emitting waves of energy, and within a certain range of frequencies we respond to these vibrations as sound. We pick up on these sound waves not only through our ears, but also through our vibrational energy field. The subtle bodies, the chakras, and the physical body all vibrate at particular frequencies. When these vibrations are out of balance, we are literally "out of tune", but certain sounds will help us to realign. When our energies are aligned we are empowered and are more easily able to manifest magical results.

Singing bowls can produce a variety of sound vibrations that can have a powerful healing effect.

Using the Voice

One of the easiest and most effective ways of using the voice magically is with mantras and chants. These sacred sounds have been used in ritual for thousands of years to create a harmonious inner and outer environment. In India, for instance, the sound of "Om" is said to contain the vibrations of the universe; it is the primordial sound from which all others arise. Tibetan overtone chanting is also very powerful, particularly when done with a large group of people. Teachers of this technique usually run regular workshops and courses, so look out for some in your area. One of the beauties of mantras and chants is that everyone can do them, regardless of their singing ability. However, if you have a natural talent for singing it is a good idea to develop your skills – you will have plenty of chance to use them in connection with magic at festivals, rituals and on ceremonial occasions.

Drumming

A well-known symbol of shamanism, the drum is also used in many sacred traditions. The beat of a drum carries primal memories of the heartbeat in the womb, and the Earth herself, reaching deep into the atavistic recesses of the human soul. The sound of drumming is

Rhythmic sounds, especially in the form of drumming, are used in shamanic ritual to summon the assistance of the spirit world.

helpful for entering a spirit body, journeying to the otherworld or accessing cosmic energy. The optimum drumbeat is around 200 beats per minute (bpm), so practise until this is your natural rhythm. The sound of rhythmic drumming helps to raise the Earth element. If it is played loudly and with authority, it also helps to dispel any unwanted negative energies.

The most desirable drum is one made by hand, using natural materials, because a well-made drum is a powerful tool, holding not only the energy of the materials used in its manufacture, but also some of the energy of its maker. Although it is possible to buy hand-made drums, a great deal of satisfaction can be gained from making one yourself.

Rattles

Together with the drum, a rattle has many associations with shamanism and is used in magic and sacred ceremony all over the world. The sound of the rattle is said to wake up the spirits and is a good way of opening a ceremony or ritual, naming those whom you wish to call upon. It is also a good complement to any singing or chanting. A rattle can also be used for healing purposes, to call in allies to help with a problem, or like the rattlesnake, to warn intrusive energies that they should step back and withdraw.

You can buy a rattle or you can make your own. A very simple version is to put a handful of dried peas in a jar or tin, but you may be able to find a workshop where you can make one from hide mounted on a wooden handle and filled with dried beans or pebbles.

Sounds and the Elements

Each element can be invoked by using particular types of instruments. Percussion instruments such as drums and rattles will strengthen Earth energy, while wind instruments, as one might expect, are connected to the element of Air. The Aeolian harp, which is actually "played" by the wind, has long been associated with magic. Stringed instruments, bells and crystal singing bowls are linked with water, while the brilliant sound of brass instruments invokes Fire. If you have no instrument, even hand clapping will generate sound vibrations and raise energy. As a general rule, fast or loud sounds increase energy, whereas quiet, slow, rhythmic sounds induce peace and tranquillity.

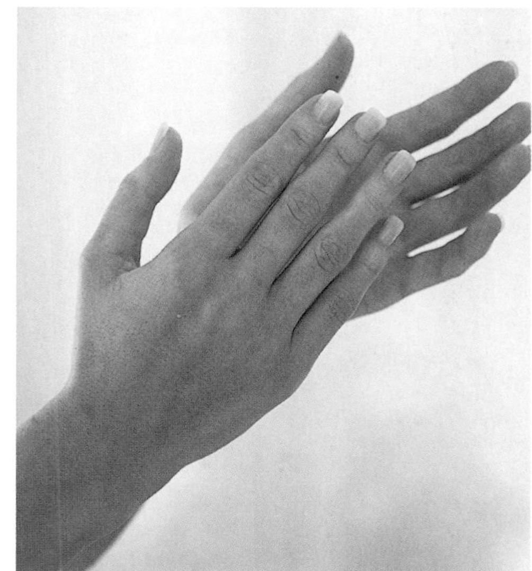

In the absence of any musical instrument, clapping the hands will raise Earth energy.

Mantra to Lord Shiva

The Om Namah Shivaya (pronounced 'Omnarmar Shiv-eye-yah') mantra to the Hindu deity Lord Shiva is a powerful way to clear negative vibrations, remove obstacles and to give you inner strength.

Light a candle and sit behind it. You may like to have a statue of Lord Shiva in front of you. Begin chanting the Om Namah Shivaya mantra rhythmically, and continue for at least ten minutes. If you have a mala (a string of 108 beads used in the Hindu tradition), you can perform the chant the traditional 108 times, moving one bead along with each repetition, or adapt a Christian rosary to help you keep count.

Animal totems

A totem animal could be any kind of creature, and each brings its own special characteristics.

To people who live close to the land and the natural world, animals have always had a great significance. All over the world, certain animals are thought to embody particular traits and strengths that are relevant to the history and geography of the particular culture. Because there is such a diversity of creatures and cultures, a number of animals have come to represent the same characteristics. For example, the tribes of the northwest Pacific coast of America revered the orca (killer whale) as a holder of great strength and wisdom, whereas to the plains tribes of North America, who had never seen a whale, that quality was fulfilled by the mighty bison. Animals can be adopted as a totem or emblem on an individual or group level and used in magic as allies or helpers, sharing their qualities to empower us and make our magic more successful.

Moon Animals

Certain animals have long and deep links with the moon and for this reason are often favoured as totems by natural magic workers. They include the wolf, hare, frog, cat, cow and owl, although any animal linked to water – such as various types of fish, for instance – will be pertinent to the moon to some degree. Moon totem animals can be carried as charms or talismans, which should ideally be made of silver, the metal of the moon. Dreams about any of the moon totem animals could well signify that an important change is imminent, or may signify a time of increased fertility (such as ovulation), a birth, the death of an old person, or a time for learning and growth.

Discovering your Totem Animal

If you feel drawn to the idea of enlisting the help of a totem animal you might want to follow the shamanic tradition and make a journey in your mind to find your own personal power animal. As with any kind of creative visualization, or mind travel, its intensity and power depends on how much mental energy you devote to the process. The more detail you add, and the better your concentration, the more real the experience will be.

Once you have found and made contact with your power animal you will be able to summon her or him whenever you need their guidance. Don't try and force an image into your mind, let your animal totem find you, whether it is a mighty eagle or a humble hedgehog it will have its own virtues and qualities.

When working with your totem animal, spend a few moments tuning in to its particular medicine. Bears have a strong connection to the earth.

The lesson of the wolf totem is about loyalty, trust and devotion.

The horse represents nobility of spirit, freedom and also endurance.

You can perform the following simple meditation to discover which animal is your totem at any particular time.

A MEDITATION FOR A TOTEM ANIMAL

Sit somewhere quietly where you won't be disturbed. Burn a little copal resin or incense such as sandalwood or frankincense. Attune yourself to the rhythm of your breathing, and as you do so, start to visualize yourself in a secret garden. This garden is your own special place and no harm can ever come to you while you are here.

As you sit in the garden, feel the warmth of the sun on your skin and a soft breeze through your hair. You can hear the sound of a fountain in the background. Now see yourself walk over to the fountain and a beautiful pool of water. Look down into the water and see your face mirrored back to you.

Keep looking at your reflection and as you do so, notice the image change from human to animal form. What animal is looking back at you? See it in as much detail as you can.

This is your totem animal. Carry its image with you as you step away from the pool and out of your garden, back into the room where you are sitting.

Animal symbolism

To get you started, the following list represents a few of the more common totem animals and some of their counterparts from different cultures. If you want to find out more, invest in a good book on the symbolism of animals.

Bear: lives fully in the summer, retreating in the winter to hibernate and renew earth-connection. Represents the receptive female energy, having the ability to go within to seek answers. A similar totem is the badger.

Bison: evokes the strength and wisdom of the elders, who are providers for and protectors of the people. Similar totems include the bull, the reindeer and the orca.

Coyote: related to the wolf, the coyote exhibits the trust, innocence and playfulness of the child that is present in all of us. It is also the trickster, and, through mischief, can expose pretensions and foolishness in others.

Dolphin: represents understanding and awareness, and is possessed of a gentle, loving energy. Similar totems are the manatee and the deer.

Eagle: associated with the ability to fly high and free, without fear and with the gift of far-sightedness. The eagle symbolizes the restless male energy and the quality of seeking and striving for higher goals. Similar totems include the buzzard and the condor.

Horse: runs like the wind and is capable of covering distance with endurance. The horse symbolizes swiftness, freedom and faithfulness. A similar totem is the elk.

Lion: the king of the jungle and a powerful hunter is associated with the powers of the sun. Proud, regal and dignified the lion establishes his authority and has few enemies. His consort, the lioness, a protective mother, nurturer and fierce hunter, is associated with the moon. Similar totems are the panther, tiger and other big cats.

Owl: hunts by night and is able to see in the dark, flying on swift silent wings. Symbolically it represents the ability to see that which is indistinct, to pierce the veil of reality and understand hidden truths.

Wolf: fiercely loyal and true, yet maintains its freedom and independence. The wolf is particularly associated with the psychic aspects of lunar lore. A similar totem is the hound or dog. Seek wolf medicine when in need of protection and support.

Cats in myth and magic

The cat has long been known as a "familiar" to magical practitioners, especially those who work with lunar magic – the cat is a symbol of the moon and represents her mystery. During the time of the witch hunts the black cat was relegated to the realms of sorcery. In mythology, the cat is associated with the Greek goddess Artemis, known in Roman mythology as Diana. In ancient Egypt, where harming a cat in any way was punishable by death, it was a sacred animal. The Egyptian cat goddess, Bastet, daughter of the sun god Re, was believed to have the power to ripen crops. Shosti, the Hindu goddess of childbirth, is depicted riding a cat, and Freya, the Norse goddess of love and fertility, rides in a cat-drawn carriage. Seek cat medicine when you want to improve your psychic abilities, or during psychic protection ceremonies.

Charms and Talismans

In natural magic, certain objects act as mystical "telephone numbers", summoning a specific power, be it god, angel, elemental force or a kind of luck. These mystical objects differ for witches and for ceremonial magicians. Witches tend to use natural objects as charms or amulets. Ceremonial magicians, however, make talismans specifically for their workings. Traditionally made using astrological principles and with particular thought for the purpose in mind, talismans are a means of drawing down the power of the planets into a scroll, or an object, which can then be used as a powerful magical tool.

Holey stones were used in witchcraft as a means of protection for animals.

Charms, Amulets and Talismans

A charm should be something from the natural world that you respond to, a simple stone you found that you felt compelled to keep for example, and can really be anything at all. An amulet is more likely to be a precious piece of jewellery that you can wear while you are working. A talisman is usually made for a specific magical purpose.

Magical Charms

Charms are always a natural substance, perhaps a plant that has a strange shape, such as four-leaved clovers, said to bring luck, or pebbles in the shape of an eye, which are thought to be protective.

Stones with natural holes in them are a classic example of magical charms. Known as holy or holey stones, these perforated flints or fossils were traditionally used to protect animals. The stones were collected from a beach or riverbank, and hung on red wool or ribbon over the doors of barns or stables to stop elves milking the cows, or to prevent the horses being stolen by night-hags during the hours of darkness. It was thought that the hole in the stone would trap any bad spirits. After seven years, the stones were thrown into running water so that any harm trapped in them could be washed away, then new stones were found and hung up.

Some fossils were thought to have magical powers: belemnites were believed to be "elf shot", arrows fired by spirits to make cattle sick; and ammonites were snakes turned to stone by the magic of wizards. Such charms were carried for protection, to bring health or luck.

Other charms include plant materials, such as herbs: for example, mint is a charm for money if carried in the purse, and sage is for wisdom. Oak is believed to protect from lightning when it is put into a red charm bag and worn every day.

Amulets

Similar to a charm, an amulet has a single purpose and may be worn or carried all the time. Amulets can take all shapes and will have particular relevance for the person who carries one. They are often made in the shape of a hand, like the Arabic Hand of Fatima, which is said to ward off harm.

Talismans

A talisman is used to focus magical powers on a particular short-term aim, such as healing sickness or for success in finding a new job or house. Ideally they

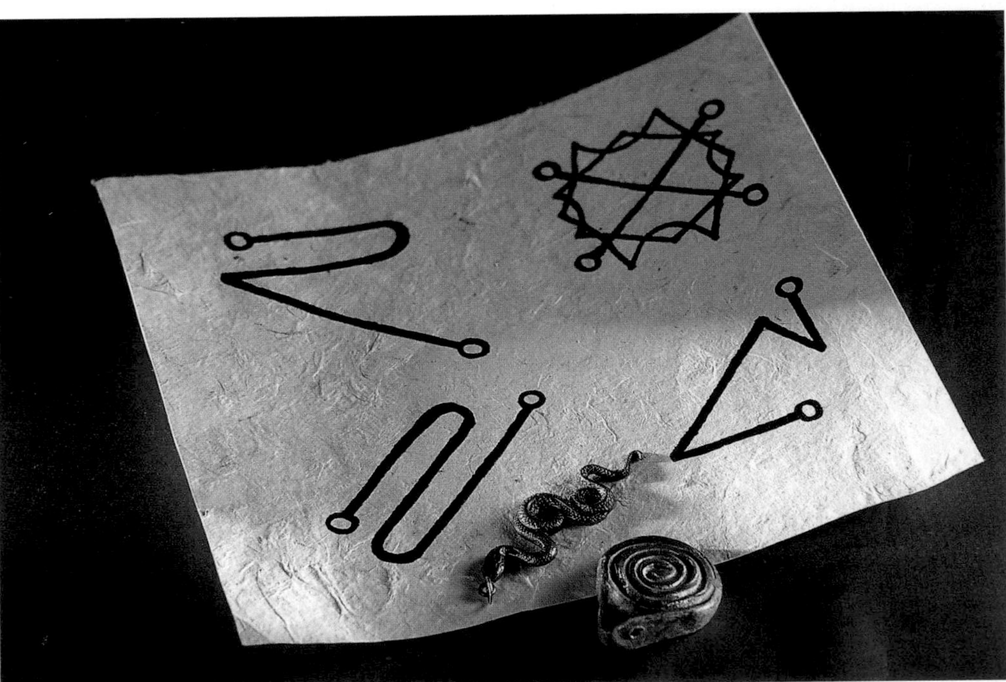

Talismans are still written in ancient alphabets, or use magical symbols that summon the help of angels or gods and goddesses.

should be made for the person whose life is intended to change. In the past they may have been made of precious metal set with jewels, written in magical ink on parchment, carved into wood or else inscribed on to clay. Today, the easiest way to make them is on coloured paper.

The art of making talismans is extremely old. Some have been found on sites in ancient Mesopotamia (modern day Iraq) that seem to predate writing, and it is possible that our various alphabets originated in the symbols used to request magical help.

USING THE ZODIAC SIGNS AND PLANETS

To make a talisman you need to understand the basic powers of the zodiac signs and their correspondences: each sign is associated not only with a particular planet, but also with a number, a colour, jewel, incense and symbol. It is also connected to a day of the week and time of the year.

CREATING A TALISMAN

Refer to the chart in the Magical Correspondences section of this book and decide on the powers that most fit with what you are trying to achieve, then work out which colours of paper, ink and silk you need, and which symbols to use for the inscription.

You will need

coloured paper
coloured inks
the correct planetary metal or a symbol of it
connecting link to another, such as a photograph, if the talisman is for someone else
coloured silk

1 Write the magical inscriptions on the paper with coloured ink, focusing as you do so on the person or situation for which the talisman is intended.

2 If it is for yourself, add a drop of your blood or saliva, or if it is for someone else, include the connecting link to that person.

3 Fold the paper and wrap it up in the coloured silk. Keep it in a safe place, until you are ready to consecrate it.

A charm or talisman should be taken great care of, and stored in a special bag or pouch.

Consecrating the talisman

You will need some holy oil; this is usually almond or olive oil with added appropriate herbs, resins, or essential oils associated with the planets concerned. You will also need an altar on which to place a bowl of water, a lit candle, incense, a stone, wine and some bread. The words you use and whom you invoke will depend on what powers you wish to invest it with: for courage, for instance, you would invoke the energies of the planet Mars, and use these words:

I call upon Zamael, Angel of the planet Mars, to lend assistance with this talisman. Please imbue it with your power, so that it may give courage to (say the person's name for whom the talisman is intended) when this is needed.

1 Work out an invocation to reflect your purpose and directed at the powers you have chosen to make your request to.

2 To cleanse the talisman, first sprinkle it with water and place it on your altar. Then energize it with fire by circling with the lit candle. Now wave the talisman through the incense smoke. This will blow life into it, so that it is fully effective.

3 Dip your index finger into the holy oil and imagine a pool of light which transfers to the talisman. Say the words you have decided on firmly and clearly.

4 Wait for a surge of energy or the incense smoke to swirl or until you perceive light around the new talisman. Place it under the stone to ground its power. Drink a cup of wine and eat the bread to complete the ceremony.

5 When you have completed the ceremony, put your equipment away, disrobe and come back to earth. Leave the talisman on the altar for one month, then give it to the person for whom it was made, or use it for the purpose you intended it.

ABSTRACT SYMBOLS

Symbols predate writing as a means of conveying ideas, and in ancient times were carved, painted, stitched or worked in metal for magical purposes, to ward off evil or to invoke gods and spirit beings. They were also worked into talismans for luck, health and inspiration. Some signs, identified as archetypes, appear to be universally understood. A symbol gains its significance from the emotional and spiritual weight it carries. It has its own energetic vibration and can influence the spirit world as well as resonate at a deep soul level with the human psyche. Among these powerful signs, or sigils, are the spiral and the circle in their various forms, which – together with other abstract symbols – have always played a central role in magic.

The natural world is full of circles, and its connotations and symbolism are numerous.

SPIRALS

Formed by tracing a point that is moving simultaneously out and around, the spiral is an evocative image, symbolic of a life path, the lessons and learning that come to us throughout life. The circular motion relates to the cyclic nature of existence, and the outward motion to the spiritual and emotional growth of a person as they progress through life, apparently repeating experiences, but each time moving to a new level.

Spirals can be combined to make double or even triple forms. Double spirals symbolize the duality of life and the natural world, seen in pairs of complementary opposites, such as light and dark, male and female, young and old, or mind and body. In Celtic lore, the triple spiral is linked with the moon and relates to the three stages of life: maiden, mother and crone. This symbol displays the cycles that are present within cycles, showing that the whole is made up of different periods of growth and development but that each stage is directly linked to the others. The spiral may also represent the pathway that a shaman may take to reach another realm.

The spiral is an inspiring symbol of the soul's journey through life.

CIRCLES

A line without end, a circle represents the continuous cycle of birth, death and rebirth as shown in the moon's journey through the sky and the seasonal cycles connected to the sun. For one cycle to begin another must end, but they do not really begin and end, merely transmute.

The circle symbolizes the cycles that are present in all of creation, the relentless progress of life in all its forms. Many traditional circular dwellings reflected this idea, symbolizing living within the whole. Circles that incorporate another solid circle speak of the totality of creation, showing that all things are connected and that creation encompasses the individual.

The cross has many meanings, including our "crucifixion" while bound to the physical world.

THE CROSS

Best known today as the emblem of the Christian church, the cross is an ancient symbol. In pre-Columbian America it was a fertility symbol related to the four rain-bearing winds. In some native American traditions, the four points of the cross represent the four directions and the four elements, with the centre point representing the source from which all life arises. The ankh, a cross with its topmost arm in a loop, was an ancient Egyptian symbol of immortality.

THE MAGIC CIRCLE

It is customary when making magic to create a circle as sacred space "between the worlds" into which divine or angelic beings are summoned. The witchcraft circle is always arranged according to the

There are many different ways of creating a magic circle. This one has been created using a ring of candles, whose light symbolizes protection and spiritual illumination.

cardinal points of north, south, east and west. Each cardinal direction has certain attributes that relate to the natural world, thus the circle is usually opened in the east, because this represents the first light of dawn. In the centre of the circle stands the cauldron, representing transformation of the "raw" into the "cooked", or on a spiritual level, of changes of consciousness within the natural rhythms of nature.

Whether you are working indoors or outside, you should visualize the magic circle as a place of stillness beyond normal time and space. It may be outlined with a wand or staff, created with cord or stones, or visualized.

The Pyramid

A geometric structure with five points, a pyramid synthesizes the symbolism of the square with the triangle, and the numbers three, four and five. The square at its base has four points and represents the Earth plane and the material world – structure, order and stability. The number four not only reminds us of the four elements, the four seasons, and the four directions, but also the four stages of life – childhood, adolescence, adulthood and old age – and even the four stages of the alchemical process – origins (or creation), division, opposites, and union of opposites. The four upward-pointing triangles of the pyramid's sides echo the symbolism of four, while bringing in that of three. Three is the trinity of man, woman and child, of body, mind and spirit. There are also many examples in mythology of the gods appearing in triad groupings, or having three aspects – such as the mother, maiden and crone aspects of the triple goddess.

At the apex of the pyramid, the four triangles meet to form a fifth point, suggesting the fifth element: ether or spirit. As the pyramid reaches up to the sky, this point represents the strivings of the human soul towards perfection, the attempt to reach up to the heavens to unite with the One.

The medicine wheel

Many shamanic practices are based on the teachings of the Native American Indian medicine wheel, which offer a framework for understanding the way these people see the world. The medicine wheel has many meanings and manifestations, ranging from structuring ceremonies and a means for the expression of dreams and visions, to methods for healing. The path of personal transformation on the medicine wheel is said to take the "knower" and the "known" through a spiral of experiences that link the individual, and his or her own course from birth to death, with the seasons and the wider whole.

Also known as the sacred hoop, the medicine wheel is a circle bisected by two lines (forming a cross), which symbolize the blue road of spirit (east to west) and the red road of life (south to north). The four sections of the circle represent the seasons of the year. As with the magic, or stone, circle, each point is associated with a direction of the compass, and with particular attributes that can be related to times and situations in your own life. The east is the place of inspiration and the inception of a new ideas. The south is related to consolidation, while the west is the place where the fruits of an endeavour can be harvested. The north is the place to recuperate and reflect.

The power generated by the pyramid shape was recognized by the ancient Egyptians.

Cosmic Forces

The mystery of the sun and moon, the stars and planets has always fascinated human beings. Over thousands of years, a rich heritage of myth and magic has grown up around these cosmic forces. Stories of solar gods and lunar goddesses exist in nearly every culture, perhaps in an attempt to understand and explain some of our most fundamental questions about life on Earth. From the earliest times people noticed that these faraway lights in the sky exerted a tremendous influence upon many aspects of our daily life, including our health and well-being (in body, mind and soul), as well as patterns in the weather, the tides of the oceans and the changing seasons.

This chapter presents an overview of these cosmic forces – the sun and moon and the constellations of the stars and planets in the zodiac. It shows how the sun is linked with health and vitality and how the mysterious moon affects our moods, intuition and psychic senses. It looks at the cardinal points of the compass and the symbolic power and meaning of these "Four Great Powers". It also includes a breakdown of the symbolism of the elemental energies of Fire, Water, Earth and Air, and looks at ether, or spirit, the intangible "fifth element" that plays such an important part in natural magic.

THE SUN

Throughout the ancient world the sun, the centre of our solar system and the source of light and heat, was worshipped for its life-giving energy and healing powers. Today, magicians and witches take the light of the sun into account when they are working magic, and as you become more aware of it, you will notice how it affects your life, your dreams and your magic. The sun is often seen as a representative of the individual in his or her world, the light radiating is the way he or she is seen by friends and family. If someone is ill, it is as if the light of their personal sun is dimmed and so spells that encourage the light to shine are sung.

Ancient societies worshipped the sun as the source of life and prosperity.

BRINGER OF LIFE

The power of the sun is concerned with life. It is the motor that drives this world and any change to the energy we receive on the surface of the earth is like a change in gear that speeds up or slows down all life processes. It is not a matter of choice: life has evolved to take advantage of the energy of the sun and so is automatically connected to its cycles – the seasons of the year and the shifting rhythm of day and night, light and dark.

Before the invention of electric lighting and the rise of our modern "indoor" culture, we would have been very aware of these cycles. In the past, people spent a great deal more time working outside and ate a diet largely based on seasonal produce. Now we can eat sun-ripened fruits in the middle of winter and are active far beyond the hours of natural daylight. To a large extent our natural connection with the sun's energies and the balance between light and dark has been lost, which in turn affects our health and well-being.

Studies have shown that spending a great deal of time in artificial fluorescent lighting increases fatigue, hyperactivity, and irritability, while the reduction of sunlight on a cloudy day, or more profoundly, in the long months of winter, has a significant effect upon our mood. For some people, the lack of sunlight can be seriously debilitating. Seasonal Affective Disorder (or SAD syndrome) causes mood swings, low energy levels and depression that begins as the days grow shorter and only gradually improves with the onset of spring. The sun is an energizing, active, dynamic force whose light is necessary for health, and makes us feel brighter, happier and well.

The sun not only has cosmic powers, its effect can be felt in a very real way in many aspects of our life, from the food we eat to the way we structure our waking hours.

SUN MAGIC

Observing the path of the sun through the year, and celebrating the seasons, is one way of working with the sun's energies. This is described in more detail in The Wheel of the Year, but two of the most important festivals of the sun are at the summer and winter solstices, when the power of the sun reaches its peak and nadir respectively. You can also work with these cycles on a daily basis: the first rays of sunlight appear at dawn, gaining in strength to peak at midday, and then fading and disappearing at sunset each evening. Tailoring your activities to suit this natural pattern can help you make the most of the sun's power: this would mean being active and outgoing through the morning and early afternoon, and then gradually reducing your activities and energetic output as evening approaches.

Eating a diet consisting largely of seasonal produce is another way to attune yourself to the sun's energies. Freshly grown, locally harvested food is ideal, as the energies contained in the

Sun legends

Within northern European mythology, the Sun God is born at the dead of winter soon after the solstice. He grows with each passing day, and receives his sword and arrows from his Mother, the ever-virgin Earth Goddess. Later, as the year turns, he becomes her lover. At midsummer he is at his height and yet, to feed the people, as the corn king, he has to be cut down at harvest. The Earth Goddess receives him and takes him into her house, symbolized by the corn dolly, made from the last sheaf of standing corn. Autumn brings the bonfires of Halloween, Summer's End. One tradition holds that on this ghostly eve, all the dead return to join the revels, and unborn children meet their parents in spirit. As the king of winter, the Sun God at his lowest ebb rules with his queen, the Lady of the Night, and at midwinter he is born again, the star child, the Child of Promise, the bringer of hope in darkness.

These legends form part of the ritual pattern of many modern covens of witches, with the high priest and priestess acting out the story of the God and Goddess. The Druids follow this cycle, and many other pagans also work their way through the cycles of stories of the old gods.

You don't have to sit in the sun to feel its regenerative powers. Try a meditation that calls on them in order to transform your negative energies.

If you have a sick friend, encourage them to spend a few moments feeling the sun's healing rays.

food will most closely match your own energy patterns, rather than foodstuffs that have been grown in another place hundreds or even thousands of miles away. You can also use "sunny" colours such as gold, oranges, yellows and reds in your clothing and surroundings as well as in your magic when you wish to connect with solar energies. Sun metals and gemstones include gold, diamonds and amber, the sun's incense is golden frankincense resin and its number is six.

The Sun's Healing Power

To use the sun directly as a healing force requires little in the way of equipment or preparation. If you are feeling low or tired, then simply sitting quietly in a sunny spot and relaxing for twenty minutes can work wonders. If this is not possible, then use your magical powers of imagination instead.

1 Sit quietly and visualize yourself surrounded by golden light beams.

2 Now imagine the beams entering your body at the crown of your head. Feel the warmth of the golden light circulating through your entire system. See the light reach into all parts of you, driving out any darkness and releasing stuck energy.

3 Finally, imagine the light leaving your body through your feet, travelling down deep into the earth where any negative energies will be transformed.

The moon

The moon is intimately linked with fertility and a woman's reproductive cycle. The full moon is a particularly potent time for women.

Mysterious, magical and ever changing, the moon shines her silver beams upon the shadows of the night. Many ancient civilizations venerated her because they observed how she influenced the germination and growth of crops, the tidal flows of the oceans, and weather patterns as well as a woman's "moontime" cycle. She also affects our moods, our sleep and dream patterns and our mental health. But perhaps more than any other celestial body, it is the moon that is most intimately linked with magic weaving and the occult. She is associated with intuition and psychic sensitivity, and her changing rhythms offer the magic-worker great scope for understanding life's mysteries.

Lunar Power

The moon is strongly associated with the imagination and psychic, intuitive powers. She is also particularly associated with women and the production of children: many ancient civilizations performed fertility rituals and celebrated the moon at annual festivals dedicated to the goddess, to seek her help and favour with conception. The time of ovulation, when a woman is at her most fertile, is most likely to occur during a full moon. During menstruation, women's powers of perception are heightened, and in many traditional societies it is customary for a woman to remove herself from the rest of the community at this time. In societies that revered the goddess, this was never intended as a punishment, but a chance for a woman to nurture and protect herself and to reconnect with her inner wisdom. Often all the women in a community would menstruate at the same time, so it was also a time of fellowship and bonding.

Developing an awareness of the moon and her phases helps to increase trust in the more subtle aspects of the psyche, including perception, intuition and psychic awareness.

Moon lore

There are many folklore sayings and warnings about the moon, from many cultures around the world, reflecting her mystery and power. These are some of the ones that have survived down the years.

- Do not leave your washing out at night – if the moonlight shines upon it, it shines upon clothes for a funeral.
- If you touch a silver coin when you see the moon, it will bring you good luck.
- Move house on a new moon.
- It is considered unlucky to marry during the month of May or during any of the waning/ dark quarters. Conversely, it is considered lucky to marry in June and during any waxing or full moon phase, but do not let the light of the moon fall on your marriage bed, or you will be courting bad luck.
- A baby that is born at the time of a full moon is a child of fortune.
- It is lucky to hold a newborn child up to the light of a new moon, and give thanks as well as offer up prayers for a long life.

Dedicate a Moon altar with white or clear stones, sandalwood incense, and riverside flowers.

Lunar Magic

The moon has four phases: waxing, full, waning and dark. Understanding these phases and what they represent is an essential part of natural magic. These are discussed in greater detail in The Cycles of the Moon, in the following chapter, but essentially the waxing phase is when the moon's energy is growing and so is a good time to initiate new projects. Full moon is a time of great fertility and powerful magic, while during the waning phase the moon's power is decreasing, so it is a good time for completion and letting go. The dark moon (or no moon) is a time for rest and retreat. The colours to use when working with moon energies are silver, white and dark blue, and the gemstones are pearls and moonstones. The scent of jasmine is associated with the moon and her number is nine.

The Moon and Dreams

Once you start to observe the phases of the moon and her movements in the sky, you may begin to notice the rhythms in your own life. There are natural peaks and troughs of energy, feelings and inspiration or creativity, and to some extent these may be reflected in the way you dream. Many people have difficulty remembering their dreams, or even fail to remember any at all, but it usually helps if you make a deliberate decision to write them down each morning. At first the dreams may drift away, but if you tell your subconscious to recall your dreams, just before you go to sleep, you will find memories start to remain. To enhance your connection to the inner world of dreams, try placing an aquamarine or other moontime crystal, such as a moonstone or piece of clear or smoky quartz, under your pillow as you sleep. Or to develop sensitivity to the dreaming aspect of the moon, you could try meditating with the moon and/or High Priestess Tarot cards. As you hold the card in front of you, softly gaze on the image, letting its wisdom speak to you.

Although the moon appears as a beacon in the night sky, it is actually a large reflective surface mirroring the light of the sun.

Moon legends and deities

Known by many names and in different guises, the moon has been depicted in many ancient legends as both the giver and the taker of life. Because of her ever-changing yet regenerative cycle, she was seen as immortal and as the place to which souls departed at death. She could bring gentle rains to water the fields, but because she could also raise storms and ruin crops she was considered unpredictable and potentially destructive. Goddesses chosen to represent her were therefore double-sided as well, endowed with both destructive and creative powers.
In Aztec mythology, the moon was named Xochiquetzal, companion to the sun and protector of lovers. She was also linked to the family and to childbirth. The Mayan moon deity was Ixchel, who was feared as the bringer of floods and storms. She wore a skirt decorated with bones, and her crown was a serpent. Despite this she was also considered a protector of women in childbirth. The life-giving qualities of the moon are universally linked to the spider, and in the mythology of many native tribes of North America, the spider is the weaver of the web of creation, producing the physical world, and then supporting and nurturing life on earth.

THE ZODIAC'S INFLUENCE

In magic, all astral or psychic energies are intimately connected with the influences of the zodiac. The zodiac is a series of starry constellations, each of which is rich in symbolic associations that can be used in magic to make predictions or influence the outcome of an event. While the earth makes its annual orbit of the sun, from earth we perceive this movement as if the sun is travelling along an imaginary line across the sky, called the ecliptic. The zodiac is the name given by astrologers to the band of constellations that appear along the ecliptic through the year. During each 30-day period of the year, or thereabouts, the sun appears to rise against the background of one of these groups of stars, and that constellation is said to be the sun sign of anyone born in that period.

Astrologers take into account the position of the moon, as well as the sun and all the other planets, when constructing a horoscope.

THE SIGNS OF THE ZODIAC

In Western astrology there are 12 signs of the zodiac. Each sign has a planetary ruler and is governed by one of the four elements. The moon travels through these constellations approximately every 27–28 days, whereas the sun takes a year. The dates shown for each sign refer to the approximate time when the sun is in that sign, although this can change by a day or two depending on the year. If your birthday falls near the beginning or end of a sign, it is on what is known as "the cusp", and it is worth checking to find out your correct birth sign. To find out when the moon is travelling through a particular constellation, you need to refer to a book of planetary tables known as an "ephemeris". This is available in specialized astrology bookshops or over the internet.

THE HOROSCOPE

To construct your natal horoscope, an astrologer needs to know not only the time and date of your birth, but the exact geographical location in longitude and latitude. From these data a unique chart can be constructed that will not only establish your "star sign" (which merely shows the position of the sun at birth), but also the position of the moon, the "ascendant", or rising, sign and all the other planets, and the complex relationships between them. For instance, some planets may appear next to one another, while others may be diametrically opposite, some planets may be moving forwards, while others have an apparent backwards or "retrograde" motion. All of these things are very important when reading a horoscope and can explain why popular astrology of the type found in newspapers and magazines is usually far from accurate as it only looks at one particular aspect of the horoscope – the position of the sun.

The starry night sky has fascinated humankind since the dawn of time. Before the invention of the compass, people looked to the stars to help them navigate.

LEARNING ABOUT ASTROLOGY

Each sign of the zodiac has certain qualities and influences, as do each of the planets, and it is the individual configuration at a person's birth that shows their potential, highlighting their strengths and also areas of difficulty or challenge. An astrologer will be able to interpret a horoscope in great detail and show hidden potential, possible illness and positive or difficult times in a person's life.

A guide to the signs of the zodiac

Remember that when consulting a horoscope, it is not only the position of the sun in the zodiac that is important, but the moon and all the other planets too. Here is a little information about each of the zodiac signs, each of which is governed by one of the four elements: earth and water are feminine and fire and air are masculine.

Star Sign	Emblem	Ruling Planet	Element	Quality
Aries (21 March – 19 April)	The Ram	Mars	Fire	Cardinal
Taurus (20 April – 20 May)	The Bull	Venus	Earth	Fixed
Gemini (21 May – 21 June)	The Twins	Mercury	Air	Mutable
Cancer (22 June – 22 July)	The Crab	Moon	Water	Cardinal
Leo (23 July – 22 August)	The Lion	Sun	Fire	Fixed
Virgo (23 August – 22 September)	The Virgin	Mercury	Earth	Mutable
Libra (23 September – 23 October)	The Scales	Venus	Air	Cardinal
Scorpio (24 October – 21 November)	The Scorpion	Pluto/Mars	Water	Fixed
Sagittarius (22 November – 21 December)	The Archer	Jupiter	Fire	Mutable
Capricorn (22 December – 19 January)	The Goat	Saturn	Earth	Cardinal
Aquarius (20 January – 18 February)	The water bearer	Uranus/Saturn	Air	Fixed
Pisces (19 February – 20 March)	The Fishes	Neptune/Jupiter	Water	Mutable

In astrology, the planet Saturn is concerned with teaching us life's lessons. Many say its position in the horoscope is connected with karma and past lives.

Horoscopes can also be constructed for many other purposes apart from the birth chart. For instance, it is possible to draw up a horoscope for a new business venture or a relationship, based on when and where the thing first started, in just the same way as the birth of a child. Studying such horoscopes, as well as the birth charts of individuals, can be useful for many kinds of magical work.

Sun and Moon Signs

In astrology, the position of the sun is said to represent your inner or life essence, whereas the moon indicates how you respond emotionally and intuitively and is a barometer of your feeling world. So an Aries moon, for instance, can indicate someone with a quick temper who "sees red", whereas a Cancer moon would be more placid and easy-going.

THE FOUR GREAT POWERS

The four cardinal points of the compass – north, south, east and west – are honoured in many ancient traditions, and over time a litany of knowledge attributing specific qualities to each direction has been built up. Together, the four points symbolize balance and wholeness, the horizontal west-east axis representing the formative, receptive force or the feminine principle, the vertical north-south axis representing the active or conceptual force, which is masculine. Various cultures have referred to these four points as the Four Great Powers and have associated them with gods, angels and spirit beings. Understanding these great powers and their particular symbolism is fundamental to practising natural magic.

The medicine wheel of Native American Indians is a cross within a circle, representing the cycles within nature.

The Medicine Wheel

There are many different approaches to understanding the four directions, but the Native American medicine wheel is particularly rich in symbolism and magical ideas. Unlike the typical modern European approach to life, which is based on linear thinking, to the Native American life is thought of in terms of circles and cycles, symbolized by the medicine wheel. It is a physical thing, typically made of stones or rocks, with four directions – east, south, west and north. Understanding the four directions can help us to realize our connection with the earth's cycles and with all of life.

The East

At the beginning of each day, the sun rises in the east. The power of the east is light: it is the arising of dawn whose light dispels darkness; it is the arrival of spring after the dormancy of winter. The east is the place of enlightenment or awakening, symbolism that is understood in Christian churches and Buddhist temples where the altar is positioned in the east. The east is the triumph of rebirth over death, and is new beginnings, fresh ideas and inspiration.

The colour of the east is yellow, the colour of the rising sun and of illumination. Its element is Air and its totem animal is the eagle. The eagle is prized for its clear vision, linking to the quality of perception or seeing, which is associated with the east. The eagle also flies higher than any other bird and is therefore closest to the sun, the source of light and sustainer of life. Eagle feathers are highly prized in the Native American tradition and often used in headdresses, to connect them to the eagle's powers of vision and closeness to the Great Spirit.

A magic circle is usually opened in the east. It is the direction to work with when seeking enlightenment or illumination, when beginning a new project, when looking for original ideas and inspiration, or when starting a new phase in life.

The South

It is customary to move around a magic circle clockwise from east to south, symbolizing the movement of the sun from dawn to high noon, or from spring to summer. The power of the south is exploration, investigation and experience; it is the curiosity of the growing child who wants to find out about things. The south is a place of blossoming and unfolding as purposes become clear. It is also connected with trust and intuition.

The east's colour is yellow, and its power is light. Its association with enlightenment means that it is used in Christian and Buddhist places of worship to position the altar.

The Wheel of the Four Winds

Each of the four compass directions relates to a time of day, to a particular element and to an angel. Use this Wheel of the Four Winds to help you place your offerings or materials in the right place within a magic circle, or on an altar.

East
Direction of the infant, of beings and creatures of Air. Its time is dawn, its season is spring, and its angel is Raphael. Its animal totem is the eagle and its colour is yellow.

South
Direction of the child, of beings and creatures of Fire. Its time is midday, its season is summer, its angel is Michael. Its animal totem is the mouse and its colour is red.

West
Direction of the adult, of beings and creatures of Water. Its time is sunset, its season is autumn and its angel is Gabriel. Its animal totem is the grizzly bear. Its colours are black, dark blue and purple.

North
Direction of the elder, of beings and creatures of the Earth. Its time is midnight, its season is winter and its angel is Uriel. Its totem animal is the buffalo and its colour is white.

The element of the south is Fire and its colour is red, the colour of our lifeblood and vital energy. Its totem animal is the mouse, which may seem an unlikely creature to represent such a powerful force, but a mouse is very sensitive to any vibrations in its environment. The wisdom of the mouse tells us not to confuse power with size and ferocity, and to learn how to develop a finely attuned "felt-sense" by trusting in our feelings and emotions.

South is the direction to work with for growth and development. It is a place to consolidate ideas, to build on what was started in the direction of east. South is the place of gathering experiences and learning from them.

The West

Journeying around the wheel, the west represents the time of day when the sun sets, and the annual movement from summer to autumn. The power of the west is consolidation and strength; it is where the fruits of an endeavour can be harvested. It is also the time to look within, a time for self-examination and reflection, allowing transformation of experience into knowledge, or matter into spirit.

The totem animal of the west is the grizzly bear, the strongest and fiercest of all the bears. The grizzly eats well in autumn, strengthening its body in preparation for the sleep of winter. It also makes careful consideration before taking action, hence its association with the qualities of introspection. The element of the west is Water, and its colours are black, dark blue and purple.

West is the direction to use when you need to take stock and evaluate a situation; it is a time for self-evaluation as you prepare for new action.

The North

Final resting point on the wheel, north is the place of rest and renewal. It is the power of winter, a time when nothing appears to be growing but inwardly the earth is gathering her energies for the new life to come. The north is the power of night, the time when the body lies sleeping but the spirit is active, dreaming and learning. North stands for focus and clarity, the white snow of purity; it is wisdom and knowing.

The element of the north is Earth, and its colour is white, the sum of all other colours and the essence of perfection. Its totem animal is the buffalo, an animal that gives totally of itself to sustain life. Sometimes the north is represented as the White Buffalo, a rare animal with sacred significance, associated with the legendary White Buffalo Woman who is said to have brought the Sacred Pipe to the Native American people.

North is the path that is used to gain strength of will and clarity in one's intentions. It is also a place of refuge, the place where you are able to retreat to find rest and rejuvenation.

THE ELEMENT OF AIR

The universe is made up of the four elements of Fire, Water, Earth and Air. Life is a balance between these forces, both as energies in the outer world and within every human being. When weaving spells and making magic, witches work with these elemental energies, each of which has particular characteristics and symbolic correspondences. The element of Air symbolically corresponds to a spring dawn: a light breeze whispers through the trees, the sky is blue and the day is just beginning. The lightness and clarity of the invisible air element governs the realm of the mind and all structured mental activity. The air element has the following magical associations or correspondences.

THE BREATH OF LIFE

Air is the element of life and breath; to breathe is to be alive, and when we take our last breath, our life expires. The speediest and most ethereal of the elements, Air rules the east, the direction of sunrise, and its season is spring. Because it is associated with the new day and with the freshness of the new year, Air symbolizes new beginnings, enterprise, infancy and the generative energy of the seed. It is creative, focused and aware. In the form of wind, air may be a gentle, cooling breeze or it may have the destructive force of a hurricane. Its energy is directed outwards. Because Air is the element of the wind, it governs all movement and is associated with travel, freedom and new discoveries. It is also the element of thought and ideas – the fresh moving force of the open mind, of intellect and the imagination.

In daily life the areas governed by Air include workplaces, meeting rooms, schools and libraries, as well as places concerned with travel, such as railway stations, airports and bus terminals. In terms of professions, Air is connected with the law, mathematics and science.

Air presides over the eastern quarter of a room or building, while in the natural world, Air's places are mountain tops, windy plains and clear or cloudy skies.

Air is manifest everywhere, from fiercely raging storms to the gentle stirring of grass in the wind.

Air presides over the mountain tops of the world, and also over clear and cloudy skies.

GODS OF THE AIR

Deities associated with the Air include Shu, Thoth, Hermes and Mercury. Shu was the Egyptian god of the Air who, with his consort Tefnut (the goddess of moisture), created the earth and sky. The Egyptian moon god Thoth was the scribe of Osiris, the god who ruled the underworld and judged the dead. As god of wisdom, Thoth was endowed with secret knowledge. It was said that his book of magic contained spells that

Air correspondences

Direction: east
Season: spring
Time: dawn
Moon phase: new
Planets: Mercury, Uranus
Gender: masculine
Colours: light blue, yellow
Senses: hearing and smell
Magical tools: wand, athame (sword)
Musical instruments: wind instruments
Creatures: birds, winged insects
Natural symbols: feathers, fragrant flowers
Celtic sacred trees: alder, birch
Trees: elder, eucalyptus
Herbs: comfrey, lavender, mint
Incense: sandalwood, lemon
Minerals: mercury, aventurine, topaz
Zodiac sign: Gemini, Libra, Aquarius
Archangel: Raphael
Alchemical symbol: upright triangle with a horizontal line

Altars dedicated to the Air element can include the colours violet and yellow, and objects such as feathers and fans. Smoke and smell are also associated with air, in particular the scent of sandalwood and of lavender.

would give the user power over all the gods, and that together his books contained all the wisdom of the world. He eventually became associated with the Greek god Hermes, messenger of the Olympian gods, who could travel as fast as thought.

In many ways, Hermes is the personification of Air. He was versatile and changeable, eloquent and inventive. His lively mind, quick wits and slippery character made him the patron of thieves and merchants as well as travellers. Hermes' Roman equivalent was Mercury, whose cult spread widely among the Celtic and Germanic peoples of the Roman Empire. The Norse people identified him with their most powerful god Wotan or Odin, the god of speech, breath, wind, storm and magic. Mercury gave us the word "mercurial" to describe a volatile, lively, quicksilver character, all of which qualities are associated with Air.

Exploring the air element

The best way to understand the qualities of an element is to explore it for yourself. Try going outside and notice how it feels to be out in the fresh air. What difference does it make if it's windy or if the air is still? Do all winds feel the same or are some easier to be in than others?

You could also try sitting indoors and working with your breath. In India, the concept of prana, or the sacred breath, plays an essential role in learning mastery over the mind. Adepts have discovered that when the rhythm and length of the breath are controlled, specific changes in consciousness occur. Attuning yourself to your own breathing patterns and learning how to change them will lend greater power to your magic. A simple way to start is to sit with your eyes closed and breathe in to a count of six, hold for a count of three, and then breathe out. Hold again for a count of three and repeat. Vary the counts to suit your breathing, as it is important to do what works for you without causing strain or shortness of breath.

The Air Personality

When Air features strongly in a person's horoscope, they will have a tendency towards being rational and analytical, preferring logic and carefully thought out ideas over irrational impulses. Air types enjoy mental stimulation in their relationships, and their idea of a good evening would include a lively exchange of ideas. However, the key to working with any of the elements is balance. Too much or too little of a particular element creates problems and challenges that need to be overcome. When Air is out of balance it can become critical and judgemental. It has a tendency to nit-pick and over-analyse until it almost literally blows a thing apart. This tendency can be particularly destructive when a creative idea or project is in its infancy, when maybe a little tender, loving care is what is needed. Too much Air (talking, discussion) and there is a danger that things can become "airy fairy" and plans will never materialize. In many ways Air is a tricky element to work with as its mercurial nature is not to be pinned down.

The element of Fire

Associated with the sun, Fire is the spark of life. It governs the realm of passion and intensity and is the element that ignites our desires. It is the intuitive flash of understanding, the leap of imagination that creates exciting new possibilities. Fire is both creative and destructive: it can cleanse and purify, but it also consumes. It is the only one of the four elements that cannot exist without feeding on something else. It makes our homes warm and welcoming, and cooks our food, but it is dangerous and can get out of control. It has the power to transform everything it touches.

Creator and Destroyer

Fire rules the south, the direction of the sun's fiercest heat in the northern hemisphere, and is related to motivation, creativity and passion. Its energy is fast, forceful and positive and its power can be frightening. It symbolizes the inner child, the spirit within and the creative spark. Because it is the element of the passions, it gives courage and strength to fight for quality of life. Those in whom it is dominant are passionate and intense. Fire consumes obstacles to faith, and banishes negativity. Fire governs the sense of sight; it also inspires the need to offer and accept the power of touch. It is the element of physical challenge, sensation and sexual energy.

The cleansing force of Fire makes it a powerful symbol of change and transformation, in many levels of magical thought and philosophy.

Fire is a creative force, and has been used for industry ever since it was discovered.

Areas governed by Fire are kitchens, fireplaces and boiler rooms, gyms and athletics fields and creative spaces such as studios and playrooms. Professions in the arts and entertainment industry are all linked with Fire. Fire presides over the southern quarter of a room or building. In the natural world its places are deserts, hot springs and volcanoes.

Gods and Goddesses of Fire

Some of the deities associated with Fire are Re, Sekhmet, Apollo and Lugh. The ancient Egyptians worshipped Re as their pre-eminent solar deity. As a creator god, he brought order out of chaos and from his tears were formed the first human beings. Reborn each morning, he journeyed daily across the sky in his solar boat, entering the underworld each night to do battle with the cosmic serpent, Apep. "Son of Re" was one of the titles bestowed on the pharaoh. Re's daughter was the sun goddess Sekhmet, "the Powerful One", usually portrayed with the head of a lioness. She was the terrifying aspect of Hathor, the goddess of joy and maternal love. Re sent Sekhmet as his "Eye", the terrible burning power of the sun, to punish the wickedness of humankind, but at the last moment saved his creation from total destruction by diverting Sekhmet's frenzied rage.

In Greek mythology, Apollo, who represented light, truth and clarity, guided the sun across the sky. He was the god of medicine and music and the patron of the nine Muses, the mythical embodiments of the creative imagination. The Celtic sky god Lugh was a deity of the sun and the weather, and his spear was sometimes seen as a fork of lightning. As the god of skills and arts, he could be honoured by an offering of a creative work. The pagan festival of Lughnasash, celebrated at the beginning of the harvest, is held in his name.

Iron as a Fire Metal

One of the Fire metals, iron is found on earth in its pure form only in meteorites. It is present in our blood, and is essential for physical energy and clear thinking. Wearing it as a talisman is said to increase physical strength. In some cultures an iron talisman is worn as protection against evil or negative energy: for this reason Sikhs wear an iron or steel bangle called a kara on their right wrist.

Exploring the Fire Element

One of the best ways of getting to know the Fire element is to sit in front of an open fire. Notice how it warms and energizes you, its variations in colour and how shapes alter and shift in the flames. Hear the sound that it makes as it burns. If you don't have access to an open fireplace, then an outdoor garden bonfire would be fine. If neither of these options is practical, then try a candle flame meditation. Light a red or orange candle and sit in front of it. Soft-focus your gaze on the flame for a few minutes, as if searching for its centre. Feel yourself a part of its vibrant, dancing energies. Then close your eyes and form a mental picture of the candle flame in your mind's eye. As you breathe in and out, imagine you are inhaling and exhaling the qualities of Fire through every pore of your body. Let yourself merge with its essence. Remember when working with fire to make sure that it is always properly contained: never leave a burning candle unattended.

Fire is vital for humanity's survival, and when under control is a nurturing symbol of the home.

The Fire Personality

Fire types are warm and extrovert, with a strong sense of fun and playfulness. Often charming and charismatic, passionate and intense, they like to live life to the full. They are usually very intuitive and tend to base decisions on their "gut instincts" rather than on careful consideration and deliberation. They are often attracted to creative pursuits or leadership roles where they have a chance to shine. In relationships they enjoy risk-taking and adventure and can feel trapped or bored by too much domestic routine.

When Fire is out of balance it becomes destructive, too much Fire can cause "burn-out" at work, and needs boundaries, and control: setting limits and saying "no" rather than taking on too many projects, for instance. Fire enjoys drama and the limelight, but too much of this and it becomes selfish, feeling that others only exist to fan the flames of adoration. Too little Fire, however, can be linked with a lack of vitality and low energy, which can lead to hopelessness, depression and lack of motivation.

Fire correspondences

Direction: south
Season: summer
Time: midday
Moon phase: first quarter
Planets: Mars, Pluto
Gender: masculine
Colours: red, orange
Sense: sight
Magical tools: wand, candles, lanterns, all solar icons
Musical instruments: stringed instruments: guitar, harp
Creatures: dragon, snake, lion, ram, phoenix
Natural symbols: flame, lava
Celtic sacred trees: oak, holly, blackthorn
Herbs: basil, bay, garlic, hyssop, juniper, rosemary, tobacco
Incense: frankincense, cinnamon, basil
Minerals: brass, gold, iron, fire opal, garnet, hematite, red jasper sardonyx, flint
Zodiac signs: Aries, Leo, Sagittarius
Archangel: Michael
Alchemical symbol: upright triangle

The element of Water

In the realm of the subconscious, dreams and emotions ebb and flow, exerting their subtle influences on our conscious thoughts. The element of Water is connected with our feeling world and it is the power that shapes all our relationships. Water is the element of love and the emotions because it is as fluid as our feelings. It rules friendship and marriage. It also relates to the subconscious mind, constantly shifting and active beneath the surface, and affecting our moods and emotional responses. It influences sleep and dreaming, as we sink down into the swirling depths of the subconscious to discover our deepest desires.

The still waters of a lake remind us of Water's hidden and mysterious depths.

The Ebb and Flow

The moon tugs at the oceans of the world to create the tides, which follow her ever-changing cycle. She exerts the same pull on the fluids in our bodies, affecting our emotions, moods and a woman's menstrual cycles. Thus the ebb and flow of water is mirrored in the cycles of our own lives.

The energy of Water is feminine and receptive. It rules the west, the direction of the setting sun, and its season is autumn. Water is an element of purification and healing; this can take the form of healing counsel leading to emotional release, sweeping away stale feelings and inducing us to face the truth about ourselves. Water is cleansing and essential to life, and our own lives begin in water. The element is thus symbolized by the womb and is related to fertility.

Areas of the home ruled by Water are the bathroom and the kitchen sink. Because it presides over friendship and relationships, it also governs the living room, the arena of social interaction. In its cleansing and healing role, Water is also the element of medical rooms and hospitals. Those in caring professions, psychotherapy and those with a strong aesthetic sense are connected with Water. In the natural world its places are seas, lakes, rivers, marshes, pools, wells and rain-drenched lands.

To appreciate the power of the Water element, spend some time in nature next to running water.

Gods and Goddesses of Water

Deities associated with Water include Tiamat, Venus, Neptune and Epona. In Mesopotamian mythology Tiamat represents chaos and the raw energy of the salt ocean, she was the primeval mother whose salt waters mingled with the fresh water of Apsu to initiate the creation of the gods.

Neptune, the Roman god of the sea, was revered by seafarers whom he generally protected, but they feared his temper: his mood could change in an instant, giving rise to perilous ocean storms. Venus, the Greek equivalent of Aphrodite, archetype of love and beauty, was said to have been created from the foam of the sea, and to have been carried on a seashell to Cyprus. As she stepped from the sea, the drops of water that fell from her body turned into pearls at her feet. The goddess had the power to calm the sea and ensure safe voyages, just as she could bring balance and harmony to human instincts and emotions. Epona was a Celtic horse goddess worshipped during the period of the Roman Empire. She was portrayed carrying fruit or corn to show her connection with fertility and the earth's abundance. She was also a goddess of Water and healing, and the presiding deity of healing springs.

Exploring the Water Element

The best places to connect with Water are in nature: spend some time by the sea or at natural pools, streams, rivers or lakes. If it is safe for swimming, then that would be ideal. Being out in the rain is another good way of experiencing the Water element. Notice how it feels as you get wet: is it a pleasant feeling or are you unable to let yourself go into it because you are afraid to get wet?

A convenient way of connecting with Water in our own homes is, of course, in the bathroom: take a long soak in the bathtub, or enjoy a refreshing wake-up shower. Don't think only of the purpose of getting clean, but immerse yourself fully in the water and notice how you feel before and after the experience. As you soak in the bath, close your eyes and visualize yourself as a fish: as you breathe in, imagine the element of Water suffusing your body; let yourself melt into the water and become one with it.

Water correspondences

Direction: west
Season: autumn
Time: dusk
Moon phase: full
Planets: moon, Neptune, Venus
Gender: feminine
Colours: black, dark blue, purple
Sense: taste
Magical tools: chalice, cauldron, mirror
Musical instruments: stringed instruments, gongs, bells
Creatures: cat, frog, turtle, dolphin, whale, otter, seal, fish
Natural symbols: shells, water, river plants, watercress
Celtic sacred trees: willow, alder, yew
Plants: camomile, hops, lemon balm, seaweeds, yarrow, belladonna, lotus
Incense: jasmine, rose, vanilla
Minerals: silver, copper, amethyst, aquamarine, turquoise, tourmaline, opal, jade, pearl, sapphire
Zodiac signs: Cancer, Scorpio, Pisces
Archangel: Gabriel
Alchemical symbol: downward pointing triangle

The Water Personality

People dominated by Water are emotional, sensitive and spiritual. They often have a well-developed "sixth sense" and incline towards mediumistic tendencies. Water types are the poets and dreamers, approaching life from a felt sense, rather than from thought (Air), spontaneity (Fire) or practicality (Earth). In relationships they are romantic, nurturing and empathic but can be prone to imagine insults where none exist.

Lack of Water creates problems in forming relationships. The person keeps an emotional distance and finds intimacy and close contact difficult, possibly because they find it hard to access and share their own feelings. A lack of empathy and poor psychic and intuitive skills are also indicated.

Too much Water, on the other hand, leads to being awash in a sea of emotion; flooded by feelings that can't be contained, it becomes difficult to function and operate in the everyday world. This can also happen when the conscious mind is overloaded by psychic material, so it is particularly important to be well grounded or earthed when dealing with this element.

Water is essential to life and its powers are healing, rejuvenating and refreshing.

The humours

At one time, it was accepted as fact that everything in the universe – both animate and inanimate – was made up of a combination of the four elements. Formulated by the Greek philosopher Empedocles in the 5th century BC, this theory of the "humours" classified individuals into one of four character types. People of the earth were said to be "melancholic", fiery people were "choleric", watery people were "phlegmatic" and airy people were "sanguine". Until the 19th century, doctors, philosophers and other professionals employed these words as technical medical terms, and would treat illness by trying to balance the humours, but they are now widely used to describe character types.

The element of Earth

Densest of all the elements and the one most closely linked to our physical world, the Earth element governs stability, security and material concerns – whether these relate to the physical body and health, money or property, business affairs or anything that is connected with our material well-being, such as food, clothing and shelter. Stability, loyalty and reliability are the qualities of the Earth element, keeping us grounded and secure in loving families and comfortable homes.

Like rocks or soil, the Earth element is connected with matter and is the densest of all the elements.

The Root of our Being

Earth is the element of all physical and material things and its energy is grounding. This feminine element is the realm of the Mother Goddess, and her body is where we sink our roots as we reach out toward new experiences. Whether it is represented by hard rock or fertile moist soil, Earth stands for stability and growth. It is the solid foundation over which all the other elements move.

Gardening is one of the best ways to get to know the Earth element.

Earth's energy is receptive, teaching patience, endurance, self-sufficiency and reliability. It helps us to recognize and accept the limitations and potential of our characters. Earth shows us how to take responsibility for our lives and our destiny. Its symbol is the wise elder.

Earth's season is winter and its direction is north, where in the winter darkness the shifting, moving waters are frozen into ice. In the natural environment, Earth's place is a cave, the primal symbol of shelter. The cave's womb-like magic makes it a symbol of birth and rebirth, where oracles speak and enlightenment is achieved. Forests, valleys and fields are other places of the Earth element. In the home, Earth governs areas of physical needs (the dining room and toilet) and practical tasks (the workshop, greenhouse and garden). It is the element of buildings and their construction, and presides over financial institutions. Professions that are connected with the Earth include catering, gardening, farming, business, and anything that involves making things or working with the hands.

Gods and Goddesses of Earth

Some of the deities associated with earth are Gaia, Pan and the Horned God. Gaia is the ancient Greek Earth goddess whose name has been given in modern times to the life force of the earth. The daughter of Chaos, she gave birth to Uranus, the sky, and Pontus, the sea. Her union with Uranus produced the Titans, including Cronos (lord of Time), father of Zeus. Gaia, pre-eminent prophetess, was the first deity of the great oracle at Delphi. Even the other immortals were subject to her law. The Greeks worshipped Gaia as the giver of dreams and the nourisher of plants and children.

In Greek mythology, Pan was a shepherd; his name may derive from a word meaning "pasture". Easy-going, lazy, sensual and unpredictable, he represents the spirit of untamed nature. He was usually said to be the son of Hermes, and was portrayed with the hind legs and horns of a goat (one of the first animals to become domesticated). Pan was a very ancient god of wild things, and his importance increased until he came to be worshipped as the Great God and father of all living things.

Grounding meditation

Being grounded is very important in any piece of magical work. If you are not grounded your power will be considerably less. Try this grounding meditation before or after a spell. Sit in a quite spot and imagine yourself in a leafy forest glade; feel the earth supporting you. As you breathe in, imagine yourself drawing the energies of the earth up through the soles of your feet, like roots coming up into a tree. Feel the element of earth run through your whole body. As you breathe out, imagine the energy returning through your feet and 'roots' back down into the earth. Repeat this cycle several times until you feel strong and grounded.

The pagan Horned God, who is related to the Celtic fertility deity Cerunnos, represents sexuality and vitality. He is the consort of the Triple Goddess. Like Pan, he is represented as half-man, half-animal. As lord of the woods he is the hunter, but he is also identified with the sacrificed and hunted animal.

Earth correspondences

Direction: north
Season: winter
Time: midnight
Moon phase: dark
Planets: Earth, Saturn
Gender: feminine
Colours: natural "earthy" colours: browns, ochres, burnt orange, olive green, black; white
Sense: touch
Magical tools: pentacle
Musical instruments: percussion
Creatures: ox, dog, wolf, goat, stag
Natural symbols: fossils, stones, grains and seeds, salt, earth
Celtic sacred trees: ash, hawthorn, pine
Herbs: pennyroyal, lovage, sage, mugwort
Incense: vetivert, patchouli, myrrh
Minerals: lead, emerald, aventurine, pyrites, coal, onyx
Zodiac signs: Taurus, Virgo, Capricorn
Archangel: Uriel
Alchemical symbol: downward pointing triangle with horizontal line (reverse of Air)

Exploring the Earth Element

Spending time outside connecting with nature is the best way to get to know the Earth element. Any outside activities, but especially walking and gardening, are very good ways of coming into contact with Earth, particularly the latter as it involves getting your hands dirty. An awareness of the seasons and the weather is essential when you are gardening, while physical contact with plants and soil is very "grounding". Even if you don't have access to a garden or an allotment, keeping plants in the house or tending a window box will help you connect with Mother Earth.

The Earth Personality

People in whom the Earth element is dominant are home-loving, dependable and loyal, and happiest when surrounded by their family. Physical touch and affection are important to them and they enjoy the pleasures of the senses – food, material comforts and a healthy sexuality. Too much Earth element is stodgy, plodding and dull. Overly concerned with security and material possessions, negative Earth is unable to take risks, to branch out and try something new, for fear of the unknown. It becomes easy to get stuck in a routine, staying in a job or relationship where we no longer really want to be because it seems the easiest and safest option and to do otherwise presents too much of a risk to our material comfort.

Too little Earth can be associated with someone who is unable to focus properly or concentrate for very long. Lacking determination and perseverance, they may dream up ever more wonderful schemes (especially if strong on Fire or Air), but never bring them to fruition.

The physical formations of the landscape remind us of the Earth element, where change takes place very slowly and over a long period of time.

THE FIFTH ELEMENT

Usually we think of there being only four elements, but in many systems of thought there is also a fifth element – ether or spirit. Because of its nature, this is the hardest element to define. Spirit is intangible, ineffable and mysterious. It is the divine soul, the magical "x" factor that in the end cannot be explained, categorized or defined, although mystics and artists through the ages have attempted to express the divine language of the soul.

The fifth element is the spirit of the universe, which can be evoked by the starry night sky.

ETHER OR SPIRIT

The word for spirit in the Sanskrit language is *akasha*, from which we get the "akashic records", a sort of mystical "log book" that occultists claim contains knowledge of everything that has ever happened in the material plane, existing as an energetic "imprint" in the astral world. In Latin, the word is *aether*, derived from the Greek *aithein*, which means "to kindle". In the Middle Ages ether was referred to as the quintessence (*quint* meaning five or fifth), and it was the alchemists' goal to find this fifth essence, which they believed contained the secret of everlasting life. Early European occultists regarded ether as the substance that made up the heavens, which filled the void in space.

Spirit does not have a place or location in any occult system: it is perceived to be everywhere and also nowhere, for as soon as we say "it is here" we have lost it. Unlike the other four elements, it is not possible to tie up the fifth in a neat package and attribute to it qualities that we can work with. Spirit perhaps is not so much an element as a force; it is the centre of the web that unites and animates all other emanations.

THE POWER OF SPIRIT

The qualities of the spirit are often best expressed through media other than words: musicians, poets, artists, saints and sages have used the power of sound, visual image, metaphor, prayer and feeling to try to convey what can only be described as the "religious" experience, an experience of something so sacred that we are transported beyond the narrow confines of how we normally define ourselves into something much bigger. The fifth element is concerned with the timeless and the universal, with the cosmic and the mysterious. It is the

Dream-like images, such as these mountain tops above cloud height, are a way of reminding us of the connection with spirit, which is the most difficult element of all to define.

source of all, the One that permeates the cosmos. Some traditions call this God, others refer to it as Great Spirit, while in the East it is sometimes known as the Tao, or the Way. Spirit is the empty space between the stars, the blank canvas of the mind that is untroubled by thoughts and emotions. In the Buddhist tradition, experience of spirit has been likened to the moment that a dewdrop disappears into the ocean of infinite being.

Magical Correspondences

Spirit is the path or channel along which magic travels from the otherworld to this. Although there are no standard magical tools used to represent spirit, it is sometimes associated with any item that connects or unifies disparate things. For this reason spirit may be represented by magical cords, cloaks or medicine bags.

In the chakra system spirit is associated with the crown, or 7th chakra, while in the Tarot deck it is represented by The World, the last card of the Major Arcana.

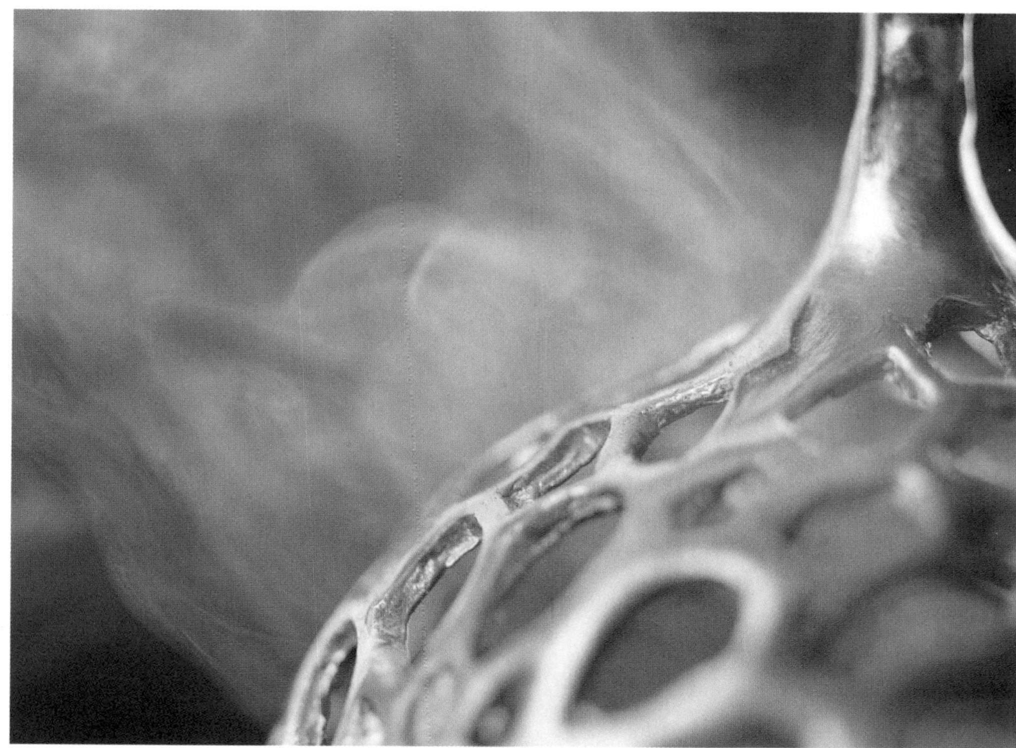

Swirling clouds of fragrant smoke can transport our thoughts from the everyday world to the invisible world of spirit.

Spirit's colours are white and/or black, as these essentially contain or reflect all other vibrations of light and dark.

Connecting with Spirit

For ceremonial magicians, the goal of magic is essentially to connect and become one with spirit, and magic is a path that is used to achieve this end. However, we all connect with spirit in our own way and it reveals itself to us only when we are ready.

The traditional magical symbol of spirit is the six-pointed star, also known as the Star of David or Solomon's Seal. It is one of the oldest symbols of the divine source from which all life is created (sometimes referred to as the One, the All, or God), and when broken down it contains all the other alchemical symbols for the four elements.

Working with the six-pointed star can be one way of helping you to connect. You could do this by drawing the symbol, wearing it, studying it each night before you go to sleep, or using it as an aid to meditation. When you meditate, imagine the symbol residing in your heart. Ask it to teach you its secrets and be open for any learning that follows; you will need to trust your "inner voice" rather than your rational mind for this.

Another magical symbol that recalls the fifth element is the pentagram. The five points of the pentagram represent Air, Fire, Earth, and Water, with spirit at the apex. Its symbolism reminds us that all four elements emanate from spirit in the astral world, and in a sense, that spirit is the cosmic "glue" that binds everything together.

The Star of David is an ancient symbol that represents the divine source of all life.

Connecting with the otherworld

Incenses have traditionally been used to help us connect with the otherworld and the realm of spirit, transforming the mundane into the sacred.

You will need

10 ml (2 tsp) frankincense resin
10 ml (2 tsp) mastic resin
5 ml (1 tsp) dammar
5 ml (1 tsp) sandarac
pestle and mortar
charcoal

1. Light the charcoal and place on a heatproof surface. Crush the frankincense and mastic resins into small pieces and mix together, along with the dammar and sandarac.

2. Sprinkle a little of the incense over the hot charcoal. Sit back and relax, allowing yourself to drift away.

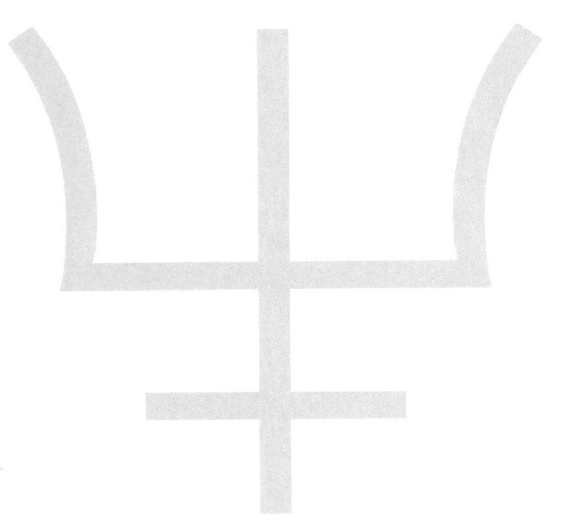

CYCLES AND SEASONS

All life on earth is governed by cycles. These vary in length; for instance, there is the 24-hour cycle of day and night, the moon's cycles last roughly 28 days, while the sun waxes and wanes through a whole year. Each cycle has its use in magic, and every time and season has benefits and strengths that can be used to gain insight, develop skills and assist the magic-worker to grow in wisdom. Being in touch with these natural cycles, rather than struggling against the tides of the world, makes our way through life smoother and our magic more effective. For no matter how good or powerful our magic, if our timing, or synchronicity, is wrong then all our efforts will be in vain and what we are capable of manifesting will be much diluted from our original purpose or intent.

This chapter considers the timing of magic, looking in particular at the cycles of the moon and the journey of the sun through the "wheel of the year". It gives information on the major festivals and celebrations in the magic-worker's calendar and also looks at the distinct qualities of each of the four seasons, the lessons we can learn from them, and how best to use them in natural magic.

Nature's timing

Just as day follows night, and spring follows winter, everything in nature happens in a certain chronology. This chronology is very important when working with natural magic because everything has a point or place of greatest power. The lunar and solar cycles influence energy patterns over short and long periods of time – through the days, months and seasons of the year. They are also present within human beings. By harmonizing with the cycles of the moon and sun your magic will be in harmony with the natural forces of the cosmos, rather than going against them.

Monday, or "moonday", is the day of the week that is dedicated to the Moon.

Telling the Time

Before the advent of clocks and calendars, people measured time, or the passing of the year, by the patterns of movement in the starry night sky. Because the stars appear to move on cyclic paths, time can be marked as they return to an earlier position.

It is thought that the first henge monuments, technically ring-ditches and embankments, were fixed observatories. By standing in the ditch, the astronomers would have had a flat circular horizon against which the moon or stars could be observed. Posts could be driven into the top of the bank so that patterns of movement could be gradually traced.

Aligning with Nature

Our modern lifestyle is pushing us further and further away from the natural rhythms of nature and we are losing contact with her cycles and seasons. Furthermore, as the delicate balance in the earth's biosphere is disturbed through man-made "greenhouse gases", the ozone layer is being damaged and the earth is getting hotter. This is disturbing the harmony of nature and causing changes in climate and weather patterns that could have a catastrophic effect if nothing is done to reverse the trend. Consequently many modern-day witches and magicians are using their magic to try to realign energies in the environment.

The wisdom of Saturn

Ancient astrologers knew Saturn as Rex Mundi, Lord of the World. He was also known as Cronos to the ancient Greeks, and Geb, god of earth, to the Egyptians. These gods governed time, one of life's limitations and restrictions. Saturn is the leveller or teacher. He teaches that we are subject to the cycles and rhythms of nature as we move from one stage of life to the next.

It is thought that megalithic monuments, such as Stonehenge, were used to help monitor the passage of time by observing the movements of the sun, moon and stars in the sky throughout the year.

Days of the week

Each day of the week is dedicated to a particular kind of magic and is governed by one of the "inner" planets.

Day	Planetary influence	Magical use	Colour	Incense	Number	Metal
Sunday	Sun	Use the power of the sun for personal healing or for a new impulse to assist your life.	Gold/yellow	Cedar Frankincense	6	Gold
Monday	Moon	Use the silvery light of the moon to strengthen psychic or dreaming powers, enhance meditation, and for inner work.	White/silver	Jasmine Water lily	9	Silver
Tuesday	Mars	Use the energy of Mars to end conflicts, for lack of motivation and for self-assertion. Also for anything that needs to be kick-started or needs physical work.	Red	Tobacco	5	Iron
Wednesday	Mercury	Use the energy of Mercury for communication: writing letters, talking, connecting with friends.	Orange	Mastic	8	Mercury
Thursday	Jupiter	King of Gods, Jupiter rules business, material growth, justice and legal matters. Energy of expansion and good fortune.	Royal blue	Cedar	4	Tin Brass
Friday	Venus	Goddess of love, Venus rules all kinds of partnerships, harmony and beauty. Use her energy to beautify yourself and improve your life. She is not a goddess to ask for help if you are wishing someone else to fall in love with you – you can use her powers only for yourself and to influence someone else would be a misuse of magic. If you want love, be loveable.	Green	Rose Patchouli	7	Copper
Saturday	Saturn	End of the week, ruled by Saturn, father of the gods. Use Saturn for anything to do with old age, with setting up or breaking down boundaries or limitations. His magic works slowly but it can be gentle and extremely powerful; patience is needed.	Black	Myrrh	3	Lead Pewter

Magical Hours

Several hours of each day are dedicated to each planet's power. These are not ordinary clock hours but represent one-twelfth of the time between local sunrise and sunset, and sunset and sunrise. This means that in summer the day hours are more than 60 minutes long and the night hours less. The first hour of each day from sunrise is dedicated to the planet whose day it is, and the following hours are ruled by the planets in the following sequence: Moon, Saturn, Jupiter, Mars, Sun, Venus, Mercury; returning to Moon, Saturn, Jupiter and so on for the night-time hours. From this you can calculate Moon or Mercury hours in any day, should you wish to work on a talisman at that time. The Moon hour on the Moon day is the strongest available lunar force, especially if it falls during the sign of Cancer (governed by the Moon). To bring in the greatest energies to a talisman, you would ideally also look at the actual planetary positions within the signs of the zodiac, and take into account your own birth sign, and the various aspects between your chosen planets.

Biorhythms

The forces of the sun and the moon are also present within human beings. The male solar energy is focused on action in the world outside, while the female lunar energy is inwardly focused. According to the theory of biorhythms, we all have an internal solar cycle and lunar cycle that affect us physically, emotionally and intellectually. These cycles produce a pattern of "highs and lows", so that some days we have lots of energy and feel able to do anything, while at other times we are more introspective.

CYCLES OF THE MOON

Because the moon has such a strong daily influence upon the rhythms of ebb and flow in our lives, its phases are closely observed when working with magic. Teach yourself to understand how the positions of the earth and the sun cause the moon to wax and wane, and change her rising and setting place and time throughout her cycles – which are actually 18 or 19 years long – before the earth, moon and sun return to their starting places. Find out how she affects your moods and the tides. The difficult phases of the moon are conducive to different kinds of magic work.

The phases of the moon are a way of recording the passage of time as she moves through her cycle.

WORKING WITH THE MOON'S CYCLE

Moon times are shown in many diaries or in *Old Moore's Almanac* (*The Old Farmer's Almanac*, in US). If you wish to utilize the powers of the moon more precisely when casting spells, refer to the lunar calendar or an ephemeris; it will take you deeper into working with the four faces of the moon. The best time of the year to remove an obstacle, for instance, is in autumn or early winter, whenever the moon is in Capricorn, or during a waning moon. If you wish for love, the best time would be when the moon is in Taurus or Libra, and during her waxing moon face.

THE BLUE MOON

Very occasionally, two full moons can occur in the same calendar month. Known as a "blue moon", this occurred only 40 times during the 20th century – on average once every two or three years and usually during a month that has 31 days. The event signifies a special time: a doubling of the moon's powers during the month that she appears. Considered unlucky by some, the blue moon is seen by many as a magical moon, when long-term objectives can be set. So a blue moon can be used to sow seeds for your future, giving them time to germinate and grow until the next blue moon rises. But you should be careful if you intend to weave magic during a blue moon. Be very clear about what you ask for, because this moon will be potent, doubling your wish and intent.

MOON-DREAMING

Many of the mental arts of magic are similar to inducing dreams to happen when you are awake, so the clearer the

Observing the moon's cycles can help attune us to the ebb and flow of natural energies, which is easy to lose touch with in the modern world.

The four phases of the moon

The moon has four phases – waxing, full, waning and dark – each of which is associated with one of the four winds. Witches observe the phases of the moon and time their magic in accordance with her cycles, tapping into the specific powers associated with each phase.

The first phase: waxing (new) moon
Wind: East
Timing: beginning of a new cycle; development and growth; new opportunities.
Lesson: to invoke – knowing.
Magic for: health and personal issues; put plans into action for the month ahead.

The second phase: bright (full) moon
Wind: South
Timing: the moon is full and ripe; a very fertile time, but care is needed as the energies are very powerful.
Lesson: to expand – manifesting.
Magic for: increase and expansion in your day-to-day affairs; a good time for personal power and magnetism.

The third phase: waning (old) moon
Wind: West
Timing: the moon's power is decreasing; release and letting go.
Lesson: to let go – courage.
Magic for: letting go of the past; a powerful healing time. It is also the time for insights and increasing psychic power.

The fourth phase: dark (no) moon
Wind: North
Timing: the moon disappears; time for retreat and withdrawal; recharging energies before the new cycle begins.
Lesson: to learn – to keep silence.
Magic for: gaining wisdom, understanding and insight. This time is best spent in contemplation, meditation and preparation, or seeking guidance; destructive magic is often practised at this time.

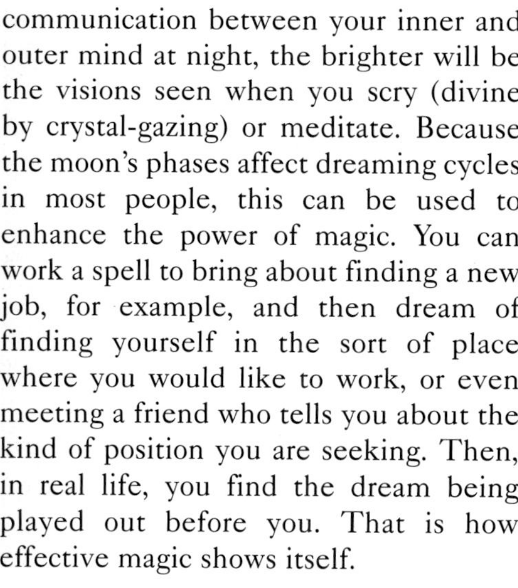

communication between your inner and outer mind at night, the brighter will be the visions seen when you scry (divine by crystal-gazing) or meditate. Because the moon's phases affect dreaming cycles in most people, this can be used to enhance the power of magic. You can work a spell to bring about finding a new job, for example, and then dream of finding yourself in the sort of place where you would like to work, or even meeting a friend who tells you about the kind of position you are seeking. Then, in real life, you find the dream being played out before you. That is how effective magic shows itself.

The Triple Goddess

The goddess of the moon is also known as the Triple Goddess. The Triple Goddess represents the maiden, the mother and the crone and is also known as the Great Mother or by her Latin name, Magna Dei.

The Maiden is associated with the new moon. She is everyone's daughter, playmate and inspirer. To the ancient Greeks she was Artemis, the huntress with her silver bow, protector of animals and children, the spotless maiden.

The Mother is associated with the full moon. She guides our lives, teaches us the skill of living, heals us. In Classical Greek mythology she was Aphrodite, the goddess of love and beauty, born of the foam of the sea.

The Matriarch or Crone is associated with the waning and dark moon. She gives wisdom, magical knowledge and the power to see into the future. The ancient Greeks worshipped her as Hecate, the dark goddess of the underworld, who teaches magic and ancient wisdom when the sky is dark.

Moon magic

The three phases of the moon are related to the Triple Goddess: new or maiden moon; full or mother moon; and waning or crone moon. Using moon magic often involves the use of three candles, which may be white or silver, or perhaps the colours associated with each of the three moon goddesses – white for the Maiden, red for the Mother and black or dark blue for the Matriarch.

Esbats

Lunar festivals are called "esbats" and are held on the first night of the full moon. They are times of celebration and power, when requests and dedications are made and a feast is shared to honour the Mother aspect of the moon goddess and her great abundance and fertility.

THE WHEEL OF THE YEAR

In natural magic, the seasons and cycles of nature show that life is a never-ending journey of birth, growth, death and rebirth. This journey is represented by the wheel of the year, which is divided into eight festivals or sabbats. Four of the sabbats are solar festivals (solstices and equinoxes) while the other four are Celtic in origin. Celebrating the sabbats is a chance to sharpen our awareness of the changing season, and to fall into harmony with the rhythms of nature. Any one of the festivals can be treated as a time for endings and beginnings as we move from one cycle to the next.

The colours of autumn are a reminder that the wheel of the year is turning and that the sun's powers are fading.

THE EIGHT SABBATS

The sun and the moon represent the polarities of light and dark, or yang and yin. When one is at the height of its power, the other is at its nadir and vice versa, and so the universe is held in a state of dynamic tension. The solstices and equinoxes are key moments in the solar cycle, while the other sabbats, or festivals, are more linked with agriculture and humans' relationship to the natural world.

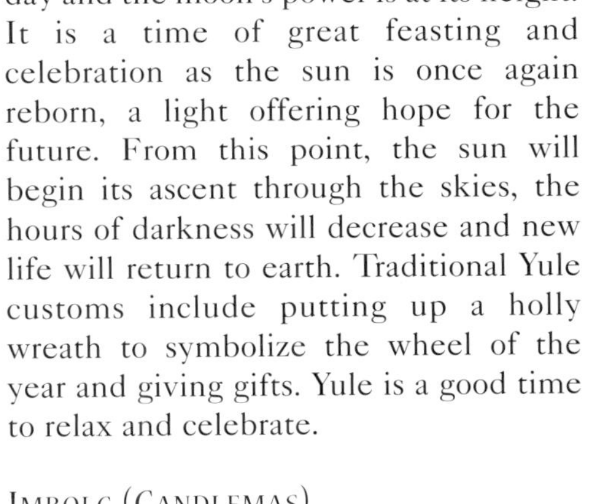

WINTER SOLSTICE (YULE)

The midwinter solstice, or Yule, is the shortest day of the year, when the sun is at its lowest point. Night overshadows day and the moon's power is at its height. It is a time of great feasting and celebration as the sun is once again reborn, a light offering hope for the future. From this point, the sun will begin its ascent through the skies, the hours of darkness will decrease and new life will return to earth. Traditional Yule customs include putting up a holly wreath to symbolize the wheel of the year and giving gifts. Yule is a good time to relax and celebrate.

IMBOLC (CANDLEMAS)

The Celtic word *imbolc* means "ewe's milk" and this festival heralds the beginnings of new life. It is the start of the lambing season, when the first green shoots appear, and the sun's strength is slowly increasing as the days grow longer. To celebrate the return of the light, a traditional custom is to light candles (hence "candlemas"). This is a good time for spring-cleaning the temple, and throwing out any lingering mental, physical and emotional baggage.

SPRING EQUINOX

Day and night are equal, but from this point the moon's power is waning and

The power of the sun is weakest during the winter, when the weather is cold and the hours of daylight are at their shortest.

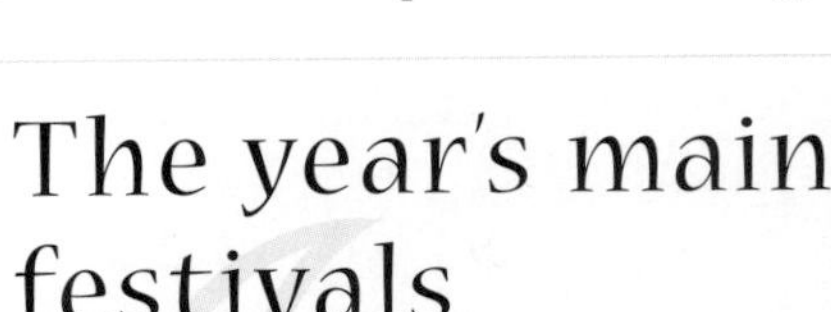

Different regions of the world have different seasonal and directional patterns, but the sabbats can be celebrated anywhere following the seasons, rather than the specific dates given here.

Winter solstice: (Yule) December 21 or 22
Imbolc: (Candlemas) February 2
Spring equinox: March 21 or 22
Beltane: April 30 or May 1
Summer solstice: June 21 or 22
Lammas: August 1
Autumn equinox: September 23 or 24
Samhain: (Halloween) October 31 through November 11

the sun is getting stronger as the hours of daylight increase. Fertility returns to the land as the life force gathers strength and the sap rises. At this time it is customary to plant the first seeds. Now is a good time to symbolically plant the new seeds for your life, to make plans and lay the foundations for the future.

BELTANE

The name for this festival of light and life comes from a Celtic word meaning "bright fire". It heralds the first day of summer and was traditionally marked by the lighting of bonfires to symbolize the strength of the rising sun.

May Day festivals and fairs, maypole dancing and other fertility rites are some of the customs associated with this sabbat. This is a good time to take part in creative projects, to socialize and have fun. Beltane is also associated with fertility magic.

SUMMER SOLSTICE

The sun's power is at its strongest at midsummer and it is the time when crops and fruits ripen. The longest day is celebrated at summer solstice, an occasion marked by the stones of many of Northern Europe's ancient megalithic monuments. At this time the mystical marriage between earth and heaven is celebrated as the God and Goddess make love. This is a time of perfection, but we also know that on its heels is the ascendancy of the dark. Healing herbs were harvested at midsummer, and it is a good time to be dynamic and active. Use magic to help with material matters, such as jobs, houses or money, or for fulfilling sexual relationships.

LAMMAS

Traditionally Lammas (or "loaf mass" in the Saxon language) was a time when the first grain was baked into bread. This festival celebrates the giving of thanks to nature for all her bounty, a time to reap what has been sown. Lammas is a good time for reflection, to go within and "count your blessings", to be grateful for what you have, and to understand why there may be a lack in certain areas of your life and how you might address this.

Celebrating the sabbats

The word "sabbat" comes from the Hebrew word, *shabbath*, which means to rest. In natural magic, the sabbats are holidays that mark important turning points of the sun's journey through the wheel of the year. They fall roughly every six weeks and are normally celebrated with feasting and rituals, using the energies of the changing seasons for peace, prosperity, health and good luck. The celebrations usually last from sunset until sunset the next day.

AUTUMN EQUINOX

Once again, day and night are of equal length, but now the sun's power is diminishing, giving way to the power of the moon. According to ancient Greek legend, this is when Demeter, goddess of the harvest, mourns the loss of her daughter Persephone, as a result of which the earth becomes barren. It is customary at this time to gather orchard fruits and the later harvest, celebrating nature's goodness yet being aware of the cold, dark months ahead. This is a good time to prune your life of non-essential activities; gather your energies and turn your attention inwards. It is also a good time to develop magical powers.

SAMHAIN (HALLOWEEN)

Also known as the Witch's New Year, Samhain marks the end of summer proper and the start of winter. It is a time when the veil between past, present and future is thin and it is possible to see beyond into the otherworld.

In Christian times, Samhain became the Feast of All Saints, a day when the dead heroes of the Christian church were commemorated. Traditionally, Samhain is associated with divination, being a good time to seek guidance for the coming season. It is also a good time to look back over the past and see how it has shaped the present; see what is holding you back and let go.

Spring is a time of renewal as daylight hours increase and the sun's life-giving energy grows stronger.

Spring and Summer

The four seasons of the year are nature's moods, each with its own unique characteristics. Following the seasons is at the backbone of modern magic, whether Wiccan, Druid or pagan, and there are many different ways of working with the gifts of the seasons. These include seasonal altars, ritual and celebration and many different kinds of magic, all of which are linked with other magical correspondences such as colours, incenses, the elements and so forth.

The yellow and violet flowers of spring can inspire us to begin new ventures in life.

Fresh Beginnings

After the long, dark days of winter, the first green shoots of life reappear in spring, a sign that life goes on. It is a time of birth and growth, of hope and optimism for the future.

The element of spring is Air, its direction is east and it is heralded in nature by bursts of fresh, vibrant colour: lively yellows, verdant greens and shots of bright blue, purple, pink and white adorn gardens, parklands, woods and hedgerows. Some of nature's sweetest perfumes scent the air – the delicate yet intoxicating scents of narcissus, bluebell, jonquil and hyacinth for instance. When using incense and incense oils at this time, all the citrus scents are fresh and uplifting; bergamot in particular is good for calming the feelings of insecurity that can accompany new ventures, and grapefruit is helpful for procrastination. Fresh green herbal scents, such as coriander, basil, sweetgrass, rosemary and thyme, are also stimulating and can help shake off any sluggishness left over from winter.

A Spring Altar

Set your altar in the easterly quarter of a room, and, if possible, arrange it under a window so that it is bathed in the morning sunshine. Invoke the element of Air to inspire you with confidence and hope for a new beginning. To symbolize new growth and natural energy you could add a vase of spring flowers or a planter containing spring bulbs. For a spirit of hope and new beginnings, burn a little elemi resin. Its spicy, lemony scent combines well with lemongrass or other citrus scents.

A summer altar for creativity can be as over the top as you wish, with vibrant pinks, purples and blues.

Ritual for a New Start

The best time to begin this springtime ritual is at new moon, or failing that when the spring moon is still in its first quarter. You will need a piece of yellow paper cut into a triangle, and a large circular piece of violet or sky-blue paper or cloth. You will also need a bell, an appropriate incense, and a few spring flowers. As you meditate before your altar, focus on your hopes and wishes for the future, allowing whatever thoughts or images come to mind to be there. Next write these down on the yellow triangle (this symbolizes the Air element). Put the triangle face down on the paper or cloth circle and place a bell on top. Each morning during the waxing moon, and as near to sunrise as possible, come to the altar, burn a little incense and ring the bell three times. As you do this, you can either ask your chosen deities or angels to help you, or else visualize your hopes and wishes being realized and achieved.

Summer's Abundance

As the sun's power increases, the season ripens and almost imperceptibly spring becomes summer, the time of nature's bounty and abundance. Summer is the season of relaxed and easy living, a gift to be enjoyed. It is a time to recharge and enjoy the sweetness of life. The element of summer is Fire, its direction is south and everywhere in nature a riot of colour and fragrance assaults the senses. These aromas include wallflowers, roses, sweet peas, honeysuckle, lavender, jasmine, carnations, clove, pinks and sweet Williams, while in the evening, night-scented stocks and nicotiana (tobacco plant) add their heady perfume. The colours of summer are hot pinks, crimson reds, royal purples, rich yellows and golden oranges, tempered by cool whites and creams and pale blue, pink and lilac.

Focus incense

If you are having trouble deciding on or setting your goals for the year ahead, this incense mix should help you to focus and clarify your thoughts.

2 parts dried rosemary
1 part dried thyme
1 part lemongrass
few drops rosemary essential oil
pestle and mortar

Pound all the dry ingredients together using a pestle and mortar, then add the rosemary oil, mixing it in well. Burn a few pinches of the mix on your altar, on a charcoal block.

The yellow triangle and violet circle on this spring altar both symbolize the Air element, which will help to inspire confidence and hope for new beginnings.

A Summer Altar

Position your altar in the south and invoke the element of Fire for creativity, fertility, expansion and growth. Remember that creativity is not the same as having artistic ability: rather the spirit of creation flows through every one of us, and may be described as the quintessential energy that we put into everything that we do. Use orange, red or deep pink candles and fabric, and images associated with solar power. Make the altar a place to try out your dreams and bring your own creations to beautify it.

Summer Rituals

Bonfire celebrations are a traditional way to celebrate summer. In Cornwall, England, a ritual is enacted whereby a bunch of nine good herbs and nine useless weeds is tossed into a fire by a young woman representing the goddess of the land. The idea is that the good plants will be increased by the fire and the weeds destroyed. Other summer rituals often re-enact the story of the Goddess and the God, who having mated at the spring equinox, marry at Beltane, so that their Child of Promise may be born at midwinter. Some Beltane rites reflect this idea of the sacred wedding, or allow couples to renew their vows, often by jumping over a bonfire, or casting bunches of sacred herbs into the fire as a kind of sacrifice.

Work with the magic of the full moon during summer to encourage fertility, passion and abundance. In ancient times, women would rise before dawn on the day of the full moon and go to the fields. There they would wash in the morning dew, asking the moon to bless them with children. If you want to have a baby, then you could also include a figure of the Goddess on your altar to ally yourself with her fertile power.

Aphrodisiacs

Certain fragrances are associated with love and romantic longing and even said to stimulate sexual desire. Best known of these are the distinct scents of summer flowers, especially rose, jasmine, ylang ylang and neroli (orange blossom). Sandalwood and patchouli are also renowned aphrodisiacs. Use any of these to stimulate love and fertility magic.

Autumn and Winter

Early morning mists and cooler days signal the advent of autumn. There are many ceremonies and rituals built around autumn's harvest, a time to give thanks for summer's bounty as resources are garnered and stored for the long winter months ahead. The long, dark days of winter are rich in magical tradition and mystery, having a unique quality and flavour associated with the moon and darkness, as well as feasting and celebration for the rebirth of the sun god at the winter solstice.

Some of the negative associations of autumn are decay and barrenness.

Harvest and Decay

After the glorious crescendo of summer, everything in nature begins to contract. Russets, golds, amber, dark reds and nut-browns are the paint-box of autumn as leaves change colour and fall, blown about by the season's blustery winds. Autumn is a rich tapestry of colour and the earthy scents of decay, a time to reap nature's bounty at the harvest as the old withers and dies. It is a season of endings and completion, a turning point on the wheel of the year between the free and easy living of summer and the restrictions of winter. The element of autumn is Water and its direction is west. Any earthy, or woody fragrances will represent the mood of autumn; suitable incense and oils include myrrh, cedar, patchouli, pine, or rosewood.

An Autumn Altar

Position your altar in the west and use rich autumnal colours for candles and fabric. You might like to use nuts, fruit or berries as an offering to the deities, angels or other powers that you are working with. As well as the abundance of the harvest, autumn is also associated with death, loss and mourning and so is a good time of year to reflect on the past and to come to terms with any unfinished business.

Water, autumn's element, is linked with emotional healing and letting go, so make sure this is symbolized on the altar too. To heal emotional hurts and disappointments, incenses such as frankincense, myrrh, sandalwood and agarwood are all helpful. Burn them during the time of the waning moon.

An autumn altar of abundance and thanksgiving could include harvest fruits as an offering to the deities. Position it in the west and use rich autumnal colours.

Harvest Rituals

Traditionally, magic was worked to keep the weather dry and calm so that the harvest could be gathered in. At this time, the God, as Spirit of the Corn, becomes Lord of the Underworld, a place of magic and eternal youth. The last sheaf of standing corn was sometimes cut in a ritual way to keep his spirit of fertility alive until the spring sowing. Today, ears of wheat are still saved and woven into corn dollies or "kern kings", then decked with red ribbons, the colour of blood and vitality, to be set over the hearth until spring.

The saving of the seed for next year's crop thus symbolizes the hope for the future that is kept alive during dark and seemingly barren periods of life.

Using Mushrooms

In addition to being a source of food and medicine, mushrooms can also inspire visions of the past and the future. A great number of mushrooms and other fungi are edible, but require expert guidance to be gathered safely; they vary from the expensive truffles, traditionally hunted by dogs or pigs, to the common horse mushrooms and puffballs that are found in many places. Some of the poisonous toadstools, however, are considered to have special properties. One of these is the fly agaric, the red and white mushroom typically shown in fairytale books. Shamans in Lapland would traditionally feed these mushrooms to their reindeer, then drink a potion made from the reindeer's urine. Having got rid of the dangerous toxic effects via the reindeer's metabolism, the potent potion causes visions of flight. It is thought that this might be the origin of the flying reindeer associated with Santa Claus.

Frost and snow outside signify the indoor months of winter, the season of introspection.

The Power of Winter

As the harvest draws to a close, the weather changes and winter takes over, bringing with it cold days and long nights. Crisp icy weather and clear open skies reflect winter's radiance, while the stark silhouettes of trees stripped bare remind us that nature is ultimately uncompromising: what is born will one day die and return to the earth. Winter is the indoor season. It is time to close the shutters and spend more time alone or with those closest to us, away from the busyness of the world. It is the season for introspection and reflection in preparation for the rebirth of spring: this means nourishing ourselves in mind, body and soul and the focus is on wholesome food, plenty of sleep, brisk walks and generally taking care of ourselves. The direction of winter is north and its element is Earth. Its moon is the dark or no-moon phase. Warming, comforting, or spicy scents such as orange, cinnamon, cloves and nutmeg are all appropriate for winter rituals.

A Winter Altar

A minimalist style for your winter altar will reflect the stark simplicity of nature. Ice white, silver and black are all winter colours, while adding a touch of crimson or dark blue links with the moon's symbolism. Position your altar in the north and choose maybe one or two beautiful objects to represent the Earth element: a fallen branch, a piece of driftwood, or twisted willow branches. Appropriate incenses include vanilla, benzoin resin, sandalwood, frankincense and dammar (cat's eye resin). Spend time each day at your altar, meditating and journeying deep within yourself.

Yuletide Myths and Rituals

In some traditions, the winter solstice (on or around 21st December) is known by its Saxon name of Yule. Yuletide is a time of feasting, when the Yule log, made of the root of a great oak tree, or the Ashen Faggot (a bundle of sticks from an ash tree) burns in the hearth for the 12 nights of the festival. It should be as big as possible and is lit from a piece of the previous year's log. As many homes no longer have an open fire, today's Yule log is usually symbolized by a log-shaped chocolate cake.

A stark, minimalist winter altar could be as simple as a stone pot and sandalwood incense.

For pagans, Yule is the time of the birth of the Star Child, Modron, also known as Mabon, the sacred Son of the Mother. He is the Child of Promise, whose coming brings hope to the wintry world. Like the birth of a real child, his coming is eagerly awaited within the ritual, and gifts of magical significance are offered to the young boy who takes his part in the Mystery Play of Mabon. The ritual tells of the magic child's birth and as he ages one year for one day, by Twelfth Night he is old enough to earn his magical instruments and symbols, which are shown to the whole company. This time of year can also be a time of initiation for other young people into the tradition of the clan. It is customary to exchange gifts at Yuletide.

MAGIC IN ACTION

Having become apprenticed to magic, by now you are doubtless keen to try putting what you have learned into action, and to start testing your powers as a magic-worker. So prepare to cast reason and logic aside as you shape-shift into the world of magic. This is where the boundary between this world and others begins to dissolve and the impossible becomes possible. It is where dreams can become reality, for magic becomes a tangible force that touches on many different areas of your life.

Although the otherworld is a place of magic and mystery, it nevertheless operates according to its own internal rules or logic. These rules are known as metaphysical laws and magic workers need to recognize and respect them. One of the most important of these principles is the law of karma – whatever you sow, so shall you reap. Misuse of magical power is not recommended, for whatever you give out returns to you threefold. So before creating magic always make sure it will harm none and is done for the highest good of all.

PLANNING AND PREPARATION

Before you undertake any piece of magic, there are certain set procedures that must be followed, more or less, all the time. For magic to be successful adequate preparation is essential, and putting in the effort during the initial stages will set the scene for the magic itself. It is worth making the time to track down all the correct ingredients and also to prepare yourself and your workspace so that you are in the right frame of mind for making magic. Contraindications to making magic would be when you feel tired or drained, or when your mind is busy and won't switch off.

This chapter will give you a good grounding in all the practical information you need to start working magic, beginning with ethics and responsibilities. It goes on to explain how to consecrate yourself, your space and your equipment through bathing and cleansing rituals that include smudging and the use of herbs and oils. It also describes techniques for raising energy, invoking spirits, angels and other beings, and for aligning yourself with higher powers. It finishes with instructions for opening and closing a magic circle – the sacred space in which magic happens – and how to make offerings and give thanks to your magical allies for their support.

The Power of Magic

When you work with magic you are working with powerful forces for change, and it is important to realize this before you begin to send wishes and weave spells. The energy you put into magic increases as it is released and what you give out returns to you threefold. So be careful with what you wish for, as you might have to live with the consequences for a long time. It is important not to be fearful of magic, however, but instead learn how to be humble and ask for the right things in the right way. When you ask with sincerity, and from the heart, you ask from the right place, and this is the way to exercise the true power that you hold within you.

Ethics and Responsibilities

The witches' law states that "if you harm none, do what you will." At first, this may appear like a licence to do whatsoever you like, and magic-workers are often criticized for having no moral code. However, it actually means that as long as you cause no harm to any person, animal or thing, you may follow your True Will. True Will is not a personal choice or desire, but the purpose of your existence here on earth. The reason you are alive is to discover your True Will, or purpose, and work towards realizing it. Furthermore, it is a universal law that whatever we give out is reflected back, hence the biblical saying, "as you sow, so shall you reap".

Reaping the consequences of our actions – good or bad – is inevitable, if not in this life, then in another incarnation. Consequently, it is always a good idea to align yourself with the divine will of the universe before starting to perform a magical act. You may think of the divine will as the God or Goddess, your Higher Self, the ultimate source, or the One – whichever description best works for you.

When making the Spellweaver's Pledge imagine golden light filling your whole being.

Making the Pledge

Before starting to weave magical spells or rituals, it is important that you pledge yourself and your actions to the light. This is a way of reminding yourself of your intentions and should be done simply and from the heart.

1 Place your hands upon your heart and ask that you be filled with the light of love. Imagine the golden light and feelings of love filling your heart and then your whole being.

2 Open your arms and raise them above your head, palms facing up towards the heavens, and say the pledge. Then bring your arms down to your sides.

The energy and concentration you devote to your magic making will return to you threefold.

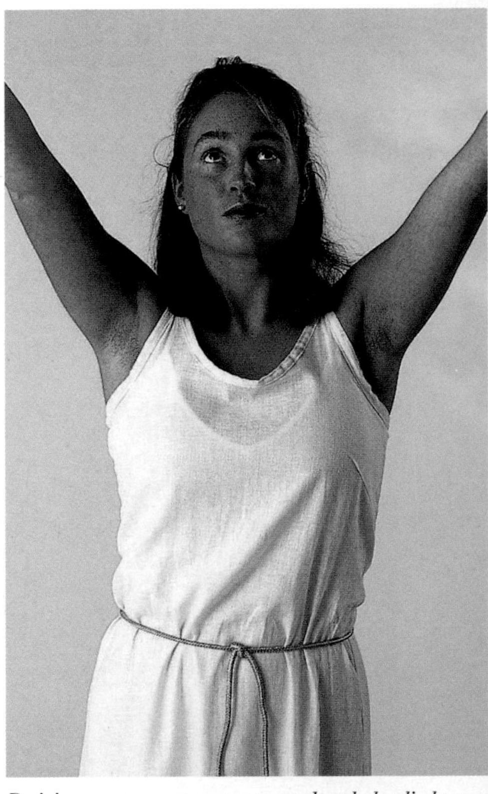

Raising your arms as you say the pledge links you with the heavens.

The Spellweaver's Pledge

I call upon the divine will of the universe to send a blessing upon my heart, so that I may be filled with the light of love and truth in all that I do. I pledge that from this day I will do my best to harm none with my thoughts, words or deeds. I pledge that any magic I perform will be for the highest good of all. So mote it be!

Hedgewitches

Of course, it is not necessary to work with others or to belong to any recognized group in order to practise magic. A magical practitioner who works alone and according to his or her own individual style and belief is sometimes known as a hedgewitch. In days of old, the hedgewitch, or country witch, or wise woman, would have been called upon regularly by members of the community. They would have performed such things as house blessings and clearings, to help with the protection of vulnerable people, property and personal possessions, and also to act as an oracle for discovering the reasons behind particular problems or hindrances.

Hedgewitches, who live in harmony with nature, use their knowledge of herbs, flowers, roots and leaves to make up concoctions for such purposes as healing, protection or fertility. The country witches of today seldom write anything down, relying – as did their predecessors – on memory and inspiration for their workings, which are usually conducted in a sacred place. Their knowledge is passed on in the old way, by apprenticeship, whereby a newcomer is gradually taught magical rituals, healing spells, chants and movements, or else may be self-taught. A hedgewitch is so named because she is able to keep one foot in the material world and the other in the world of spirit, and the "hedge" represents the veil between the worlds.

Covens and Lodges

Many practitioners of magic like to work with others, either within a coven or group of witches, or in a magical lodge. Traditionally, these organizations have been kept secret, but one way of discovering other like-minded people is to look for announcements in popular occult magazines, which may list societies or training schools. Alternatively, seek out publications written by specialists in the area of magic that most interests you. It has never been easy to find a way into the Mysteries, but these basic steps are open to all.

Having found a suitable coven or lodge, the next step will be to undergo a ceremony of admission, or initiation. The word "initiation" means beginning, so this is a first step, rather than the conclusion of a magician's work. No one should accept initiation into a group unless they are certain that it is right for them, and that the group is trustworthy. If there are any doubts in your mind about a group, it is far better to wait than to rush into a situation.

Commitment and Secrecy

Although society is far more tolerant now than it was in the past, it is still best to keep some things secret and go about your magical work in privacy and silence, both of which will add to its power. Effective magicians never speak of some things, including who is working magic, when and where any magic or ritual is being done (unless it is some sort of public festival) and any magical names and mottos used. These are only ever known to the magicians and the gods. While you can read books on most techniques or activities, it is the practical experience of magic that makes it work, and that is a particular secret that cannot be shared.

Go about your magical work in quiet privacy: it is not a sideshow or something to do in public, but a personal commitment that you should take seriously.

TIME AND PLACE

Before you rush into any piece of magical work you need to consider timing and location. Timing is important because everything has a point of greatest power and therefore a right time and purpose. By utilizing the season, the correct phase of the moon, the four winds, the right planets, herbs, minerals and affirmations, you can increase the efficacy of your magic. Similarly, every place has a certain energy field, or spirit of place, that will be naturally better suited to some types of magic than others.

An offering on an outside altar can be as simple as a few flowers on a tree branch.

TIMING

To plan the best time for your magic you need to use your knowledge of the phases of the moon, the time of day and the season. Current positions of the planets and the kind of "energetic pattern" they are creating are also worth noting. You can consult an ephemeris, a table showing the movements of the planets, for this kind of astronomical information.

Consider whether the purpose of your magic is to attract or create something, or to reflect or dissolve something. The waxing phases of the sun or moon are for the former, while their waning phases are associated with the latter. The moon's cycles last roughly 28 days, while the solar cycle takes 365 days, or a calendar year; the sun is waxing, or growing in strength, from the winter to the summer solstice, and waning thereafter. To find out about the phases of the moon you can consult a diary or almanac.

PATIENCE

Modern society is fast-paced and based on instant gratification. We are not accustomed to having to wait for things and even the length of time it takes to cook our food is getting shorter and shorter. Yet magic does not work in this way. It takes time for things to manifest on the material plane, and we must resist the temptation to think it is not working if, once we have set magic in motion, we don't see an immediate result.

One of the golden rules for every magic worker is patience. Just as it takes time for a sown seed to germinate and develop into a healthy plant, so it is with magic – and the bigger the plant you are trying to grow, the longer it may take to come to fruition. So once you have set your magic in motion, leave it alone. Do not keep repeating the spell or ritual without need as this shows a lack of faith in its original power. Another thing to remember is that magic can move in mysterious ways, so try not to be cynical or disappointed if the results are not exactly what you had planned or envisioned; they will be exactly what your inner self called for to meet your true needs at this particular time.

INSIDE OR OUTSIDE

You have two choices about where to perform your magic – indoors or outdoors. Traditionally, spells are cast outside. Some covens meet out of doors, in woods or high hills, in all weathers. These outdoor witches use whatever is around them for their symbols: water in a seashell from rain or a spring, a small

One of the most important elements of your magic work is patience. If you are naturally impatient then you will need to work on your ability to wait.

Woodland clearings, or the tops of hills, are traditionally places where magic is made, but anywhere outside will do, so long as it is quiet and secluded and you can be sure you will not be interrupted.

bonfire, a tree branch for a wand and their hand for a sword. If you want to work outside it is helpful to find a natural beauty spot that is peaceful and secluded, where you won't be disturbed. Such a place could be part of a garden, near a particular rock or tree, or in meadowland. It will be somewhere that inspires a feeling of being part of creation and where you feel safe. You may also want to set up a natural altar in your chosen spot, using "found" objects that you come across, such as stones, feathers, nuts, flowers, leaves, pine cones etc.

If you do not have access to an appropriate place outside, you can use a room in your home. If you have the space, it should be a room or section of a room that is primarily dedicated to making magic. If this is not possible, you will need to create a magical space each time you work, but in any case, it is important to keep the atmosphere clean and balanced. This can be done by cleaning it regularly with salt and burning purifying herbs.

Natural objects or representations of them are good for working magic outside.

Visualizing sacred space

Sometimes it is not possible to travel physically to a special place for magic work. However, everyone has the ability to create an inner sacred space that can become a sanctuary or temple, a retreat from the everyday world where magic can happen.

Your inner sacred space can be any kind of place in which your spirit feels happy and at home – a woodland clearing, a cave, a deserted beach, even a corner of your own garden. Concentrate on creating the place and remembering it in detail. You will need a candle and some incense.

1 Take five deep breaths to centre yourself and focus your mind on what you are about to do. Voice your intent out loud. Light a candle and burn some incense, holding your intention in your mind. Contemplate the candle flame for a while, imagining it lighting up the recesses inside you, so that you may find a way to the place you seek more easily.

2 When you feel ready, sit in a comfortable position and focus on your breathing. With closed eyes, take deep, slow, relaxing breaths from your diaphragm. Now picture an opening, a natural doorway such as a hole in the ground or the mouth of a cave. This will lead you to the sacred space you seek.

3 When you pass through the doorway, and enter your sacred space, pay attention to details that will make the place seem more real. Notice what you are standing on: is it grass or stone, sand or pebbles? Pause to smell the fragrance of a flower, reach out and touch trees or rocks, hear the sound of birdsong and the sighing of the wind, sit by a freshwater spring and drink its water.

4 When you feel it is time to leave your sacred space, give thanks and promise to return. Retrace your steps through the entrance and come back to your physical body.

PREPARATION RITUALS

Taking the time to prepare yourself before you start working magic is an important part of the magic itself. If you work spells or rituals when you are feeling tired or when your mind is busy with other things, then you can't expect to achieve good results. In fact, because magic involves connecting with powerful energies, it is not recommended that you attempt to perform magic at all when you are like this. Wait instead until you have more vital energy and are able to switch off your thoughts and become like an empty vessel. Magical energies will then be able to flow through you without you becoming drained or too attached to the result of your work.

Add some essential oils to your bath and bathe by candlelight as preparation for magic work.

PREPARING YOURSELF

There is a saying that "cleanliness is next to godliness", and it is an esoteric belief that harmful negative energies will fasten on to any dirt on the body of an individual engaged in magic work. Traditionally, initiates fasted, refrained from sexual activity, bathed and anointed themselves with oils and herbs to prepare themselves for magic. While it is not necessary to go to such extreme lengths, some level of deliberate preparation will give your magic work more significance. Eating a light, plainly cooked meal rather than one that is rich in spices and sauces is preferable before you begin, for example. When we have sex our energies mingle with those of the other person, so make sure that any sexual contact is especially loving and nourishing as it can affect our magic – for better or worse, depending on the qualities of the relationship.

After your bath you might like to anoint yourself with rose water or an oil blend containing rose geranium essential oil before performing a ritual.

Bathing is highly recommended; an invigorating shower or a long soak in the bath are both appropriate. Water not only cleanses the physical body but also washes away psychic dirt from the subtle bodies. We pick up this psychic dirt all the time – from negative energies in the atmosphere created by our negative thoughts, anxieties, stresses and petty jealousies as well as from vibrations in the environment. If you do not wish to bathe, simply washing your hands and face is helpful.

While you are bathing, imagine that you are cleansing away all impurities from your body, mind and soul, and as the water drains away visualize all those impurities draining away from you. Using essential oils or herbs in the bath is

Cleansing herbal bath mix

The ingredients for this mix are associated with purification and cleansing. Use fresh herbs if possible.

You will need

7 basil leaves
3 bay leaves
3 sprigs oregano
1 sprig tarragon
small square of muslin (cheesecloth)
10 ml/2 tsp organic oats
pinch rock or sea salt
thread

Pile the herbs in the muslin, then add the oats and the salt. Tie the corners of the muslin with thread. Hang the sachet from the bath tap so that the running water is infused with the essence of the mixture.

Golden light breathing exercise

The more concentrated and positive effort you fill your magic with, the more potent it will be, so to be successful as a worker of magic you need to know how to raise or increase energy. Energetic breathing will help you build up your concentrated energy. This technique is cleansing and empowering; it increases energy in the body and gives you more resources to work with.

1 Stand with your feet hip-width apart and feel them make contact with the ground. Rest your hands on your stomach and take a few deep breaths into the stomach area.

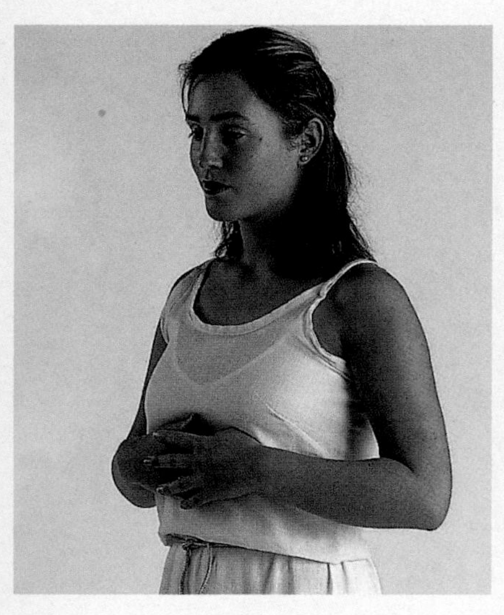

2 Place your hands just below your sternum. Begin to breathe, not too deeply, but slowly and with concentration.

3 Breathe in through your nose and visualize drawing golden light into yourself. Hold the breath for a short time (do not strain) and imagine your heart opening. Breathe out through your mouth, letting the golden light circulate around your body.

4 Continue breathing in this way until you feel energized and wide awake. Then rest your hands on your heart for a few moments, letting the breath gradually return to normal.

Spend some time preparing yourself mentally with a period of meditation to achieve the right frame of mind before you begin your magic work.

also helpful: lavender, geranium or rose are good choices, or look for any others that are particularly purifying.

Next, choose what you are going to wear. A robe is ideal, otherwise select loose-fitting garments that do not constrict the flow of energy through your body. Don't worry about looking fashionable – comfort is much more important when making magic. In fact, many witches like to work "sky clad", or naked, as they feel much freer and closer to nature like this, but this is up to you.

Mental and Psychic Preparation

When undertaking any magic work it is important to be in the right frame of mind, so mental and psychic preparation is recommended. After you have bathed, a period of meditation immediately preceding the start of a ritual will help to achieve calm composure. Meditation can be accompanied by some quiet, spiritually inspiring music and the burning of a suitable incense. A light fragrance such as geranium or a head-clearing scent such as rosemary is best, leaving the heavier aromas for the ritual.

Preparing the Temple

Whether or not you have an actual "temple" room in your home, you will need to create a sacred space for working magic. Again, this needs to be properly prepared. The first step is to create a "clean slate", as any psychic impurities or negative energies present when magic is performed can intrude and interfere, contaminating the result and perhaps changing it completely. As a modern analogy, we might think of such impure energy as a kind of occult computer virus, with a purifying and cleansing routine acting like an anti-virus program.

Every culture has its own favoured purifying and cleansing methods, many of which date back thousands of years. In Old Testament times, for instance, brooms made of hyssop were used to clean out temples and other sacred buildings. Today, many occultists like to use the Rose Cross ritual. This involves lighting an appropriate incense and carrying it around the room while wafting the smoke in a pattern from corner to corner in a cross shape, then making the shape of a circle in the middle of the cross. This shape represents a cross with a rose in its centre, which is the symbol of the Rosicrucian Brotherhood, a secret occult order that dates back to the fifteenth century.

A feather can be used in smudging, fanning the fragrant smoke around your body to cleanse your aura of any negative energies.

Smudge sticks are densely packed and can burn slowly for a long time.

Smudging

One of the most popular purifying and cleansing techniques, smudging is a shamanic practice that has enjoyed widespread revival in recent years. Its shamanic origin means it lends itself to just about any magical path without causing contention. It is very simple but extremely effective, and because it needs a little input from the practitioner, it encourages magical thought and activity while the basic tools for the ceremony – a smudge stick and a smudge fan – are being put together.

A smudge stick is a densely packed bundle of herbs, which usually includes sage – a plant that smoulders when lit, producing clouds of fragrant smoke. The fan should be made of feathers, or else a single feather can be used. The purpose of the fan is to waft the smoke all over the area being cleansed – over the walls, floor and ceiling and around the doors, windows and any other openings into the room, such as the fireplace or air vents. The nature of the herbs, the intention of the person who gathers and ties them together, and the action of the fan will drive away any negative thought-forms lingering in an area.

Making a Smudge Stick

It is very rewarding to grow and dry your own herbs, thus ensuring that their magical qualities are tended during all stages of growth, and that you honour the spirits of the herbs when cutting them. The three herbs suggested here are all for purification. The best variety of sage to use is American white, or mountain, sage (*Salvia apiana*). All the herbs must be thoroughly dried.

You will need
dried sage stalks
dried lavender flower stalks
dried thyme stalks
natural twine

Gather all the dried herb stalks together and arrange them in an intertwined bundle. Tie the stalks together at the end, and then wind both ends of twine upwards around the bundle until it is bound together. Light one end, extinguish the flame and let the smoke rise to fill the area. As you fan the smoke, strengthen the action by visualizing the herbs' cleansing qualities.

Blessing your Equipment

In the same way that you prepare yourself before performing magic, all equipment and materials that you intend to use should also be cleansed and consecrated beforehand. Once blessed, the items can be stored, ready for use. The blessing described here is for a cord, but you can adapt it for any other item. You can also perform this ceremony on an altar if you prefer.

you will need
compass
incense
candle
bowl of spring water
bowl of sea salt
cord

1 In a cleared space outside or on the floor, mark out a circle with the four points of the compass. Put the incense in the east quarter, the candle in the south, the bowl of water in the west and the bowl of salt in the north.

2 Begin with the east quarter. Light the incense and say the first line of the blessing. Pass the cord through the smoke rising up from the incense, while imagining a clear, cool breeze passing through the cord.

If you do not have a smudge stick or dried herbs, then you can use incense sticks for your cleansing and purification rituals.

3 Turn to the south quarter and say the second line of the blessing, passing the cord through the candle flame as you do so.

4 Turn to the west quarter and say the third line of the blessing, while sprinkling the cord with water.

5 Turn to the north quarter and say the fourth line of the blessing, sprinkling the cord with salt. Finish by saying the final lines of the blessing.

The Blessing
I cleanse, bless and consecrate this cord with the powers of Air.
I cleanse, bless and consecrate this cord with the powers of Fire.
I cleanse, bless and consecrate this cord with the powers of Water.
I cleanse, bless and consecrate this cord with the powers of Earth.
Finish with
May this cord now be cleansed and purified for the highest good of all.
And so mote it be!

Thought-forms

In occult terms, an atmosphere can contain "thought-forms". These subtle vibrational patterns are produced by the workings of the mind and are picked up at a subliminal level, rather like how a radio set receives broadcast messages. A received thought-form reflects the nature of the original broadcast: happy, sad, gloomy, cheerful, and so on. Thought-forms that are deliberately created by a magician can be extremely valuable and they form a major part of magic. But unconsciously produced thought-forms tend to be negative and can get in the way of making successful magic, which is why purification rituals are so important.

CASTING A MAGIC CIRCLE

Whether you work inside or outdoors, it is traditional to create a magic circle before starting a ritual, spell or other piece of magic. The circle will help you concentrate on your work and will banish any unwanted thoughts or influences. With practice, you will come to know it is there, protective and empowering, each time you begin your ritual. You need to visualize the area within the circle as a place of stillness beyond normal time and space. It is a place where physical, social and spatial boundaries are redrawn, and represents the wholeness of the human, the natural and the divine. It is where the internal and external are connected and where all is incorporated into one – matter and spirit reunited. You may outline the circle using a wand or staff, and as you turn to draw the line in the air you may see it burning with golden fire.

The working place is a circle of light, whether visualized, or made with physical elements.

Making Your Circle Magical

A legacy from ceremonial or high magic, the circle traditionally recognizes the four points of the compass. North is the place of Earth; west is the place of Water; south has the heat of Fire; and east possesses the breath of Air.

It is customary to open the circle in the east, which through its association with Air symbolizes intellect and rational thought. Its magical tool is the athame (dagger) or sword, although a feather may also be used. The next point on the circle is Fire in the south, the energy of the magical will that desires to create. Its magical tool is the wand, which can be a slender branch of wood; hazel is especially appropriate as it has the capacity to bend, although a candle may also be used to represent this point. The south is the quarter of the circle for energizing, for setting in motion a course of action. Through its association with Water, the west is associated with emotions and feelings. While the east separates and divides, the west flows and merges; beginnings are initiated in the east, while letting go is the theme of the west. The west's symbol is the cup or

Making a magic circle

You can make a magic circle in many different ways. It can be visualized in your mind's eye, drawn in the air with a wand, a dagger or just your hand, or created physically – with stones, candles, or other symbolic objects. One popular way is to use a length of white, silver or gold cord, laid out on the ground. This will need opening and closing down before and after the spell.

You will need

2.7 m/9 ft length, 5 mm/¹/₄ in thick white cord
salt water

The Light Invocation

By the powers of Heaven and Earth, I cast this circle in the name of love, wisdom and truth, for the highest good.

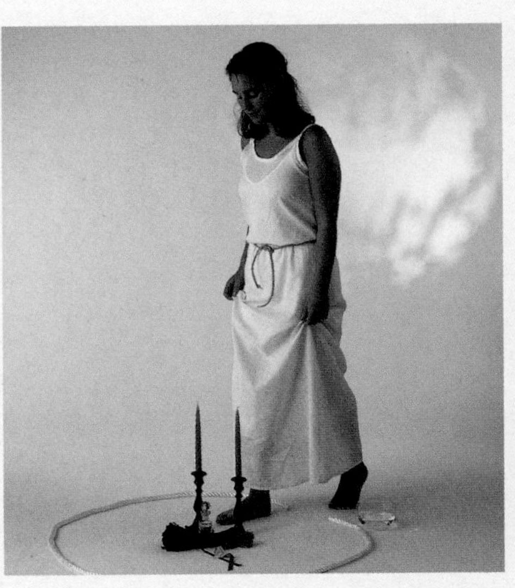

1 Place the cord in a circle with an opening in the east. Step through the opening with whatever items you are going to use for your spell or ritual. Place them in the centre of the circle. Close the circle behind you and seal it with a sprinkling of salt water.

2 Go clockwise around the circle, sprinkling salt water on the cord as you go. Visualize yourself surrounded in golden light and say the light invocation. The circle is now ready to work within. When you have finished your spell, close the circle as detailed on the opposite page.

chalice, or else a bowl of water. The north corresponds to darkness and winter, the polar opposite of the south's fiery heat. It is the quarter for containment and inner reflection and is represented by the pentacle or sometimes salt.

Casting the Circle

There are many different ways of casting a magic circle. It may be drawn in the air with an athame or with your hand, visualized as a ring of fire, or you may prefer to create an actual, visible circle, such as a cord circle – if you are new to magic, you may find this easier to work with. If you are working outside, you could make one out of rocks, pebbles, pine cones, pieces of wood, or even flowers: choose objects that seem to "speak" to you in some way and are in harmony with your magic.

One of the most versatile circles is a basic cord circle, which can be used indoors or outside. Remember that a magic circle is always opened in the east and should be cast in a deosil (clockwise) direction. It should always be closed before any magic work takes place, and you should not step out of it until you have finished. When you are finished, you must ritually take the circle apart or dissolve it.

Closing the Circle

At the end of your magic it is important to take the circle apart. This is to keep the magical energy pure and contained, marking the boundary between magical and everyday activity. Doing so also acknowledges that endings are part of life's cycles. Work "widdershins" (anticlockwise) until you end up where you began. For instance, if you started working a spell or ritual in the south, you would close the circle by beginning in the east and moving round through north and west until you reach the south. Gather up your tools from each quarter as you go round and as you do, say the following words:

I give thanks to all who have helped me
and leave my magic with you.
And so mote it be.

One way of making a magic circle is using candles or tealights.

Nature's circles

If you are creating a circle from natural objects, use 12 items. Ask permission to use each object in your magic before taking it. Purify each item with a pinch of salt and say:

I bless this stone/rock/flower or whatever with love, light, wisdom and truth.

Then sprinkle salt on the object, asking for a dedication to the light. Welcome it to the circle and explain what you are going to do.

Some magicians and witches visualize a circle to create a place between the worlds, and trace it with their finger at the beginning of a ritual or spell.

INVOCATIONS AND OFFERINGS

Once you have created your magic circle, it is customary to invoke the spirit beings that you wish to call upon to assist you in your magic. Their subtle yet powerful presence will help to connect you with the otherworld and make your magic more effective. At the same time, every magic worker knows that magic is a give-and-take relationship, so will always give thanks to these unseen helpers as well as to the spirit or energies of the place and the equipment that has been used. In this way, you ensure that your magic is aligned to the highest good of all.

A sacred herb in the Native American Indian tradition, tobacco is often used as an offering.

GUARDIANS OF THE WATCHTOWERS

In casting a magic circle, great importance is attached to astral beings called the Guardians of the Watchtowers. The "watchtowers" are the four quarters of north, south, east and west. The purpose of the powerful guardians is to protect those who invoke their aid and ensure the security of the circle. They will be with you while you work and should be thanked at the end.

The guardians may be seen as angels, totem animals, gods and goddesses, holy living creatures, elementals or any other kind of otherworld beings – every tradition has its own set, but it's up to you what you choose to work with. Cabbalists, for instance, often invoke the four archangels: Raphael (Healer of God) in the east; Michael (Like unto God) in the south; Gabriel (Strength of God) in the west; and Uriel (Light of God) in the north. Some practitioners may prefer to work with the Arthurian legends: King Arthur, master of the mysteries, in the east; Gawain, defender of all that is good, in the south; the Lady of the Lake, guardian of the secrets, in the west; and Merlin, the archmage with the power of vision, in the north.

INVOKING THE GUARDIANS

There is no single right way to invoke your heavenly powers, what matters is the spirit with which you do it, so be creative. Just remember that you cannot command or order these powers to be with you, but only ask or invite them from a humble heart. The following invocation calls upon the Guardians of the Watchtowers (the four directions), but if you are working with a different

Angels and Arthurian heroes are both called upon in magical working as guardians and helpers. Here Sir Galahad achieves the Grail, a potent magical symbol, watched by other knights of the Round Table, and three archangels.

An offering of salt is made on a very simple and impromptu altar.

Leaving an offering outside

When you are taking something from the natural world, show your gratitude by leaving something behind. If you are taking something from the land, always ask its spirit for permission first. Remember it is illegal to pick wild flowers or disturb protected species.

1 To make an offering, hold your gift in your hand and present it up to the sky.

2 Present your offering to the earth to show appreciation to the Great Mother.

3 Hold it out to each of the four directions – north, south, east and west – keeping in mind the connection between all things.

4 As you leave the offering in your chosen place, voice your thanks and intention. Speaking the following words aloud will help to focus your attention and energy:
I offer this in gratitude for the gifts given, in honour of creation and my part in it.

set of guardians, then you may insert their name after "I call".

1 Stand inside your magic circle, close your eyes and take a couple of breaths to centre yourself.

2 Face north, raise your hand and say:
I call the Guardians of the North to protect this place from earthly wrath.

3 Turn to face the east and say:
I call the Guardians of the East to calm the airs and bring me peace.

4 Turn to the south and say:
I call the Guardians of the South to protect me from the fire's red mouth.

5 Finally, turn to the west and say:
I call the Guardians of the West to lay the stormy seas to rest.

6 When you have completed the circle and are again facing north, say the following words. As you do so, imagine the circle you have cast is spreading through the universe like ripples in a pool, bringing tranquillity and peace to its centre, which is you and your circle.
Let blessings be upon this place
And let my Circle clear this space
Of spirits wicked, cruel or fell,
So that in peace I may dwell.

Giving Thanks

It is always advisable to give thanks to your unseen helpers. One way to do this is by making an offering to the spirits. This must be natural or biodegradable. Not only will this acknowledge them as important, it will also encourage a cooperative relationship, for when you make an offering you exchange energy as well as giving thanks. You may also make an offering if you need special help, or in gratitude when your magic bears fruit.

You can make offerings on your altar or shrine, in your magic circle, or outside. In the North American Indian tradition, tobacco is often used, while the Celtic tradition favours salt. The offering can be anything that has special meaning to you and is in harmony with your magic – flowers, stones or coins, or something made especially for the purpose, such as a loaf of bread you baked, or a cake.

Elementals

Archetypal spirit beings associated with each of the four elements are sometimes known as "elementals". Believed to inhabit the realm of Faerie, they are sylphs, salamanders, undines and gnomes. Sylphs are the fairies of Air in the east, and their name is taken from the Greek *silphe*, meaning "butterfly". Salamanders rule Fire in the south, and their name is from the Greek *salambe*, meaning "fireplace". Undines are the ruling spirits of Water in the west, and their name is derived from the Latin *unda*, meaning "wave". Finally, gnomes are the creatures of Earth in the north; their name comes from the Greek *gnoma*, meaning "knowledge".

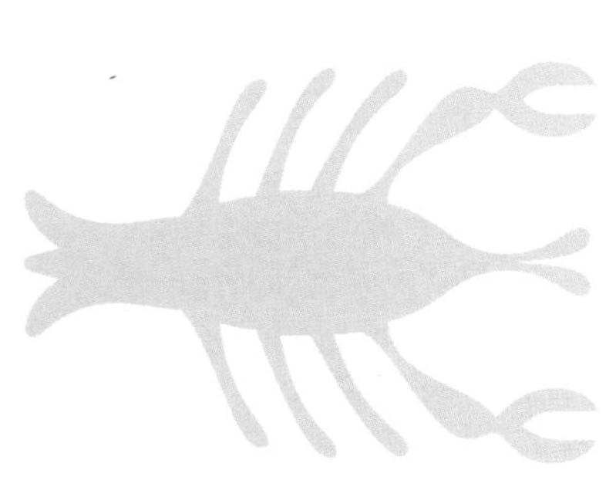

Ritual Through Life

A ritual is a way of making contact and communicating with the otherworld, thereby bringing transformation – or magic – to the individual and to the wider cosmos. Traditionally, it is a way of honouring transitional states as we move from one stage of life to another, and it provides an opportunity to step outside routine ways of thinking and behaving in order to connect with the unseen forces of the cosmos that shape our lives. Major life events, such as birth, marriage and death, are usually acknowledged by some kind of ritual ceremony, while seasonal festivals are also acknowledged by ritual acts. It is also possible to transform everyday events into something special through ritual.

This chapter looks at the power and purpose of ritual, differentiating between rites, ritual and ceremony and the role they have to play in magic. It includes a variety of rituals that can be performed to assist with many different aspects of life. These include the banishing ritual of the pentagram, a traditional magical ritual to clear psychic energies, as well as rituals for inner calm and healing. It looks at how we can use rituals for blessing ourselves and our homes and how to make rituals a part of our daily lives. It concludes with information on rites of passage and how magic is being used to create meaningful rituals for the modern world.

THE POWER OF RITUAL

Since ancient times, rituals have played an important part in magical and sacred ceremonies. Rituals are patterned acts, performed to bring about specific objectives. For our earliest ancestors, they were often accompanied by sacrifice and were an attempt to placate, if not to control, forces that were potentially life-threatening, such as wild animals or extreme climatic conditions for instance. In magic, rituals are a way of connecting with the otherworld to give thanks, make offerings, ask for guidance or make requests. The tools that are used in ritual, the elements and the powers that are invoked, all have particular meaning and significance and must be used with care.

Lighting a candle focuses the mind, and acts as a signal to all present that the ritual is beginning.

The Pattern of Ritual

A ritual is a patterned activity. This means that it follows a recognizable structure and sequence of steps, time after time. What is important is that you engage with it in mind, body and soul and do not just "go through the motions". The latter would make it an empty gesture devoid of meaning and therefore it would lack any real power to make magic happen.

To begin with, it is essential that a clear and precise objective is outlined and that everyone who is involved is fully aware of this purpose, which is often stated at the start of the work. Most magical rituals follow four basic stages: purifying mind, body and soul; getting dressed or robing; preparing the place; and creating the circle. Whether the ritual is for divination or a celebration, to consecrate a talisman or work for healing, its purpose is then said aloud so that all those taking part are clear about why they are there, and agree to its purpose.

Preparation for a ritual often begins with cleansing or purification. This can be symbolic, such as passing round a bowl of warm water, scented with essential oil, and floating flowers.

Working the Ritual

Once you have made the necessary preparations, opened the sacred space and stated your purpose, you can proceed to magically do whatever you have decided upon. This could be creating a talisman, weaving a spell, sitting in meditation, enacting a traditional myth, or celebrating a special time of year. Towards the end of the ritual it is usual to have a sacred sharing, or communion, with the deities, angels

Outdoors or indoors?

Old-fashioned village witches often performed their rites and rituals alone or else with a close group of family and friends, and as far as possible they would work outdoors. Modern-day magic workers tend to hold their rites, rituals and ceremonies indoors for the sake of convenience.

and otherworldly beings who have been called upon to help your magic, as well as with any other people who are enacting the ritual with you. Something to eat, which may be bread and salt, biscuits, fruit or any other sacred food, placed on a platter, is blessed, often in the name of the Earth Mother who provided it, and eaten. Then wine, water, milk or any other drink in the chalice is blessed in the name of the Sky Father, or by the power of the Sun God, before being drunk. The chalice is taken with both hands to show complete involvement.

After the communion there is often a pause to meditate on what has been begun by the ritual, or if you are with others, to discuss business or any other matters. Then it is customary to say "thank you" and release the higher powers that you summoned to your ritual and to unwind the circle widdershins (anticlockwise), the opposite direction to the one used at the beginning. You may feel a shift of energy and gentle return to ordinary awareness at this point. When you are clearing up, you might find it useful to discuss the ceremony, although if you are working for an ongoing purpose it is best not to talk about it so that the magic has time to develop in the silence of secrecy. If it was a festival, then that has been completed and may be shared.

Food is often a part of a ritual, and preparing it – such as dividing up bread or pouring out glasses of wine – can become part of the ceremony.

If you are passing round a chalice, hold and take it with both hands to show involvement.

Rites, Rituals and Ceremonies

There is sometimes confusion over the difference between rites, rituals and ceremonies. The words "rite" and "ritual" are often interchangeable, but rites tend to have shorter and simpler workings, and are often performed by someone working alone. Much less emphasis is placed on the preparation and the closing of a rite, with the concentration instead on the central stages. They come in many shapes and forms, which vary depending on their source or tradition and on their purpose. Simple rituals veer more towards a rite, while those that are more elaborate and complex could more accurately be described as a ceremony.

A ceremony usually involves several people, and has a more complicated pattern and more elaborate equipment. Ceremonies may be held in public or in front of an audience. They are used by many traditions worldwide to mark special times – to celebrate birth and naming, to join two people in marriage, or to lay the dead to rest. Some ceremonies are performed by a priest before a congregation, while others allow the wider participation of the faithful, in processions, public offerings, hymn singing or ritual dance.

Stick with It

It can take time before you can perform rituals and ceremonies with ease and confidence and at first you may feel embarrassed and rather self-conscious, particularly if there are others present. However, most people feel like this when they start doing something new and out of the ordinary, so persevere. It is worth putting up with a few uncomfortable feelings in the beginning, as these will begin to subside once you start to reap the rewards of natural magic.

A BANISHING RITUAL

A highly respected ritual that has been used by a number of the main magical disciplines for hundreds of years is the Lesser Banishing Ritual of the Pentagram. It is called "lesser" only to distinguish it from its counterpart, the Greater Ritual of the Pentagram, which is used for magical invocation rather than for banishing or clearing. The Banishing Ritual involves invoking angelic powers for the purpose of purification and is often used to space clear a place of unwanted energies or create higher vibrations for magic.

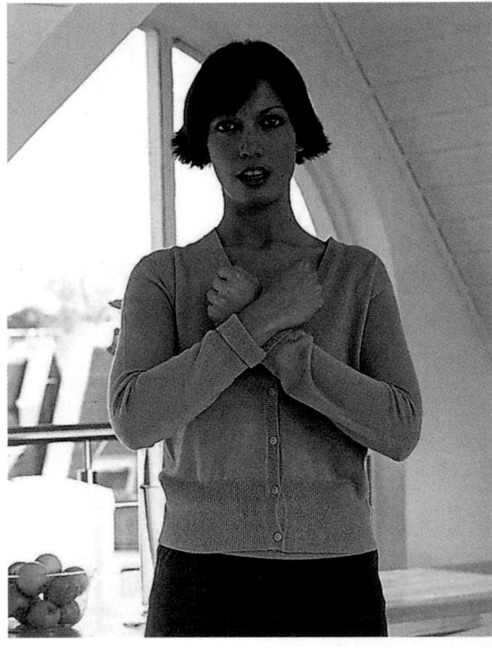

The traditional gesture of the god Osiris completes the cabbalistic cross part of the ritual.

Cabbalistic Influences

Because the banishing ritual is Cabbalistic in origin, much of its wording is in Hebrew (including some words from the Lord's Prayer) and it calls upon the archangels of the Judaeo-Christian tradition. The ritual is divided into three sections: the Cabbalistic cross; the drawing of the pentagrams; and the invocation of the angels. To close the ritual, the first section – the Cabbalistic cross – is repeated.

The first movement of the ritual is to reach up to an imagined sphere of light above your head.

The Higher Self

The main reason for performing the Cabbalistic cross as part of the Banishing Ritual is to enable the magic-worker to get in touch with his or her "higher self". This higher self is visualized as white light that is present above the head, and is drawn down by the ritual. The higher self is able to bridge the gap between the everyday world and the higher astral planes, the source of infinite knowledge and wisdom.

Performing the Ritual

Before you begin, prepare yourself by bathing, drinking spring water and sitting quietly in meditation for a while. You should be dressed in clean, comfortable clothes. Make sure you will not be disturbed at any time. Unplug or switch off phones, close the curtains if you are overlooked. When you are ready to begin, place yourself in the middle of the space you are working in. Work through the following steps slowly with reverence and respect.

1 Visualize a sphere of pure, clear light, about the size of a football, a little way above your head. Reach up to it with the fingers of your right hand and visualize that you are drawing a shaft of this light down to you by touching your forehead. Say:
Ahte (pronounced "Ach-tay" and meaning "Thou art").

2 Touch your fingers to the centre of your chest, visualizing the shaft of light travelling down to infinity through the floor, as you say:
Malkuth (pronounced "Mal-koot" and meaning "the Kingdom").

3 Touch your right shoulder, saying:
Ve-Geburah (pronounced "vay-Geboorah", meaning "the Power").

4 Touch your left shoulder, saying:
Ve-Gedulah (pronounced "vay-Gedoolah", meaning "and the Glory"). As you do this, visualize a shaft of light emanating from infinity to your right, crossing your body as you perform the action and plunging away into infinity again on your left.

5 Now cross your wrists at the centre of your chest with the right wrist outermost in the "Osiris risen" position. As you do this, say:
Le Olahm (pronounced "lay-Ola-chiem" and meaning "Forever").
Now bow your head and say:
Amen ("So be it").

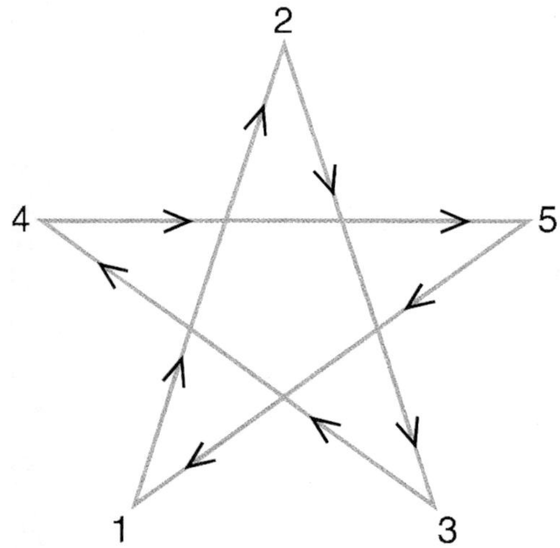

This diagram shows the order you should trace the pentagram. Begin at point number one.

DRAWING THE PENTAGRAMS

The next part of the ritual consists of drawing four pentagrams, one in each direction of the compass, starting with the east. The particular pentagram used here is called the "earth banishing pentagram". Each pentagram should stretch from about shoulder to knee height and is best drawn with the arm at full stretch if possible. As each one is completed, it should be "fixed" with a stabbing gesture of the fingers into the centre, accompanied by a Hebrew word.

1 Face the east to draw the first pentagram. When it is complete, fix it while saying the names of the letters that spell the name of God – Yahveh in Hebrew, or Jehovah in English:
Yod-He-Vau-He.

2 Turn to face the south and draw the next pentagram. Fix it by saying:
Adonai ("Lord").

3 Then draw the western pentagram, fixing it with the name by which God identified himself to Moses, pronounced Eeh-heh-yeh:
Eheieh ("I am that I am").

4 Finally, draw the northern pentagram. The word to fix this with is pronounced "Ah-geh-lah". It is made up of the initial letters of the phrase Aith Gedol Leolam Adonai:
Agla ("Thou art mighty forever Lord").

As you invoke the archangel Gabriel, turn your palms to face you.

THE INVOCATION OF THE ARCHANGELS

The third part of the ritual involves the invocation of the archangels.

1 Raise the palms of your hands to face forward and say:
Before me, Raphael (pronounce the angel's name "Raff-eye-ell").

2 Turn your palms to face behind you, saying:
Behind me, Gabriel (pronounced "Gab-rey-ell").

3 Lower your right hand, palm upwards, and say:
On my right hand, Michael (pronounced "Mick-eye-ell").

4 Lower your left hand the same way and say:
On my left hand Uriel (pronounced "Ur-eye-ell").

5 Finish by saying the following words. Raise your hands above your head and put them together as you utter the last line:
For about me flame the pentagrams.
Above me shines the six-rayed star!

The Cabbalistic Cross

It should be noted that the hand makes the cross from right to left, not from left to right as in the Roman Catholic crossing gesture.

EVERYDAY RITUALS

Rituals help strengthen our connection with the universe. Just as vibrations spread across a spider's web or ripples radiate across water, a simple ritual can have far-reaching effects on you and those with whom you relate. By performing simple rituals based around your daily activities you can consciously choose to strengthen the connection between your everyday self and your higher self, and life itself becomes a ritual for living.

Ritual food can be chosen so that it embraces the essence of the four elements.

HABITUAL ACTIONS

In everyday life habitual actions such as cleaning our teeth or making a cup of tea are sometimes referred to as rituals, yet we do not generally associate them with magic. What differentiates habit from magical ritual is the consciousness we bring to the action. Performing an act with awareness has the effect of increasing the efficacy of that act. This is because the intent carries to other levels of our being: for instance, if you take a shower with the intent of cleansing your spirit as well as your body, the overall cleansing effect is greater. It will empower you and make you stronger. It will also "charge" your energy body with spiritual vibrations so that you will radiate a certain aura wherever you go and life becomes a magical experience.

Even the most ordinary activity can have ritual significance. Taking the time to buy and arrange some special flowers, for example, gives your home love as well as decoration.

FOOD AND DRINK

Preparing and eating food are powerfully symbolic activities and mealtimes provide a very good opportunity to incorporate ritual with day-to-day practicality. When you are preparing food, do it with love and appreciation of what has been supplied by Mother Earth to give you nourishment. Choose your ingredients carefully – ideally you should always use organic, locally grown and seasonal foods, and those that you have grown yourself are even more special.

Tea ceremony

Throughout the world, there are many customs associated with the brewing and serving of tea. The most notable of these comes from Japan, where the classic tea ceremony is a complex ritual that elevates drinking tea into a spiritual experience. The tea ceremony has many rules and set procedures and is presided over by a master of ceremonies. It is a good example of how a daily activity can be transformed into a magical experience.

Making food for rituals

Although for rituals many people just use commercial bread, broken into pieces, and any kind of wine, mead, cider or fruit juice as a drink, you may wish to try the old ways where special biscuits or scones and your own home-brewed wines or beer are made for rituals. Any type of food or recipe will do; it is the act of making it that adds power to your ritual. As you become more experienced, you can adapt traditional recipes by adding favourite or appropriate ingredients. Although not everyone has the time to make wines for rituals, it is a pleasing skill to master. Country wines can be made with fruits, vegetables, herbs, berries and dried fruits. It is very important that you sterilize all the equipment before use.

Baking bread yourself for a specific magical purpose gives the ritual greater power.

Eating foods that are as close to their natural state as possible is not only beneficial for your body, but is also helpful from a spiritual point of view. Remember we are what we eat, and the plants and animals are all gifts of Mother Earth, so by sharing her bounty at mealtimes, we are also taking in some of the eternal blessings of creation.

In magical ritual, it is customary to bless our food or drink before taking it into our body. You can do this by holding your hands over the meal, closing your eyes and inwardly saying thank you to Mother Earth for her goodness. Make time to eat away from your normal activities, even if this is a quick snack. Take time to experience the different tastes, colours and textures of your meal. Don't work, read, watch TV or talk excessively to others while you are eating as this only takes energy away from eating. When you eat with awareness, even ordinary meals can become a ritual that nourishes body and soul.

Food for Festivals

All over the world, special dishes are served at festival times throughout the year. These can range from a simple kind of special bread eaten occasionally to elaborate feasts with many courses to celebrate a major event such as a wedding or seasonal festival, like Yule. But you may not want to wait for big occasions, and could make one meal a month (at new moon for example) an opportunity to share some simple dishes with others on your path, to discuss the arts of magic, and celebrate the passing seasons. It can be a time when you decorate your shrine with new flowers and symbols, and use that as the centrepiece of your gathering.

Home-brewed wine and mead are free from chemicals and full of goodness, and have the added value of having been made yourself, so adding to their magical purpose.

Ritual through the Day

Just as everyday acts can be transformed into ritual, it is also possible to use rituals throughout the day to help strengthen your connection to your magical powers. Morning and evening are two especially potent times of day for ritual activity. Morning is the beginning of a new day and rituals performed at this time will set up a pattern of energy that you can take with you throughout the day. Evening is about endings and winding down; rituals performed at this time will help you come back home to yourself.

As you touch your forehead to begin, say clearly and firmly, "I am Spirit!"

Morning Rituals

Greeting the morning puts you in touch with the rhythms of nature and is a great way to start a new day. You can work out your own simple ritual involving a few stretches or breathing exercises to wake up the body, perhaps followed by a moment of quiet or meditation to collect yourself for the day. Taking a shower is also energizing and refreshing and changes your energy from sleep to awake; use fragrances such as rosemary, all the citrus scents, peppermint or eucalyptus in your shower products.

It's good to make time for a period of quiet contemplation or meditation, accompanied by purifying incense, to prepare you for the day.

Start-the-Day Ritual

The following ritual summons a fresh charge of personal psychic energy to strengthen your being and encourage you to appreciate the joy of a new day.

1 Light your chosen incense or vaporize your essential oil. Stand facing a window, towards the east (during warm weather this ritual can also be performed outside facing the morning sun). Take some slow, deep breaths.

2 When you feel calm, make the sign of the pentagram on your body. Touch your forehead with the fingertips of your right hand, and say:
I am Spirit!
Then touch your left hip and say:
I am Earth!
Touch your right shoulder and say:
I am Water!
Touch your left shoulder and say
I am Air!
Touch your right hip and say:
I am Fire!
Finally, touch your forehead again to complete the figure of the pentagram and say:
Thus I seal my affirmation.

3 Inhale the fragrance of incense or oil for a few moments before beginning the new day.

Wake-up herbs

For protection and purification: frankincense, juniper
For success: cinnamon, carnation, cloves
For a clear mind: rosemary, basil, peppermint
To dispel sluggishness: grapefruit, lemon, lime, bergamot

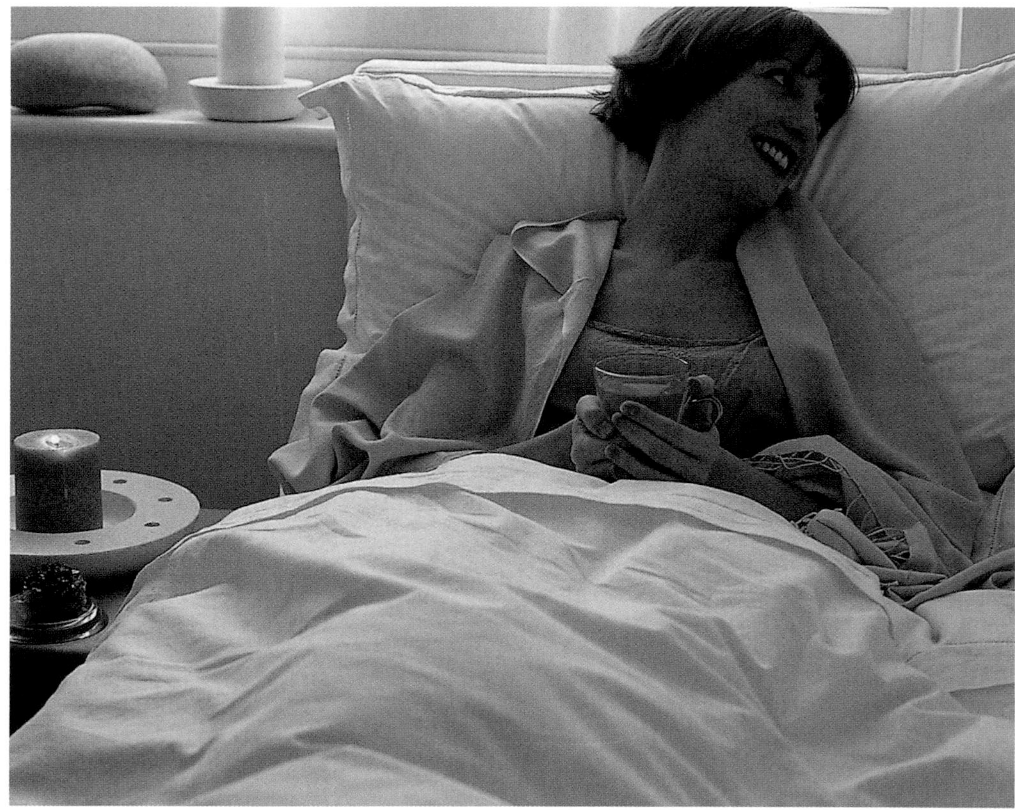

After you have finished your bedtime ritual, relax with a cup of dreaming herb tea and allow the tensions of the day to disperse.

Evening Rituals

Just as you began with energizing and empowering rituals to greet the day, evening time is about winding down and relaxing and giving thanks for the day that has passed. It is a time of transition between wakefulness and sleep, and it is important that you allow yourself to slow down before going to bed. A simple night-time ritual is to make an offering on your altar last thing at night using incense and candles to give thanks and let go of the day that has passed. Useful herbs, incense or oils for encouraging peaceful sleep include lavender, marjoram, hops, camomile, rose and passion flower.

End-the-day Ritual

To end the day, you can use this specially modified version of a much more elaborate ritual known as the Middle Pillar Exercise, which has its origins in the teachings of the Cabbala. To add to its effectiveness and enhance your ability to sleep, place an amethyst or clear quartz crystal under your pillow before you settle down to sleep.

Placing an amethyst under your pillow will help you achieve a deep and untroubled sleep.

1 Before you begin, calm and centre yourself. Stand facing west – the direction of the setting sun – and for a few moments focus on the sun setting on the horizon, whether it is actually still daylight or already dark.

2 Imagine a beam of brilliant white light shining down on you from an infinite height. As it touches your head and enters your body, it transforms your entire body into light-filled glass, like a clear bottle of human shape.

3 As the light courses down through your body, see it changing hue, moving through all the colours of the rainbow. As these colours flow down, imagine any dark areas of your body being cleansed by the rainbow light, pushing the blackness downwards and out through the soles of your feet.

4 As the rainbow-coloured light flows out of your body through your feet, imagine that it is forming a pool or puddle of black mire, and that this pool is then draining away into nothingness, leaving you clean and filled with brilliant opalescent, rainbow hues.

Dreaming tea

Mix the following herbs to make yourself a goodnight tea. It can help you to recall your dreams and have a restful night's sleep. (It is not advisable to drink this tea if you are pregnant.)

1 heaped tsp dried jasmine flowers
1 heaped tsp dried camomile flowers
2 sprigs fresh marjoram
a large cup or mug of freshly boiled spring water
honey (optional)

Place all the herbs in a jug and pour over the boiled water. Infuse for 5 minutes, strain into a cup and sweeten with honey if desired. Sip this tea about half an hour before you go to sleep.

A RITUAL FOR INNER CALM

When you are flooded with emotion, desires and restless thoughts it will be difficult to focus on making magic, as all you will be able to think about will be yourself. A magic-worker needs to be able to switch off from their personal concerns in order to connect with the higher self and the cosmos. This means being calm and still inside with your energies contained and focused. Methods to achieve this state form an essential part of Eastern sacred traditions, most notably Zen Buddhism, from which this ritual has been adapted.

Meditation is an ideal practice to help you move towards a clear-minded state.

Zen Philosophy

The word Zen is derived from the Chinese *ch'an*, which in turn originates from the Sanskrit *dhyana*, meaning "meditation". A philosophy of Chinese origin that was adopted by the Japanese in the 12th century, Zen has its own unique identity within the wider practice of Buddhism. Its essential concept is that perfection (nirvana) can only be achieved when all is reduced (or expanded) to nothing. Zen rituals therefore tend toward simplicity, quiet, stillness and deep inner reflection to create an atmosphere of intense and almost tangible peace.

Ritual for Inner Calm

This ritual is ideal when you are feeling stressed and anxious and are unable to settle yourself by your usual methods. To perform it, you will need as much silence and stillness as your surroundings permit. Ideally your space should be as empty and clutter-free as possible, as this will help to induce calm and composure. Remember to turn off your phones.

If possible, use a gong to mark the beginning and end of the ritual; otherwise find something else that will produce a similar clear, simple sound. You will also need a low table or altar covered with a plain black cloth and a few sticks of sandalwood incense in a suitable container. Set up the altar so that you can sit or kneel before it facing east.

The Ritual

Light the sandalwood incense. Kneel on a cushion or sit on a straight-backed chair before the altar. If you prefer, you may sit cross-legged in a half- or full-lotus position. When you are comfortable, perform the fourfold breath to still your thoughts. To do this, breathe in to an unhurried count of four, hold your breath for a count of four, breathe out for a count of four and hold your breath again

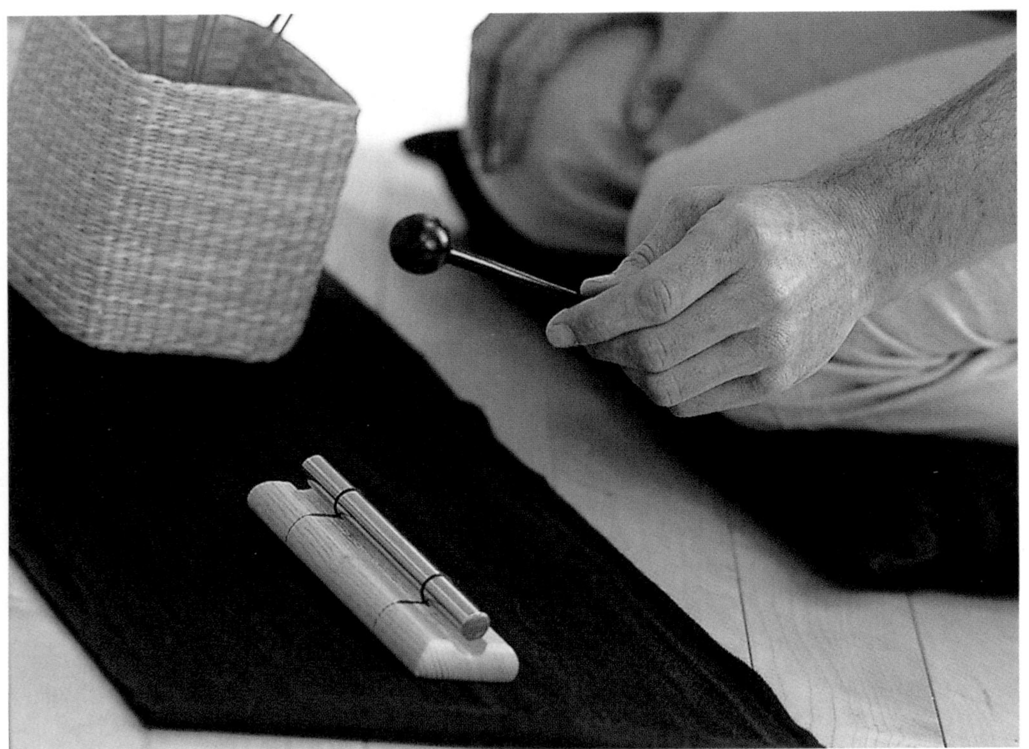

A simple sound is used to mark the beginning and ending of a Zen ritual.

The sound of Om

"Om" is spoken after taking as deep a breath as possible. It begins with the sound "ahh", moving into "oh" and ending with "mm" for as long as the out-breath lasts. All of these three sounds should merge into one. The sound of Om is said to symbolize all the sounds in the universe.

Zen koans

Koans are exercises in paradox, used in Zen teaching, and are designed to baffle the mind until it is defeated and reduced to nothingness. They take the form of questions that defy reason; perhaps the most famous is "What is the sound of one hand clapping?" When everything is reduced to its ultimate state of non-being, then the perfection of union with the higher spiritual forces of the cosmos becomes possible.

for a count of four. Take the next breath and repeat the sequence. Continue to practise the fourfold breath for a few minutes until you feel a state of great calm begins to unfold.

When you feel sufficiently calm and at ease with your surroundings, gently sound the gong once. As the sound fades, begin to chant the single word "Om" as slowly as possible. Keep your head bowed towards the altar. Repeat the chant 10–12 times, taking care throughout to avoid any feeling of "hurrying things along".

Once you have reached the end of the chanting, take two or three more fourfold breaths, then slowly bow towards the east, with your hands held at your chest in an attitude of prayer. In this position, repeat a single long "Om". Your mind should now be clear enough to concentrate your thoughts. Close your eyes and visualize a circular ripple of light in the centre of your abdomen, slowly spreading out horizontally, like the ripples from a stone tossed into a pool filmed in slow motion. As this circle of light reaches the horizon, it continues out into the universe and to infinity. Continue to observe this visualization for several minutes. As you do so, make your mental image as sharp as you can, ideally you are aiming for a reality equivalent to having your eyes open, but this takes a little practice.

To end the ritual, stand up, place your hands in the prayer position at your chest as before and bow deeply from the waist. Sound the gong one more time to close the meditation.

The Zen philosophy epitomizes simplicity, and ritual in the Zen style will therefore also be very simple and unadorned.

Incenses for inner calm

In the East, several incenses are particularly valued for their affinity with meditation, but two of the most noteworthy are sandalwood and agarwood (or "aloes"). Hindu temples were often made from sandalwood, while yogis (masters of yoga) use a yellow sandalwood paste to mark the "third eye" chakra. This paste is cooling and helps calm restless thoughts. Burning sandalwood incense has the same effect. Little known in the West, agarwood has been valued in Middle and Far Eastern countries for thousands of years. Its indescribable fragrance has been compared to a blend of sandalwood and ambergris and is reputedly one of the finest (and most costly) fragrances in the world. Agarwood is used in Japanese incense and is said to open up the heart to compassion while calming the mind.

A HEALING RITUAL

In many traditional societies, it is the medicine man or woman who performs healing rituals for the sick – whether this is a person, situation or even an environment. The healing ritual described here is based on traditional shamanic practices in its use of herbs, drums and chants to summon the assistance of the spirit world for the purpose of healing or rebalancing energies.

The Role of the Shaman

The word "shaman" comes from the Tungusic dialect of the Ural-Altaic tribes of Siberia. Shamans were the priest-doctors of the tribes, responsible for officiating at ceremonies and rituals, tending the sick and caring for all aspects of the spiritual wellbeing of the people. The term is now used more broadly to describe individuals who commune with the natural and supernatural world for the good of their community using traditional shamanic practices, such as drumming, journeying and dreaming.

A Shamanic Healing Ritual

The shamanic ritual outlined here calls upon the powers of the drum, of sacred herbs, and of the Inyan (the stone people of the Native American Indians) to summon dream spirits for healing, cleansing and purification. Have a representation (such as a picture) of the person, situation or place that you are doing this healing ritual for and place it on your altar or shrine. This ritual is best done in a fairly large open space so that you are able to move around, or if possible outside.

Sit for a moment in front of the burning sage, and breathe in its cleansing smoke.

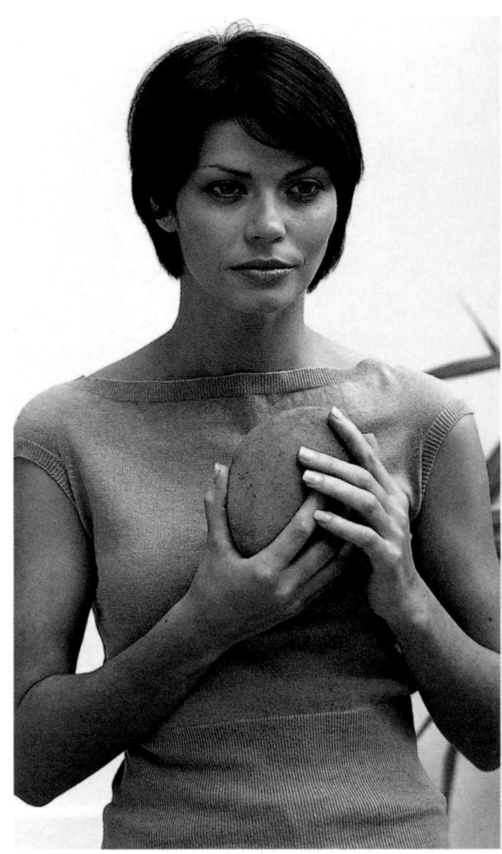

As you hold the stone to your heart, visualize the person you are working on.

You will need
loose dried sage
heatproof bowl or shell
black or dark feather
large stone chosen for its individuality
tobacco
drum

1 Place the sage in the bowl and light it. Use the feather to fan the smoke around yourself and over the large stone. This is known as "smudging".

2 Take a pinch of tobacco and stand in the centre of your space facing north. Say the following words, then place the pinch of tobacco at the centre.
Great Spirit I honour you and humbly seek your presence within this grandfather rock.

3 Pick up the large stone and, holding it to your heart, ask it to help you clear any negative energies from the person, situation or place you are working on. Set the stone down on top of the tobacco saying the words:
Mitake oyasin ("For we are all related").

The shaman's drum

The drum is one of the shaman's most powerful tools. Its primal sound touches the deepest recesses of mind, body and soul, connecting us with the heartbeat of Mother Nature and life itself. Before using a drum for a ceremony, it is customary to make an offering to the spirit of the drum. The spirit is made up of the essence of the animal that gave its hide, the tree that gave its wood and the maker who gave his or her skill and intent. The offering is given to honour the separate units that came together to make the whole. To make an offering, sprinkle a little tobacco over the drum before you begin to use it, saying thank you.

Drums play an important part in shamanic rituals. The sound of the drum is said to call healing spirits, while driving away sickness.

4 Take another pinch of tobacco and, still facing north, hold out your hand in that direction. With feeling and respect call out "Buffalo" and place the tobacco on the floor to the north.

5 Repeat the gestures for the east, south and west, calling out "Eagle", "Mouse" and "Bear" respectively.

6 Turn to the north again and say the following words, then stand the smudge bowl on the stone so that the smoke coils up through the room.
Guardians of the four winds, I, your brother/sister, do call your presence here.

7 Take up the drum and, beginning at the edge of your space, walk deosil (clockwise) in a spiral until you reach the centre, drumming the atmosphere towards the stone. Drum over the stone into the herbs, visualizing any negative energies coiling away in the smoke. Thank the Great Spirit, grandfather rock, and the four totem animals for their help.

8 Repeat the words "Mitake oyasin" and then remove the smudge bowl from the stone. Take the stone outside to rest on the earth so that any remaining energy can be safely discharged into the ground.

Rituals for Blessing

One of the most essential arts in the witch's or magician's set of skills, is the ability to perform blessings. As well as blessing yourself, sometimes you may also need to bless places. You may sometimes have felt, when entering a place, that the atmosphere did not feel right or, when moving somewhere new, that it still had psychic disturbance caused by the previous occupants. Performing a blessing can change this and put the atmosphere right.

When you are performing a ritual to change an atmosphere it is important to use a new candle.

Blessing Yourself with Colour

Before dealing with a difficult situation or if you need healing, or want to work a particularly powerful piece of magic, you might find the following ritual very helpful. It will help you to feel balanced, protected and able to deal with problems. Work through it slowly, really seeing or sensing the colours and their different energies. You can also use it to bless another.

1 Sit comfortably upright and close your eyes. Imagine that you are standing on a dark, black, curved surface. It is so intensely black that you could almost imagine it is the night sky, spangled with brilliant stars. Moving up your body from your feet, watch the colour changing to a dark, peaty brown, fading gradually as you move up your legs to a russet brown.

2 At the top of your legs, the colour is crimson red. Above that is a band of orange across your stomach, fading into a yellow band in the region of your solar plexus. Above the yellow, the colour changes to a rich leaf-green over the heart region. At the top of your chest and throat, the colour changes through turquoise to a bright blue at your Adam's apple. From the bright blue, the colour changes to deep violet on the level of your "third eye", in the centre of your forehead, and finally there is a change to brilliant diamond white at the top of your head.

When blessing yourself with colour you need to be sitting comfortably before you begin the meditation.

3 Allow these colours to become vivid and definite and try to discover a gradation of tone, from very dark at your feet to a brilliant white light above the top of your head.

4 See the vivid and shining white as a great ball above your head and then imagine drawing this force downwards through each colour band. It comes from beyond you, for it is the healing power of the creative force, or perhaps one of the healing angels.

5 As the light flows down through you, have a sense of it opening up like a rose unfolding. The chakra at the crown of your head is the link with your higher self through which you may work magic.

Blessed colours

The colours that you visualize during the blessing have the following significance.

At the forehead the intense violet-purple represents your psychic faculty. As the brilliance flows downwards through your body, the blue rose of communication and speech flowers at the throat. Below that there is a green flower at the heart centre, from which the power of love and compassion flows to others. Next is the main healing centre of the solar plexus, through which the magical life force of the universe may be directed, in rays of golden sunlight, to those in need.

Across your abdomen is the orange-coloured flower that helps you cope with the mundane aspects of healing the sick, and will assist indigestion. Below that is the crimson blossom filled with the brilliance of white light that enlivens your most basic urges of sex and true unity. This can be used to heal and balance your own life, but you shouldn't use this healing power with others until you have fully mastered control of this centre of energy. Below that is a darker region of stability and strength. It is the strong base on which the blossoms of sacred light grow. This is a mysterious firmament, often envisioned as sprinkled with stars.

A large number of candles placed in the corner of a room will dispel stagnant energies.

Traditional tools for changing an atmosphere: words recited from a book of power, the sound of a bell, and the cleansing power of a candle flame.

Changing the Atmosphere

When someone moves into a new home a common problem is that they feel disturbed by the atmosphere left by the previous occupants. You can deal with this matter fairly easily, if you are just changing the atmosphere to suit the new tenant, not trying to shift a ghost or a haunting – that is a job for the highly experienced.

You will need
twig of rowan wood
piece of red ribbon or thread
new white candle
candle holder

1 Bless yourself with colour as described in Blessing yourself.

2 Tie the piece of red ribbon or thread around the rowan twig, and then carry it around the whole dwelling clockwise in every room and space, from top to bottom, mentally sweeping out old energies. Sweep these out of the front door as if they were dust.

3 Go outside, light the new white candle and carry it in. Carry the candle around all the rooms and spaces, clockwise, visualizing bright, new light entering.

4 When all feels well, stand in the centre of your home and stand quietly for a few moments. Before you snuff out your candle, you can recite this Navajo blessing:

This home will be a blessed home.
It will become the house of dawn.
Dawn light will live in beauty in it.
It will be a home of white corn,
It will be a home of soft goods,
It will be a home of crystal water,
It will be a home dusted with pollen,
It will be a home of life-long happiness,
It will be a home with beauty above it,
It will be a home of beauty all around.

Psychic upsets

Many psychic upsets are the result of people playing with the occult when they don't know what they are doing, such as using a Ouija board or attempting to set up a séance without knowing how. These actions can open a crack between the ordinary self and the inner one, and if people have fears or phobias, or repressed memories, these will be the first through the gap. These methods for contacting magical powers are not recommended for the novice, and should be left to trained witches and magicians.

RITES OF PASSAGE: BEGINNINGS

Life is a journey with many milestones along the way. Different cultures around the world have many different ways of acknowledging these phases with ritual and celebration. Also known as "rites of passage", these rituals are designed to acknowledge the transition from one stage of life to another, and usually involve not only the individual but also their family and sometimes the wider community. For instance, most traditions have a way of naming a baby, others have rites at puberty or first menses, while marriage is almost universally acknowledged as one of life's major stepping stones. These rites of passage are usually embedded in the established religion of the society, although many customs also have their roots in magic.

A ring is an excellent symbol of commitment, as it is the unbroken circle without beginning or end.

WEDDING RITUALS

Although a traditional church "white wedding" is still the favoured option for many people, others are looking for ways to unite in marriage that do not involve the church. There are other marriage ceremonies, which although they may not be recognized by the state, suit many couples, particularly as they can decide for themselves the words and format of the ritual rather than following a fixed set of procedures. Weddings over the broomstick have taken place in many parts of the world, in which the couple step over a besom to indicate they are entering a new phase of a shared life. Pagans have a ceremony called "hand fasting" where the bride and groom have their hands bound together with a ribbon and there is an exchange of rings.

Although a priestess and priest officiate at pagan ceremonies, the format of the actual ceremony is always directed by the couple, allowing them to promise to love, support and remain with each other for a traditional "year and a day", or

The pagan ceremony of hand fasting involves tying the couple's hands together with a ribbon to signify their commitment to each other.

for a lifetime or forever. They usually have a pair of wedding rings blessed by the priestess and priest, and exchange these as a sign of long-term commitment. There is often a ceremonial sharing of bread and wine, and often the bride and groom break the wine glass to show that no one else can break their union. Many pagans like to conduct these marriage rites out of doors, in a sacred circle, ringed by lighted candles, flowers and ribbons. Their guests are instructed as to what may happen, as they may be from many faiths, perhaps being asked to light a candle of their own, to offer gifts or to speak personal blessings and wishes for the future of the couple. There is a wedding feast with a special cake, usually followed by a party.

Naming Ceremonies

Many parents today in more modern, secular societies, are not comfortable with having their baby baptized or christened into the Christian faith and are looking for other options. In former times one of the tasks of the village midwife was to bless a baby at its birth, before the priest of the orthodox religion named it. Today, pagan priestesses trained in these arts are much in demand. Within the blossoming pagan religions, new ceremonies are being constructed which can be offered to adherents, so that their children can be named and blessed in the power of the old gods and goddesses.

Affirm the life you are living now and keep mementos and reminders of the days that are passing. The stages of childhood in particular should be marked and recorded with reverence and joy.

Coming-of-Age Rituals

In the Jewish religion, a boy's coming of age is marked with the "bar mitzvah" ceremony, symbolizing the end of childhood and an initiation into adulthood at puberty. For the most part, however, coming of age is not officially recognized within modern society and many people are once again looking to the pagan tradition for meaningful rites that honour the young person's passage. By officially recognizing their status in society, a young person is given a more clearly defined role and a sense of belonging that is often lacking among modern teenagers whose "difficult" behaviour can be connected with a struggle for identity.

Rituals are being set up so that young people can be seen to have passed into adulthood, and they are given the symbols of the responsibilities they are taking on. These rituals are different in character from those of earlier traditions, which might have involved a hunting ritual for boys, or a time apart for girls, but in content they can still be part teaching session and part celebration.

In a magical community, at the chosen age in years, or moment in life, a ritual is organized where the young person is presented with their own magical tools, their Tarot pack or symbol of the clan or community. They will be told of their responsibilities, which may increase if they are initiated into the Mysteries of their family, and they are shown the kind of assistance and support that is available to them within the community.

In most magical and witchcraft groups young people do not receive full initiation until they are adults. Some groups take 18 as the age of adulthood, others wait until the age of 21.

Traditions of marriage

The wedding ring: having no beginning or end, the ring symbolizes the unbroken circle of lives and the couple's commitment to each other for eternity.

The bouquet of flowers: this is a vestige of the sacrifice, which in days gone by would have been an animal or bird, offered on the altar and then becoming part of the wedding feast. Flowers symbolize beauty and perfection, with particular blooms having different meanings. Brides cast their bouquet over their shoulder to pass on the expectation to be the next to be wed.

The stag and hen night: the Stag is reminiscent of the Horned God and a symbol of male sexual potency and authority, while the Hen, with her power to lay eggs and create new life, symbolizes the fruitful mother aspect of the goddess. The traditional stag and hen parties, or bridal shower, may have evolved from the competitive games that were once held. Often, the bride had to be "stolen" from her family and taken into the groom's community, and the groom would swoop into the bride's territory on a horse and carry her off to a new life, chased by her family and his friends.

Rites of passage: endings

While most of us welcome beginnings and the start of something new, we tend to find endings more difficult. This is partly because of the way we are taught to see life, as something that progresses from start to finish. In magical thinking, however, an ending is not something final but is merely another stage in the infinite cycle of birth, growth, decay and rebirth. It is yet another transition from one stage to another as we journey through the wheel of life. It is important to acknowledge endings as this helps us to move on to the next stage of the soul's journey.

In magical thinking, an ending is not seen as final, but as another stage in an infinite cycle which is reflected in the cycles of nature.

Divorce Rituals

In the past, people struggled to make a marriage or partnership last, trying to hide their differences or finding ways of respecting them and continuing to live together for a variety of practical reasons. Today, people are more ready to separate if they have grown apart and there is less social stigma to being divorced, but as yet, mainstream society does not have any official rituals, other than legal ones, that acknowledge this transition.

For this reason, rituals of division have been created by modern pagans, which try to signify an ending that is peaceful and not acrimonious. In a ceremony, the couple acknowledge that they cannot reconcile their differences, have fallen out of love, and desire to part. Then the wedding rings are taken off, and possibly thrown into running water, or given to a goldsmith who can melt them down, undoing the magic of joining. A ribbon that has been tied around the couple is cut and they are set free, perhaps by burning a paper on which their original bonds or promises were written. A cake may be cut in half in the presence of those assembled, or some other symbolic representation of the parting performed, to help at this difficult time.

Funerals

In orthodox places of worship, a funeral is usually a rather sombre and gloomy affair. While the death of a friend, family member or colleague is very sad for those that are left behind, pagan funerals try to focus on celebrating the dead person's life. Many pagans choose a woodland burial in a biodegradable coffin and to have a living tree planted over their grave, rather than a cold headstone, as a memorial. Others are cremated so that their ashes may be ritually scattered at some sacred or beloved spot by their friends. Some funeral centres will allow for a magical circle to be cast about the coffin and floral tributes can be offered in the shapes of stars, moons or circles. Ritual prayers or poetry may be read at the service. Symbolic acts of casting off mortal life for an eternal spiritual one can be shared by family and friends, and anecdotes of the deceased's life, including photographs of them at different life stages, are often included.

Other Endings

As we go through life, we will encounter many endings. Some of these, like death and divorce, are fairly major, but "smaller" endings, like leaving home, changing a job, or moving to a new area, all signify the ending of one phase of life and the start of something new. These endings are often acknowledged by the people we are leaving behind with cards

Severing the ties

When relationships are no longer able to sustain themselves, a ritual severing of the ties that bound the couple together helps to set them free and to heal any bitterness or uncertainty. In earlier times, the partners' names were written on a log which was then split; each partner would burn the half log bearing the partner's name on their own fire to release any lingering bonds.

As in any kind of ending ritual, splitting a log with the couple's names written on it was a way of letting go and moving on from a painful situation, and marking its passage.

For those who are left behind, a remembrance shrine can bring comfort, and a feeling of continued closeness to someone who has died.

A funeral poem

The following poem is a comforting reminder of the immortality of the soul, present in all things in creation.

Do not stand at my grave and weep,
I am not there, I do not sleep.
I am a thousand winds that blow,
I am the diamond glints on snow,
I am the sunlight on ripened grain,
I am the gentle autumn rain.
When you wake from sleep in the
morning's hush,
I am the swift, uplifting rush
Of quiet birds in circling flight.
I am the soft starlight at night.
Do not stand at my grave and cry,
I am not there, I did not die.

This is a version of a poem written by an anonymous soldier in Northern Ireland.

and gifts, but we can also acknowledge them for ourselves. We can light a candle on our shrine or altar and say goodbye to the old life, acknowledging and giving thanks for all it has given us, before we embark on our new journey.

Rebirth

Many occultists believe that after death the immortal soul is drawn towards a great light. People who have had a near-death experience often describe passing through a dark tunnel towards a place of brightness, and perhaps encountering a divine or heavenly being or spirit guide who leads them to a glorious garden. But when it is not their time to die, they return to complete their life on earth, usually as changed people. Occultists believe that when we die, after a period of rest the soul once again prepares for rebirth into the temporal plane.

Those who have evolved through many thousands of lives and, according to the Buddhist belief, have been able to step off the wheel of incarnations, may still choose to return to earth, to teach others, or to act as a beacon, guiding lost souls towards their heavenly or divine heritage. Some people seem to return quickly to a new life; it depends on the purpose of each particular incarnation, and time as we understand it in the physical world has no meaning in the realm of spirit. Others return after long intervals of earthly time.

Immortal Life

In magical thinking, a burial or scattering of ashes is essentially returning the person's physical remains to the Great Mother, which is part of all life. Through the food we eat and the air we breathe, our lives are created with the substance of earth, which is also part of the cosmos. Along with the earth, moon and stars, the sun and planets, we are part of this vast creation, ever changing but immortal.

Remembrance shrine

When someone has died, the ones who are left to grieve may find comfort in marking a particular place in the house where they can go to remember and celebrate a life that has moved on. A remembrance shrine can be made using photographs, a lit candle, some burning incense, some fresh flowers or a keepsake that reminds you of that person. Make the shrine an affirmation of the person's life rather than a continual mourning for a loss.

SPELLWEAVING

Magic doesn't just happen all by itself: spells are woven, crafted, worked and cast in order to bring about a desired result. This means making spells is an active process that requires effort, energy and commitment on the part of the spellweaver.

Essentially, a spell is a magic recipe containing many different ingredients and needs careful thought and planning. Before you start, you need to be clear why you want to cast a particular spell and to make sure your intent is in line with your highest purpose. You also need to assemble all your ingredients – and this may take several hours or even days as you search for exactly what the spell requires. And even once the spell is cast, you will need to back up your magic on the physical plane by taking whatever action is necessary to set things in motion.

This chapter contains 27 spells to bring magic into all areas of your life. The spells begin with meeting angels and guides, and then you can start to work magic for healing and protection, self-empowerment, luck and prosperity, love and romance, friends and relationships and more. It will show you how to work with a variety of magical ingredients including talismans, charms, spell bags and an assortment of stones, plants, herbs, trees and oils. You will also learn to record your efforts by creating your own spell book or Book of Shadows.

THE SPELLWEAVER'S ART

The art of weaving, or casting, spells is what attracts many people to magic. Spells are magical formulae that are designed to change or adapt reality to the magic-worker's will. They are serious matters, so be sure that your motives are pure and that your object is both achievable and desirable. You should never use magic to interfere with the free will of another, and whatever you give out in magic is returned threefold, so always make sure you are working for the highest good of all concerned. Spells are usually cast once the magic circle has been created and the otherworldly beings have been summoned. Always have your spells planned out in advance and make sure you have all the equipment gathered together before you step into your magic circle.

Spells are usually worked in a circle that is large enough to hold you and your equipment.

SIX STEPS TO SUCCESS

Natural magic requires six basic components for success, so before you embark on a spell, check that each one is in place. The first requirement is desire and need. This may sound obvious, but if you don't truly desire what you are working for then your energy won't really be behind it and your thought-forms won't take shape in the astral plane.

The second requirement is emotional involvement. This fuels your desire and need, and further strengthens the links between the astral and the physical planes: once your thought-forms are strong enough on the astral level, they cannot help but manifest themselves on the physical.

Thirdly, you need to have enough knowledge and to have set realistic targets. Knowledge is power. It includes knowing which tools to use and when and how to use them. For instance, in a spell to attract love, some herbs will be more suitable than others, and certain times will be more favourable than others. Having realistic expectations means knowing which magical goals are naturally within your reach, and which are not. No spell can make you superhuman and achieve the impossible.

How many spells?

If you are new to working spells it is likely that the first one you perform will use up a lot of psychic energy, so try not to wear yourself out. In the beginning it is probably best to confine yourself to one or two spells in a session, although as you become more practised you may do three or four.

A magic circle can be made out of individual items as well as an unbroken cord. If you are doing this kind of circle, use numbers and symbolism to add power to your spell.

The fourth component is belief. This can be difficult in the beginning, but having enough confidence and belief in the outcome of your spells is crucial. Lack of belief and negative thoughts about it will undermine what you are doing. The popular tag on the end of spells, "so mote it be"("so may it be"), is an affirmation of belief and has been used for centuries to assert a spell's reality in the here and now.

In the spirit of the old occult saying that declares "power shared is power lost", the fifth requirement is the ability to keep silent. This helps to protect the energy you have put into your spells from outside influences, some of which may be negative. Lastly, you need to be willing to take whatever practical steps are necessary to back up your magic in the everyday world. For instance, it is no good doing a spell for prosperity and then sitting around waiting for money to shower down on you from above. You will have to create and work your spell by taking appropriate action, being confident that your magic will guide you in the right direction.

The Book of Shadows

The traditional name for a witch or magician's spell book is a "Book of Shadows". Its title may allude to the shadows cast by the flickering candlelight that the practitioner worked by as they wrote up their magical diary, in the days before electricity. On another level, it may also refer to the fact that the book, like the magic itself, should be kept hidden and out of sight in the "shadows". According to legend, these books were once written in secret alphabets in case they fell into the wrong hands. The first time such a book was ever made public was when Gerald Gardner, founder of the Wicca movement, published his own early in the 20th century.

Making your own collection of precious and symbolic items will help you to be more creative with your spells. Invest time in your equipment to imprint them with emotional energy.

Keeping a Spell Book

Get into the habit of recording your spells and other magic work in a personal magical diary, or spell book, usually known as a Book of Shadows.

Originating in the late Middle Ages, when literacy became more widespread, the practice of keeping a log has become a standard tool in modern magic. It is traditional to write up the diary by hand and to record in detail your spells and magic work, including the words that you used and any equipment, as well as the outcome. Many people also like to include transcriptions of dreams and astral travel, insights gained during meditation and other discoveries on their personal journey in their spell book. Over time, it will prove an invaluable record of your findings, failures and successes. Today, there are an infinite variety of beautiful notebooks available in the shops, made with handmade paper, coloured paper, tissue leaves and so on. Look for something that appeals to you, or spend some time making your own record book, and enjoy transforming it into a magical treasure trove.

Be Creative

Once you have grasped the fundamentals of how magic works and the different attributes of the various magical tools and helpers – be they herbs, oils, gemstones, colours or deities – you can begin to create your own spells. The possibilities here are endless; it is a question of experimenting and trying out different combinations until you find something that is effective. In many ways your own formulae will be more potent, as you will have invested time, thought and emotional energy to give them an energetic imprint that is uniquely yours.

Golden rules for spellweaving

- Work from the heart and do what you do with gentleness and responsibility.
- Seek no revenge and send no ill will – for whatever you send will return to you.
- Do not manipulate the free will of another, or attempt to control events to suit yourself.
- Keep yourself, your working space and equipment clean and free of psychic dirt.
- To insure against negative influence always include the words "for the highest good of all" in a spell.
- At the end of every spell affirm your belief in its power by saying "*And so mote it be!*".

Undoing a spell

If you wish to undo a spell, write it down on a piece of paper. Light a white candle and some frankincense then burn the written spell in the candle flame and say:
This spell is undone. So mote it be.

Spirit and Angel Spells

There are many different ways of connecting with angels and celestial beings, but weaving spells is an excellent method. You can use these spells whenever you are seeking guidance, clarity or inspiration from on high, during times of vulnerability or for blessings. Always remember to thank the Beings of Light; whether you sense their presence or not, they will be there.

The six-pointed star used in the Spell for Connection is a powerful mystical symbol.

A Spell for Connection

Sitting within the six-pointed star will help to develop your connection with celestial beings. Bless your equipment before you begin.

You will need

rhythmic spiritual drumming music
lotus oil
natural sea salt
6 violet candles
6 amethysts
gold candle

1 With spiritual drumming playing in the background, face east and anoint your head, hands and feet with lotus oil.

2 Draw a six-pointed star, made of two overlapping equal-sized triangles, in salt around you. The star should be big enough for you to sit in the centre.

3 Sit or stand in the centre of the star and place a violet candle on each of the six points, beginning at the south. Light the candles in turn, saying the following. As you light the first, say:
O Angel Gabriel, lift my spirit to Levanah, to draw down her magic into my heart.

Light the candle to your right and say:
O Angel Raphael, lift my spirit to touch Kokab that I may draw down his wisdom and truth.

Turn to the next candle, light it and say:
O Angel Zamael, lift my spirit to touch Madim that I may draw down courage and strength.

Light the next candle, and say:
O Angel Cassiel, lift my spirit to touch Shabbathai that I may draw down understanding and patience.

Light the next candle, and say:
O Angel Sachiel, lift my spirit to touch Tzedek that I may draw down righteousness.

Turn to the last candle, light it and say:
O Angel Anael, lift my spirit to touch Nogah that I may draw down love and beauty.

4 Then place an amethyst next to each candle, in the same order as above. Put the gold candle in front of you, inside the star, light it and say:
Mighty Michael, Angel of the Sun, lift my spirit to touch Shemesh that I may be drawn closer and closer to the light of the Divine. This I ask of you, that I may grow ever closer to the truth. Adonai, Lord of Light, Adonai, Adonai.

5 Now close your eyes and sit with your hands in your lap, palms up. Stay here for up to 20 minutes and feel the essence of spiritual light filling your body, mind and soul.

6 To close your spell, pick up the amethysts and blow out the candles, starting with the last one you lit and ending with the first. Close your cord circle, saying:
May divine will be done.

The colour violet, and the amethyst, are both connected to the crown chakra, the chakra of spirituality.

The angel blessing can be spoken on its own, if you feel it is needed, without candles and incense.

An angel altar should be left for 24 hours, and then dismantled.

Angel Blessing

This spell can be performed as a way to bless and consecrate yourself.

You will need

2.7 m (9 ft) white cord
white candle
frankincense
charcoal burner

1 Open your cord circle and place the candle, frankincense and burner in the centre. Turn to the south and set light to the candle and the charcoal. Sprinkle some frankincense on to the hot charcoal saying:
Lord of Light, this offering I make.

2 Next, say the Angelic Invocation. While you say the first line, touch your head, as you say the second line touch your stomach, as you say the third line touch your left shoulder, and say the remainder of the invocation as you touch your right shoulder:
Uriel above me
Michael beneath me
Raphael to my left
Gabriel to my right
By the power of these Great Angels
Surround me with light.

3 Visualize an angel in each of the four directions. Bow your head and say "thank you" to each one. Ask them for what you feel you need; humility, an open heart, strength etc.

4 When you have finished thank each angel again and let him depart. Blow out the candle and close your circle.

An Angel Altar

You can use this altar for someone you know is in need of angelic protection or healing, but never perform spells for another without their permission.

Cast a circle of salt on your altar, then place a white candle, some frankincense and a photograph of the subject within it. Light the candle and the frankincense and say the Angelic Invocation while touching the head and relevant parts of the person's body in the photograph and saying their name rather than your own. Leave the altar as it is for 24 hours, then remove the circle of salt, gathering it up so that it can be sprinkled on the earth outside, or over a pot of earth. For serious situations, leave for 48 hours, repeating the invocation after 24 hours.

A spell seeking guidance

Spells can be used as oracles when you need an answer to an important question. This simple version uses a 'magical book', which could be any book containing spiritual teachings. It is best done during a waning moon.

you will need

blue candle
your thickest magical book
sheet of paper
black ink

1 Light the candle and place it beside the magical book. Concentrating on your question, write it down on a new sheet of paper in black ink. Fold the paper into a narrow bookmark shape. Say:
In this book I seek; in this book I peek.
Reveal a clue, now heed me.

2 Slide the paper into the book at random, then read the words next to the paper. This should help answer your question if it was clear. Pinch out the candle.

Spells for Psychic Help

Round white stones are used to represent the full moon, or increase your connection with her.

Psychic powers can be developed by learning to trust our instinctive, intuitive responses rather than rationalizing and analysing everything that we do. Traditionally, women are said to be more in touch with this aspect of themselves than men, but this is not a hard and fast rule. Regardless of our gender it means cultivating a relationship with the "feminine" or "yin" aspect of the life force, and one way of doing this is by drawing on the powers of the moon when casting spells and working magic.

Drawing Down the Moon

Draw on the powers of the moon to refresh and rejuvenate you for the month ahead and help you get in touch with your sensitivity and powers of intuition. The best time for this spell is 2 days before the full moon.

You will need
13 circular stones of any size
salt
aromatherapy burner
jasmine essential oil
9 white or cream candles

1 Beginning in the south, make a circle of 12 of your chosen stones in a clockwise direction. Place the 13th in the centre.

2 Sprinkle the stones with salt. Light the aromatherapy burner and put in 3 drops of jasmine oil.

3 Place 8 candles around the circle and one by the centre stone. Then light the candles as you say these words:
Magna Dei, Light of the Night, I light these candles to guide your moonrays here. I ask you to come and bless this circle.

4 Stand facing south, with your arms outstretched above your head and your feet quite wide apart. Reach towards the sky and say this lunar invocation:
Hail to thee, Sophia, holy spirit of the wise moon. I call upon you to enter and fill me with your light. Protect me and guide me on the moonway. Teach me your wisdom and truth as I seek your clarity and guidance.

5 Draw down the powers of the moon. Allow yourself to be refreshed and refilled with the feminine virtues of wisdom, beauty and grace. Let the moon bless your feelings and perceptions until you feel energized and content. Lower your arms.

6 Finish by saying "thank you". Blow out your candles and close the circle.

The spell is particularly of benefit to a woman, as the moon cycles reflect her own.

Psychic Dreams

You can encourage psychic dreams with an aquamarine crystal. Store your dream crystal in a little pouch made of shiny pale blue or silver material, decorated with moon charms and sequins. Before you use the aquamarine you need to clear your dreamtime by first using jet in your pouch under your pillow, until any nightmares you may have been suffering from are gone. Then dedicate or bless your aquamarine, place it in the pouch, and put the pouch under your pillow for perceptive dreams.

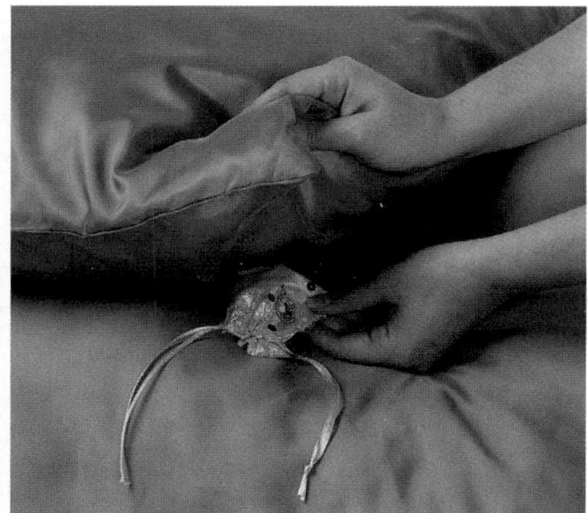

You can dedicate or bless your dream crystal every month, at the full moon, for extra potency.

Opening the Inner Gates

The gate of inner vision is situated at the 6th, or brow, chakra, also known as the "third eye", which is located just above the eyebrows. Seeing with this "inner" eye is associated with clairvoyance. Best time: Monday, waxing moon.

You will need

2.7 m (9 ft) white cord
flower
red candle
small bowl of water
stone
sandalwood incense
picture of an open door or gate, or the Moon Tarot card

1 Open your cord circle and place the flower in the east, the candle in the south, the bowl of water in the west and the stone in the north. Light the incense in the centre of the circle.

2 Sit in the centre of the circle with the picture or Tarot card on your lap. Close your eyes, centre yourself and focus on the intention; be sure that your wish to work with inner vision is for the highest good of all.

3 Stand up and make an opening gesture to each of the four quarters in turn, saying the appropriate sentence as you pick up each object. Light the candle as you speak the following words about candle fire:
Open my mind like a growing flower, may my vision now empower.
Open my mind to the candle fire, may my vision now inspire.
Open my mind to the water's flow, that on vision journeys I may go.
Open my mind to this stone so cold, that visions I shall safely hold.

4 Pick up the picture or card and hold it out in front of your heart. Circle or turn around four times, saying:
Open gates that I may roam,
Safely bring my knowledge home.

5 Sit down and close your eyes again. Relax and sit in meditation for a while, letting any pictures or images come and go freely.

6 When you are ready, open your eyes and put out the incense. Close the circle widdershins and dispose of your equipment appropriately.

Psychic protection

As you become more sensitive to spiritual energies, you need to make sure that you are protected. Feeling excessively tired and drained is often a sign that you are picking up too much psychic dirt. Best time: Saturday, waxing moon. Carry this spell with you for the next few days.

You will need

12 tealights
indigo blue candle
myrrh incense
carnelian stone
vervain Bach flower essence
15 cm (6 in) square of indigo cloth
red thread

1 Arrange the tealights in a circle, then open it deosil, lighting the first tealight in the east. Sit in the centre of the circle, facing west, and light the indigo candle and the incense.

2 Close your eyes and visualize yourself in a golden globe of pale blue light with orange flames around the surface.

3 Take the carnelian stone and bring it to rest on your hara, the body's life energy centre about 5cm (2in) below the navel. Hold the stone here and repeat this invocation three times:
Bright angels of the astral plane, please come and bless this stone and fill it with your power, love and protection.
After the third repetition, say:
Thank you (to the angels). And so mote it be!

4 Add two drops of vervain essence to the stone and wrap it up in the cloth. Tie the parcel with the thread. Extinguish the candle and incense then close the circle widdershins, pinching out each tealight, starting in the east. Dispose of the candles with respect and do not reuse.

The carnelian is connected to the hara, the personal power centre or Shaman's Cave.

Carnelian

This deep red or orange stone has the ability to protect you from negativity. It links to your own inner power and strength during times of psychic stress.

SPELLS FOR HEALING

There has always been a strong link between magic and medicine, and any distinction between the two is often very blurred. In many cultures, spells and incantations have been used for a variety of healing purposes. Traditionally, knowledge of healing spells was the province of the village wise woman, the shaman or the medicine-man. However, it is accepted that recovery from illness has much to do with state of mind, and with a little knowledge of the art and craft of magic, it is possible for you to practise healing magic for yourself or those who are close to you.

A SPELL FOR HEALING

This is a spell to bring healing. Ask permission if you are doing it for another. Before you perform this spell, find a suitable tree – ash, birch, juniper and cedar trees are all good. You may prefer to cast your circle outside next to the tree, and work within nature. The best day for working this spell is a Sunday.

You will need

2.7 m (9 ft) white cord
gold candle
gold pen
15 cm (6 in) square of natural paper
knife
lime
gold thread
15 cm (6 in) square of orange cloth

The colours of gold and orange, used repeatedly in this spell, are colours of the sun, which is renowned for its healing powers.

Binding the spell with gold thread (the colour of the sun), before burying it under your chosen tree, helps to invoke the sun's healing powers.

1 Open the circle and honour the four directions. Light the candle and say these words:
Angel Och, healing spirit of the sun,
I light this flame to honour your presence
And ask you to hear this prayer.

2 Write the name of the person to be healed on the paper, visualizing health and wellbeing surrounding them.

3 Cut the lime in two lengthways. Fold the paper three times and place it between the two halves. Bind it together with gold thread and say:
Powers of lime
Health is mine/thine
Cleanse the body, cleanse the mind
Spirit pure, fill my (or say another person's name) being
With health, with health, with health.

4 Place the bound lime in the orange cloth and bind it with gold thread. Close the circle in the usual way.

5 Now take the spell and bury it near the base of the tree. Ask the spirit of the tree to help you (or another person) to return to good health. Thank the tree, and depart.

A Spell to Heal the Earth

Modern magic workers like to use their skills to help heal the damage that we are causing to our planet. Choose a place where the Earth's resources are being used or abused, such as a polluted river or a quarry. This is a spell of atonement.

You will need
moss agate crystal
white rose

1 Holding the moss agate crystal in your right hand and the rose in your left, repeat the following prayer of atonement. As you say the last line, lay down your moss agate.
Spirits of this place, I come in peace but with a heavy heart. I wish to say how sorry I am for what my brothers and sisters are doing to you in their ignorance. I come to make an offering to show you that I am sorry for taking from you without respect. I ask your forgiveness. I ask you to help humanity to see how precious all life is.
I make this offering to you.

2 Transfer the rose to your right hand. Hold it to your heart, say the following:
Creator, guide us all in the ways of peace, love, wisdom and truth. I call you here to (say the name of the place) to bring the Divine to this area, to bless it with your healing love. May (say the name of the place) now be sacred again.

3 Lay down the white rose on the earth. Visualize the whole area filling with white light, embracing it with illumination. End the spell with the Native American saying:
"*Mitake Oyasin*" (we are all related).

The white rose stands for purity and innocence, and is an appropriate gift for the Earth.

Frankincense is the incense associated with the sun. It is not difficult to see why when you see the rich ambers, yellows and golden colours of the loose resin.

A spell for good health

Each planet has its own magic symbol, which can be used to harness its powers. The sigil of the sun is used in this spell for health; it can also be used for success and prosperity. Sunday is the best day to perform this spell.

You will need
2.7 m (9 ft) white cord
gold candle
frankincense and burner
gold pen
15 cm (6 in) square of natural paper
a lock of your hair

1 Open the circle, taking with you all the ingredients for the spell. Light the candle, and begin to burn the frankincense, and say these words:
Angel Och, healing spirit of the sun,
I light this flame to honour your presence
And ask you to hear this prayer.

2 Take the piece of paper, and write the name of the person whom the spell is for, visualizing health and wellbeing surrounding them as you do so.

3 On the other side of the paper draw the sigil of the sun, and write the words 'Angel Och'. Hold the piece of paper to your heart, with the name facing inwards, and visualize golden-orange light filling your heart, and then the whole of your body. Repeat:
I am healthy and well.

4 Take the lock of hair and lay it on the spell, on the side of the sigil of the sun. Fold the piece of paper six times so that it forms a small packet. Keep it in a very safe place, or preferably, carry it with you, close to your heart.

The sigil of the sun is often used for healing.

SPELLS TO EMPOWER

The path of magic is the road towards self-empowerment. Instead of being a victim of circumstance, magic encourages us to use our free will to make creative choices for ourselves, in line with our soul's highest purpose. A universal law is that "like attracts like", so whatever we give out returns to us. Lack of self-confidence and negative self-beliefs stand in the way of us getting what we want for ourselves, but we can use spellweaving to help remove these obstacles and increase our personal power and magnetism.

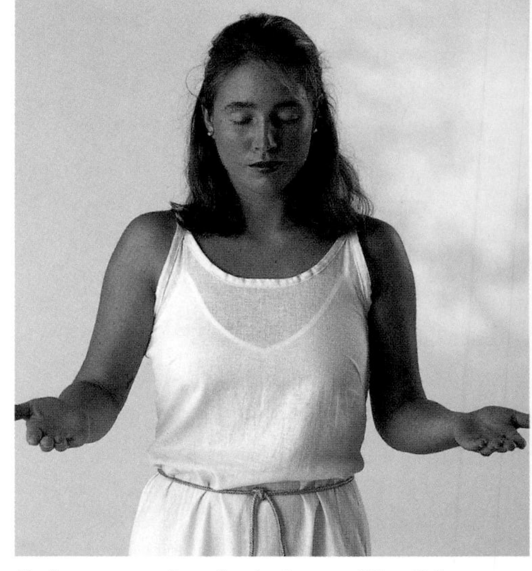

Before you undertake the Aura of Confidence spell, you should perform the Golden Light Breathing Exercise, to energize yourself.

A SPELL TO REMOVE AN OBSTACLE

If you feel that you are stuck and unable to move on for some reason, and can identify the cause, try this spell to remove the obstruction in your life. For this you will need to create a gift to Mother Earth, it should be something you have made yourself, like a cake or painting, or it can be a loving action such as clearing a stream, picking up litter, or planting a tree. This spell needs to be performed outside.

You will need
a gift for Mother Earth
a fossil or a blessed stone
natural sea salt

1 Take your gift and fossil to the place you have chosen to perform your spell. Beginning with the east, with the salt draw a deosil circle around yourself, large enough to sit in, repeating the opening circle invocation.

2 Place yourself comfortably on the ground, facing north. Say the following invocation three times with as much feeling as possible.
Mother Earth, I bring you a gift of (state what) because I have come to you today to ask you to help me. I wish to remove (state your obstacle).
I ask you with all my heart if you will talk with the Angel Cassiel on my behalf, and that together you help me to lift the condition. Please help me to understand why it is there, so that I may move forward, safe in the knowledge that I am part of a loving universe. Teach me, Mother Earth, to be wise and to trust in the beauty of all life. Show me the way to remove this obstacle so that I may grow in understanding and wisdom.
(Take your fossil).
I ask that this fossil, when it is buried in your being, may take away my burden and help me to endure, because it is within you and you are with me.

3 Add "thank you" at the end of the third time. Bury your fossil. Send the energies home by saying "So mote it be", while visualizing the completion of your task.

4 Leave the earth your gift, or tell her your pledge has been done, or will be done on a certain day. It is important to give, or you may not receive.

5 Starting with the west, break your circle of salt widdershins and brush it away into the surrounding area, until you are back at west again. Walk away, leaving your troubles behind you. Do not look back.

If you have a weakness for chocolate cake, make this your gift to Mother Earth.

AURA OF CONFIDENCE

Tap into the sun's powers to radiate self-confidence. If you are not confident, then it is unlikely that your magic will be very successful. Make sure you practise Golden Light Breathing (see Preparation Rituals) before you work this spell to energize you. The best time for this spell is Sunday during a waxing moon.

You will need

2.7 m (9 ft) white cord
gold candle
gold pen
15 cm (6 in) square of natural paper
larch Bach flower essence
envelope
gold ribbon
goblet of golden drink
round, golden biscuit
tin box

1 Open a circle in the east. Sit in the centre, facing south, light the candle and say:
O Michael, Angel of the Sun, I call upon your presence and ask you to shine your golden light upon my life. Strengthen my aura with your positive rays.

2 Close your eyes and visualize yourself surrounded by an egg-shaped space. This is your aura. Breathing gently, watch as the Angel of the Sun beams his golden light rays towards you. With each inbreath, feel the light warming and energizing your whole being.

Think carefully before you write down the things you would like to achieve.

As you drink the golden drink, and eat the biscuit, visualize the sun's warming powers.

3 As you breathe out, see the egg-shaped space filling up with golden light and becoming bigger and brighter as your aura expands outwards. Repeat to yourself six times these words: *I can.*

4 Open your eyes and write down six things that you would like to achieve in the next six months. Choose things that seem out of reach at the moment, but not so far away that you feel they are impossible. Drip six drops of larch essence on the paper, fold it up and put it into the envelope. Tie the gold ribbon around the envelope.

5 Eat the biscuit and drink the drink; both represent the power of the sun. Snuff the candle, thank the angel Michael and close the circle.

6 Put the spell into the tin box. Bury the box under a hazel tree and leave it for six months, undisturbed. When this time has passed, you may unearth the spell to check your progress.

Amulet for strengthening willpower

Making magic is about focusing your will to achieve a result. The more focused and determined you are, the better the likely outcome. Keep this amulet in your pocket and carry it with you; whenever you feel weak-willed, holding on to it will remind you of your resolve. The best time to perform this spell is on a Tuesday, during a waxing moon.

You will need

wand
red candle
haematite stone
centaury Bach flower essence
12.5 cm (5 in) square of red cloth
gold thread

1 Cast a magic circle with your wand and visualize it as a ring of fire. Put your spell ingredients in the centre and light the candle.

2 Begin in the east; hold the stone in your left hand and pass it over the candle flame, saying the first line of the following words. Then turn to the south, west and north in turn saying the second, third and fourth lines respectively and passing the stone over the candle each time.
I call the Sylphs, the helpers of Air.
I call the Salamanders, the helpers of Fire.
I call the Undines, the helpers of Water.
I call the Gnomes, the helpers of Earth.

3 Then continue with the rest of the incantation:
O elemental beings, please bless this stone so that it may remind me that I have the mental power to achieve my goal (or say whatever particular goal you are trying to achieve), sticking to what I feel is right for me. For I know that I am as firm and as steadfast as a rock.

4 Place the stone on the red cloth, together with a few drops of centaury essence. Bind the stone in the cloth with the golden thread.

5 Say "thank you" to your elemental helpers and let them depart. Blow out the candle and use your wand to close the circle.

GOOD FORTUNE SPELLS

In everyday language, a lucky life is said to be a "charmed life", and good luck charms and talismans have always played an important role in natural magic. They have been worn or carried as protection against the "evil eye" since ancient times. They have also been given to those embarking on any of life's "journeys" – whether a literal journey or a metaphorical one like a wedding, the start of a new job or the birth of a child.

A SPELL FOR GOOD LUCK

Work with the magic of the oak tree when making a good luck spell. You will need a spell bag or pouch, which you should make yourself, and a suitable oak tree. The best time for this spell is on a Thursday, during a full moon.

You will need
small amethyst
turquoise stone
oak leaves
cinquefoil essential oil
sprig of rosemary
spell bag

If you make the spell bag yourself it will have far greater potency than if you buy it. It can be used again and again, and don't forget, the effort, time and energy you invest will be returned threefold.

Turquoise brings blessings, and amethyst offers protection, so these two stones make an ideal combination for a good luck spell.

1 Greet the spirit of your tree and tell it your intentions. Place the amethyst at its base as an offering. Walking deosil round the tree, repeat the following four times:
O Sachiel, Angel of Jupiter, I ask you to hear my call.
Light my path, guide my actions, words and thoughts and those of all I am yet to meet, that by the power of your might, all will be fortunate to my sight.
Good fortune growing, growing.

2 Anoint the turquoise stone and the oak leaves with the cinquefoil oil, while visualizing yourself surrounded by the arms of the mighty oak tree.

3 Place the turquoise, the oak leaves and the sprig of rosemary in your spell bag. Hold the spell bag up to the oak tree and say the following words:
Heart of Oak, you are my heart and with honour I shall carry you by my side.
Thank you.

4 Carry this spell with you for good fortune, and store it carefully when not in use. You could also do this spell as a special gift for a friend, and then give them the spell. But ask first.

A Spell to Improve Business

Repeat this spell regularly to keep your business affairs flowing smoothly. Giving a gift to the energies that are helping you with your business pleases them and encourages them to work positively on your behalf. Rice and wheat are symbols of new life, and they encourage fertile opportunities. Do this spell every month for a while. It is best performed on the first day of a new moon.

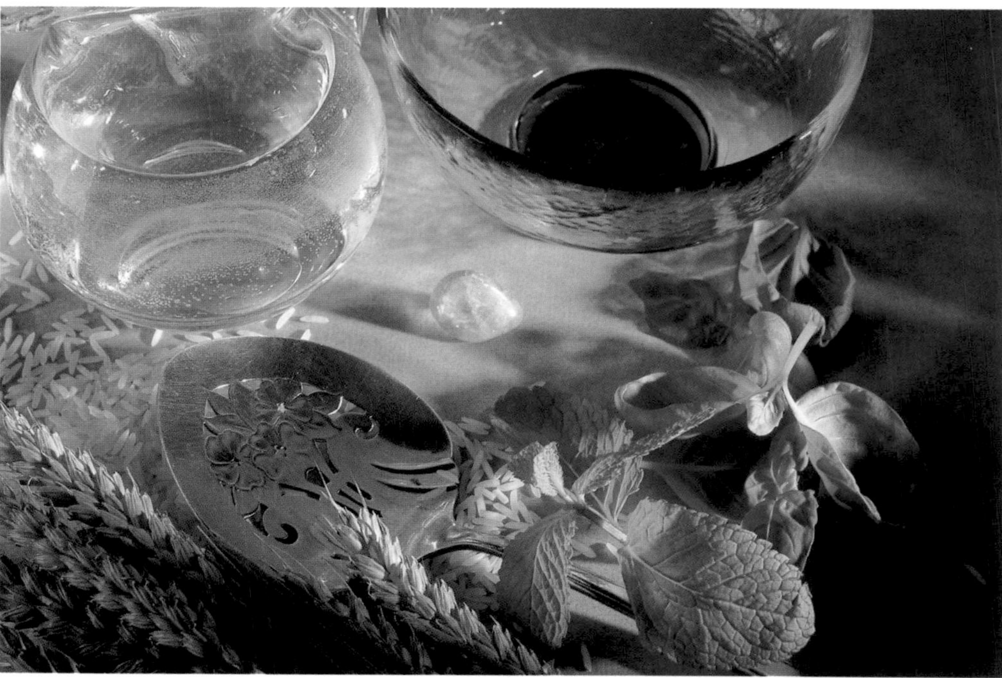

Potency is added to magic if you use special tools for the task. This beautiful silver spoon is used for stirring the water in the spell to improve business.

You will need
3, 7 or 9 fresh basil leaves
bowl of spring water
spoon
citrine stone
dried ears of wheat
rice grains
mint leaves

1 Bless your equipment and ingredients. Soak the basil leaves in the bowl of water for one hour, stirring occasionally in a deosil (clockwise) direction.

2 Beginning to the right of the entrance at your place of work, walk deosil round the building or work area, sprinkling the aromatic water as you go and repeating the following invocation until you are finished:
Business expand, business grow
secure and successful –
my dealings flow.

3 Bless the citrine stone, wheat, rice and mint leaves again, then place the stone where you keep your money or transactions. Offer the corn and the rice to the energies that are helping you with your business affairs by sprinkling them in discreet places around your office or workplace.

4 Carry the mint leaves with you in your money pocket or purse. Replace them with fresh ones each time you re-work the spell.

Spell for safe travel

For this spell you need to find a stone that is different in some way from other stones in your area. Ask its permission to be used in a spell for safe passage. Use it for yourself or another. The best time to do this spell is a Wednesday.

You will need
2.7 m (9 ft) white cord
yellow candle, blessed
lavender essential oil or incense
aromatherapy burner (if using oil)
an unusual stone from your area
yellow and violet or blue paints
artist's paintbrush

1 Open your cord circle in the east and honour the four directions (see The Four Great Powers in chapter 3). Place the candle and oil burner (if using) in the centre and light them, adding a few drops of lavender oil to the burner. Alternatively, light the incense.

2 Sit in the centre of the circle facing east and paint your stone bright yellow. When it is dry, paint a triangle in violet or blue, with a line near its base as shown. This is the alchemical symbol for Air.

3 Hold the stone up to the east and repeat the following invocation eight times, making sure that you say "thank you" to the angel Raphael after the eighth time.
O Raphael, Angel of the East, fill this stone with your blessing and protection. I pray to you for a safe journey for me (or say someone else's name). Guard me (or say someone else's name) and guide me (or another name) on the path this journey takes, until I (or another name) can return.

4 Close your spell and circle in the usual way. Carry your stone with you on your travels, returning it to Mother Earth when the journey is ended and you are safely home.

This is the alchemical symbol for Air that you need to paint on the stone for the travel spell.

Spells for the Home

Our homes and possessions are like an extension of ourselves. In magical terms they are connected to us along fine energy pathways and we can use magic to make things happen in our physical surroundings. Traditionally, many home spells are concerned with blessing and protection, although we can also work spells to help us find things that are lost and to buy and sell property successfully.

Sweep your house with a birch broom to cleanse the physical and spiritual environment.

A House Blessing Spell

If you have recently moved into a new home or there have been upheavals in your domestic life, perform this blessing to consecrate the space. The best time is on a Sunday morning during a waxing moon. You should be alone.

You will need
natural sea salt
small bowl
rose geranium essential oil
white candle
aromatherapy burner
a few grains of organic rice
15 cm (6 in) square of golden fabric

1 Bless and consecrate yourself using the Angelic Invocation. Place the salt in the bowl. Starting in the top right-hand corner of your home and working deosil through the building, sprinkle a pinch of salt in the four corners of every room, door and window. As you sprinkle, say:
I cleanse and purify this room of all unnecessary or negative vibrations.

2 Take the rose geranium oil and light the white candle. Again working clockwise around the building, place the candle in the centre of each room. Anoint all doors and windows with a little of the oil as you say:

I call upon the Angels of Light and Love to bless this home and all who enter here.
May love, happiness and harmony prevail.

3 Place the candle in the centre of your main living room. Light the aromatherapy burner and add six drops of rose geranium oil to it. Sit quietly, visualizing your home filled with the qualities that you desire.

4 Let the candle burn down almost completely, then anoint it with rose geranium oil and sprinkle with rice as thanks to the helpful energies. Snuff the candle, wrap it in the gold fabric and place the spell beneath your front door mat or as close to your door as possible, saying:
This I place so that all who enter here will be blessed.

5 Leave the parcel undisturbed until the next time you perform a cleansing or blessing ceremony, when it can be replaced by a new parcel.

Grains of rice are a precious gift from the Earth and are often used in magical spells and rituals as a symbol of giving thanks.

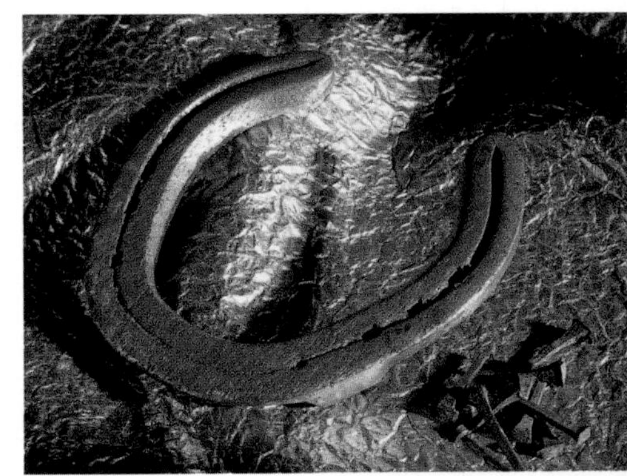

Horseshoes, hung with the open ends upwards on front doors, provide protection and strength.

A spell for finding

This spell uses your powers of visualization in which you imagine a lost object being drawn back to you. It is best performed on a Wednesday, the day of the week associated with Mercury, the god of thieves. You will need to find a hazel tree to cut yourself a wand. Ask permission of the spirit of the tree first and leave a lock of your hair as a gift. Perform this spell during a waxing moon, on a Wednesday.

You will need
20 cm (8 in) wand of hazel
honeysuckle essential oil, diluted in carrier oil
yellow cloth

1 Find a quiet place where you won't be disturbed and draw a deosil circle around yourself with the hazel wand, saying these words:
By the powers of heaven and earth I cast this sacred circle in the name of love, light, wisdom and truth.

2 Perform the Golden Light Breathing exercise (see Preparation Rituals in chapter 5), then anoint your temples, forehead and hands with honeysuckle oil. Sit or stand in the north, facing south, close your eyes and visualize yourself on a high mountain peak made of magnetic crystals. You can see for miles in any direction.

3 Now see yourself opening your hands, palms are facing upwards. Say this invocation:
Swift and sure, my (name the object) return to me.

4 Imagine that your property is being drawn back to you, by the strength of the magnetic mountain. Draw it back with as much willpower and concentrated thought as you can. Note any pictures that come into your mind and from which direction your property returns to you in the visualization.

5 To add to the spell's effectiveness, write what you have lost on a piece of paper and pin it up where you will see it.

6 Say "thank you" to the energies that have helped you. Close your spell then move your wand widdershins from the end to the beginning of the original circle, saying:
This spell is done.

7 Wrap the wand in the cloth and store it in a safe space with the rest of your magical equipment. If the lost object is in someone else's possession, he or she should feel compelled to return it. If nothing happens, try the spell again a week later, or accept that it is irretrievable.

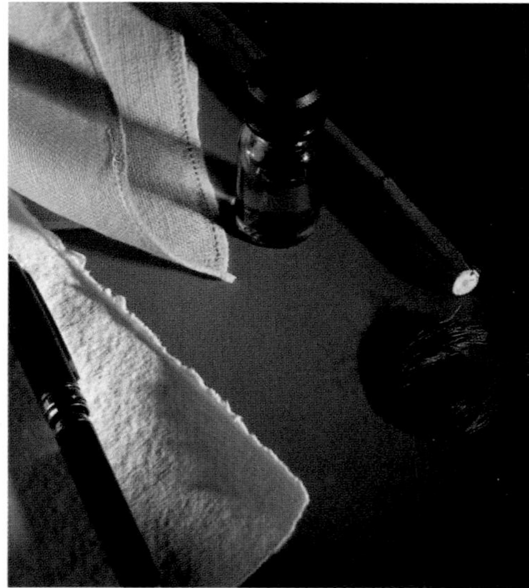

The hazel wand in a spell for finding gives magical protection during the ceremony.

Burning frankincense in a spell for selling will cleanse your home and purify it of old vibrations.

A Spell for Selling

When you need to sell your house, or any other object, work a spell to attract the right buyer. Burning frankincense will cleanse your home and purify it of old vibrations, making it ready for the next keeper. The best time for this spell is on a Wednesday during a waxing moon.

You will need
an altar
a vase of yellow flowers
frankincense and burner
item for sale, or a picture or symbol of it
yellow ribbon

1 Hold the item being sold, its picture, or a symbol of it in your right hand. Stand in front of your altar and turn to face west, the direction for letting go. Turn slowly, from west to east, moving deosil, as you say:
I let go of this (name the object), so that something new can come in its place.

2 Place the vase of flowers on the altar and burn the frankincense. Tell the spirit of the item you are selling that it is time to part company and that a new keeper is coming to take over.

3 Tie up the item or its symbol with yellow ribbon and put it on your altar in the east. Call on the east wind, saying:
Hail to thee East Wind. This (name the object) sells, this (name the object) sells. Please guide the next keeper here speedily so that I am free for something new.

4 Say thank you to the East Wind, saying:
For the highest good of all concerned, so mote it be!

Flowers to help a sale

To enhance the magic of a spell for selling, change the vase of flowers on the altar each day of the week for one week. Repeat the spell if the item hasn't sold, and repeat weekly until it goes.

Saturday: evergreens, cypress
Sunday: orange flowers
Monday: white flowers, river plants
Tuesday: red flowers
Wednesday: yellow flowers
Thursday: violet or purple flowers
Friday: pink flowers, roses

Spells for Friendship

Attracting love and friendship are among the most popular reasons for spells, but remember that when you make magic you cannot use your powers to influence the free will of another. You may ask for someone to share your love with, but do not name them: whoever answers will be right for your needs. If you are having trouble manifesting results in this area, you may need to look at what is blocking you – this may be negative self-beliefs or else others may be gossiping behind your back.

Warm pink and gold are both colours associated with love and healing.

A Love Spell

Try this spell for your perfect love match. Before you start, take a long bath or shower, then spray your whole body with rose water. Work this spell on a Friday, during a waxing moon.

You will need

bottle of rose water
2.7 m (9 ft) white cord
4 green candles
charcoal and heatproof burner
pink candle
rose petals
rose essential oil
cinnamon stick
gold pen
glass bowl of spring water

1 Open your cord circle and step inside with your equipment. Light a green candle in each direction. Invoke the four winds in turn, repeating the following words four times, each time substituting the next direction:
Hail to thee East/South/West/North Wind.
I call for love and make this offering of light to you.

2 Place some charcoal in the heatproof burner in the centre of the circle and light it. Light the pink candle next to it. Do the Golden Light Breathing exercise until you feel full of energy.

3 You are calling for new beginnings, so face east. Put seven rose petals to one side, then rub a little rose oil into the rest. Crush the cinnamon stick and place it on the burning charcoal with the scented rose petals.

4 Focus your heart upon feeling love. Write the word "love" in gold ink on the seven reserved petals. Float them gently in the bowl of water.

5 Sit in the circle and breathe in the scent of rose and cinnamon. Take time to centre yourself and build up charged energy. Open your hands, open your heart and repeat your request seven times, with genuine feeling:
O Anael, Angel of Venus, I call upon you to fill me with love, that I may feel a joyous heart. I ask that I may share this love with another who will come to me of his/her free will and together we shall know the beauty of a loving union.
I ask this for the highest good of all.

6 At the end of the seventh request say "thank you". Blow out the candles, and close the cord circle widdershins. Pour the water and petals respectfully on the earth.

Cinnamon brings success, and is also an aphrodisiac. Breathe in its warm, sensual smell as you work.

A Spell to Stop Gossip

Gossip produces negative thought-forms that can become attached to our energy field and create problems for us. You will need to find a suitable holly tree to bury your spell under – you might want to perform your spell next to it, too. Do this on a Tuesday, during a waning moon.

You will need
2.7 m (9 ft) white cord
red candle
red pen
very small square of natural paper
snapdragon (antirrhinum) flower
thorn
red ribbon

1 Open your cord circle. Light the red candle, face south and sit down.

2 Using the red pen, write the name of the person or organization that is gossiping about you on the paper square. If you do not know the source of the gossip-mongering write "whoever is".

3 Carefully take one of the larger flower heads from the snapdragon and gently open it up. Roll the piece of paper into a tiny scroll and place it inside the flower, repeating the following words five times:
Speak only goodness, think only kind. Look to your own faults and not to mine.

4 Keep the scroll of paper in place by sealing the flower head with the thorn, and as you do this say:
Flower seal, flower heal
lips that speak not from the heart.

5 Take your spell to a holly tree. Tell the spirit of the tree your intention to bury it there and ask it to protect your good name.

6 Bury the snapdragon flower head under the holly tree. Say thank you by tying a small red ribbon to a branch.

7 As you walk away, know that you are leaving the malicious gossip behind you. Do not look back.

The colour red is associated with bringing change in difficult circumstances, and with courage, while snapdragons are used to redirect negative energies into a more creative outlet.

A spell to make friends

Perform this spell in a horseshoe shape within your magical cord circle. The colour green and the apple are both sacred to Venus, and sweet peas are the traditional flower of friendship. Work this spell on a Friday, with a waxing moon.

You will need
2.7 m (9 ft) white cord
7 green candles
aromatherapy burner
sweet pea essential oil, diluted in sesame oil
5 seeds from a sweet organic apple
gold pen
natural paper
heatproof container

1 Open the cord circle in the east. Place the green candles in a horseshoe shape, with the open end facing north and you facing south in front of it.

2 Place the aromatherapy burner in the centre of the horseshoe shape and add seven drops of sweet pea oil. Lay the apple seeds in the centre too. Light the first candle to your left and say:
Nogah, Nogah, light of love,
I honour and illuminate your beauty and call upon you to help me today.

3 Using the lit candle, light the next one. Light all the candles this way, then light the burner.

4 Using the gold pen, draw the sigil of Venus on the paper. Beneath this write your wish:
By the powers of the four directions, above me and below me, within me and without,
I call for favour with Anael, Angel of Venus,
I call for friends of the same heart, that joy and celebration shall prevail.

5 Burn your spell in the flame of the last candle to be lit, dropping it into the heatproof container. Visualize the smoke carrying your wish to the sky. Blow out the candles widdershins and close your circle in the usual way. As you extinguish the last candle say: *And so mote it be!*

6 Take the apple seeds to a prepared site or pot and dedicate them as follows:
Nogah, these apple seeds I plant to honour you and please you. And as they grow, so is my life blessed with joy of friendships new.

The seal of Venus.

SPELLS FOR PARTNERSHIPS

Many marriage customs have their root in magical thinking. In some cultures, for instance, grains of rice (symbols of fertility) are thrown as confetti, while a horseshoe is traditionally associated with luck, and the wedding ring is a symbol of the eternal bond of lives. Spells for a long and happy partnership are some of the most popular of all. These not only include spells for luck and fertility but also for removing conflict and reminding a partner of your love.

Red is the colour of Mars. Call on the energies of this planet when working with conflict situations.

A SPELL TO REMOVE CONFLICT

This spell will help remove conflict in a relationship. It will work best if both people in the relationship do it together. If only one of you wishes to do it, write down what you wish to let go of, and work to heal your own difficulties. The best time for this spell is Tuesday during a waning moon.

You will need
5.5 m (18 ft) white cord
a small round table or stool
5 red candles
charcoal and burner
coriander seeds
red pen
2 pieces of natural paper
heatproof container

1 Open your cord circle. Place the round table or stool in the centre and on it position the red candles, also in a circle, and light them, remembering which candle is the last to be lit.

2 Light the charcoal in the burner. When it is hot, face west and sprinkle on the coriander seeds, saying the following dedication:
O Zamael, Angel of Mars, we call upon you to help us today/tonight and dedicate this offering to you.

3 Breathe in the aroma of the burning seeds. Both of you should then use the red pen to write down the emotion to be let go – jealousy, anger etc.

4 Swap papers and, without looking at what the other has written, add your negative feelings on the other side of their paper. Then walk widdershins around the table five times, visualizing the way you express your emotion.

5 When you have circled the table for the fifth time, each of you should burn your own piece of paper in the flame of the last candle that was lit, dropping the paper into the heatproof container.

Burn coriander seeds to invoke Zamael, angel of Mars. Coriander is sacred to this angel.

A joint wish

Write your names together on natural paper, stating a positive wish you both want. Place it between the two halves of an organic apple, seal the join with green candle wax and bury the apple near to your home in a prepared spot. If the apple pips (seeds) grow, tend them carefully because they represent new growth in your relationship that needs looking after.

A Spell for Joining

For a romance that is blossoming, work with the energies of spring to create this love token, which is inspired by the Maypole, an ancient fertility symbol. During the spring May Day festival (Beltane), people traditionally danced around the pole, interweaving coloured ribbons as they did so, symbolizing the joining of the male and female. Give the love token to your partner to represent the weaving together of your lives. Work this spell on a Sunday at full moon.

You will need
wand
straight wooden stick
two green ribbons
two yellow ribbons
thread or wool (yarn)
beads, pendants or stones for decoration

1 Find a comfortable place to work, then cast a circle around you. Assemble your materials in the centre. Sit facing south.

Green is the colour of new growth and fertility, while yellow symbolizes health and happiness.

2 Invoke the winds of the four directions in turn, repeating the following words and each time substituting the next direction:
Hail to the South/West/North/East Wind.
I call upon your assistance in the making of this charm for (say the person's name).
Please lend it your power and give it your blessings and protection for the highest good of all concerned.

3 Secure the lengths of ribbon around the top of the stick using the thread or wool. Hold the stick firmly in place and lay out the ribbons in the four directions, green in the north and south, yellow in the west and east.

4 Weave the ribbons around the stick, crossing alternate adjacent pairs in a continuous pattern, until you reach the base. Wind the north and south ribbons deosil and the east and west ones widdershins around the wood, weaving the north ribbon over the east one, and the south ribbon over the west one.

5 Secure the ends with thread or more ribbon. Tie beads, pendants or stones on to them as decoration, or leave the ribbon ends free if you prefer.

6 When you have finished, thank the Four Winds for helping you, and close the circle in the usual way.

Love's protection

In many cultures giving a cloak or scarf to a loved one signifies the offer of protection, and that the giver will always be there for the other. You can make a love charm to symbolize the cloak by using a smaller piece of fabric decorated with symbols of your love. Think carefully about the colours, patterns and fabric you wish to use. The best time to make and present this love charm is in the autumn, during a waxing moon.

You will need
square of fabric
soft pencil
needle and thread
small pieces of fabric
beads and charms
paintbrush and fabric paints or needle and embroidery thread (floss)

1 Use your hand to create a magic circle around your workspace. See it as a ring of fire and know that it protects you as you make your spell.

2 Draw out the pattern of your design on the cloth in pencil. Sew on the pieces of fabric you have chosen. You can also tie on beads and other charms if you feel they are needed, or have a particular significance.

3 Using either fabric paints or embroidery thread, fill in the pattern. Close your circle when your spell is complete.

4 Give the charm to your partner as a token of your love; remind them that you will always be there when they need you.

Spells for Separation and Endings

When relationships are no longer able to sustain themselves, many couples decide that it is best to part. This is usually the last step in a painful process that involves a lot of soul-searching and talking together. Magic can help you to achieve an ending that is peaceful and not acrimonious, that recognizes your differences without seeing one another as wrong. Ending spells may also be performed after the death of a partner to help you let go so that you are free to move on.

As you work on the talking stick, concentrate on the issues you want to resolve.

Effective Communication

Separation is a difficult and complex process, particularly if children are involved. Clear communication can help each partner let go of unspoken resentments and painful feelings, so that each can move forwards as peacefully as possible. Using a "talking stick" is a Native American technique designed to facilitate open and honest dialogue to help people move on and progress a difficult situation. The charm can be used for any problem and is particularly good for moving forward in a relationship, even if it is towards an ending rather than a reconciliation.

Making a Talking Stick

Traditionally, a talking stick was made from wood, but it can be made of any material – this one is made from paper. Decide how you are going to symbolize the relationship problem you are having, as you will inscribe this on your stick. The best time to work this charm is during a waning moon, on a Tuesday.

You will need

pencil
sheet of natural paper
coloured paints or pencils
paintbrush
coloured ribbon or string

When you and your partner have finished using the talking stick it should be burned.

1 Use your hand to cast a magic circle around your work area. Visualize it as a ring of bright fire.

2 Draw your inscription on paper. Spend time designing and choosing the words or symbols, remembering that they stand for the problem that you and your partner are going to discuss.

3 Using coloured paints or pencils, add colour to the design; think about talking and listening to your partner concerning this particular issue as you work, and about letting go of the problem so that you can both live without its shadow hanging over your relationship.

4 Roll the paper up into a scroll and tie it in place with the ribbon or string. The symbols along with your intentions are now bound up into the roll of the charm.

5 Close your circle. You are now ready to use your charm. Begin by presenting it to the person you love and suggest how it may be used.

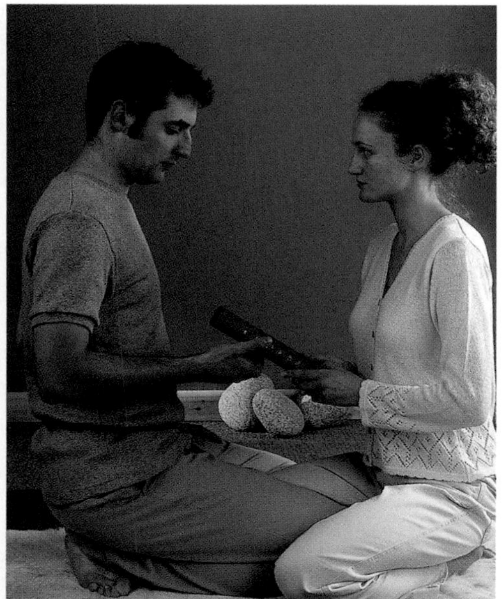

Before you begin using the talking stick, make sure you both agree on the rules.

HOW TO USE THE TALKING STICK

One person holds the stick and talks while the other person, without interrupting, listens intently and respectfully in silence. When the speaker is finished he or she places the stick on the ground for the other person to pick up. When you both feel you have finished, throw the talking stick on to a fire, or burn it in a heatproof container. Watch the flames devour it, symbolizing the ending and letting go of an issue. This talking ceremony will need to be repeated many times during a separation process, which is a series of endings, letting go a little more each time.

A spell for helping to cut the ties

This spell can help you to say goodbye at the end of a relationship, and let go of your partner. It can be performed at the end of any relationship to ease the transition from one life stage to another. The best time to perform this spell is on a Saturday during a waning moon.

You will need

purple altar cloth
aromatherapy burner
cypress essential oil
30cm (12in) black ribbon
white candle
black candle
photograph of yourself
photograph of your partner
clean pair of scissors

1 Clean and prepare your altar space and put the cloth on top. Place the oil burner in the middle of the altar towards the back. Light the burner and add three drops of cypress oil.

2 Tie one end of the black ribbon around the white candle and the other around the black candle. Position the candles on the altar so that the ribbon forms a "tightrope".

3 Place the two photographs side by side in the middle of the altar, beneath the ribbon; the photograph of you should be on the side of the white candle, your partner's photo should be on the side of the black one.

4 Light the white candle and say:
White candle, please hear my plea and represent me.
Help me to part from (say your partner's name) in a spirit of love and friendship.

5 Light the black candle and say:
Black candle, please hear my plea and represent (say your partner's name).
Help (say your partner's name) to part from me in a spirit of love and friendship.

6 Hold the scissors over the taut ribbon and prepare to cut the ribbon as you say these words, actually cutting it as you finish the second line:
Scissors shiny, scissors sharp
Make me and (say your partner's name) move apart
Neither harmed nor alarmed
May we now go our separate ways,
Scissors clean, scissors new
Make a clean break.

7 Put the white candle on top of your photograph, and the black one on top of your partner's picture. Let the candles burn for three minutes as you visualize you and your partner happily walking away from each other.

8 Move the photographs a little further apart and repeat the visualization. Repeat once more. Close the spell by saying "thank you" to the spirits and blow out the oil burner. Repeat the spell for up to seven days.

A spell for emotional healing

Try this spell to help you through the grieving process at the end of a relationship. The best time for this is a Sunday, during a waning moon.

You will need

16 tealight candles
pink candle
rose essential oil and aromatherapy burner
pansy

1 Arrange the tealights in a circle and open it in the west by lighting the first tealight, followed by the rest of the tealights.

2 Sit in the centre of the circle, facing south, and light the pink candle and the oil burner. Add a couple of drops of rose oil to the burner. Close your eyes and breathe in the soft fragrance of the rose essential oil. As you do so, imagine yourself surrounded by a pink light. This soft pink light permeates your whole being and fills the sacred circle where you sit.

3 Bring the pansy to your heart chakra. Hold it there and, speaking softly, tell it your troubles and how you are feeling. When you are finished, slowly get up and close the magic circle in the usual way, giving thanks to the spirits for listening. Take the pansy outside and bury it in an appropriate spot.

Imagine yourself surrounded by pink.

SACRED SPACE

The idea that we can connect with higher powers through the many different spaces we inhabit is an ancient one. The Romans, for instance, believed that each home has its resident *genius loci* – the individual deity of the place – and each household had a special altar, where at certain times the family would gather to give thanks for their security. The same idea occurs in traditional Chinese and Indian thought, and similar spiritual belief systems have existed all over the world throughout the ages. Today, a growing awareness of the importance of sacred space is rekindling this ancient need to sanctify our environment – whether at home, at work or in nature – and many magical and mystical practices are being put into action.

This chapter begins with hints and tips for how we can encourage good vibrations in our homes using herbs and stones as well as creating altars for household gods. It includes a hedgewitch salt cleansing ritual and a shamanic rattle ceremony to be used for clearing negative energies. Information is given on how to create different atmospheres, how to make a place feel special and how to change the function of a room by banishing the old spirits and welcoming the new ones. A special technique is given to clear negative energies in the workplace, as well as ideas on creating personal altars and placing altars around the home. Finally, a section on outdoor magic describes ways of honouring nature and receiving nourishment from it.

GOOD VIBRATIONS

A home where we feel secure is one of the most basic human needs, but what exactly gives us that feeling of security is something most of us would find hard to define. It has nothing to do with material wealth and luxury – some of the most palatial buildings can feel cold and uncomfortable. In magical thinking, this is because all locations have a spirit of place, or "genius loci" as the Romans called it. When this spirit is properly acknowledged and cared for, it can have a positive effect on the place and all those who occupy it. We can use many techniques based on natural magic to help generate positive vibrations in our everyday environments.

A bead curtain hung in a doorway adds a sense of mystery and magic to the place of transition.

DOORWAYS

In magical terms, the doorway is very important. It is not only the means by which we enter and leave a particular space, but it also symbolizes the transition between entering and leaving different psychic realities. A doorway, therefore, is an ideal setting to affirm the atmosphere you wish to create inside your home or a particular room. Bead curtains add a sense of mystery and magic, while fairy lights strung around the doorway create a sense of light and warmth, and invite the fairies into your space. Flowers and herbs encourage connections with the natural world and convey a sense of ease and relaxation, while garlands of foliage, such as rosemary, ivy or laurel, on a door symbolize protection. Many people like to hang images or charms over the door to attract specific qualities: angels invite blessings, protective deities offer strength and coins invite prosperous

Furnishings in the home

Today we choose our carpets because we like their colour or pattern, but the traditional designs from the Far East, Turkey and North Africa were woven to attract good fortune and domestic tranquillity. Similarly we hang pictures on our walls because we like to look at them, but originally the murals of ancient civilizations served a spiritual purpose in placating and invoking local deities. All these devices were originally intended to drive away bad vibrations and attract good or harmonious ones in their place.

In the Japanese sacred tradition, candlelight and flowers represent the innocence of the heart.

exchanges. You can also place spells for protection or good luck under the front doormat, so that you step on them each time you go in or out of the home.

HOUSEHOLD GODS
Many cultures have a tradition of honouring the household gods or ancestral deities. In ancient Greece, for instance, Hermes and Hestia were the twin protectors of the home. A statue of Hermes, the god of transition and exchange, stood by the front door, while one of the goddess Hestia presided over the hearth, representing stability and permanence. When a new baby was born, it was the tradition for Hestia's blessing to be sought by ritually carrying the child around the hearth. In the Chinese tradition, the spirits of the ancestors are venerated at the family altar or shrine, so that they will confer their blessings on the family.

ALTARS
The idea of having an altar at home may take a little getting used to, but in many parts of the East it is common practice. In the Japanese Shinto tradition, for instance, the *kamidana* is a small altar enshrining protective deities, where offerings of food, water and flowers are regularly placed. The tokonoma, an alcove in the north wall where scrolls are hung and flower arrangements or beautiful artefacts are displayed, also serves as a spiritual focus.

A domestic altar embodies the sanctity of home and family, and its presence helps to create a positive environment. It is a constant reminder of the search for spiritual fulfilment, anchored in the context of daily life. It can be a focus for prayer, a shrine to honour those you love, a place where you choose to meditate, or somewhere to spend a few minutes in quiet contemplation. An altar does not have to conform to any particular size, shape or colour but is your own unique creation.

DARK CRYSTALS AND STONES
Any dark crystal can be programmed to draw in negative vibrations from its local environment. Placing dark stones in a problem area can help to cleanse it before it is filled with symbols and objects of warmth and light. Flint, a dark stone commonly found throughout most of the world, is a powerful protector against negative psychic energies.

SHARP OBJECTS
To give protection against negative influences, you can place needles, pins, thorns, prickles or any other sharp objects in a jar, then fill it with a mixture of protective herbs. The jar should then be sealed and left in the area that seems to be causing problems. It can also be placed under the bed for protection at night. Another traditional means of protection against psychic opposition is to put rusty iron nails around a property, facing away from the walls.

A HORSESHOE
Iron is the metal of Mars – the Roman god of power, strength and courage. An iron horseshoe can be displayed with its "horns" facing to the left, in the shape of a crescent moon, to reflect the properties of Mars, and also of the moon goddess.

Protective herbs and spices

Many herbs and spices can be used to help banish negative spirits or energies and protect the home. These are some of the most common:
Angelica: an all-round protective plant.
Asafoetida: removes all negativity, but smells acrid, so is used only in severe cases.
Cactus: all spiny plants and tree branches offer protection. Prickly plants or stems in the home or workplace will deflect negativity from the surrounding area.
Fumitory: to expel negative thought-forms.
Garlic: a powerful psychic protector. Its strong smell and taste deters unwanted energies. Cloves of peeled garlic can be strung over door frames, or placed in strategic positions and replaced once a week with fresh cloves. In folklore garlic was used to keep vampires at bay.
Rowan: all parts of the rowan tree have magical protective properties. String the leaves and berries into a garland and place them around whatever you wish to gain protection for but keep the garland out of reach of small children or babies.
Salt: central to many magical practices, salt is one of the sacred items for all magical practitioners. It is a crystal and its cleansing powers mean that it is held in great respect.
Yarrow: a powerful psychic protector.

In the English folklore tradition it is believed that a jar of needles, pins and thorns, together with protective herbs, gives protection against negative influences or psychic opposition.

SPACE CLEARING

Any kind of good, positive atmosphere is welcome and wholesome, but we sometimes need to cure a negative, unwholesome one. Negative energies in the environment will have an adverse effect on the people who live or work there: common symptoms include feeling tired or drained of energy, poor concentration, loss of interest in present circumstances and being stuck in a rut. Space clearing is a way of clearing negative energies – it is like a psychic spring-cleaning. We can also perform space clearing ceremonies on ourselves to free ourselves from negative thought-forms and psychic energies.

Shaking the rattle as you say the words imbues them with the power of the rattlesnake.

SPACE CLEARING IN FOLKLORE

Many ancient space clearing ceremonies have persisted as part of the folklore tradition. "Beating the bounds" is an old custom whose original purpose was the spiritual protection of the community. The village boundary line was beaten with birch wands to ensure the safekeeping of the village by establishing a magical barrier around it that no evil spirit could cross. Similarly birch broomsticks were not only used domestically for sweeping the floor, but magically for clearing out unwanted psychic energies and for creating a magic circle. In the days of earth floors, a circle could literally be swept into the floor, this ring forming a visible barrier to the inner realm and a protection against any outside influences that might disrupt the work within. Sometimes today witches still sweep the area they use for magic.

Performing the fourfold breath will calm and centre you before a space clearing ritual.

Space clearing can also be about clearing negative energies from the body. For instance, the Northern European folk tradition of "wassailing" (the giving of a New Year salutation for health and wellbeing with a cup of spiced ale) was thought to clear away any evil spirits residing within a person's body. The term "wassail" comes from the Anglo-Saxon *waes hael* meaning "be whole" or "be well".

A HEDGEWITCH SPACE CLEARING

This ritual can be performed once a week to keep your home or workplace clear and clean. Sweep up any old salt and take it outside your property boundary before repeating the ritual.

Begin at the doorway and move deosil (clockwise) around the room. Take a pinch of natural sea or rock salt and sprinkle it in the first corner, saying:

Clean and clear this corner (or window, fireplace etc) be, from all that is not good for me.

Repeat these words as you sprinkle more salt in all four corners, then around the doorframes and fireplace before moving on to the next room you wish to cleanse.

Changing ourselves

Because "like attracts like", there is no point in space clearing the environment if we do not also change our own state of mind, banishing negative thoughts so that unwelcome vibrations are no longer received. Most psychic negativity is produced by our own mental and emotional states. Rituals that produce changes inside ourselves – changes of consciousness – need to be approached with care and sensitivity and work best when they are short and simple.

Rattles, such as this North American Indian one, are made from seed pods.

Space Clearing Yourself

To perform this self cleansing you will need a selection of white candles, including one large one, together with tealights and a rattle. Rattles conjure the ominous sounds of the rattlesnake as it warns of its presence by shaking its tail. When used in ceremony, a rattle can either summon the energy of the snake to protect, or can warn intrusive energies that they should step back and withdraw.

1 Distribute the candles about the floor of the room and light them, using as many or as few as you feel is appropriate but reserving the large one.

2 Sit on a cushion in the centre of the room. Light the large white candle and place it directly in front of you.

3 Spend some time performing the fourfold breath: breathe in for a count of four, hold for four, breathe out for four, and hold for four before taking the next breath. Then pick up your rattle in your right hand and repeat the following words, shaking the rattle at the end of each line except when you say "It is true":

Pay attention (shake rattle)
Snake is here (shake rattle)
It is true
Snake is coming (shake rattle)
So beware adversary – snake is ready to strike (shake rattle loudly).

4 Then repeat the following chant:

Life is love; love is life; let there be an end to strife.
Let the good replace all bad; let love release all spirits sad.
Let my will reveal the power, starting at this present hour,
To enhance the energy, so that I possess the key,
To allow all ills to go, and to let the goodness flow
Into this place where I now kneel, let love begin all things to heal.

5 Repeat the chant several times. Visualize all negativity departing from you at great speed as you chase it away and reclaim what is rightfully yours.

Making a space clearing rattle

If you don't have a ceremonial rattle, you can make one. You will need an aluminium drinks can, some paper, a handful of rice, glue, scissors and some sage for burning.

1 Wash and dry the empty can, making sure the ring pull has been completely removed.

2 Place the can on the paper and draw round the circular base to form a circle the same size. Cut out the circle. Pour the rice into the can through the ring-pull hole and place the paper circle over the top of the can to cover the hole. Glue in place.

3 Cut out another piece of paper big enough to wrap around the sides of the can. Glue it around the can, decorate it if you wish.

4 When the rattle is complete, dedicate it to Sosho (the snake) by passing it through the smoke of burning sage. Call for the powers of the rattlesnake to enter your rattle and to help you in your magic.

As with all magical equipment, if you make it yourself it has greater power.

Changing Atmospheres

Natural magic can be used to change and create atmospheres for a variety of different purposes. For instance, sometimes you may want to change the function of a room in your home, in which case you will not only need to think about how to decorate and rearrange the room, but you will also need to think about its energetic personality. If the change in use is particularly radical, like the change from a work space to a bedroom, you will need to banish the old spirits of place before the new ones can be welcomed in.

If a former bedroom, which has acquired a relaxed atmosphere over the years, is changed into a sitting room, psychically sensitive people may feel drowsy when they spend time in the room. If the planning department of a company moves out of an office and the accounts department moves in, employers may notice the accounting staff spending time in discussion. The atmospheres in these spaces are not particularly negative – they are misplaced echoes of former thought-forms, each with a residual power of subliminal persuasion, that need to be overwritten by a more appropriate one.

As you clap your hands, visualize the sounds driving away the old atmosphere of work, business and stressful activity.

This atmosphere is being changed from the masculine atmosphere of an office – symbolized by a pen – to the gentler atmosphere of a girl's bedroom – symbolized by the little pink bag.

To Change an Atmosphere

Transmuting one positive atmosphere into another can be done with a ritual in which you begin by focusing on the old atmosphere, then swing your focus to the new, whatever it may be.This could also be described as stamping a new psychic impression upon a place. Here, the aim is to change what was a home office into a bedroom for a young girl.

You will need
4 small tumbled rose quartz crystals
altar
white candle
2–3 candles in a colour that reflects the new usage of the space
a token of the original use of the space (in this case a pen)
black cloth large enough to cover or contain the token
rose geranium essential oil and burner
a token of the new atmosphere (in this case a pink bag)

1 Set up an altar in the middle of the room using colours that suit the new atmosphere you wish to create. Put the white candle in the centre of the altar with the three coloured candles arranged in a triangle around it.

Using colour to change atmospheres

Use this list to help you choose the most appropriate colours to represent the new function of the room and enhance the atmosphere you are seeking to create.

Red: best used in active areas, such as a living room or dining room, or to add a touch of energy to a more neutral backdrop
Orange: use in creative areas and for a supportive ambience
Yellow: best used in work places, its happy, sunny colour also works well in the kitchen
Green: use in areas of relaxation and harmony, such as a living room or bedroom
Blue: ideal for areas of peace and relaxation, such as a living room, bedroom or bathroom
Violet: as a combination of blue and pink it is ideal for areas where both liveliness and rest are required, such as a dining room
Pink: for inspiration and happiness, this could be used in a bedroom, living room or office
Purple: good for areas requiring stillness, depth and meaning, such as a bedroom, or any restful, contemplative 'inner' space
Silver: symbolizes magic and dreams; can bring a touch of feminine (yin) energy into a more masculine (yang) space
Gold: symbolizes happiness and abundance; can bring masculine (yang) energy into an overly feminine (yin) space
Brown: for an atmosphere that requires stability and reliable energy; ideal when changing a mentally orientated space to a more practical one

An element of red will bring energy and dynamism to a room.

2 Put everything you are going to use in the ritual on the altar for a few moments, then take the rose quartz crystals and put one in each corner of the room.

3 Take the object you have chosen to represent the old atmosphere, and place it in the western quarter of the room. Take the object that is representing the new atmosphere of the room and place it in the eastern quarter. Light all the candles.

4 Start the ritual at the east side of the altar, facing west. Take a few deep, calming breaths and say the following:
Go! Depart! Begone ye hence!
Avaunt I say, this is my will!
Be ended, finished, changed, transposed,
Leave no disturbing echoes still!

5 Clap your hands loudly, then take the cloth over to the object in the west and cover it. Return to the altar, but this time stand at the west side facing east, in the opposite direction to the earlier part of the ritual. Say the following:
Now welcome be, now welcome stay,
Now welcome is for evermore!
Be started, newborn, fresh, unfurled,
And bring thy presence to the fore!

6 Go to the object in the east that represents the new atmosphere and bring it reverentially to the altar to place it there. Sit beside the altar and leave the item there for several minutes while you meditate on it. As you do so, absorb the new atmosphere that is emerging in the room and reflect it back at the object.

7 When you feel this is complete and the atmosphere has been altered, close the ritual by extinguishing the candles. Dismantle the altar and remove the object that represented the old atmosphere from the room. Leave the object that represents the new atmosphere in a prominent position on a windowsill or shelf.

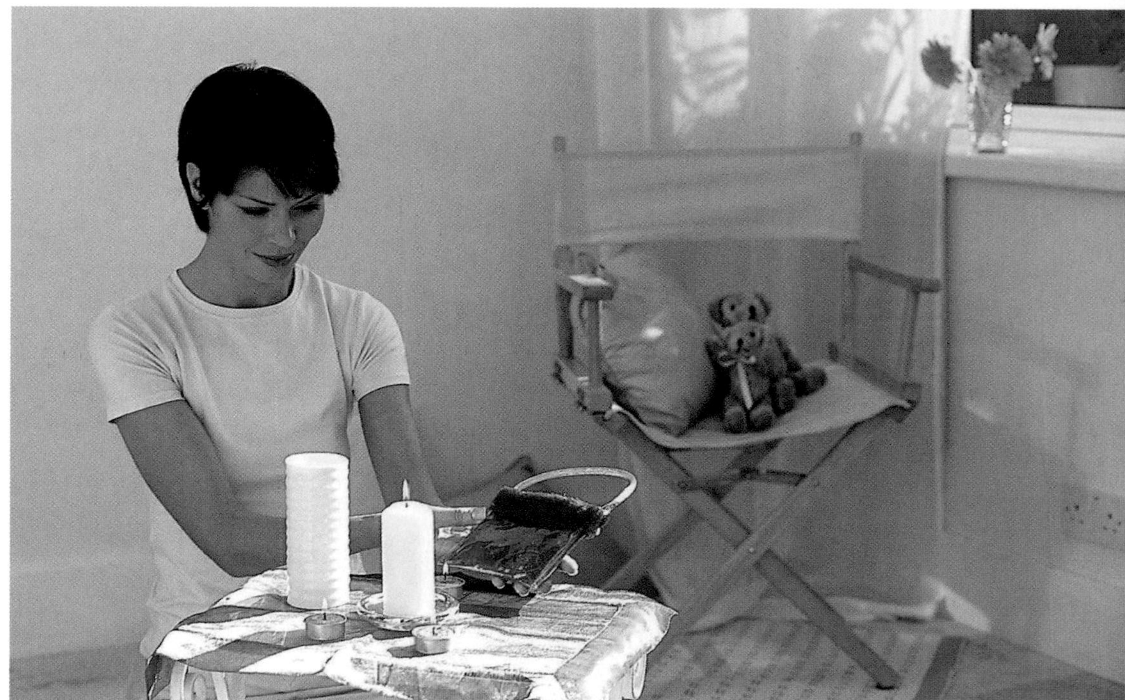

After removing the old object, bring in the new one, and place it in a central position in the room as a focal point for the new energies.

Creating a special feel

When we expect visitors and spend time preparing for their stay, our aim is to make our home feel especially welcoming. If we are holding a dinner party, we take great care both to prepare good food and to provide a pleasant atmosphere. It is important to us to provide for our guests' physical comfort, and we are also concerned about doing the equivalent on a psychic level. There are also times when a special atmosphere is called for – when entertaining friends, celebrating the season or marking some other important event, such as a wedding or naming ceremony.

There are two key words that relate to making a place feel special, both materially and magically, and these are "pride" and "respect". Without one, we will not feel the other. When both these elements are brought into play, our place – whatever and wherever it may be – will begin to fill with that special atmosphere of sparkle and excitement.

For a Special Feel

Every now and again, we want to make a place feel especially welcoming. This ceremony uses frankincense, rose water and orange candles to create a "golden" atmosphere. Frankincense is one of the most precious incense ingredients, while rose water is delicately purifying and leaves a lingering subtle fragrance.

The many candles that are randomly arranged in this ritual will brighten every corner.

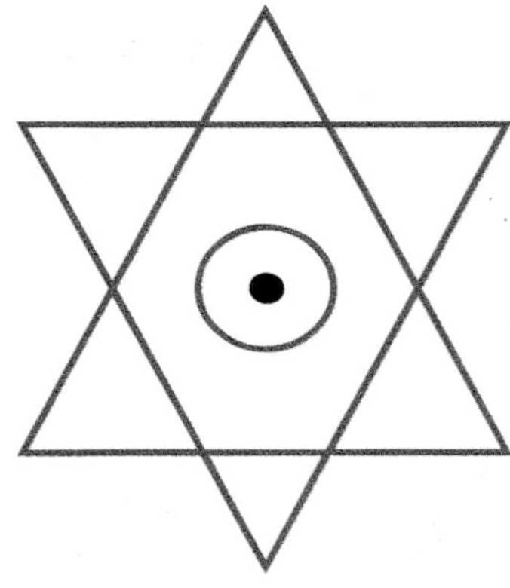

The solar hexagram is a six-rayed star with a representation of the sun in the centre.

Orange candles symbolize the life-giving, creative power of the sun. As you perform it, you should notice your space begin to change and fill with that special atmosphere of sparkle and excitement.

You will need

altar and orange altar cloth
2 orange or gold candles
frankincense and charcoal burner or essential oil and burner
wand
additional orange candles for dark areas
rose water in small bowl

1 Position the altar so that you will face east when standing before it. Arrange the cloth and the two candles in holders upon it, together with the incense or essential oil burner and the wand.

2 Place the additional candles around the room in the shadowy areas that light does not normally illuminate, and where the candle glow will enhance the richness of the room's appearance. The aim is to achieve a depth of perspective in the room, so arrange the candles in a non-linear way, and avoid having them at a similar distance from the altar.

3 Light the candles, then stand in front of the altar and bow your head. Take several deep and calming breaths.

4 Use the wand to "draw" a solar hexagram in the air in front of you, above the altar. The hexagram, a six-pointed star (identical to the "Star of

As you perform this spell, focus your mind and concentrate on what you are doing, and visualize a sphere of happiness being created.

David"), is associated with the zodiac, the planets and the sun.

5 At the centre of the hexagram, "draw" the symbol of the sun: a small circle with a dot in the middle. As you do this, visualize the outline appearing as a line of brilliant golden light. Then, in a commanding voice, say:

Let none undo the spell I cast,
For it is well and three times good;
This place is special now at last,
Be it now full understood!

6 Now pick up the bowl of rose water and, as you walk clockwise around the edge of the room, dip your fingers in the water and then brush your hand over the walls and floor areas. As you do so, say, "Blessed be this boundary". Where there are areas of the room that might be damaged by the rose water, pass your hand over the walls a little distance away. It is helpful to visualize the blessing water creating a sphere of happiness and peace, as you mark out the boundary of the room.

7 To close the ritual, extinguish all the candles, starting with the furthest away from the altar and ending with the nearest. Then give thanks and go outside to discard any remaining rose water into the earth.

Elemental imbalances

Sometimes the atmosphere of a place is spoilt by an elemental imbalance, that is to say, where there is either too much or not enough of one of the four elements. These elemental imbalances can be corrected by introducing any of these quick fixes:

Air: music, wind chimes, images of air creatures such as birds, lavender fragrance;
Fire: candlelight, gold or orange materials, fire creatures such as the phoenix, lion or dragonfly, frankincense or copal fragrance;
Water: an indoor fountain, water garden, fish-tank or bowl of water, images of water creatures or plants, jasmine fragrance;
Earth: plants, herbs, crystals, images of earth-dwellers such as prairie dogs or badgers, cypress fragrance;
Elemental lightbulbs: Another way to change the atmosphere is by replacing a plain lightbulb with one you have painted with particular designs, using glass paint. To introduce more Air use a patterned lightbulb painted with violet circles on a yellow background; to add more fire to a room use a lightbulb painted with red flames on a green background; to add Water use a lightbulb painted with blue bands on an orange background; and to introduce Earth use a lightbulb painted with citrine and russet-brown diamonds.

Painted lightbulbs add instant elemental influences to a room.

Magic in the Workplace

Unless you have a private office or work from home, it may be difficult to imagine using magic in the workplace. However, there are a number of ways of using magical tools and equipment to protect against negative energies at work. It is a good idea to do this, as we are exposed to many vibrations that can adversely affect us. Common problems include allergies, poor concentration, high stress levels and feeling tired all the time. Such problems have been linked to excessive exposure to artificial light, electromagnetic radiation (the energy waves emitted by electronic equipment such as computers, mobile phones and photocopiers), and "sick-building syndrome". The latter is a term used to describe a cluster of health problems associated with inhabiting certain kinds of buildings.

As offices are usually crowded and busy places, space clearing at work often needs to be a private, mental exercise.

The Power of the Mind

It is a good idea to perform regular space clearing rituals at work to transform negative energies. Although it can be awkward to conduct any kind of overt ceremony or ritual, there are ways around this. At its purest and most powerful level, magic needs no special equipment or physical actions, not even speech: the entire ritual, including all scents, colours and tools, can be imagined through creative visualization. An occult master can use his or her mind and willpower to achieve astonishing results using this technique, but fortunately even a shadow of this ability is good enough for your needs.

Create a scrapbook of images that represent your working environment, and use this as a focus for your thoughts.

Preparation

Try to choose a time when you are unlikely to be disturbed. Even though your outward actions will not raise any eyebrows among your colleagues, you will be better able to concentrate if you are alone. Beforehand, you will need to obtain a small notepad suitable to make into a scrapbook. You will also need to collect a number of appropriate images to represent your working environment. These could be taken from magazines and catalogues. Your tools for this ritual will be nothing more complicated than scissors, glue and paper.

Cut out the pictures you have collected and use them to assemble a collage, or compound image, of your workplace, by arranging and sticking them together. Remember that it does not need to be a realistic impression of the place, nor does it need to be artistic or to scale, or to have perfect perspective. You are simply aiming for a symbolic general impression of your working environment, not an accurate representation.

Crystals

As natural parts of the earth's structure, the energies of crystals are radiated at natural frequencies. You can use these to help balance the emissions of modern appliances by placing them around equipment such as computers and printers or televisions. To remain effective, the crystals will need to be cleansed once a month.

Sympathetic Magic

Everyone is familiar with the voodoo practice of sticking pins into a doll that represents someone you don't like. This is based on the principle of sympathetic magic: the idea is that the doll and the target become inextricably linked, so that whatever happens to one will transfer itself to the other by association. Though this practice is a form of destructive magic and is not recommended, the principle of sympathetic magic can be used in a positive way – in this instance, to clear negative energies at work.

So just as the doll is only a rough image of a real person, your workplace collage need only be an approximation of the actual place. You can make a single collage or as many versions as you like, until you find an image that you resonate well with. Once you are satisfied, sit quietly with the image and visualize it being filled with golden light. See the light filling up the picture until everything is surrounded by a golden glow – pay particular attention to areas of heavy or particularly negative energy, such as photocopiers, computers and other machines. Say these words quietly to yourself:

Darkness be gone! May this space be filled with golden light. And so mote it be!

Repeat the visualization regularly for maximum effect; each time you practise it your powers of visualization will become more powerful and effective.

Guarding Against Negativity

There are other steps you can take to repel negativity and to promote good vibrations at work. Keeping the area clean and free from clutter is one of the most basic – negativity attaches to dirt. If you are having trouble with another worker, a cactus plant positioned between you will offer protection.

If when you are at work you feel a sudden vulnerability, use your mind to project an image of a guardian figure standing next to you. This could be your guardian angel or guide, a totem animal or someone you know with whom you feel safe and happy. Remember the guardian will never take the offensive against the person or situation that is causing you to feel vulnerable, but will offer a mantle of protection around you, strengthening your auric field so that negative energies cannot get to you.

Protection Strategies

There are also other ways to keep your workplace psychically protected:

- Display plants and flowers that have protective qualities, such as fern and geranium. Put them in waiting rooms and reception areas to reduce invasive effects from the energy of visitors.
- Place smoky quartz crystals in the four corners of the room to help absorb stray energies. Make sure you clean them once a month.
- Position clear quartz crystals near computers and electronic equipment to help to absorb and transform electromagnetic radiation.
- Include plenty of green plants in the building to provide oxygen, and let their vibrations help to connect you with the natural world.

If you need protection from a difficult colleague, position some cacti on your desk between you.

If you need protection, make a display of suitable plants and keep it on your desk.

Smoky quartz crystals, placed in the corners of a room, will absorb stray energies.

Altars at work

In many parts of the East, you are just as likely to find an altar or shrine in a shop or office as at home. You can make an unobtrusive "altar" at work by creating a small display of personal objects on your desk or workstation. These could include a photograph, a natural object, such as a stone or crystal, a piece of fruit, and some fresh flowers or a plant.

Personal altars

Creating a personal altar is a way of inviting magic into your home. The sacred space it occupies is available to you all the time; it is a meeting point where the divine reaches down to touch the everyday world and where you can concentrate your intentions and desires for spiritual growth. There is a two-way flow between the individual and the world of spirit, and the altar is its channel. It can be both a setting for a journey into a spiritual dimension and a place to gain deeper understanding of your own character and place in the universe.

A personal altar is probably best used for prayer or meditation rather than spell-making, ritual or ceremony, when special altars are usually set up for that particular purpose. As it is used, it becomes energized and its influence widens, flowing out through and around you, to bless your home and everyone in it. A personal altar can be a physical expression of your deepest attachments and longings: by giving them form you bring them into your daily life and empower yourself to achieve what you desire. There is no set way of creating your own personal altar – the form it takes is up to you. What is important is that it has meaning for you.

Natural Objects

In natural magic, a personal altar would usually contain symbolic representations of the natural world. Placing natural objects on an altar helps to reinforce its connection with earth energies and underlines our commitment to preserving the natural world. It is also a reminder of our own connection with the web of life. When looking for objects for your altar, you may prefer to take only things that have fallen ("found" objects), rather than by cutting flowers or trees, for instance. Remember to always give thanks for what you have taken by leaving an offering or by a simple action, such as clearing away litter.

Feathers represent birds, who are honoured as a link between earth and heaven.

Stones represent the Earth element. Their presence on an altar can help stabilize stress-filled places.

Sacred Images

Deities from any religion may have a personal symbolism for you that you would like to represent on your altar. For instance, a statue of the Buddha in meditation could help you to focus on your own meditation, while the Goddess could be represented by a fertility figure or a statue or painting of one of her many aspects. By invoking the Goddess and seeking her ancient wisdom you will find an aspect of her in yourself. Bringing her into the heart of your home in this way upholds a tradition that has been practised throughout history. Similarly, if you call on a guardian angel for spiritual support, you can place a picture or figurine of an angel on your altar to focus your prayer.

Abstract Symbols

Symbols predate writing as a means of conveying ideas. Ancient symbols were carved, painted, stitched and worked in metal for magical purposes, to ward off evil or to invoke gods. A symbol gains its significance from the emotional and spiritual weight that it carries. Some of the most compelling symbols are the simplest, such as the circle that

Natural symbolism

The natural world is full of symbolism, whether in trees and plants, rocks and shells, or feathers, flowers and pieces of wood.

Feathers: represent the Air element and also symbolize the connection between the earth and the heavens.
Stones: bring grounding, Earth energy to the altar. A stone also brings some of the character of the place where it came from.
Fossils: even more than stones, a fossil is a striking reminder of the antiquity of the earth and carries the resonance of millions of years of history.
Seashells: a reminder of the ocean and the element of Water. Seashells are associated with the unconscious and feminine energy. They also have traditional links with regeneration, baptism and prosperity.
Fruits, nuts and grains: are a reminder of the abundance of nature and the changing seasons of the year.
Flowers, herbs and trees: plants are great healers, with particular species being linked with different properties. For instance, ash is associated with purification and cleansing, roses with love and beauty, and basil is said to protect from pain.
Driftwood: a piece of driftwood, carried by the oceans, conveys the blessings of the Goddess.

Elemental altars

Another way of creating a personal altar is through a symbolic representation of the elements. For instance, if you are working on creative issues, then you would focus especially on the Fire element, for relationship issues on Water, on Earth for stability and material prosperity, while Air represents freedom, change and new ideas.

Fire: symbolized by the colours orange or red and by yellow or gold flowers
Air: symbolized by incense, scented candles, a fan or feathers and silver-coloured cloth or ornaments
Water: symbolized by the colours blue and green, and by water, wine or any liquid
Earth: symbolized by stone or terracotta objects and earthy colours such as russet, brown and deep orange

represents the wheel of life, death and rebirth. The spiral too stands for the cycle of existence, but its outward motion also symbolizes growth and energy. The pentacle, or five-pointed star, is an ancient symbol of harmony and mystic power. Placing ancient graphic symbols such as these on your altar will bring their energy and associations into your life. By painting or carving them yourself, you will enhance your connection with them further.

Practical Considerations

A personal altar is essentially a work of intuition and imagination. Any flat surface can become an altar when it is hallowed by intent. The surface could be a shelf, a windowsill, the top of a chest or even the top of a refrigerator. Some people like to know that their personal altar is completely private to them. If you feel this way, you could arrange a beautiful shrine inside a cupboard or box. A small wooden box makes a lovely altar because you can arrange all your sacred things on the flat lid and it is also portable. Having a portable altar is a good idea if you are often travelling away from home and wish to carry the essence of home with you.

Statues of female or male figures can be used to represent the archetype you wish to honour.

A portable altar will remind you of home.

ALTARS IN THE HOME

Most people have one room that feels special, where the sense of positive energy is most complete. It could be the living room, the kitchen, or a welcoming entrance hall. Traditionally the hearth is regarded as the centre of the home and it is really a prototype altar. Deciding where to position your altar will influence its style as well as how you use it. For instance, your altar can be for you alone, or to share with others. A family altar can work for cohesiveness, like the traditional ancestral altars of the East, while a couple could share in the creation of an altar to promote a deeper commitment to one another. In each case certain locations in the home are more suitable than others.

This simple bedside altar to Gaia, the goddess of dreams, includes lilies to invoke calm.

POSITIONING THE ALTAR

All the different activities that we pursue create distinct types of energy in each room. This is why it can be very difficult to go to sleep in a room that has been full of lively conversation, for instance, or to concentrate on a piece of analytical work in the kitchen. Similarly, every altar will be influenced by the energy of its surroundings. You can use this power to create a life-enhancing altar in any room by drawing on the intrinsic energy of the space, and there is no reason why you shouldn't have several small altars around the house, wherever you feel they are appropriate.

To help you position your altar, you could look into Feng Shui, the ancient Chinese art of placement. There are many good reference books available on the subject, but essentially the different rooms in a building as well as the different corners in a room correspond to

A bedroom altar could include the scent of lavender to help promote peaceful sleep.

An office altar dedicated to Thoth, the scribe and guardian of knowledge to the Egyptian gods, encourages inspiration.

A child's altar

Children have a wonderful ability to invest all kinds of objects with magic. A handful of toffee wrappers can become jewel-coloured windows, and fragments of translucent sea-worn glass are as valuable as any precious gemstone. Young children naturally make collections of their favourite things. Creating a special place for them – or an altar – will encourage the child to build a magical relationship with their spirit, which grows and develops as they journey through life.

particular areas of life. For instance, south-west-facing rooms are linked with love and relationships, while those that are north-facing suit business affairs. Alternatively, you could use a pendulum to dowse for the most suitable spot (see Divination), or follow your gut feeling and be guided simply by your intuition.

The Bedroom

Most of us want our bedroom to be a sanctuary where we can be wholly ourselves. It is where we take our secrets and prayers, joy and grief. A bedroom altar acts as a focus for these, and for daily rituals to help you greet the day and prepare for night.

For peaceful rest, place sleep crystals on your altar: amethysts, a piece of jade or obsidian. Burning a little lavender incense or essential oil will also help you sleep. Honour the earth deity and goddess of dreams, Gaia, with barley grains or laurel, or include an image of Nephthys, who sheltered the sleeping pharaohs beneath her protective wings.

At bedtime, set a bowl of water scented with jasmine oil near your bed and place your sleep stones or crystals in it. To help your wishes come true, write what you wish to come to you in your sleep on willow leaves.

The Study or Office

An altar in the workplace will generate positive energy to help you concentrate. Wisdom and inspiration are personified by Thoth, the scribe of the Egyptian gods, who wrote down the wisdom of the universe. Yellow candles assist communication and learning. Helpful crystals include emerald to give insight, azurite for clarity, and haematite to aid reasoning and memory. There are also many fragrances that are useful for mental work. Eucalyptus, peppermint and camphor can clear muddled thinking and are an antidote to daydreaming, while rosemary and basil have head-clearing properties, aid concentration and sharpen the intellect.

The Hallway

An altar or shrine in the doorway or near the entrance to the house is traditional in many parts of the world. The Roman god Janus is a traditional protective deity, while a guardian totem animal such as a dog, lion or tiger is also appropriate. Sacred objects at the entrance to your home help to sanctify the whole of it and you and your visitors will carry blessings with you as you leave.

To create the welcoming smell of home, warm and spicy fragrances such as cinnamon, cassia, star anise and clove work well in the winter season, while summer blooms such as stocks, lilac, sweet pea or cabbage rose can permeate the whole house with their fragrance and particular characteristic.

A kitchen altar could include offerings of food in honour of Demeter, the grain goddess.

The Kitchen

At the hub of the house, the kitchen is a potent place. The magical process of preparing and cooking food transforms the energy of the earth into a form that we are able to take in. An altar for hospitality could be dedicated to Hestia, the goddess of the hearth, or to Demeter, goddess of abundance and unconditional love. Leave offerings of rice, grains, fruit or honey for the nature spirits and light the altar candles each time you prepare a meal. A shrine behind the sink would engage your attention as you work there. You could hang herbs and flowers, chilli and garlic around the window like a garland, or decorate it with evergreens.

The Living Room

To promote harmony between your family and friends, set up an altar to the four elements in the living room. This could combine salt for Earth, a red candle for Fire, sea shells for Water and feathers for Air. You could also put photographs of loved ones on the altar.

Create a prayer bowl, placing a clear quartz cluster in a bowl filled with spring water, with floating green candles for harmony. Invite members of the family to write down their prayers and tuck them under the bowl.

A prayer bowl in the living room can be a family focus for wishes and requests.

OUTDOOR ALTARS

Magic is about relating to the natural world and finding our place in it. Visiting nature is a good way to find peace, tranquillity and inspiration and most people have a particular place that they visit when they need time alone, to meditate or just to relax. Such a place could be anywhere – part of a garden, a spot near a favourite tree, a rock on a hillside, or a cool, leafy forest – it doesn't really matter as long as it is special to you. Like the traditional holy sites, these places have a natural power, but they also take on the energy of those who visit them: they become magical or sacred space.

A flat rock makes a good outdoor altar, especially when it is in a spectacular setting.

NATURAL ALTARS

You can set up an altar in your sacred outdoor space. This may be a temporary or more permanent feature depending on the location. A flat rock or a tree stump can work well, or a sacred circle can be made with stones, twigs or cones, although nothing should be done that disturbs the natural harmony of the place. An outdoor altar can be adorned with anything that has a special significance for you, such as crystals, feathers, flowers or sticks. It can show appreciation for the moment and it has the advantage that others might see it and add their energy. Remember to leave an offering on your altar when you visit.

Ritual sites in nature

Increasingly, those involved in magic today are looking to ritual sites in nature and ancient stone monuments to contact the energies of their ancestors, those who practised the 'Old Religion'. These sites, which often date from the Neolithic era, are often viewed as places of female mysteries and the land itself is thought of as the Goddess incarnate. Believed to be gateways into the otherworld, a 'dreamtime' that enables magic workers to connect with a sacred place within themselves, these places are the locations for healing, divination and the conducting of life rites, such as hand fastings (pagan weddings).

TREE ALTARS

Trees make very beautiful natural altars, pleasing to the eye and very calming when attention is focused upon them. Being firmly rooted, a tree has a deep

Salt is part of the crystal kingdom and is the blessed representation of the earth. Use salt to purify, consecrate and protect.

connection with Mother Earth, and that energy can be tapped into when you talk to it, leave offerings and pray or meditate there. You can tie things in the branches for decoration, or place tiny items in the trunk. A flat rock placed at the base of the trunk can serve as an altar stone. Be aware of which trees attract you, because they all have their own attributes and symbolism. For example, oak is the keeper of wisdom and possesses great strength; willow represents love and regeneration, being very ready to grow a new tree from a cut branch; the tall and graceful beech symbolizes aspirations to higher ideals; yew, associated with ancient burial sites, represents transformation and inner wisdom.

Rock Altars

Rocks are the bones of the Mother, supporting her and therefore us. Because they take millions of years to form, they hold ancient Earth wisdom and knowledge, power and strength. They can help you to connect with these primordial energies and you can call upon this strength when you pray or meditate at a rock altar. Feel the strength of its timeless wisdom helping, supporting and connecting you.

The Garden Sanctuary

Whatever the size of your garden, you can create an outdoor sanctuary to connect with the magical powers of nature. If space permits, this can be achieved through planting trees or shrubs to form an enclosed area. This can contain seating, such as a wooden bench or chair, as well as a shrine or grotto. A water feature is also recommended; this could be a fish pool, or some kind of running water in a stream or fountain. It does not need to be very big, but the energy of water is refreshing and cleansing for the subtle bodies. A statue of the Goddess and/or a nature deity such as Pan can be part of your garden altar. If your garden area is small, consider creating a miniature garden with Japanese bonsai trees, or arrangements of pebbles, or making a nature table to reflect the changing seasons of the year.

Trees have enormous symbolic and magical powers, and are also vital for the sustenance of life on our planet. Offer them respect and reverence in your magical work.

Making a cairn

The beauty of making something to use as an altar is that your energy is blended with the materials in a focused way. A cairn looks like a haphazard pile of stones but, to make it stable, care must be taken in selecting stones that fit together well. Take time to gather the stones.

1 Begin by selecting a few large, flat, roughly circular rocks to act as the base of the cairn. Start to build up a tapering dome by laying smaller flat rocks in an overlapping pattern.

2 As you work, keep the intent of honouring creation, and that will help focus your energy. Work slowly and methodically so that the stones are evenly balanced.

3 When the cairn is complete, decorate it with objects found close by.

Making a cairn takes time and care, and so gives the end result greater significance.

MAGIC IN DAILY LIFE

Caught up in busy schedules and coping with the demands of everyday life, it is easy to forget to take care of your own needs and to become disassociated from the core of who you are. But at the centre of everything that is going on in your life, ultimately there is only one person – you. If you don't take care of yourself then everything else in your life will suffer. Practising natural magic puts you firmly at the centre of life's wheel and encourages you to look for practical ways to nourish yourself in body, mind and soul and to reconnect with the magic of daily life.

The focus of this chapter is finding ways to use magic for everyday concerns. It begins by recognizing that care of your inner self forms the basis from which the rest of your life will grow and blossom, before turning to specific areas of life such as your goals and ambitions, the quality of your relationships and your health and wellbeing. It also offers suggestions for how to increase wealth and prosperity by focusing on abundance, and how to deal with change with the minimum of stress. It concludes with a special section on lunar gardening, which shows you how to work with the cycles of the moon for strong and healthy plants. By bringing magic to bear on all aspects of your life, you will be enriched on many levels.

The inner you

It is what you are within, rather than what you do, that is important so far as the life of your soul is concerned. The meaning and purpose of your life, and your connection with the greater whole, are to be found deep within you. There are many ways of nourishing your connection with your inner self, but before you begin you should take care of your physical, mental and emotional needs. Natural magic is based on balance and harmony between all aspects of creation, and you need to reflect this before you can succeed.

Regular meditation is a very good method of staying in touch with your inner self.

Body Care

Physically, you are influenced by your lifestyle and what you choose to eat and drink. You may like to consider changing things in your daily life that do not serve you – or are actually harmful to you – such as too many late nights, poor eating habits, or addictive patterns such as alcohol or drug consumption. On a physical level, it is helpful to be disciplined about transcending your "bad" habits, as a weak or sick physical body will significantly affect your emotional, mental and spiritual health. Taking the Bach flower crab apple essence can help you to detox, while walnut and chestnut bud can help reduce addictive cravings.

Mental and Emotional Wellbeing

Albert Einstein once said; "A clever mind is one that is trained to forget the trivial." On a mental level, being unable to switch off our thoughts is associated with many common stress-related problems such as tension headaches, anxiety and insomnia. White chestnut flower essence can be helpful, and it is also advisable to consider physical exercise, or to begin practising a spiritual discipline such as yoga or tai chi, all of which will help reduce stress levels.

On an emotional level, you need to consider "relationship" – how you relate to others and from what emotional

Take time out, find a private space, and don't let yourself be distracted by other people. Cultivating self-awareness will give you the confidence to take a break when you need one.

A woman's moontime

The female menstrual cycle mirrors the cycle of the moon in duration, and both the hormonal changes in the body and the phases of the moon have a profound efffect on the emotions. The time of ovulation, when a woman is at her most fertile, is likely to occur during a full moon. During their menstruation, women are sensitive and highly perceptive; it is particularly important at this time of the month for women to look after themselves. Book a date with yourself and use your "moontime" to let go of the past and to allow the flow to cleanse and take away any problems or difficulties in preparation for the new cycle ahead.

perspective you see things. When you look closely at your emotional responses to life, you may realize that they are outdated, linked to wounds from the past that have yet to heal. There are several Bach flower remedies that can help with emotional healing, including using honeysuckle for someone who dwells on the past, holly for jealousy, anger and destructive feelings and impatiens for irritability and excessive reactions. Understanding and sorting out your feelings will help to alleviate heated arguments, high stress levels and heavy atmospheres.

Living Life Creatively

The spirit of creation flows through every one of us. We may describe it as divine inspiration, chi, life force or quintessence, but it is the energy that we put into everything that we do – whether this is carving a sculpture, writing a letter, making a meal, or simply interacting with others. In this sense, creativity is not restricted to "artistic" pursuits, and everything you do can be approached with the spirit of creativity, giving spiritual value to all aspects of your daily life. Being mindful of this is one of the best ways of staying in contact with your inner self as you go about your daily affairs.

Mindfulness is another name for meditation, and meditation is one of the best ways of connecting with your creativity and inner self. Its benefits have been well documented: it allows you to relate to who you truly are without falling into the common traps of everyday life. It also helps you to think clearly and sharpens your intuitive, spontaneous responses. Spending regular time in meditation each day is a good discipline to foster; it is like washing your inner senses and will give you the eyes to see the magic that is all around us, ever-present all of the time.

An Altar for Inspiration

The creative process is about inspiration, hard work, discipline, exercising judgement and discernment and the courage to make mistakes and learn from them. Making an altar to inspiration will encourage you to go beyond your limits, so that your open mind will attract fresh ideas like a magnet, faster than they can be expressed. It is in this state of intuitive awareness – a form of meditation – that creativity flows and life itself becomes a magical experience.

There are really no rules for making an inspirational altar. You might like to make it very vibrant, dressing it with a variety of colours so that its flamboyance will give you the confidence to express yourself in your daily life. Or you may choose a theme or colour scheme and work with that. The objects you choose to put on the altar can reflect the creative opportunities you want to explore, such as brushes and paints for artistic endeavour, or pens and paper if you are searching for the courage to express yourself. Use this special place to try out your dreams, and bring your own creations to beautify your altar.

Playing music is just one of the ways to express the creativity you hold within you.

Harmonizing with Nature's Cycles

To a greater or lesser extent, most of us are disconnected from the natural rhythms of nature, the journey of the sun and moon through day and night, the months and the seasons of the year. Effectively this cuts us off from our own nature, our innate, inner wisdom that is central to who we are. Spending time in nature and observing the seasons through ritual and celebration, as well as changing our diet and lifestyle to adapt to nature's patterns, can help us to reconnect with nature's cycles and our central core.

Imbolc: the light of inspiration

At the beginning of February, the festival of the return of light, or Imbolc, honours the Celtic triple goddess Brigid, a fire deity, and celebrates her union with the god of light. It is a time of inspiration and creativity, when rituals are performed to bless new love, fertility and the planning of new projects. Imbolc is predominantly a female festival and Brigid blesses women's self-expression and creativity. By tradition, if a white cloth is left outside overnight at Imbolc, the goddess will bless it with inspiration.

Goal-setting

Wherever our real ambitions lie, striving for achievement is necessary if our lives are to be fruitful and valuable. If we aim for nothing, we may end up achieving just that. And if we don't set our own priorities, someone else will. So setting out the things we want to achieve over the next week, month, year or five years, is a valuable exercise in establishing what our goals are. We can then use magic to help us in our journey towards them.

If your goal is physical fitness, picture yourself running along a beach or climbing a hill.

Establishing Goals

Achieving something that we want to do is a great boost to confidence and self-esteem, helping us to raise our sights to even higher goals. Aspirations need not be set in stone: they need re-evaluating as we learn from experiences and as our outlook and priorities change. Re-evaluating current goals is therefore the first step. Very often we find ourselves pursuing ambitions that no longer satisfy us and, in some cases, maybe never did.

Asking yourself what you want from life and then thinking about the practical steps you can take to achieve it is part of goal-setting.

For instance, our work may leave too little time for relationships, family life or creativity, or perhaps we realize we are doing the wrong job altogether – a career path chosen perhaps to satisfy our parents – in which case it might be time to change track and consider retraining for something that we would really like to do. To help establish your goals you can divide your life up into different categories and look at each one in turn:

Setting goals

- Visualize your long-term goals and set short-term targets – weekly or monthly – to help you get there.
- Set specific daily goals to keep you motivated.
- Goals should stretch you, but not defeat you before you begin. If you make them too easy, they won't motivate you. Make each goal a challenging and positive one.
- Limit the number of your stated goals and make sure they don't clash or contradict each other.
- Write a list of your goals and read it at the start of every day.
- Re-examine your list from time to time; if your goals have changed or seem unrealistic, you can change them.
- Give yourself small rewards for each of your achievements.

A wishing box

One way of working towards your goals is to create a wishing or dream box. Write down your wishes and then keep them in a special wooden box on your altar. Surround the box with oak leaves to sanctify and protect your dreams. The sacred oak will aid your rituals with its strength and bring the promise of success. If you are unable to find oak leaves, you can sprinkle a few drops of the Bach flower oak essence on the wishes.

Keep some frankincense in your wishing box. This most ancient incense has been burnt on the altars of many cultures to summon the aid of the divine. Its uplifting scent banishes negative thoughts and promotes success. Burn a little each day as you visualize the goal you are working towards manifesting.

relationships, work, home, health, creativity, leisure and money. Some of these categories may overlap and you may notice that some areas are more important to you than others. Take as much time as you need, until you have found goals that have meaning for you and are going to help you create the life you want for yourself.

The Power of Now

Magic only recognizes the here-and-now: the past has gone, the future is not yet, and the point of power is in the present moment. So when working with goal-setting, always use the present tense for your targets. For instance, instead of saying "I want", begin with "I now have /am". Similarly, visualize the result you desire as if it is already happening. For instance, if your goal is to get a new job, you can visualize yourself opening the letter of appointment telling you it is yours. Or if your goal is a return to health and fitness, visualize yourself striding up a hill or running across a beach. Hold on to your vision for as long as you can, so that it sinks into your unconscious mind, forming a new pattern into which you can grow. Even when you seem to be making no progress, your spirit will still move in the direction you have chosen.

Ritual for Worldly Success

For material achievements such as making money and success at work, include Earth element as well as Fire on your altar. Earth is the element of stability and prosperity, and supports us in taking responsibility for our own destiny. Fire is the element related to ambition and creative projects and helps burn away any resistance there might be to achieving our goals.

1 To represent the Earth, use the colours of the land, such as olive green and russet, and place two green candles, and one darker one, on the altar, together with some salt or a stone.

2 Place a bowl of the Fire incense, frankincense, on the altar; it is best to use pieces of frankincense resin.

3 Now write your goals (remembering to use the present tense) on a piece of paper. Fold the piece of paper up and put it into the bowl of resin.

4 Close your eyes and visualize the realization of your ambitions, seeing the successful outcome rather than the process of getting there. When you have fixed the images in your mind, take the piece of paper and burn it in the candle flame, dropping it into a fireproof bowl.

5 To finish, pinch out the candles and take a few moments to gather your thoughts. Remember that you need to remain open to whatever happens and that you always seek the highest good of all concerned.

Burning the paper symbolizes letting go and trusting the universe to bring you a result.

When working for worldly success, Earth colours such as greens or russets and symbolic representations of Earth, such as salt or a stone, will help your magic along.

Magic as medicine

Originally, medicine and magic were not two separate disciplines but one. Medicine has largely moved away from magic, but there are many ways of using magic therapeutically, whether with herbs and plant medicines, with the assistance of cosmic powers and divine beings, or by using the vibrations of colour, sound or crystals. You can use magic as medicine to treat yourself or another (with their permission of course), to restore harmony in body, mind and soul. It is about listening to your body and working in harmony with its innate self-healing powers to restore wholeness.

A quartz crystal will help you to transmit your healing power as you voice your prayer.

A Healing Ceremony

Healing ceremonies play an important part in magic and medicine. Traditionally they are conducted by the shaman or medicine man, who uses a combination of ritual, spells and charms to drive out the bad spirits causing the illness from the sufferer. This ceremony enlists the healing energy of Water.

Set up an altar for healing in the west and stand facing towards the west to make your offerings or to say prayers. Make the altar a vision of pure watery beauty, fresh with the colour blue and decorated with flowers such as jasmine, lilies, lotus, iris or poppies, or with water-smoothed pebbles or seashells. These beautiful natural items will speak of the vibrancy of the world outside that waits to be enjoyed.

Choose sandalwood incense, which is associated with purification and healing, or camphor or eucalyptus for their cool, cleansing scents.

A healing ceremony will be most effective during the time of a waning moon – particularly in the four days following full moon. This is the time when things can be cast away or released,

The goddess of compassion

Chinese worshippers flock to the shrines of Kuanyin to seek her favour because they believe she can cure almost every sickness and alleviate every distress. Her name means "One who sees and hears the cries of the whole world" and her image stands on many family altars in the East. She is usually shown carrying a vial containing the dew of compassion, and she cures the seriously ill by sprinkling a few drops on their heads.

On your healing altar, place a bowl of water, a quartz crystal, the colour blue, and some beautiful white flowers, such as lilies, to echo the vibrancy of the outside world.

including grief and anger. To perform a healing ceremony on behalf of someone who is ill, light two blue candles on the altar and present a bowl of clear spring water as an offering.

Ask for the healing help of Archangel Gabriel or Ceridwen, the white goddess of the Celts, or try appealing to the compassion of Kuanyin, the Buddhist goddess of mercy. Using a silver pen, write down the name of the person and their ailment on white paper or a petal from the lily, and then float it in the water. Visualize the ailment being lifted out of the sufferer and give thanks for their recovery. Place a clear quartz crystal in the water, and hold a second crystal in your hands while voicing your prayer, so that the healing power is transmitted.

Magical Herbalism

Every culture has had its own tradition of plant medicine, sometimes widely known and sometimes kept as secret wisdom by certain members of the society. Today many people in the western world are turning to more natural, plant-based medicines, but to understand this vast subject fully and use plant material safely takes many years of study and commitment. It is not recommended that you try to treat serious conditions yourself, but there are some traditional herbal remedies that you can use to treat everyday complaints. Generally, the herbs are best made into a tea or decoction and then drunk. If you are unsure about the safety of any herb, seek professional advice before using it.

Moon medicine

The phases of the moon are associated with important healing energies. The new moon is for health, vitality and regeneration; the full moon for fertility and empowerment; and the waning phase is the time when unwanted symptoms and ailments may be banished. The following moon medicine combines the power of crystals with the appropriate moon phase, depending on what is being treated.

To make the moon medicine you will need to make sure the moon is in the correct phase of her cycle and perform it either outside on a calm night, or inside by the light of the moon. Choose an appropriate stone that has been cleansed. Traditionally, all white, clear or watery bright stones are associated with the waxing and full moon ("bright moontime"); examples include moonstone, pearl, aquamarine and clear quartz. Black, dark or cloudy stones are used at the time of the waning moon ("dark moontime"); examples include jet, smoky quartz, obsidian and black tourmaline.

The nine tealights correspond with the moon's magical number of nine.

You will need

9 white tealights
matches
glass bowl
appropriate moon stone
spring water

1 Place the glass bowl on the floor in front of you, then position the nine tealights in a circle around it. Light the tealights, starting with the one in the south, saying while you do so:
Hail to thee Levanah, Queen of Heaven.
I call for your blessings and ask that your moonrays fill this essence with healing.

2 Put your moon stone in the bowl and pour in the spring water until the stone is completely covered. Leave it in place for at least three hours. Do not leave the tealights burning unattended and replace any that burn out.

3 After three hours, blow out the tealights, remove the stone, pour the infusion into a glass and sip slowly while visualizing yourself being touched by the moon's gentle rays.

Traditional ways with herbs and spices

The use of herbs and spices for healing, spiritual cleansing and magic has a long history. Many remedies are tried and tested, and almost every plant is useful in some way.

Feverfew leaves: eaten in honey sandwiches these are a traditional cure for migraine. This daisy-flowered herb with its peppery scent is fairly common, growing wild in some places.
Lemon balm: this is said to make the heart merry and the soul joyful. Bees love this plant and bee-keepers traditionally rub their hives with it to keep their bees contented and settled.
Garlic: this offers protection from negative influences, including everyday infections such as the common cold, as well as bad spirits like vampires and ghosts.
Dandelions: these have a detoxifying and cleansing action. At one time, dandelions were a rustic oracle for telling the time: the flowers were said to open at five in the morning and close at eight in the evening.
Camomile: this brings down a fever, soothes the stomach, and is cooling and calming; it is also a tonic for blonde hair.
Ginger: this is warming and energizing; it is said to be a prescription for a happy love life in your later years.
Rosemary: said to be an aid to memory and concentration; it is also used as a conditioning tonic for dark hair.
Cloves: this warming spice is a traditional remedy for toothache in its oil form.

CHAKRA BALANCING

When our chakra system is balanced we enjoy good health. However, the chakras can be thrown out of balance by many things, including poor diet, lack of sleep and exercise, stress and modern medicines. Negative environmental influences such as electrical energy fields, geopathic stress and pollution also upset the chakra system. There are many ways to balance the chakras. For instance, you could work with colour therapy and gemstones, placing the appropriate coloured stone on each of the chakra points. Or you could use the healing properties of sound by intoning the mantra (healing sound) relevant to each energy centre, beginning from the base and ascending to the crown, and going down again. The box below on chakra properties tells you what colours and sounds to use for each chakra.

To diagnose which chakras are out of balance, you can use a pendulum to dowse them; you can also use dowsing after the treatment in order to check that the imbalance has been corrected.

The healing power of colour

Choose colours according to your healing need or preference.

Colour	Healing uses
Red	low energy, sexual problems, blood disorders, lack of self-confidence
Orange	depression, mental disorders, asthma, rheumatism
Yellow	detoxifying, hormonal problems
Green	antiseptic, balancing, tonic; soothes headaches
Blue	insomnia, nervous disorders, throat problems, general healing
Indigo	painkiller, sinus problems, migraine, eczema, inflammations
Violet/purple	psychological disorders; fosters self-love and self-respect
Magenta	emotional hurts and upsets, accepting life's problems
Black	for when you need to hide (such as when grieving)
White	tonic, replaces all colours
Gold	depression and low energy; digestive disturbances
Silver	hormonal and emotional balance, calms the nerves

Bottles of dual-coloured liquid can be used to diagnose colour imbalances. The bottles you are drawn to will tell you what colours you need more or less of in your life.

Chakra properties

Each chakra governs distinct organs and functions, and corresponds to a colour and sound.

1st chakra, colour; red, mantra; "lam":
Governs the gonads or ovaries, skeleton, large intestine and lower body; physical survival, energy distribution, practicality

2nd chakra, colour; orange, mantra; "vam":
Governs the bladder, circulation, sexuality; feelings, emotions, creativity and pleasure

3rd chakra, colour; yellow, mantra; "ram":
Governs the adrenal glands, spleen, pancreas, stomach; identity, self-confidence, personal power

4th chakra, colour; green, mantra; "yam":
Governs the thymus gland, immune system, lungs; relationships, personal development, self-acceptance, compassion

5th chakra, colour; blue, mantra; "ham":
Governs the thyroid, lymphatic, immune and neurological systems; self-expression, communication, trust

6th chakra, colour; indigo, mantra; "om":
Governs the pituitary gland, central nervous system; understanding, perception, intuition, spiritual "knowing", psychic abilities

7th chakra, colour; violet, mantra; silence:
Governs the pineal gland; openness, connection to higher energies, self-realization

Crystal healing

Gemstones and crystals are attributed with specific healing powers. You can use them to transform poor health (whether physical, mental or emotional) into wellbeing by placing them on the chakras. You can also programme stones to deal with specific complaints, and then place it on the relevant part of the body to draw out the sickness. It is important to use only cleansed stones in healing and to clean them again afterwards.

Amber: relieves depression
Amethyst: protects the immune system; calms fear; aids sleep
Aventurine: soothes the emotions
Bloodstone: blood detoxifier; strengthens physical body
Carnelian: increases physical energy
Chrysocolla: assists in the relief of grief, worry and pain
Clear quartz: a powerful talisman for healing, known in many cultures as the "all-healer", guards against loss of vitality and strength; draws out pain, raises self-esteem, balances emotions, increases insight
Garnet: relieves depression, boosts sexuality and fertility
Haematite: helpful for blood disorders, anaemia; eases the effects of jet lag
Jet: dispels irrational fears; protects from illness and infection
Malachite: releases trauma, relieves depression, protects against negativity
Rose quartz: comforts and heals the emotions; strengthens the heart
Tourmaline: good for psychic protection; relieves stress

Crystals whose colour corresponds to a chakra will enhance its natural qualities, whatever the situation. For a simple chakra balancing, place a stone on the relevant chakra for a few minutes.

Colour Healing

There are many different ways of harnessing the vibration of colour for health and wellbeing. You can wear it, use it in your surroundings, make colour infusions, eat coloured food or even bathe in coloured light.

A colour infusion draws on the energizing, health-giving powers of the sun. To make one, use coloured stones, fabric or any other colourfast item and soak the "colour" in a bowl of mineral water. Leave the bowl in sunlight for several hours, then pour the water into a glass and drink the infusion. Always make sure the coloured item you are using is clean before you soak it.

Coloured foods can also be used for healing. Red, orange and yellow foods are hot and stimulating. Yellow foods can help with weight loss and red foods restore energy. Green balances and detoxifies and is a tonic for the system. Blue, indigo and purple are soothing; blue curbs activity so is useful when you are trying to gain weight.

Another way of healing with colour involves shining coloured light on to the body to relieve physical, mental and emotional problems. You can try it yourself on everyday ailments. Place a coloured gel over a spotlight, making sure it is not touching the hot bulb. Turn off any other lights, and bathe in the coloured light, taking in the healing vibrations of your chosen colour. The main colour choice is often followed by its complementary opposite. For instance, if you are being treated with green, this may be followed by magenta to ensure a healthy balance in the body.

Flower Essences

The subtle vibrations of flowers and trees are contained in flower essences. These are very useful for treating negative mental and emotional states and helping to rebalance the body's subtle energy system.

These properties of flowers were first discovered in the early twentieth century by Dr Edward Bach, who found himself drawn to certain flowers when suffering from particular emotions. The essences are made from flowers that are gathered when the dew is on them, floated in water and placed in the sun to allow the water to absorb the subtle vibrations. There are 38 Bach remedies, each one representing a negative emotion, plus rescue remedy, a mixture of five essences that is used for treating shock.

Harmonious Relationships

The people in our lives can be one of the greatest sources of happiness, yet they can also present us with some of our biggest challenges. Every relationship will have its ups and downs and you should consider the effect your moods and emotions have on those around you as well as vice versa. Relationships require a level of self-discipline and a commitment to work things through if they are to be nourishing and supporting. There are many ways of using your magic skills to foster an atmosphere of love and understanding and to honour your closest relationships.

To help communication between members of your family, use blue stones on the altar.

A Family Altar

Making a family altar is a good way of celebrating and deepening the bonds between you. It is best positioned somewhere that is at the heart of family life, such as in the living room or kitchen.

An old piece of furniture that has been handed down to you through the generations could be the perfect site for an altar dedicated to your family. It will carry the blessings of those it served in the past. You could place the altar in the west where the Water element governs relationships. If you wish to observe Feng Shui principles, the area of your home or room that corresponds to the family is positioned in the west, and to love and relationships, in the south-west.

You might invite all the members of the family to help you make the altar, each bringing an object that symbolizes an aspect of themselves. Photographs of your loved ones will act as a focus for your prayers and thoughts about your

Place pictures and gifts from children on the altar, to honour their contribution to the family.

Zodiac candle colours

Each sign of the zodiac can be symbolized by a coloured candle as follows:

Aries: dark red
Taurus: green
Gemini: yellow
Cancer: silver
Leo: gold or orange
Virgo: yellow
Libra: sky-blue or rose
Scorpio: burgundy or red
Sagittarius: purple or black
Capricorn: black
Aquarius: rainbow
Pisces: sea-green or indigo

family. To honour your relationship with your partner, choose a happy and harmonious picture of the two of you together. Other items could include gifts to you from your children, especially presents or drawings made by them, which bring with them fond memories and the resonance of the love that motivated the gift. But remember to include objects that represent family members as they are now – acknowledging your children as complex teenagers, not just as enchanting toddlers, for example – so that the altar grows with the family and remains relevant. If pets are part of your family, you can also include reminders of them on the altar.

Relationship Difficulties

When you or other family members are going through a difficult time, try to stay open and talk about what is happening. Because of their link with the throat chakra, all blue crystals aid communication. You can put the stones on the altar, or else use them as a charm and carry them with you. Blue lace agate helps you express feelings, turquoise fosters partnership, light blue angel stone heals anger and lapis lazuli aids in the release of emotional wounds. Rose quartz is the stone of love.

If someone close to you is having problems in their relationship with others, perhaps with friends or at work, surround a picture of them with rose quartz crystals for harmony. While you do this, think about the person close to you and imagine them at ease with themselves and others.

Giving Blessings

When someone leaves home or begins a new life journey, write a protective blessing and tuck the folded paper into the frame of their picture on your altar. When loved ones are away, you can light candles that represent their sun sign to send them your love and support. You can also burn candles to bolster confidence and self-esteem or to celebrate significant dates such as birthdays and anniversaries.

Honouring the Ancestors

In cultures with an established tradition of family altars, the ancestors are the most honoured family members. Photographs and mementos of your forebears keep those you loved as a positive influence in your life, and provide a sense of continuity for your children, helping them to see themselves as links in a chain of existence.

In Spanish-speaking countries – particularly Mexico – the Day of the Dead is when the dead are entertained as respected members of the family. One of the most important religious occasions of the year, families have picnics in the cemeteries and build altars covered with flowers and food to welcome their dead relatives home for the night, burning candles and copal incense to help them find their way. Veneration of the ancestors is also an important tradition in the East. To prevent their spirits from becoming restless or vengeful, rituals are conducted that ensure proper respect and provide the family with a means of consulting the wise elders; the family includes past and future generations, as well as the present.

If someone in the family needs special love and care, surround their picture with rose quartz.

The symbolism of flowers

In folklore, flowers are believed to speak the language of the heart. Using flowers and herbs is another way of working with whatever qualities are being expressed or are needed in a relationship.

Apple blossom: love, friendship
Clover: fidelity
Coltsfoot: peace and tranquillity
Cyclamen: love and truth
Gardenia: peace and healing
Hyacinth: love and protection
Jasmine: friendship
Lavender: peace and happiness
Lily of the valley: peace, harmony and love
Narcissus: harmony
Passion flower: peace and friendship
Rose: love
Sweet pea: friendship and courage
Vervain: inner strength and peace
Violet: contentment

Copal

One of the most important and valuable incense burning substances used by the Mayans, Incas and Aztecs of Central and South America was copal, the gift of the jaguars. According to the Mayan's holy book, copal resin was extracted from the Tree of Life and given to humanity as a gift. There are three types of copal resin: black, golden and white.

Coping with Change

Our lives follow cycles that are continually changing, evolving and shifting from moment to moment, and nothing in the physical realm remains the same forever. In modern society, we have come to fear or abhor most endings, seeing them as associated with failure or as the loss of something we value or want to keep. However, natural magic teaches us that change is good, and when we are able to let go of things that do not really serve us, or of an experience that has run its course, our lives can open up in very positive ways.

A ritual purification of your new home, using sun-charged water and rosemary, will cleanse the psychic space to make it yours.

Endings

To attract a new beginning, we must first close the door on that which is ending. This could be a work contract, a relationship, a house move or perhaps grown-up children leaving home; whatever the situation it is important to create an ending that honours the change, while remaining positive about it. The simplest way to honour an ending is to voice the fact, and give thanks for what you have experienced as you indicate your intention to let it go and move on to a new beginning. The ceremony can be as simple or as elaborate as you wish. For instance, you could light a candle on your altar and say a prayer, or give some other offering as a thanksgiving for what is ending. Water is the element associated with letting go, so you could also include this on your altar.

A traditional witch's broom made from birch twigs can be used symbolically to sweep away the old to make way for the new.

Moving House

If you are moving house, cleaning and clearing out is something that you will do naturally in the process of moving on. After the physical clearing and cleansing has been finished, an ideal way to acknowledge the act spiritually is to sweep the house symbolically with a bundle of birch twigs or a birch broom, imagining each area being purified as you do so. In ancient times, brushwood from the birch tree was used to sweep out the spirits of the old year, preparing the way for the beginning of the new one. Let the house know of your intentions in performing this act and thank it for having been your home. You can also use the birch broom to sweep the new house you are moving into, as a first step to claiming it as your new home. Here, it will have the effect of sweeping away the atmosphere created by the previous occupants, making space for your own spiritual energy.

To prepare your new home for the beginning of your life there, you can bless it by walking around all the rooms and sprinkling them as you go with drops of water that you have charged with the energy of the sun. Use a sprig of rosemary to sprinkle the water, as it is a protective herb that favours new beginning. This will add vitality and vigour to your new environment.

A Talisman for Change

Endings and beginnings may be accompanied by feelings of insecurity, fear, and sadness, and you can use this talisman to help you come to terms with your feelings. Make it during a waxing moon if you are more concerned with beginnings, during a waning moon for endings and letting go.

You will need
2 silver or white candles
silver pen
23cm (9in) square of natural paper
moonstone

1 Light the candles, saying these words as you do so:
Hail to you Levanah, I light these candles in your honour and ask for your help with the endings/beginnings (whichever you are working on) in my life at this time.

2 Draw the symbol for Alpha (beginnings) or Omega (endings) in the middle of the paper, depending on whether you are working with endings or beginnings. If you want to work with both, then draw both symbols.

3 Fold the four corners of the paper into the centre to make a diamond shape, then fold in the same way twice more.

4 Pinch out the candles, place the moonstone on your talisman and leave it in moonlight for several hours. Afterwards, put it in a safe place or carry it with you.

Symbols of new beginnings

Add a wish to a bowl of pumpkin seeds.

A white lily holds a rolled-up wish paper.

There are many ways in which you can call for a new beginning, once you have recognized and acknowledged an ending in your life.

- A pair of lodestones placed together in a central area of a room will call for the attraction of a lover.
- If you see shooting stars and comets together in the sky, wishing upon them calls the Sky Father's protection and blessing for any wishes you make.
- The cowrie shell is sacred to the Goddess and empowers wishes for love, friendship and family. Decorate a small pouch with cowrie shells and drop your written wish inside.
- A bowl of seeds (such as sesame, sunflower or pumpkin) with a wish tucked into them, placed on an altar or on the kitchen windowsill, will encourage the growth of whatever you have called for.
- A birch broom propped up beside a doorway will encourage the old to depart and the new to arrive, and will also provide protection for your home.
- When you are seeking new work or prosperity opportunities, turn silver coins in your pocket on the first night of a new moon to invite growth in your finances.
- Write a wish on a piece of paper, fold or roll it and place the paper within the cone of a white lily flower; this bloom is sacred to Ostara, the goddess of birth and new life.
- Written symbols, such as Beth from the Druidic tree alphabet, or the Greek letter Alpha, will encourage new beginnings. Write them in places of significance, such as over a written wish, or trace them in the air in a space where new beginnings are being called for. You could also include them on a talisman.

A talisman to the moon can help you cope with change.

Abundance and Prosperity

Prosperity is not only a matter of material possessions, physical or otherwise – feelings of satisfaction with our lot often bear little relation to what we actually possess. Abundance is about tuning in to the blessings of life, shifting emphasis away from personal limitation and all that we lack, and opening ourselves to new and prosperous possibilities. It has long been acknowledged that if you have a clear idea of what you want you are far more likely to achieve it. Magic recognizes that thought is a form of energy, and positive thinking contributes energetically to the fulfilment of your desire: ideas are the first step to abundance.

An altar of abundance, dedicated to Lakshmi, should reflect Earth colours and scents.

Personal Belief Systems

When you want to focus on creating abundance a good place to start is to examine your belief systems. For instance, many people believe that material wealth is at odds with spirituality, and that being poor is somehow virtuous. Another widely held view is that you have to work hard in order to have wealth, or that only money that is "hard won" is deserved. Similarly, many wealthy people are unable to enjoy their riches as deep down they harbour a sense of guilt, alternatively some people are actually afraid to have more money for fear that they won't be liked or won't fit in any more with their social group, or even that they will become a target for people's jealousy.

Most of us have many barriers that stop us from receiving the abundance that we deserve – whether on the material plane (money), on the emotional (love) or on the spiritual (godliness). The first step in bringing more abundance into your life is to feel that you are worth it and deserve it: a person living in abundance has much more to offer than someone who is living in lack or "poverty consciousness".

One way of increasing your feeling of self-worth is to practise "affirmations", sayings that you use to help redirect your thoughts from negative to positive. The words you use for attracting abundance can be whatever you feel fits the situation, but here are two suggested affirmations;

I (say your name) am now open to receive (say what it is you are wishing for),
or *I (say your name) give thanks for the ever-increasing blessings in my life, now, today and always.*

One of the best ways to find abundance is to have gratitude for everything you have, as well as anything else you may receive.

An Altar to Abundance

Dedicating an altar to abundance is a powerful symbol of your intent to welcome more of life's goodness and to give thanks for the gifts you have already received. As Earth is the element associated with the material plane, use warm earth colours such as russet, deep yellow, rich browns and olive greens. Add spicy scents to your altar to attract prosperity, scents such as patchouli, star anise, clove and cinnamon are ideal – or make up some prosperity incense mix.

Make an offering of some silver coins, and as you do so, think of all the things that already enrich your life and represent them on the altar to create a positive reminder of what you have already been given and to express your gratitude. If you focus your attention on what you have, and keep giving thanks for it, you will find greater abundance being drawn into your life, based on the "like attracts like" principle.

Hindu Gods of Abundance

If you are seeking to manifest greater wealth, call on the Hindu goddess Lakshmi and/or the god Ganesha.

In the Hindu tradition, Lakshmi is the personification of abundance, wealth and harmony. She is portrayed as a beautiful woman seated on a sacred lotus throne; with two of her four hands she offers blessings of love and joy, while gold coins fall from the other two into the ocean of life. She is a symbol of everything that is fortunate and it is the nature of good fortune that it is distributed randomly. Deepavali, the third day of Diwali (the Festival of Lights), is dedicated to her worship; lamps are lit inside every home to welcome her and fireworks are exploded in her honour.

Ganesha, the elephant-headed god and lord of obstacles, helps to clear the path of anything that stands in the way of us receiving Lakshmi's blessings, so his presence can also help to bring abundance into your home.

A Prosperity Box

To help you focus on what you want to bring into your life, choose a suitable container to be your "prosperity box". Using black ink, make a list of what you wish for. Be specific with what you are asking for – for instance, if you would like more money, state how much you need. Then write another list using energy-enhancing orange ink: this list should contain all the things you are prepared to do to help you achieve your desires. Remember: you have to take practical steps to help magic happen.

Fold the pieces of paper and place both lists in the box, together with a handful of prosperity incense, a few silver coins and a small piece of jade. Keep the box on your altar. When you receive a gift, place it on the altar for a while and give thanks to sustain the flow of abundant energy.

Chai Shen, the god of wealth

For generations, Chinese families have set up an altar outside their homes on the eve of the Lunar New Year, in the hope of receiving the blessings of Chai Shen, the god of wealth, for the coming year. Each year, the god arrives from a different direction and this must be carefully calculated to make sure the altar is correctly positioned, otherwise it would welcome the god of evil instead.

All the family members say prayers and make offerings that symbolize abundance and good fortune, including sweets, fruit and wine. Everyone writes their wishes for the year on red paper, which is burned with offerings of incense. The previous year's portrait of Chai Shen is burned, and firecrackers are set off. After the ceremony, the god's portrait is carried inside to watch over the household for the year to come.

Prosperity incense

1 part cassia bark or cinnamon
1 part grated nutmeg
1 part finely grated orange rind
1 part star anise
few drops orange essential oil
2 parts frankincense grains

Pound the first four ingredients using a pestle and mortar, sprinkle on the oil and mix in the frankincense resin. Burn small amounts of the mixture on a charcoal block placed in a heatproof bowl.

A mixture of frankincense and rich spices can help in your prosperity magic.

Prosperity boxes can be filled with wishes for others, and offerings to a wish-granting power.

LUNAR GARDENING

Watery or fleshy plants, like courgettes and cucumbers, should be planted during a full moon.

Because the moon has such a strong influence over crop yields, for hundreds of years farmers, agriculturists and gardeners have all observed the moon's phases when planting, tending and harvesting crops. The phases of the moon, and also the zodiac sign that it is passing through, seem to affect the way plants grow, so timing gardening activities according to the moon helps make them more effective. The principles of lunar gardening take a while to adjust to, but after a while, you will find that your flowers bloom brighter, crops grow more succulent and flavoursome, and trees have stronger roots. In fact your whole garden will benefit from this ancient way of gardening and be filled with healthy plants that are a joy to behold.

Gardening by the Moon

If, to begin with, you find it a little too complicated to check the zodiac signs for your gardening tasks, you can simply follow the moon's phases of waxing and waning. The moon is increasing in influence between the new and full phases (brightmoon) and decreasing in influence during the waning and dark phases (darkmoon).

New Moon

Seeds of plants that flower above the ground should be sown at the new moon. This is also the time for farmers to sow cereals such as barley and sweetcorn (maize), and for leafy and fruiting crops such as asparagus, broccoli and Brussels sprouts, squash and tomatoes to be planted. This is also the time for fertilizing and feeding anything that you wish to flourish.

Full Moon

Because full moon has the strongest influence over the Water element this is the best time to plant watery or fleshy crops like marrows (zucchini) and cucumbers. This is also a good time for harvesting the leaves, stems, or seeds of herbs for drying, especially when the moon is transiting a Fire sign. It is important to pick your herbs on a dry day, so that they dry quickly, without rotting. The best time to harvest is just before midday. String the stems together and hang them upside down in an airy, cool but dry atmosphere, until ready for use. The full moon is also an excellent time for baking bread. The influence of the full moon proves the yeast better and encourages the dough to rise.

Traditionally, mushrooms are picked at full moon, the best time being just after dawn, when the dew is still on the grass. Take them home and have them for breakfast. Remember that some fungi are poisonous, so be very careful that you pick only edible mushrooms and do not eat anything you are unsure about.

Waning Moon

The waning moon is the time in the moon's cycle for root vegetables, peas and beans, and garlic. Anything undertaken during this time will benefit

Tend leafy plants and feed the garden well during the new moon. This is also the best time for sowing many types of seeds.

underground development or retard growth. This is therefore an excellent time to mow the lawn, as its new growth will be slowed, or to plough and turn the soil. Gather and harvest crops during the waning moon, especially in late summer, the traditional harvest time. This is an excellent time to prune trees, roses and shrubs, and to water the garden. Making jams and pickles should also be done during a waning moon, for best results.

Crops that are suited to planting during the waning moon are endive (chicory), carrots, garlic, onions, potatoes, radishes, beetroot (beets) and strawberries. All flowering bulbs, biennials and perennials should be planted during this time, especially when the moon is in a Water sign. Saplings also benefit from being planted during the waning moon, when it is in Cancer, Scorpio, Pisces or Virgo.

Darkmoon

The fourth quarter, or darkmoon, is the best time for garden maintenance: for weeding, cultivation and the removal of pests. Start a compost heap during the darkmoon time, or harvest and dry herbs and everlasting flowers, especially if the moon is in a Fire sign. A watermoon is the best time to water fields and gardens.

Elemental gardening table

When gardening according to the moon's sign of the zodiac, your timing needs to be a little more accurate than is the case with the moon's phases. The moon takes only about a couple of days to pass through each sign, so to coordinate both factors will take careful planning. For details on the moon's phases and when it is passing through a particular star sign, you will need to refer to a lunar almanac or an ephemeris. Then check the chart below to discover which zodiacal sign is most appropriate for each activity.

AIR
Gemini (barren and dry): weeding, clearing, pest control
Libra (moist): plant fruit trees, fleshy vegetables, root vegetables
Aquarius (barren and dry): garden maintenance, weeding and pest control

FIRE
Aries (barren and dry): weeding, clearing, garden maintenance
Leo (barren and dry): bonfires, ground clearance, weeding
Sagittarius (barren and dry): plant onions, garden maintenance

WATER
Cancer (very fruitful and moist): best sign for planting, sowing and cultivating
Scorpio (very fruitful and moist): very good sign for planting, sowing and general cultivation, especially vine fruits; start a compost heap
Pisces (very fruitful and moist): excellent for planting, especially root crops

EARTH
Taurus (fertile and moist): plant root crops and leafy vegetables
Virgo (barren and moist): cultivation, weeding and pest control
Capricorn (productive and dry): good for root vegetables

Carrots and other root vegetables develop best during the time of a waning moon.

Lunar Plants

Particular plants and trees come under the influence of the moon. These have been used in ceremonies and rituals to the moon goddess, and were also depicted in traditional art and sculpture. Flowers of the moon include all aquatic plants like waterlilies, seaweed and lotus, as well as jasmine and poppy. All flowers that are white or that blossom at night, such as jasmine or night-scented stock, are also moon flowers.

Trees of the moon include sandalwood and camphor, both of which were used in the ancient world in ceremonies to attract the attentions of the moon goddess, as well as the willow, aspen, eucalyptus, pear, plum and lemon. The willow is also known as the moon's wishing tree, and calling for favour by tying white, silver or light blue ribbons to her branches on lunar festival days can help to empower a wish.

Foretelling the weather

Because the moon influences weather patterns, it is possible to predict changes in the weather according to where the moon is in her cycle, or her appearance.

- a new moon always brings a change in the weather, and if the horns of the moon are sharp it indicates the onset of windy weather
- a crescent moon cupped and on its back means rain
- if you can see a star close to the moon, expect to have "wild weather"
- a bright full moon heralds good weather and a mottled full moon will bring rain
- storms and other dramatic weather patterns are more likely just after a full moon

ARTS OF DIVINATION

The word divination shares the same Latin root as divine, meaning sacred, godly or pertaining to the heavenly realm. Divination is a sacred art; it is the means by which we can discover the unknown (or what is hidden) by means of intuition, inspiration or magic. In ancient times, it was very much a part of both religious and secular life. In Old Testament times, for instance, the priest would cast stones or lots when important decisions had to be made, while in the Ancient and Classical world, oracles were regularly consulted to assess the best time for an undertaking or to predict the outcome of a course of action. In all cases it was believed that God or the gods were speaking through the divining tool.

Divination embraces a number of arts that use symbols or patterns to help you focus your clairvoyance or psychic vision on matters that may be occurring at a distance, back and forth in time, or simply at a deep level within yourself.

There are a variety of different methods by which the doors to your own psychic abilities are opened in a way that permits intuition to work. This chapter includes some of the most widely popular systems of divination in use, including numerology, astrology, the Tarot, the I Ching and runes. Dowsing, a relatively straightforward art, is also included, along with scrying, which is perhaps one of the trickiest to master.

DIVINATION

Above the entrance at the celebrated Delphic Oracle in ancient Greece was carved the inscription, "Know Thyself". Indeed, increasing self-awareness can be said to be the ultimate purpose of divination. Rather than being a method to predict a future that is already certain, it is a way of seeking guidance from the gods or our "higher self" about possibilities. If we accept that we are the creators of our own destiny, it follows that the more information we have at our disposal, the more we are able to make choices that are in line with our highest purpose or destiny.

The I Ching can give you greater insight into your situation and help you make wise decisions.

High and Low Magic

At its most elevated level, divination is a sacred art designed to exalt the consciousness of the individual seeking guidance (the inquirer) and to increase self-acceptance. At the other end of the spectrum, divination is also associated with "fortune-telling" and prediction. This can place the inquirer in a passive position, a victim in the hands of fate. Practitioners of natural magic are more inclined to use divination for its original sacred intent. This puts the onus of responsibility firmly in the hands of the inquirer and means that the divinatory arts are approached with the same care and respect as any other aspect of natural magic. When interpreted correctly, a reading will direct the inquirer's attention to the forces shaping his or her path in life – and present choices or suggest a course of action.

Divination can be done for yourself and for others. If you undertake to perform any kind of reading for someone else, be careful about how you give them difficult or challenging information.

Synchronicity

The practice of divination stems from a desire to know in advance what is going to happen. Through the ages many

Uses for divination

Divination can be used to:

- analyse problems
- clarify a decision-making process
- help you to understand yourself and others better
- reveal aspects of a situation that are out of conscious awareness
- stimulate intuition
- open up your mind
- assist healing
- predict future patterns or trends

Ethics – the dos and don'ts of divining

Traditionally the divinatory arts were taught by oral and practical exposition, where the student would naturally assimilate the level of responsibility needed to stand as mediator between the inquirer and the spiritual realm. Whenever you undertake to perform any reading for another person, you should treat them with respect and compassion: do not give them more information than they can handle, and do not frighten them if you see difficult or challenging aspects in their reading. The following guidelines may also be helpful:

1 Do not use divination for guidance obsessively: this can be counter productive and indicates giving away your power and responsibility.

2 Always obtain the permission of another person before doing a reading for them.

3 Do not use divination for entertainment or in inappropriate circumstances.

4 Respect your spiritual allies; seek their advice seriously and remember to give thanks.

5 Don't divine when you are low in energy or feeling upset; wait until you feel balanced and centred.

6 Remember that divination is a means of spiritual clarification, not sorcery.

7 Dedicate your art to the highest good of all.

8 Encourage the inquirer to see the reading as a pattern of possibilities based on their current situation; remind them that they have choice.

different methods have been used to foretell the future, from signs and portents in the sky to the patterns made by tea leaves or the innards of slaughtered beasts. Sticks, coins, coloured stones, pictures and dreams have all been used to predict events, often with an uncanny accuracy. No one really knows how divination works, but the theory of "synchronicity" may come close to giving us a plausible explanation.

It was the twentieth-century psychologist, Carl Jung, who used the term synchronicity to account for "meaningful coincidences". In rational thinking, mysterious or amazing coincidences are ascribed to chance, but during the course of his work Jung noticed a pattern of coincidences in seemingly unrelated events that caused him to challenge the predominant scientific view of cause and effect. He ascribed this to a deeper level of the mind, which he referred to as "the collective unconscious". Archetypes and symbols operate at this level.

According to magical thinking, nothing happens at random; everything is connected and has meaning, as events in one area of the web of life correspond to patterns in other areas. This means that in theory, almost anything can be used for divination; it is all a question of being able to read the signs or patterns. A divinatory reading can reveal a minute part of the greater pattern; during that moment, it is as though a veil is twitched aside and we glimpse the otherworld.

Palmistry has been used as a divination tool for centuries and can take years of study and practice to perfect.

Preparation

Before divining, it is important to create a calm environment with soft lighting. Too much background noise or bright lights can disturb your concentration. Privacy is also vitally important because quite personal and intimate subjects may be discussed while doing any kind of reading. Eye contact and a friendly smile always helps the other person to feel at ease. Before you start, the inquirer should focus on the subject or issue that they are seeking guidance with. If you are using any tools – such as Tarot cards or the Rune stones – let the inquirer handle these as they focus on their issue. Some people will take only a short time to get their issues clear in their minds, while others will take longer to focus. The inquirer should then pass the cards, stones or whatever is being used back to you so that you can begin.

Numerology

Aside from their practical use in counting, numbers also have a symbolic value. Numerology is the art of understanding life by studying the symbolic value of numbers and the relationships between them. Since time immemorial, cultures and religions all over the world have either devised their own system of numerology or borrowed from and expanded on existing ones. All of them have been used to explain and gain a deeper understanding of ourselves in relation to the cosmos, and numerology has always played a part in magic and divination.

Life Cycles

The numbers 1 to 9 form the basic building blocks of numerology. Aside from zero, all other numbers can be reduced to arrive at one of these single digits. For example, 39 reduces to 3; this is arrived at by adding 3+9=12; 12 is then reduced to 1+2=3. Numerology is based on the principle of reduction, which mirrors the process of life. For instance, our time in the womb from conception to birth is nine months, which consists of three terms, while traditionally our lives are said to be made up of three cycles of three nine-year periods. The first cycle (ages 0–27) is concerned with the birth and growth of the individual; the second cycle (ages 28–54) is about how we engage with the world; while the final cycle (ages 55–81) is about engaging with the spirit. Similarly the numbers 1 to 9 form three nests of three with their symbolic meanings fitting within this bigger framework.

The personal year number helps us all to work in harmony with unfolding events.

The numbers of our birth date help us discover and express our core personal qualities.

Numerology and You

Numbers affect every area of our lives and almost any set of numbers can be broken down and have meanings assigned to them. Many numbers are uniquely ours, from our telephone or house number to the number on official documents such as passports, driving licences and bank accounts. Many people also have a number that they consider "lucky". In numerology, however, the most significant numbers are those that relate to your date of birth (the life path number) and to the letters of your name (personality number).

The Life Path Number

Everyone has a life path number that represents their potential. It is derived from the sum of the digits of their birth date. For example, a birthday of 9 November 1968 (9/11/1968) has a life path number of 8, reached in the following way: 9 + 1+1 + 1+9+6+8 = 35, then 3 + 5 = 8. Your life path number is a guide to what you need to do in life.

The Cosmic and Personal Year

Like astrology, numerology can also provide a clue for the best timing of events. Every year, the calendar changes and different possibilities are available to us. The cosmic year number is calculated by adding up the digits of the current year. For example, the year 2004 is a 6 year, showing that there will be a potential for universal peace and harmony (the vibration of 6) that year. While the number of the cosmic year symbolizes the potential that exists around you, there is also a personal year number that relates more directly to you. To calculate this, you use your birth date, substituting the current year for the year of your birth.

Numbers and their Meanings

Traditionally, the symbolic meanings of numbers are ascribed as follows:

0: The lens; the all-seeing eye that encompasses everything but cannot act; reflective; withdrawal from life to take stock before embarking on the next adventure.
1 Initiative and independence; the leader; goal-setting and ambition; Great Father; the sun.
2 Nurturing and relationship; balance; carer, mediator; Great Mother; moon.
3 Creativity; self-expression; the birth of ideas; aspiration; Cosmic Child.
4 Structure and order; stability; material structures; discipline and consolidation.
5 Breaking free from limits imposed by structures leading to growth and change; restlessness; adventurous; exploring new possibilities; self-discovery.
6 Emotional harmony and sensitivity; perfection and ideals of family life; love of heart and home.
7 Spiritual transformation; meditation, mysticism; spiritual learning and development; life and spirit combine.
8 Strategist and organizer, regulating relationship between spirit and matter; moves between spheres of heaven and earth; connects with cycles of life. Karmic number.
9 Wisdom gained through experience; the great teacher; completion and ending before a new cycle begins.
11 Speaking with inspiration; channelling the spirit; visionary; the prophet or seer.
22 Building the dream; the master builder; systematic approach combined with gentleness and sensitivity.
33 Unconditional giving; devotion to great causes; saint or martyr; the tireless helper.

Personal year numbers

Your personal year number is calculated by adding the day and month of your birth with the current year.

1 Fresh beginnings, both in your personal and professional life
2 Finding peace; revising and strengthening what you have started
3 Self-expression; personal as well as professional development
4 Discipline and consolidation; application, hard work and self-discipline
5 Exploring new possibilities; change
6 Self-esteem; love and romance
7 Soul-searching; self-awareness and personal spiritual growth
8 Go with the flow; try to connect more with inner self and others
9 Resolution; assess the past and note and enjoy your achievements

The personality number

Although many people will have the same life path number, the unique path that their life will take will be influenced by their personal attributes. A clue to these can be gained from the personality number. This number represents your identity; by recognizing and using its inherited qualities, you are better able to express yourself. In numerology, every letter of the alphabet has a numerical equivalent. The personality number is obtained by finding out the numerical value of every letter in your full name and reducing it to a single digit. For example, the name Ann Helen Myers consists of the numbers 1+5+5 + 8+5+3+5+5 + 4+7+5+9+1 = 63 which reduces to 9. Name changes and nicknames will reflect the personality number most representative of you at the time.

Numerical equivalents of the alphabet

1	2	3	4	5	6	7	8	9
A	B	C	D	E	F	G	H	I
J	K	L	M	N	O	P	Q	R
S	T	U	V	W	X	Y	Z	

The letters of our names can give us clues to our inherited patterns.

ASTROLOGY

Before the modern scientific age, it was widely believed that the movements of the celestial bodies regulated life on earth. The cycles of day and night, the waxing and waning of the moon and the movement of the planets across the starry night sky follow regular and predictable patterns. Our ancestors related these patterns to natural phenomena, including not only the weather and seasons, but also different kinds of destiny. Astrology is the study of these cosmic patterns pin pointed in the continuum of time and space and represented symbolically on an astrological "chart" or horoscope.

The universe is constantly evolving and new planets are still being discovered today.

ORIGINS OF ASTROLOGY

Astrology is one of the most ancient of all the magical arts. It seems to have evolved in Mesopotamia, where it was practised by priests who concerned themselves with the prediction of major events, from whether or not the harvest would be good to the destinies of kings and princes. Later it became the province of mathematicians, and the Greeks and Chaldeans used their knowledge of the heavens to delineate

The zodiac signs

In modern-day Western astrology, there are 12 signs of the zodiac, each related to a constellation.

Aries: The leader; "me first"; loner, pioneer, go-getter; enjoys action, adventure; quick to anger; ruled by Mars

Taurus: The builder; practical, patient, steadfast; enjoys material comfort and wellbeing; ruled by Venus

Gemini: The talker; quick-witted, restless, easily bored; enjoys travel, new ideas; constantly on the look-out for new experiences; ruled by Mercury

Cancer:  The nurturer; empathic, sensitive to needs of others; imaginative; enjoys home and family; ruled by the Moon

Leo: The actor; plays centre-stage, dramatic, generous, warm, affectionate; enjoys good living, romance, and "to play"; ruled by the Sun

Virgo: The perfectionist; precise, meticulous, pays attention to detail; enjoys work in the service of others; sincere, dependable; ruled by Mercury

Libra: The adjuster; seeks to bridge or reconcile opposites, to balance; relationships important and need for peace and harmony; enjoys aesthetics and beautiful things; ruled by Venus

Scorpio: The transformer; death and rebirth, endings and beginnings; going to the depths, emotional intensity; enjoys the occult, the mysteries of life; ruled by Pluto and Mars

Sagittarius: The traveller; journeys to expand horizons; free spirit, adventurous, buoyant and exuberant; enjoys humour, having fun, new experiences; ruled by Jupiter

Capricorn: The climber; works hard to achieve ambitious and lofty goals; patient, cautious, responsible, committed; enjoys the status of success, black humour; ruled by Saturn

Aquarius: The reformer; intellectual revolutionary, seeks social justice, a "brotherhood of man"; freedom of thought, originality and emotional independence; enjoys gadgets, machines, electronic media; ruled by Uranus and Saturn

Pisces:  The dreamer; impressionable, imaginative, sensitive and artistic; psychic development, meditation, spiritual transformation; refines and idealizes; enjoys the arts, but also has a tendency towards escapism; ruled by Neptune and Jupiter

certain characteristics associated with each pattern that could be applied to life on earth.

Uses of Astrology

A horoscope involves plotting the position of the celestial bodies at a given moment in time. It is possible to draw one up for almost any life situation: we can use it to help us determine the best time or place for an event, such as a wedding or business venture, or we could also examine the potential of a relationship by comparing two charts and looking at the symbolic interaction between them. However, the most useful place to start with astrology is with your own birth chart.

The birth chart can be used as a tool for self-awareness: personality types and psychological traits as well as information on the building blocks of life – such as career, health and relationships – are all covered in the birth chart. It can also be used to predict future life-trends, although be aware that these are "trends" and not absolute certainties. Drawing up a birth chart involves complex numerical calculations and unless you want to spend the time learning how to do this, it is a good investment to get your chart drawn up by a professional astrologer. Once you have your chart, it is yours for life. The next step is learning how to make sense of it.

Understanding Astrology

Your horoscope will be drawn as a circle divided into twelve sections, each section representing a sign of the zodiac (Aries, Taurus, Gemini and so on); the word zodiac itself comes from the Greek meaning "a circle of animals". Each of the celestial bodies (referred to as "planets" for convenience) will appear in a sign of the zodiac. Most probably you already know your "Sun sign" (often referred to as your "star sign") but in addition you will find that you will also have a zodiac sign for the Moon, Venus, Mars and all the other planets. The basic layer of the birth chart shows the disposition of the planets and how they are influenced by the nature or character of the signs in which they fall. The next layer is to look at the relationships or "aspects" made by these planets to one another; some of these aspects will be easy and harmonious, while others will be stressful and present challenges. On top of this, the chart is further divided into twelve "houses". These represent areas of life – such as work, relationships, creativity and health for instance – that show us where the energies of each planet are expressed.

Astrology is the study of the patterns made by the planets and how these can influence life on Earth.

The symbolism of the planets

The word planet is derived from the ancient Greek "wanderer". In ancient times, the planets were regarded as mysterious wanderers of the night sky and linked with the gods and goddesses of classical mythology. Each of these divinities is contained within the horoscope, and can be seen to represent different energies or aspects of the psyche. How these are expressed will vary according to which of the 12 zodiac signs the planet falls in, and whether this is a Fire, Water, Earth or Air sign.

Planet	Symbol	Function
Sun	☉	Wholeness; integration of the self; inner purpose; vitality; conscious authority; the heroic impulse to "be"
Moon	☽	Emotional response; imagination; receptivity; rhythm and mood; memories
Mercury	☿	Thought and communication; mental faculties; intelligence
Venus	♀	Love, beauty, art; relationships (friends and lovers); harmony; money and resources
Mars	♂	Action; self-assertion; desire, ambition, competition; physical energy; ego
Jupiter	♃	Expansion, freedom, opportunity; search for meaning; luck, learning, philosophy
Saturn	♄	Limitation, structure, perseverance, responsibility; life's lessons; karma
Uranus	♅	Originality and inventiveness; eccentricity; urge to reform; radicalism; change, the unexpected, intuition
Neptune	♆	Idealism and inspiration; spiritual values, transcendence; clairvoyance, the subconscious
Pluto	♇	Transformation; death, rebirth and regeneration; intensity, power

The Houses

Just as there are 12 signs, there are also 12 astrological houses that closely reflect the meanings of the signs. The houses are "areas of life", compartments of experience that indicate where the energies of each planet are expressed. If the planets show us "what" then the houses indicate "where".

The first house is concerned with childhood and the development of personality. It governs physical appearance and is the way we present ourselves to the world. The second house represents possessions and values; it is the domain of accumulated wealth, income and everything to do with material comfort. It is connected with a person's capabilities and resourcefulness. The ability to communicate is contained within the third house. This house also governs neighbours, relatives and the immediate environment. Home is the domain of the fourth house; this includes our homeland, as well as the actual building in which we live. The fifth house is about pleasure and creativity, and includes love affairs, our sex life and children, as well as creations of an artistic sort. Our health and wellbeing falls into the sixth house, which also includes our work and how we fulfil our role in society. Close relationships and partnerships (both marriage and business) fall into the seventh house, while the eighth house is the house of transformation and covers endings, death and rebirth. Inheritances, wills and life's challenges and upheavals are found in this house. Travel, higher education and spiritual voyaging are ninth house matters, while the tenth is concerned with public position, our reputation and status in the world. Friends and social groups are contained in the 11th house, while the 12th house is the area of spirituality and transcendence.

Aspects

Reading a birth chart is extremely complex. Not only does the astrologer take into account the position of the planets in the signs and houses and where they fall in the circle, they will also look at the "aspects" or relationships between the planets. Like relationships, some aspects are easier to handle than others. The challenging aspects are often what motivates psychological growth. The main astrological aspects are as follows:

The conjunction (0°): planets are in close proximity to one another. The conjunction is like a marriage, with each planet strongly influencing the other; it is usually a harmonious aspect, depending on the planets and houses involved.

The opposition (180°): planets are placed on opposite sides of the circle, suggesting tension and confrontation. The opposition is a challenging aspect and means that we will struggle to integrate these opposing forces.

The trine (120°): planets are in a harmonious relationship forming one (or more) sides of a triangle, enabling easy synthesis. If all three points of the trine (or triangle) are completed, it is known as a "grand trine".

The square (90°): planets are in tension with one another, forming one (or more) sides of a square. The square produces restless striving in order to get to grips with the planetary energies involved; being at right angles to one another, the planets involved may also go off at a tangent, causing blocks.

The sextile (60°): planets are in harmony; sextiles produce motivated activity, a working relationship between the planets and the angles involved.

The first of the 12 astrological houses is concerned with childhood.

Our love affairs and our sex life are governed by the fifth house, which is also about pleasure and creativity.

Work comes under the governance of the sixth house, which also includes our role in society.

THE ASCENDANT AND DESCENDANT

The houses of your horoscope begin with the ascendant. This is the precise degree of the sign on the eastern horizon at the time and place when you were born. Also known as the rising sign, the ascendant is very influential; it is like the outer mask or persona that we present to the world and is largely how we create a first impression with others. So, for instance, someone with Leo rising but with a moon in Pisces may seem bold and brash, but their moon sign indicates sensitivity and that they are liable to be easily hurt. Opposite the rising sign is the descendant; this marks the cusp of the seventh house (the house of relationships) and describes the "other", the natural partner. The ascendant and the descendant form a polarity, so that neither can be understood without the other. The ascendant-descendant axis divides the circle into upper and lower halves, the upper part symbolizing the "world out there" and the lower part our subjective, inner experience.

THE MIDHEAVEN AND THE IC

The uppermost point of the chart is known as the "midheaven"; this point symbolizes the height of worldly success and public position, and with most house systems is on the cusp of the 10th house. It describes our aspirations and the type of career we are likely to develop.

At the other end of this axis is the IC, or *imum coeli* (Latin for "bottom of the sky"), on the cusp of the 4th house. It describes the least exposed parts of ourselves and is a link to our personal and ancestral past. The IC and the midheaven form an axis of innermost and outermost life experiences, which further divides the circle into eastern and western hemispheres. The eastern hemisphere is concerned with the self, while the western hemisphere is linked with the impact of others.

The moon through the signs

Unlike the Sun, the moon travels through all the signs of the zodiac in a month, spending two or three days or so in each sign. Because the moon is so important in magic and ritual, it is especially useful to understand how it functions through the different signs.

Moon in ...	Key word	Magic for ...
Aries	energy	starting new projects, leadership, goal-setting
Taurus	dependability	love, money and material things
Gemini	communication	talking, writing; travel (short journeys)
Cancer	nurturing	home and family, emotional support; issues to do with motherhood
Leo	courage	creativity and fertility; daring to take risks
Virgo	self-improvement	work (on self or in the world); health; attention to detail
Libra	balance	emotional harmony, giving and receiving; artistic and spiritual work; legal matters
Scorpio	transformation	making real changes in your life; sexuality and desire
Sagittarius	exploration	travel (long journeys); pursuit of spiritual values
Capricorn	achievement	getting organized; pushing forwards with career, ambitions; status in the world
Aquarius	revolution	freedom and originality; any work that involves creative expression, problem-solving
Pisces	compassion	healing; working with dreams, psychic abilities, clairvoyance and telepathy; trusting intuitive powers

The 11th house governs our friends and our social groups.

The Tarot

The origins of the Tarot are shrouded in mystery. Some say it dates back to ancient Egypt, while others see strong links with Hebrew mysticism. However, we do know that in fifteenth-century Italy the wealthy Visconti family commissioned an artist to paint a set of 78 unnamed and unnumbered cards that depicted religious allegories, social conditions and ideas of the time, to celebrate a family marriage. These cards formed the deck for an Italian gambling game called "Tarocchi", and by the late eighteenth century we find them being used as a divinatory tool. Since then, hundreds of different Tarot decks have been produced but the core meanings of the cards remains largely unchanged.

Pick a Tarot card each day and meditate on the image, or think about what you feel it shows.

What is the Tarot?

Essentially the Tarot is a deck of 78 cards, which divide into two clear parts: the 22 cards of the Major Arcana and the 56 cards of the Minor Arcana. The Minor Arcana is further sub-divided into four suits, each of which is related to one of the four elements: Wands (Fire), Swords (Air), Cups (Water) and Pentacles (Earth). The Minor Arcana closely parallels a normal pack of 52 playing cards with its suits of clubs (wands), spades (swords), hearts (cups) and diamonds (pentacles). It is therefore possible to transpose the meanings of the Tarot cards on to a deck of playing cards and to use these for readings.

The word "Arcana" is related to arcane, which means mysterious or secret, and the Tarot has also been known as a "Book of Secrets". The Major Arcana deals with archetypal themes and reflects the major turning points in our lives: our commitments, triumphs and tragedies, our greatest challenges and most powerful impulses. The cards of the Minor Arcana deal with more day-to-day aspects of life, such as work, relationships, our ideas and our ambitions. Taken together, they constitute a guidebook to the incidents and issues that we have to handle in our lives, from the past, in the present and looking to the future.

Decoding the Tarot

Most modern Tarot decks have a picture on every card, and the best way to learn the meanings is to shuffle a new pack thoroughly and take one card each day. Place it somewhere you can see it and think about what it seems to show, or meditate on the image. Write down your conclusions in a book kept for the purpose, and next day go on to another card, until you have examined all 78. You may simply focus on the name or number of the card, or try to decide what the picture shows at first, but gradually meanings will start to emerge.

Many books on interpreting the Tarot system are available and they take a wide variety of approaches – from light-hearted fun to a deep magical or psychological orientation. It is best not to rely too heavily on the meanings given in books, however, but to use your own intuitive understanding.

Understanding the cards

This numerical guide can be used as a quick reference to the Minor Arcana definitions, by cross-referencing the generic numerical meaning for any card with the general background to a particular suit. Take the Nine of Cups, for example. The suit of Cups is concerned with emotional issues, whilst a general definition for any of the number nine cards concerns fulfilment. By combining these two pieces of information, you can work out a general definition for the Nine of Cups to signify emotional contentment.

King: Competition, realization
Queen: Fulfilment, deep satisfaction, skill, maturity
Knight: Focus, single-mindedness
Page: Information
Ten: Culmination and change
Nine: Integration, contentment
Eight: Organization, evaluation, experience, commitments
Seven: Imagination, options, variety of choice
Six: Poise, contentment, relaxation, victory
Five: Adjustment, challenge, possible conflict
Four: Manifestation, creation of a plan
Three: Clarification, plans made public
Two: Affirmation, some sort of choice, commitment
Ace: Potential, new beginnings; the "raw" energy of the suit

The Minor Arcana

The 56 cards of the Minor Arcana are divided into four suits. The suit of Wands is concerned with energy and ambition, our goals and desires; it is also connected with sexuality. The suit of Swords is concerned with the mental realm of thoughts and ideas; it is also the area where conflicts are likely to surface. Emotions are connected to the suit of Cups dealing with love relationships, artistic endeavours and contentment. Lastly, the suit of Pentacles is concerned with everyday material matters, such as money and property.

The Major Arcana

The cards of the Major Arcana represent the powerful cosmic forces at work in our lives and are always the most important cards in a reading. These cards represent archetypal forces and have traditional astrological correspondences.

Number	Card	Correspondence	Traditional meaning
0	The Fool	Uranus	Fresh beginnings; spontaneity; taking risks and stepping into the unknown; change
I	The Magician	Mercury	Manifesting results in the material world; communicating; bringing different elements of life together
II	The High Priestess	Moon	Trust your intuition; don't take things at face value but look behind the scenes; patience
III	The Empress	Venus	Fertility or pregnancy; domestic bliss; abundance and the good things of life; enjoyment of sensuality. The "mother" principle
IV	The Emperor	Aries	Power and authority. Established structures and organizations: banks, schools, offices, companies. The "father" principle
V	The Hierophant	Taurus	Traditional ways of doing things; seeking advice from figures in the establishment or a higher authority (a teacher or spirit guide)
VI	The Lovers	Gemini	Intensity and choices in relationships; instant chemistry and attraction between two people; the feeling that something is "meant to be"
VII	The Chariot	Cancer	Moving forwards on the path through life towards success; staying focused on goals
VIII	Strength	Leo	Recognizing and using your inner strength; having self-confidence
IX	The Hermit	Virgo	Look before you leap; take time out to be alone; cultivating wisdom and self-awareness; the guide
X	The Wheel of Fortune	Jupiter	Luck, expansion and growth; fate taking a hand in your life and possibly redirecting the path you are on
XI	Justice	Libra	See what is out of balance and make necessary adjustments; reaping what is fair and just
XII	The Hanged Man	Neptune	Sacrifice and letting go; reversal of fortune, a time to sit back and wait until circumstances improve
XIII	Death	Scorpio	Changes and endings (not usually a physical death), followed by regeneration and rebirth
XIV	Temperance	Sagittarius	Testing the waters before diving in; compromise and cooperation, allowing feelings to flow. Treading a middle way and not jumping in where angels fear to tread
XV	The Devil	Capricorn	Trapped by fears, compulsions and addictions; being overly attached to security; can also be rediscovery of passions and sexual energy.
XVI	The Tower	Mars	Disruptive changes that are sudden and unexpected; life will never be the same again; a radical upheaval
XVII	The Star	Aquarius	Realizing dreams and visions, a wish comes true; renewal of hope and faith
XVIII	The Moon	Pisces	Dreams and illusions, everything may not be as it appears at face value; the power of the subconscious
XIX	The Sun	Sun	Extremely positive card denoting growth, life and an increase of potential in all or many areas of life; vitality, joy and happiness
XX	Judgement	Pluto	Decisions are pressing and need to be made; coming to terms with the past. Moving forwards with a more positive attitude; the lifting of karmic restrictions
XXI	The World	Saturn	The most auspicious card in the deck. You have come a long way and can now enjoy great success in all areas of life; completion of a cycle

Using the Tarot

One of the main differences between using the Tarot compared to other divinatory tools, such as astrology or numerology, is that it is a pictorial system. The visual images give this system an impact that is real and immediate. It is even possible for some people without any knowledge about the Tarot to give accurate readings simply by looking at the images, having an instinctive response and then conveying what is seen, felt and understood.

We can use the Tarot for many purposes: to ask for advice about a best course of action, to gain insight into life's spiritual "lessons", as a tool for meditation and self-discovery, and also to develop our psychic ability and interpret what we see for others.

Tarot for Yourself

It is possible to do readings for yourself. One way of doing this is to begin each day with a simple question such as "What kind of day is in store?" Shuffle the pack, then pick a card. At the end of the day you may be able to understand how the card related to the day's events; it will also help you come to terms with a card's meaning, as experience is the best form of learning there is.

A quick three-card reading is also useful. Shuffle the pack and pick three cards, laying them out from left to right. The first represents yourself and your current situation; the second and third cards represent the situations and people you are about to encounter, respectively.

Reading for Others

When giving a Tarot reading, almost as much thought needs to be put into the preparations as into the actual reading itself. It is important to create a calm environment, preferably with soft lighting and no disturbing background noise. Privacy is also very important because quite personal and adult subjects may be discussed while doing a reading for another (the inquirer). Eye contact and a caring smile can help the inquirer to feel at ease when you are reading their cards, and remember it is not part of your remit to make scary predictions or give negative feedback. Always focus on the positive messages of the cards.

Ask the inquirer to concentrate on the subject or issue of their reading, as they shuffle the cards. Some people will take only a short time to get their issues clear, while others will take longer to focus. When the inquirer feels they have shuffled for long enough, they should pass the deck back to you. Now you are ready to lay out a spread. There are many different types of spread you can choose from, with two of the most popular being the "Celtic Cross" pattern, or one based on astrology. There are many good books on the Tarot, which will give information on different spreads for you to try.

Lay out the cards, face up, in the correct sequence. Notice any patterns or clusters of cards (for instance two or more

Before you begin to work with your Tarot cards, take some time to get to know them.

Care of your cards

Many people like to keep their Tarot cards wrapped in silk or in a special pouch or box. Do not loan out or let others handle your cards (except when giving a reading), as they will absorb your psychic impressions and become special to you.

of the same number, or a predominance of a particular suit), as this will give you a clue to the overall theme of the reading. You should also pay particular attention to any Major Arcana cards.

When you have interpreted all that you can from the cards, draw the reading to a conclusion and gather them together.

A Tarot Spell for Insight

The Tarot is a powerful divination system. Use this spell to empower a new pack of cards, or before doing a particularly important reading.

1 Take your cards and a square of silk, either red or bright blue, and a large surface with a clean flat cloth on it. Place a tall yellow or gold-coloured candle in a gold-coloured holder and light it.

2 Place the cards face down on the cloth and, with both hands, mix them up very thoroughly, saying the following:

Cards of wisdom, cards of grace, cards with magic on their face,
Open in me the holy power, to answer truly at any hour.
Open in me the skill of sight, to speak the truth by day and night.
Let the knowledge in me rise,
Let all I speak be good and wise.
Help me, Lord of the Tarot,
Help me.

Keep your Tarot cards in a safe place, and don't let anyone else use them.

3 Clap your hands over the cards three times, then select three cards and turn them over. These will show how well your spell has worked by their meanings. Snuff out the candle.

4 Collect up all the Tarot cards, wrap them in the silk square, place them in their box and put it in a safe place to retain their power.

The Celtic Cross formation is one of the best Tarot spreads to use.

Tarot meditation

One of the best ways of getting to know the Tarot is through meditation. To do this, sit quietly and comfortably with your eyes closed and take a few deep breaths to calm and centre yourself, allowing your thoughts to settle. Keeping your eyes closed, reach out and pick a card, feeling its energy in your hands. Open your eyes and allow your gaze to softly focus on the image, absorbing all its details, colours and characters.

Now close your eyes again and start to re-form the image in your mind's eye. Let it become bigger and bigger, until it becomes like a doorway. See yourself walking through it and into a living world peopled with the characters and symbols of the card. Notice your thoughts and feelings, and let yourself interact with the figures you find there. When you have finished, say goodbye and step back through the doorway. See the scene you have visited shrinking until it is once more the size of a card. Take a deep breath and open your eyes. Record your findings in your Book of Shadows.

The I Ching

Paradoxically, the only certainty in life is change. In all change, however, there are certain patterns, and it is this predictability that the shamans of ancient China referred to when they were called upon to give advice and divinations on forthcoming events. Originally, an answer to a question was divined from the patterns on animal hides or tortoise shells; later this developed into the I Ching, or the Book of Changes. As the I Ching developed, it became more than an oracular device; the ancient sages saw that it could be used as a blueprint for understanding the way the whole universe works in all its complexity.

What is the I Ching?

At its root, the I Ching is made up of eight trigrams, said to represent the eight fundamental forces of nature. At some point they were arranged into an octagonal form known as the Bagua, showing opposing pairs or forces, and were given specific names taken from nature. As its name suggests, a trigram is an arrangement of three lines, with a solid line used to represent yang energies, and a broken line to depict yin. In Chinese thought, yin and yang are the two opposing principles that underlie all of creation, the complementary opposites that are apparent in everything. When combined with one another, the trigrams make up the 64 hexagrams of the I Ching.

When you are consulting the I Ching, light a candle to help focus your mind.

Throw combinations

3 heads	= 9	_·_	changes to _ _
2 heads, 1 tail	= 8	_ _	
1 head, 2 tails	= 7	___	
3 tails	= 6	_x_	changes to ___

Consulting the Oracle

A physical way of constructing a hexagram is needed and the most common is to throw or cast three coins. It is a good idea to dedicate your coins to the I Ching and only use them for this purpose. The "heads" side of a coin is considered yang, and is given a value of three, while the "tails" side is thought of as yin and has a value of two. When the coins are thrown, a total of six, seven, eight or nine is obtained, giving lines that are either yin (even numbers) or yang (odd numbers).

Begin by preparing yourself and letting go of everyday thoughts and concerns. Light some incense and burn a candle to help put you in the right frame of mind. When you are ready, hold your question in your mind's eye and then drop the coins on to a hard surface, making a note of the pattern to give you a number. Repeat this process a further five times until you have six totals. The hexagram is then constructed upwards, following the path of organic growth, so that the first total makes up the bottom line.

You may be able to obtain some old Chinese coins to use for divining, but any coins will do.

Changing Lines

A line totalling six (old yin) or nine (old yang) changes to its young opposite. The changing lines give deeper insights into a reading, being used to produce a second hexagram. The initial hexagram relates to present conditions, while the second hexagram relates to the future outcome of a situation, or can help to clarify the original question.

The eight forces of I Ching

Ch'ien/Heaven: the creative
Chen/Thunder: the arousing
K'un/Earth: the receptive
Sun/Wind: the gentle and penetrating
Li/Fire: the clinging
Ken/Mountain: the stillness
K'an/Water: the abysmal
Tui/Lake: the joyful

The 64 hexagrams

Hexagram	Name	Meaning
1 Ch'ien:	The Creative	Masculine, dynamic, inspiring
2 K'un:	The Receptive	Feminine, yielding, receptive
3 Chun:	Difficult Beginnings	Immaturity, new growth, sprouting; perseverance
4 Meng:	Youthful Folly	Inexperience, guidance, enthusiasm, tuition
5 Hsu:	Waiting	Correctness, patience, perseverance, nourishment
6 Sung:	Conflict	Opposition, disengagement, communication
7 Shih:	The Army	Unity, harmony, acting in concert, strength, division
8 Pi:	Holding Together	Union, bonding, cooperation
9 Hsiao ch'u:	The Taming Power of the Small	Patience, yielding, strength; gentle action
10 Lu:	Conduct	Caution, courtesy, simplicity, innocence
11 T'ai:	Peace	Balance, harmony, new growth, prosperity
12 P'i:	Standstill	Lack of progress, barriers, stagnation
13 T'ung Jen:	Fellowship with Others	Cohesion, bonding, strength in numbers, co-operation
14 Ta Yu:	Possessing Plenty	Feminine, yielding, receptive, gentle, providing, bountiful
15 Ch'ien:	Modesty	Quietly progressing, steadfast, deepening, developing
16 Yu:	Enthusiasm	Energy, opportunity, support
17 Sui:	Following	Acceptance, following, joy
18 Ku:	Work on Corruption	Disruption, decay, disorder, spoiled, repairing
19 Lin:	Approach	Advance, waxing power, strength, benevolence
20 Kuan:	Contemplation	Meditation, understanding, perceiving, example
21 Shih Ho:	Biting Through	Clarity, decisiveness, obstacle, unity
22 Pi:	Grace	Adornment, beauty, simplicity
23 Po:	Splitting Apart	Strong, enduring, patient, non-action
24 Fu:	Return	Change, turning point, improvement
25 Wu Wang:	Innocence	Purity, innocence, sincerity, intuition
26 Ta Ch'u:	The Taming Power of the Great	Keeping still, tension, practice, staying firm
27 I:	Corners of the Mouth	Nourishment, discipline, meditation, fulfilment
28 Ta Kuo:	Preponderance of the Great	Pressure, regeneration, growth, cautious progress
29 K'an:	The Abysmal	Depths, despair, danger, alertness
30 Li:	The Clinging	Dependence, passion, brilliance, creativity
31 Hsien:	Influence	Harmony, mutual benefit, coming together, courtship

Hexagram	Name	Meaning
32 Heng:	Duration	Persistence, progress, endurance, stamina
33 Tun:	Retreat	Withdrawal, conserving strength, stillness, order
34 Ta Chuang:	The Power of the Great	Self-possession, strength, heaven, patience
35 Chin:	Progress	Advancement, dawning, rising
36 Ming I:	Darkening of the Light	Oppression, damping, sunset, inner light
37 Chia Jen:	The Family	Harmony, togetherness, loyalty, health, balance, structure
38 K'uei:	Opposition	Misunderstanding, contrary resistance, adversity
39 Chien:	Obstruction	Obstacles, barriers, blockage, stuck
40 Hsieh:	Deliverance	Relief, release, growth, progression
41 Sun:	Decrease	Discipline, simplicity, limited, drawing in, restriction
42 I:	Increase	Improvement, gain, progress
43 Kuai:	Breakthrough	Resoluteness, determination, resistance
44 Kou:	Coming to Meet	Caution, awareness, temptation, tolerance
45 Ts'ui:	Gathering Together	Peace, harmony, cooperation, prosperity, leadership
46 Sheng:	Pushing Upwards	Direction, ascending, growth
47 K'un:	Oppression	Exhaustion, stretched, adversity, endurance
48 Ching:	The Well	Spiritual nourishment, counsel, guidance, wisdom
49 Ko:	Revolution	Change, advance, devotion
50 Ting:	The Cauldron	Growth, sacrifice, nourishment
51 Chen:	The Arousing	Shock, movement, stimulation
52 Ken:	Keeping Still	Stillness, observing, quietness, clarity, readiness
53 Chien:	Development	Gradual progress, patience, steady growth
54 Kuei Mei:	The Marrying Maiden	Impulsiveness, disturbance, desire, proper conduct, discipline
55 Feng:	Abundance	Fullness, power, wise actions, plenty
56 Lu:	The Wanderer	Moving, restless, temporary, transient
57 Sun:	The Gentle	Gentle, penetrating, wind, persistence
58 Tui:	The Joyous	Inner strength, fulfilment, harmony, joy
59 Huan:	Dispersion	Division, dissolution, rigidity, stubbornness
60 Chieh:	Limitation	Restraint, moderation, guidelines
61 Chung Fu:	Inner Truth	Prejudice, understanding, acceptance
62 Hsiao Kuo:	Preponderance of the Small	Non-action, caution, patience
63 Chi Chi:	After Completion	Order, balance, awareness, culmination
64 Wei Chi:	Before Completion	Caution, regeneration, potential, clarity

THE RUNES

A system of sacred writing from northern Europe, Runes are said to have appeared to the Norse god Odin, during a shamanic initiation rite. The runes then became his gift of knowledge to humanity and as such they are empowered with ancient wisdom. The word "rune" comes from the Middle English *runa*, meaning "a whisper" or "a secret", and traditionally knowledge of the runes was granted only to a runemaster, who guarded it closely. A runemaster performed a similar role in Norse communities to the shaman, or medicine man or woman.

Runes can be written on small round pebbles, or on specially cut rounds of wood.

RUNE LAW

Runemasters underwent many initiatory experiences to discover the secrets of rune lore. They knew how to use them for divination, but also for magical and healing work. Runes can still be used as guides for meditation, as protective talismans, and in spells and charms.

THE RUNIC ALPHABET

The angular script of the runes points to the fact that they were not intended for writing but for carving. Many stone memorials bear runic inscriptions and it is likely that the earliest alphabets were inscribed on to pieces of wood, stone or bark. There are many different varieties of runic writing, but the most widely used runic alphabet is the Early Germanic or Elder Futhark. The word "futhark" refers to the first six runic letters f, u, th, a, r and k, just as our word "alphabet" refers to the first two letters of the Greek alphabet, Alpha (or a) and Beta (or b). The Elder Futhark has 24 letters and some scholars believe it was probably in existence as early as the 2nd century BC. Traditionally, it is divided into three "families", or aetts, of eight runes each, which were named for the Norse gods Freyr, Hagal and Tyr.

In the ancient runic alphabet, each inscription (also known as a glyph) possessed a signifying sound and a meaningful name. Over time, they have also become associated with particular trees, colours, herbs and gemstones.

A rune bag is essential for storing your runes, and it is also important that you keep them cleansed and that no one else uses them, as they are imbued with your unique energy.

Care of your runes

The following guidelines will help you take care of your runes:

- cleanse them regularly with spring water, salt or by smudging
- to empower your runes, leave them outside for 24 hours to let the sun and moonlight energize them
- keep them in a special bag or box, and do not lend them to anyone

A guide to the runes

There are 24 rune symbols, each of which stands for a different letter of the Early Germanic, or Elder Futhark, alphabet. Each of these inscriptions has a divinatory meaning, as well as tree, colour, herb and gemstone associations.

Sign	Name	Meaning	Divinatory meaning	Tree	Colour	Herb/plant	Gemstone
ᚠ	Feoh	Cattle	Spiritual richness	Elder	Light red	Nettle	Moss agate
ᚢ	Ur	Auroch (recently extinct cattle)	Strength in time of change	Birch	Dark green	Sphagnum moss	Carbuncle
ᚦ	Thorn	Thorn	Contemplation before action	Thorn/oak	Bright red	Houseleek	Sapphire
ᚨ	Ansur	A mouth	Messages and new opportunities	Ash	Dark blue	Fly agaric	Emerald
ᚱ	Rad	A cartwheel	The wheel of life, a journey or quest	Oak	Bright red	Mugwort	Chrysoprase
ᚲ	Ken	A torch	Enlightenment and inspiration	Pine	Light red	Cowslip	Bloodstone
ᚷ	Geofu	A gift	A spiritual gift, love and partnership	Ash/elm	Deep blue	Heartsease	Opal
ᚹ	Wynn	Happiness	Success and achievement; balance	Ash	Yellow	Flax	Diamond
ᚺ	Hagall	Hail	Strength to face a challenge	Ash/yew	Light blue	Lily-of-the-valley	Onyx
ᚾ	Nied	Need	Everything is as it should be; your needs are met	Beech	Black	Bistort	Lapis lazuli
ᛁ	Is	Ice	Standstill, preparation before moving on	Alder	Black	Henbane	Cat's eye
ᛃ	Jara	Harvest	Harvest, reward for past effort	Oak	Light blue	Rosemary	Cornelian
ᛇ	Eoh	A yew tree	Transformation; letting go, endings ready for beginnings	Yew	Dark blue	Mandrake	Topaz
ᛈ	Peorth	A dice cup	Choice, taking charge	Beech	Black	Aconite	Aquamarine
ᛉ	Elhaz	An elk	Protection within	Yew	Gold	Angelica	Amethyst
ᛊ	Sigel	The sun	Good fortune	Juniper	White/silver	Mistletoe	Ruby
ᛏ	Tyr	The god Tyr	Initiation	Oak	Bright red	Sage	Coral
ᛒ	Beorc	A birch tree	New beginnings	Birch	Dark green	Lady's mantle	Moonstone
ᛖ	Ehwaz	A horse	Progress	Oak/ash	White	Ragwort	Iceland spar
ᛗ	Mann	A human	Destiny	Holly	Deep red	Madder	Garnet
ᛚ	Lagu	Water, sea	Attunement to creation	Willow	Deep green	Leek	Pearl
ᛜ	Ing	The god Ing	The inner spark	Apple	Yellow	Self-heal	Amber
ᛞ	Daeg	Day	The light	Spruce	Light blue	Clary	Diamond
ᛟ	Othel	A possession	Focus and freedom	Hawthorn	Deep yellow	Clover	Ruby

The three-rune spread

A line of runes is referred to as a "spread", and a three-rune spread is helpful for giving an overall picture of an issue by placing it in its context. It is like a signpost at a crossroads showing where you are, where you have been, and where you can potentially go if you learn the lessons you need to learn. Focus on the situation and pick out three runes from your bag. Lay them one by one in a row, and read them in turn as follows:

1 The past: this provides background to the situation and shows events that led up to it.
2 The present: the issue as experienced now.
3 The future: the most likely developments given 1 and 2.

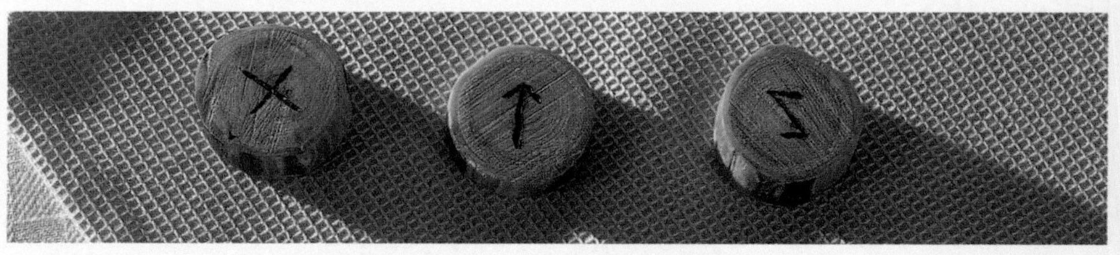

Consulting the Runes

The runes can be used in a variety of ways. A single rune may be picked to give you guidance for the day ahead or to help clarify a problem or issue. The message of a single rune can help bring you back down to earth when you are losing touch with reality, or reassure you about a course of action you have already decided upon, confirming what you already know. You can also draw a rune to honour significant events, such as birthdays, anniversaries, a wedding, or getting a new job, or to celebrate the changing seasons and festivals throughout the year. The most common issues or questions on which people seek guidance, whether from the runes, Tarot, I Ching or any other divinatory method, tend to fall into categories such as love and relationships, work, home and family, health, and general life guidance.

When using the runes for clarification or guidance, avoid asking "closed" questions that demand a "yes/no" answer. Instead, turn the question into an "issue" statement: for instance, the question "should I change my job" becomes "the issue is my job". The runes will never tell you what to do, but what they can do is comment on a situation, giving you a new perspective.

Keeping your issue in mind, focus your thoughts on it while holding your runes. This will send a vibration of your thought-forms into the runes, and then you will unconsciously be attracted to pick out the rune that resonates with you. You can pick a rune directly from the bag or box, or else lay them all face down in front of you and then pick the one you are most drawn to. You may notice your body becomes warmer as you are drawn to the right rune; you will just need to trust that whichever one you pick is right for you for this moment.

Advanced Divination

As well as providing insight into everyday situations, the runes can also be used to give deeper insight to help you on your spiritual path. The following spread is based on the World Tree and is designed to act as a guide to the next stage of your spiritual journey. Similar to the Tree of Life, the World Tree is one of the very oldest and most universal symbols in the world. Known as Yggdrasil in the Norse tradition, its roots are said to connect to the underworld, home nature spirits and elementals, while its upper branches ascend to the sky and the realm of angels, advanced souls and supernatural entities.

Beginning at the base of the tree and working upwards and from left to right, lay the runes out in the correct positions,

Rather than picking the runes one by one from the bag, you might prefer to spread them all out in front of you and then pick the one you are most drawn to.

For guidance for the day ahead, simply pick one rune from the bag.

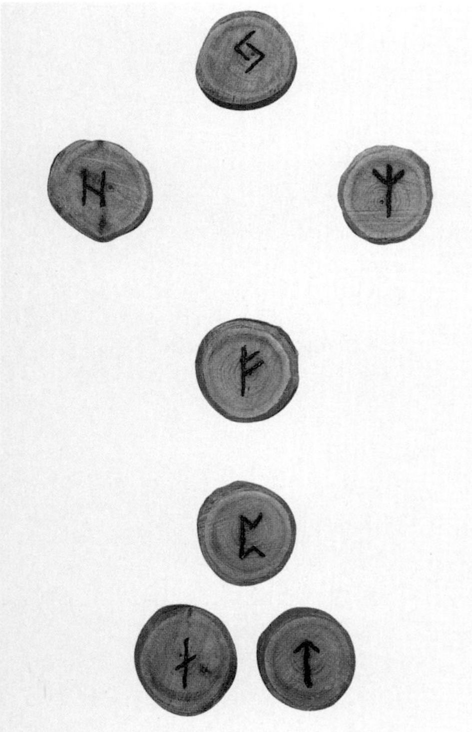

The layout of the World Tree spread of runes.

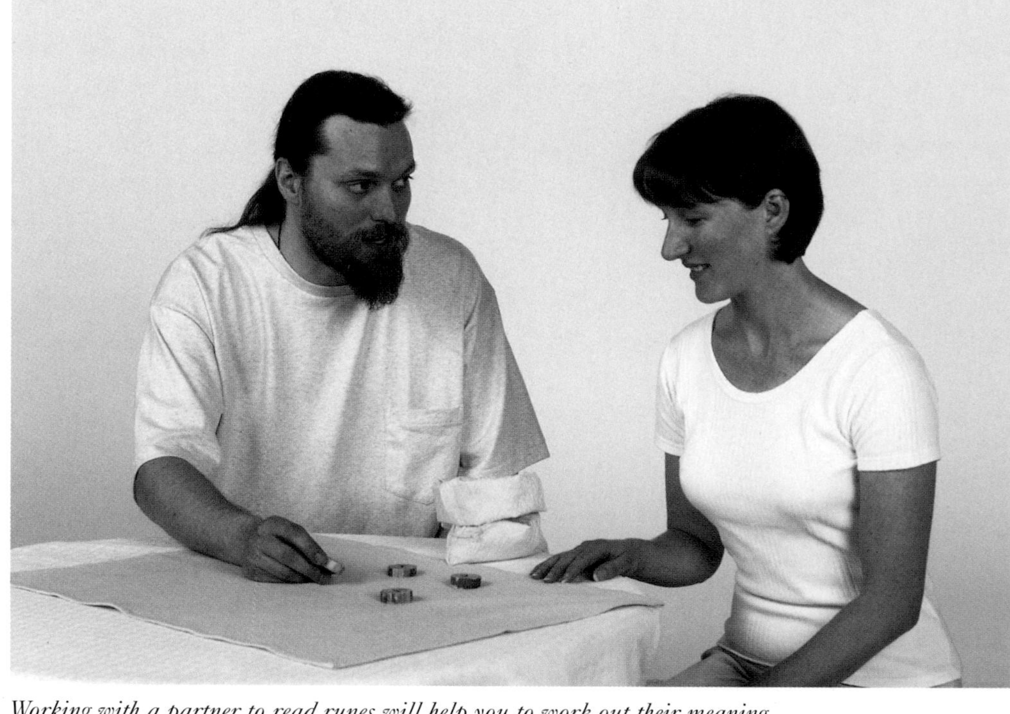

Working with a partner to read runes will help you to work out their meaning.

asking the following questions of the runes as you pick each one:

1 *What do I need to learn?*
2 *What will challenge me?*
3 *What is my guiding rune?*
4 *What power will help me?*
5 *What comes to warn me?*
6 *What do I need to let go of?*
7 *What will be the outcome of learning this lesson?*

Interpreting the Runes

The meaning of a particular rune may change depending on whether it is picked upright or upside down (reversed). This is largely a question of individual preference, and there are many books available with more detailed meanings for each of the runes, including upright and reversed meanings. However, as with any other method of divination, to become adept at interpretation you need to train your intuition. This is the connection to your higher self, the part of your being that knows everything, including your purpose in life and how it can best be achieved. Meditation is one of the best ways for training intuition.

At the beginning of each day, pick out a rune and sit with it quietly in meditation for ten minutes or so. As you go through the day, reflect on its symbol and notice any particular themes or patterns to your day; at the end of the day, you can check the rune's official meaning and see if it relates to your experience. When checking the rune's official meaning, pay attention to any particular passages or words that seem to jump out at you, as these will be the ones that have the most relevance for you at this time. When we look up a meaning, a lot of what is said doesn't seem to apply, but then suddenly we will come across something that strikes a chord and that seems to speak to us directly. This is when divination is at its most powerful.

Creating your own rune set

If you want to get to know the runes, a good way of doing this is by making your own set. The two materials from which runes are commonly made are wood and stone, although other materials such as crystals, glass beads or clay can also be used. If you are using stones, you will need to collect 24 of a similar size. Some of the best stones for rune making can be found on beaches and in streambeds; remember to leave behind an offering in thanks for what you are taking.

For stones: using a fine paintbrush and an acrylic paint in your chosen colour (preferably a neutral, earthtoned shade), paint the runic inscriptions on each stone. When the paint is dry, apply a coat of varnish over the stones to protect the paint. For wood: you will need a long branch. Ask permission from the tree before you cut it. Use a handsaw to cut the branch into 24 slices. Burn the inscriptions into the runes with a soldering iron. Rub over with beeswax to protect the wood.

Making your own runes makes them personal.

Dowsing

Everyone has the ability to dowse and it is a skill that every witch and magician should hone and perfect. Dowsing is essentially the art of asking a "yes/no" question and using the movement of a dowsing device – usually a pendulum or rod – to divine the answer. It is a simple process that connects the rational, intellectual part of ourselves with the intuitive, wise part. It is like a doorway between the mind and spirit, using the body as a threshold. The more respect we bring to our dowsing, the more reliable and effective it will be.

When holding a pendulum, keep your fingers pointed downwards, to allow it to swing freely.

How Dowsing Works

A genuine need to know is a key factor for dowsing to work well. You ask a clear and unambiguous question in your mind, to which the answer can only be "yes" or "no". The second important step is then being able to let go of the question and any emotional attachment to the answer one way or the other, and waiting with a "detached curiosity", or an open mind, for the answer to come back from your inner self.

The most familiar tools that are used in dowsing are the pendulum and L-rods, although other devices such as Y-rods and "bobbers" are also used. The movement of the dowsing tool occurs involuntarily, in the same way as a yawn or a laugh, without your needing to make it happen. But before dowsing can start, you need to establish your personal basic dowsing responses.

Crystal pendulums are widely available and are also very beautiful objects to work with.

Pendulum Responses

Before you begin, you need to establish the pendulum motions that will mean "yes" and "no" for you, as these vary from person to person.

1 Sit in a relaxed, upright position and hold your pendulum in a central position just above the height of your knees. Start swinging it in a to-and-fro motion towards and away from you. This is the "neutral" position and indicates that you are ready to start.

2 Now move your hand over your dominant-side knee (right for right-handers, left for left-handers). State clearly to yourself the following words: *Please show me my "yes" response.*

3 Notice what the pendulum does; it may swing in a clockwise or anti-clockwise direction, or from side to side, or even diagonally. Whatever it does, this is your signal for "yes".

4 Take the pendulum back to the neutral position and move your hand to the other knee. Repeat the procedure as in step 2, this time asking for your "no" response. It should be something clearly different to "yes" and will be your signal for "no".

5 Repeat the exercise several times to become confident and familiar with your responses. After a short period of time, your chosen responses will become automatic and spontaneous and you will be able to dowse with confidence.

Choosing a pendulum

Almost anything that swings freely can be used as a pendulum, but ideally it should be symmetrical and attached to its cord centrally so that it can swing in any direction. Natural materials such as wood, stone, metal or crystal can all work well, but find one that feels right when you pick it up and swing it, or make your own from whatever you feel is appropriate.

Dowsing and Health

There are an infinite number of possible situations in which you can use dowsing, but using it as a tool for information and

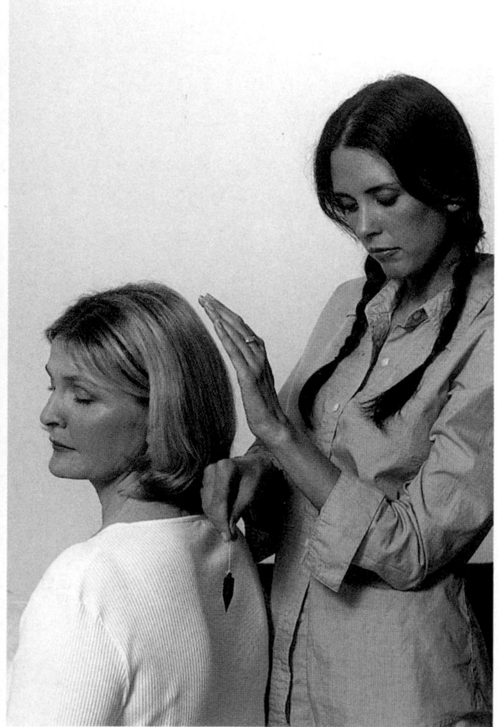

With practice, you can learn to detect problems in specific parts of someone's body.

You can use a pendulum for sensing the energies around a person's aura to judge their health.

guidance around your health is one of its most valuable uses and also one of the best ways to build up experience and confidence. You can experiment with lists of herbs, vitamins, massage oils, Bach flower remedies or forms of treatment with which you have become familiar, so that you can dowse along the list, picking out things to try in a particular case.

You can also dowse for someone else, but you should always get their permission first. Unless you are very experienced and able to hold them in mind as you dowse, it is a good idea to obtain something from them, such as a lock of hair or a ring, to help "link" you to them while you investigate. If they are present, you can ask questions while swinging the pendulum over their hands, or you might feel more confident if they supply the sample and allow you to work on their problem by yourself. Always be sure that you are dealing with an ailment you can handle, and if either of you are in any doubt, seek medical advice.

Typical dowsing responses

This is the kind of pattern of responses that you might establish:
Anti-clockwise for "no"
Towards and away for "neutral"
Clockwise for "yes"
Diagonal to the left for "no"
Diagonal to the right for "yes"

Dowsing the life-force in food

As well as its nutritional properties, our food carries the "life-force", or vital essence. This is most intensely present when the food is at its freshest and diminishes over time. Food that has high life-force tastes better and gives us more nourishment; we may find that we need to eat less of it. You can dowse over your food to assess its vitality, using a scale of 0–10, with 0 being absence of life-force, and 10 being the optimum. As you dowse over the food, ask questions such as "is the vitality of this (say what it is) higher than 5? Higher than 8? Does it have a vitality of 10?" and so on to assess the score. You will find that freshly picked fruit and vegetables have the highest score, while packaged foods and ready-meals will be at the lower end of the scale.

Divining the Land

In magical thinking, etheric energy (known as "chi" in Chinese thought) flows through every energy system, including that of the earth. We can use dowsing to detect energy patterns in nature and to observe the different effects they have on us. We can also use dowsing to repattern chi paths and to bring healing to traumatized environmental energies.

Although you can use your pendulum for dowsing in relation to earth energies, it is often more useful to use another of the basic dowsing tools, the L-rod. So called because of its shape, the L-rod can be constructed from any material, including an ordinary wire coat hanger, cut and bent into shape. You will need a pair of rods, one for each hand. Mostly used for searching for things while the dowser moves around, they can also be used for "yes/no" questions in a sitting or standing position.

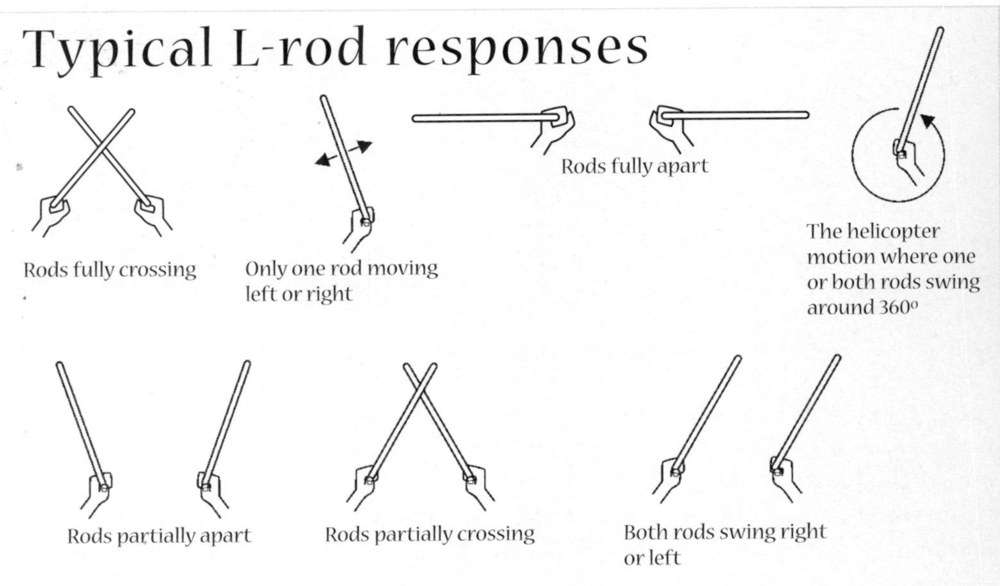

L-rod Responses

To establish your "yes" and "no" responses, stand in a comfortable upright posture, spine straight and shoulders relaxed, and hold the shortest "handle" part of the rods. The rods should be pointing straight out and away from you, parallel with each other. This is the neutral or search position.

Keeping the rods the same distance apart, move them over to the dominant side of your body and ask to be shown your "yes" response. Return to neutral and repeat on your non-dominant side to be shown "no".

Dragon Energies

In traditional Chinese thought, the chi paths of the earth's subtle body are known as dragons. Dragons inhabit every landscape. Typically described as having the body of a serpent, the scales of a fish, wings of a bat and claws of a bird, they symbolize the energy that is present in all animals and throughout nature. Sinuous and mercurial by nature, their energies fluctuate and change with sunrise and sunset, with the waxing and waning of the moon, with the passing of the sun through the seasons and with the deep, quiet cycles of planetary time. The West recognizes its own dragons or energy lines, referred to as ley lines, which form more or less rectilinear grids across the earth. Where ley lines cross are points of power. In addition, there are energy paths for each of the elements of Earth, Air, Fire and Water.

Searching for Dragons

Centre and calm yourself and standing comfortably with your rods in their neutral position, say the following:

I wish to dowse for earth energies; is this timely and appropriate?

To establish your own responses, first hold the rods straight out and away from you, parallel with each other; this is neutral.

Saying in your mind, "please show me my response for yes", move the rods over to the dominant side of your body and note the signal.

Go back to neutral, then to the opposite side of your body, asking for the "no" response. Observe the signal. Test the responses several times.

If the response is "yes", ask:
Please show me any energy paths of significance to my health.

Walk forwards at a slow but steady pace. When you reach the first path, your rods may start to split apart as though meeting something solid like a wall. Once they are completely apart you have arrived at an energy line. Conversely, you may find that the rods cross – this is an equally valid "here it is" sign. You can continue to dowse to find out more about the dragon, such as how big or small it is (some lines are very narrow while others are several metres wide). You can also ask if the line is predominantly yin or yang, and find out how strong it is, using a scale of 0–10. The effect of being in a predominantly yin chi path slows us down, rather like a glass of wine or heavy meal. Predominantly yang chi, on the other hand, acts like coffee, stimulating and speeding us up. These effects increase with the intensity of the etheric field, and are more extreme the more strongly the etheric field is polarized to yin or yang.

Healing Traumatized Energies

Traumatic changes to the surface of the landscape, such as quarrying or excavation or new construction projects, can create stress and trauma in an otherwise healthy energy field. If the chi has been traumatized it is likely that one or more blocked, stagnant or overly stimulated chi paths runs through the space. Let your dowsing guide you to where to work.

Place your hands where your L-rods indicate and visualize yourself channelling healing energy from the divine source, asking that the etheric field receive whatever healing energy that it needs in order to regain a state of health and balance.

At the end of each session, visualize yourself filled with golden light and give thanks for the healing that has occurred.

Dowse intermittently to see if the process is complete. It may take several healing sessions over a period of days, weeks, or even months, the earth's cycles of time being much slower than those of a person.

Repatterning energies

If you find a chi path that is detrimental to your health, you can ask the spirit of place that the energy be repatterned. Remember that the energy itself is neither good nor bad, and that something that may be harmful to us, can be helpful to other species. Repatterning may take hours or days, but once you have begun the process you don't need to stay. You can return to the place every few hours and check with your dowsing to find out when it is complete. You can use a pendulum to do this exercise.

1 Hold your pendulum and begin by checking with the spirit of place if it is timely and appropriate to communicate with it. If the answer is "Yes", continue by saying:
I wish to spend time in this space and need the energy here to be supportive to my health. Are you willing to repattern the energy here to be supportive of my health?
If the spirit of place is not willing, then you might want to ask it to suggest an alternative place where you can work.

2 If the spirit is both willing and able, make a special request almost like a prayer. You may also visualize golden light filling the entire space as you make your request:
I request that the energy in this space be repatterned at this time to be supportive of human health at every level, and that it may remain so for as long as may be the divine will.

3 Once your dowsing indicates that the repatterning has occurred, give thanks to the spirit of place by leaving an offering.

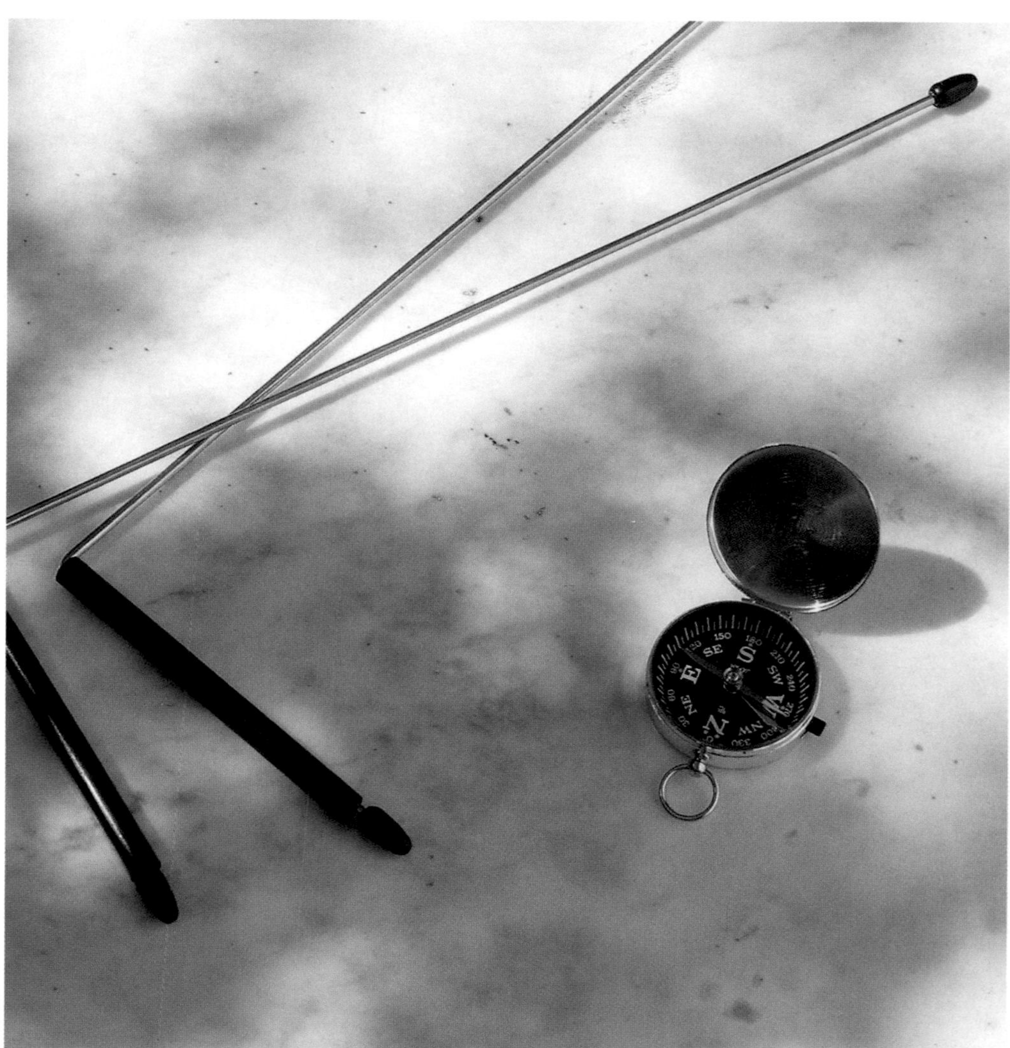

L-rods are probably the most popular and widely used tools for water dowsing.

SCRYING

From the earliest times, people have seen supernatural images in shiny surfaces such as a pool of dark water, a black stone, a concave mirror or a crystal ball set against black velvet. In Tibet, seers sometimes gaze at a wetted thumbnail. The process is called "scrying", which means "perceiving", and it is an art that many magicians aim to master as a way of answering questions about the future. To be able to scry you need to be able to switch off from the distractions of everyday life and enter an altered state of consciousness. It uses the same kind of inner vision as dreams, so you may find that by improving dream recall, scrying gets easier, or conversely if you learn how to scry you will remember your dreams.

FINDING YOUR RELAXED STATE

To improve your success at scrying, it is necessary to be able to enter a deeply relaxed state, so performing this preparatory exercise might help.

Find a time and place where you won't be disturbed for at least half an hour. You will need an upright chair and a notebook and pen for keeping a record – you may wish to use your Book of Shadows or else create another magical diary which you keep for recording your work with dreams and/or visions.

Scrying within a magic circle of candles will protect you from harmful or negative visions.

1 Sit with your feet flat on the floor or on a thick book so that your knees are at a right angle, and find a comfortable relaxed position. Close your eyes.

2 Breathe out fully and then, counting at your own speed, breathe in for a count of four. Hold your breath for a count of four, breathe out for a count of four, then hold your breath out for another count of four.

3 Repeat this entire breathing cycle at least 10 times. If you lose count, it will be necessary to start again from the beginning. You may find this pattern difficult, in which case you can try a slower 10–5–10–5. You can count quickly or slowly or, if you can feel your pulse while sitting in a relaxed position, count that.

4 Focus all your mental attention on breathing slowly and rhythmically, and relaxing physically. Gradually, you will find that this helps you to become calm and focused.

5 Bring your attention to the scrying glass, and gently open your eyes. You are in your relaxed state and ready to begin scrying.

An ordinary picture frame can be turned into a scrying vessel by placing a piece of black paper behind the glass.

Steps to scrying

You can learn to develop your ability to "see" by following these steps.

1 Allow yourself to sink into a relaxed state. Open your eyes to regard the glass, crystal, sphere or other "speculum".

2 Look within the glass, ignoring any reflections or points of light on its surface. Sink within it, forming the question in your mind. In a while, you will find that the glass seems to cloud over, or become dim. Through the mist, a dark patch may appear.

3 You might find yourself sinking into this dark patch, then pictures, signs, numbers, words or other symbols may appear before you. This will probably not happen in the first experiments you perform but will come with practice.

4 Continue for a number of regular sessions and you will gradually master this ancient and very valuable skill.

Learning to Scry

Scrying is not a skill that you can learn automatically. Like riding a bicycle or swimming, there is a knack to it and it takes time, practice and concentration. A common mistake in beginners is that they try too hard, which only creates tension. Rather relax, and you will see words, images, still pictures or actions flitting through your mind's eye, rather like watching a film. The trick is not trying to hold on to what you see, but to let it go.

After a while, you will find that the film slows down and the images or non-visual concepts remain visible long enough for you to study them. Like remembering dreams, you may need to tell yourself what is happening in order to fix it in your longer-term memory, but it does get easier with practice. You may find that it helps to cast a circle around yourself and the table with the scrying vessel (known as the "speculum") on it, or that to light a candle and some sweet incense will bring on a more psychically open state of mind. Really it is a matter for patient experimentation to see what works best.

Trust What You See

In order for scrying to work, there must be no distracting reflections on the surface of the object, so the ambient light where you are working should be soft and diffuse. If a vision is to emerge, the mind and body need to be stilled and calmed by a period of quiet contemplation, with the eyes closed so that residual images fade from the retina.

Once you feel you have reached the right state of mind you are ready to begin to gaze into your scrying object. Gazing into the speculum induces a trance-like state and allows ideas to emerge from the unconscious mind, as they do in dreams. The first impression may be of a mist, which eventually darkens and resolves into colours, shapes, symbols or complete images. Like the images seen in dreams, these are likely to relate to deep-seated issues and offer information that the conscious mind does not have access to. They may seem inexplicable at first, but become relevant later.

Making your own scrying vessel

Real crystal balls are difficult and expensive to obtain, so before you decide whether to get one you can make your own scrying vessel. Use black enamel spray paint to coat the outside of a balloon-shaped wine glass. You may need several coats. Alternatively try scrying in a clear glass bowl of water. You can also make a simple mirror by painting the glass of a picture frame, or as follows, using a sheet of black paper.

1 You will need a picture frame, a piece of black paper and a pair of scissors. Take the frame apart and cut out a piece of black paper to fit. Place the paper in the frame behind the glass and put the frame back together again.

2 Once the frame is properly secured, polish the glass thoroughly with a soft cloth. Your scrying glass is now ready to use.

Crystal balls are closely associated with magical arts, especially the ability to see into the future.

Interpreting visions

Although visions in a scrying vessel can only be interpreted by the individual who sees them, like the symbols perceived in dreams they sometimes seem to represent archetypes that have universal significance. Some visions are simply a mist of colour.

White: good fortune
Yellow: obstacles to come
Orange: troubled emotions, anger
Red: danger
Blue: business success
Green: health and happiness
Grey/dark: misfortune
Rising clouds: affirmative
Sinking clouds: negative
Far-off visions: the distant past or future
Foreground visions: the present or near future

DEVELOPING THE SUPER SENSES

From ancient times, every worker of magic has made use of psychic abilities of one kind or another. Some of these are immediately available, inherited perhaps as a gift from the gods, from ancestors, or from past lives; others may be less accessible, but can be developed just like any other skill. Most magical training is aimed at working with these "super senses", but it will require commitment, dedication and hard work.

The ability to enter an altered state at will is probably the most important key to developing psychic abilities. Meditation and creative visualization are two of the most powerful tools in this respect and this chapter begins with a variety of techniques designed to develop these skills. This is followed by information on psychic training using games and experiments to develop telepathy and intuition, as well as how to sense auras and chakras. Astral travel and dreamworlds – including information on dream control and lucid dreaming – are also included, as well as how to journey to the otherworld and inner planes. Through psychic powers it is possible to meet spirit guides, teachers and angelic beings, while exploring past lives can provide many valuable insights into your current situation here on the Earth plane.

MEDITATION

Psychic ability may be seen as the gift of the Goddess, the great Earth Mother. A heightened sensitivity to the unseen relies on a strong intuitive sense that we can develop through cultivating a strong relationship with the Goddess or "feminine" aspect of ourselves. For men and women alike, this means learning to trust our body sensations and having a "felt sense" that is accurate and reliable. To be able to do this we need to be as relaxed and free in body, mind and spirit as possible. Meditation is one of the best ways of achieving this; it helps to ground and centre us in the root of our being and opens up the doorway to the otherworld.

Burning white sage before you begin to meditate clears the head and promotes insight.

THE POWER OF MEDITATION

Many ancient religions and many cultures in both East and West have practised the art of meditation, and today we have a huge variety of techniques at our disposal – some active, some passive. What is important is to find a method that works for you and to practise it regularly; over time, you will be able to "switch off" from everyday concerns and enter an altered state more readily, while along the way you will be developing an increased sensitivity, heightened perception and intuitive awareness.

Essentially, meditation is the quality of awareness that we bring to an act. It is about raising our levels of consciousness so that we are aware of our activity and of any thoughts and emotions that we are experiencing in the moment as we do it. In which case, any act can become a meditation; if you enjoy walking for instance, you can make this activity your meditation. Instead of hurriedly rushing to be somewhere, slow down and take the time to feel your feet connect with the earth as you take each step. If you enjoy dancing or jogging, you can also make this your meditation, allowing yourself to relax ever more deeply into your body's natural rhythm and movement.

Active meditations such as these are particularly helpful when you are feeling stressed and find it difficult to sit still

Meditation is the best gateway to inner wisdom, opening you up to previously unknown dimensions.

Going in

Meditation is a way of 'going in' to meet yourself. As everyday concerns begin to fade and your conscious mind quietens, the deeper more subtle senses begin to awake and inform your conscious awareness. Unless you can withdraw from the everyday world for a few minutes each day, there is no way that these inner forces can develop.

The three "S's" for meditation

56

Follow this checklist of the "three S's" – Stillness, Silence and Sensitivity – to help make meditation easier.

Stillness. If you sit relaxed and completely still, this helps you to drift into the poised state of awareness where inner material can begin to flow. As soon as you start to wriggle about, or become aware that you are not comfortable, you will break the stream of concentration.

Silence. Don't be tempted to use background music to blot out noises in the environment. It is far better to find a quiet time of day and learn to create inner silence. This matters because as well as seeing images many people also hear sounds, and any music will make this much harder. The more you focus inward and allow any images or feelings to surface, the less you will be distracted.

Sensitivity. You need to listen, watch and perceive whatever images, sounds, symbols or other sensations start to occur in your mind. These will be vague and fleeting to begin with, but the more physically and mentally still you become, and the quieter the background noises are, the sharper your own awareness will be.

and relax; they help to "burn off" your outer layers of energy and bring you back into contact with your inner self.

Letting Go

Meditation teaches us to relax and let go of everyday concerns as we move into deeper levels of our being. It is from these deeper places in ourselves that we are able to experience our connection with the universe; the more deeply we can let go, the more powerful our experience of the hidden realm and cosmic oneness. Many meditation techniques are based on passive "non-doing" states. Bringing awareness to the breath is a good way of bringing attention into the here and now, using each out breath to relax a little more deeply. Many meditation practices involve working with the breath in a sitting or lying down position, as the mind and body can most easily unwind in these positions.

Active and Passive Meditation

Active meditations can include dance, walking, jogging or any day-to-day activity, providing it is performed with conscious awareness. With a modern sedentary lifestyle, there are many advantages of using active meditation methods. They help to burn off excess energy, which if it is not used, has a tendency to produce an imbalance in the mental body, making it much harder to quieten the mind. They also help to move energy through the body's subtle energy system. Passive meditations usually involve sitting or lying down in a comfortable position and letting go of tensions held in the mind or body through focusing on the breath.

Embracing Darkness

From a seed that sprouts in the soil to a child growing in the womb, all life begins in the dark. The darkness is a place of mystery and tremendous power; it is the realm of the Goddess and is associated with the "feminine" creative force. In modern society, we have become afraid of darkness and have created many sources of light to help us escape from it; but being able to embrace darkness is a necessary part of life. It is also essential if we are to develop as a worker of magic and to feel comfortable entering the otherworld, itself a place of mystery.

A Darkness Meditation

This guided meditation is a good way of connecting with the beneficial power of darkness; it may be a little tricky to master at first, but with practice it does get easier. It is best done in the evening.

Using the flame of a candle to help your mind to focus is a good meditation technique.

1 Sit in a relaxed, upright position in a darkened room. The darker it is, the better, with no chinks of light coming in through the curtains or under the door. Breathe gently and, keeping your eyes open, stare into the blackness. Feeling at ease, imagine the darkness that is all around you entering your open eyes. It should give you a deep, soothing feeling.

2 At this point, you may like to close your eyes and imagine yourself disappearing into the darkness, just as a shooting star disappears in the rich dark of the night sky. Feel yourself being absorbed, so that just for this moment in time, you don't have to be or do anything. Allow yourself to fully experience the deep relaxation of letting go.

3 Come out of the meditation slowly, lighting a candle to allow your eyes to get used to the light, before you turn on electric light or allow daylight in.

4 As you go about your usual activities following the meditation, imagine that you are carrying a patch of this darkness within you; silent, deep and relaxed. If you do the darkness meditation before bed, try and carry this patch of dark silence with you into sleep.

THE MIND'S EYE

Perhaps the most powerful tool of any witch or magician is their mind. It is estimated that we use only a tiny percentage of our mental powers, leaving vast reservoirs untapped. Learning to train and use the mind is one of the most basic yet far-reaching skills of any magic worker. The ability to exert control over our thoughts and to direct the focus of our attention is a necessary prerequisite for successful magic; it is also how we can develop the extraordinary powers of the mind to travel in space and time. One of the best ways of doing this is through the faculty of imagination. This is because the imagination deals in pictures, not words, and can influence the unconscious mind on a much deeper level.

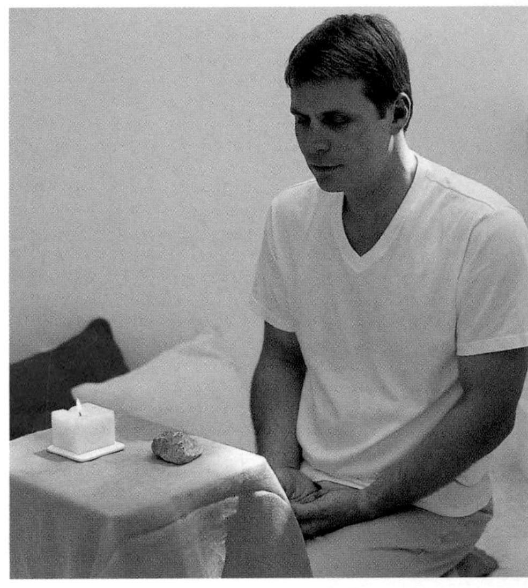

Meditating with lapis lazuli helps promote a lively silence, and aids thought processes.

THE IMAGINATION

The words imagination and magic share the same root. To imagine is to allow our thoughts to wander freely and conjure up pictures or concepts that are not actually present but seen in the mind's eye as though they are – and the more vivid our imagination, the more real these things seem. Imagination can be seen as the ability of the mind to be creative or resourceful. William Wordsworth, the eighteenth-century English poet, described it as "another name for absolute power and clearest insight".

A vivid imagination, directed by magical training, is the most effective tool we have for changing the world from within, yet for most of us it is something that has lain dormant since childhood. Creative visualization is a way of accessing and training the imagination and beginning to harness its power.

Using creative visualization

Creative visualization can be used in many areas of life, including personal relationships and health and business situations, as well as to improve memory, overcome problems and counter negative thinking. It is also one of the most powerful tools for developing psychic abilities.

A grounding visualization is helpful whenever you feel unconnected to reality, or to the natural world. Sit in front of a green candle on a wooden table to represent the earth.

Creative Visualization

Essentially, creative visualization uses the power of the mind to consciously create pictures at will. For instance, if you are sick, you could use creative visualization to imagine or see yourself healthy and well; this is much more effective than simply using positive thinking, although accompanying a visualization with a positive thought or affirmation increases its power. Techniques similar to creative visualization have been used for centuries in some parts of the world to heal or prevent disease, although it can be used for any aspect of life.

For instance, creative visualization is a good technique to use for grounding and protection. When developing your mental powers it is particularly important to take care of yourself. Being grounded (or "earthed") is essential; a lack of grounding makes you unable to channel higher energies successfully. You can become overwhelmed by extra-sensory perceptions and get swept away. Similarly it is also a good idea to learn how to protect yourself so that you don't become drained or tired, or else vulnerable to negative energies.

Holding a grounding stone can reduce feelings of confusion and anxiety.

Grounding Visualization

Practise the following grounding visualization before undertaking any work on the mental plane. It will help to connect you with the natural world and to focus, stabilize and renew your positive energies. To do it, you will need a green candle and a dark stone, such as black onyx or smoky quartz.

1 Light the candle and sit on the floor in front of it, or else sit on a chair with your feet on the ground. This is to connect you with the earth. Take the stone in both hands.

2 Breathing slowly and deeply, visualize the roots of a tree gradually growing down into the earth. Think of the strength of numerous small roots, locking themselves into the fertile soil, anchoring the tree firmly and working silently down towards the earth's core. See yourself connecting with the earth.

3 Concentrate on your out-breaths and with each one, feel the energy flowing downward through your body into the ground. You can also see it as a stream of light, passing through you and "earthing" through the soles of your feet. Become aware of the constant, sustaining strength that lies beneath you, supporting you.

4 Now on each in-breath, feel the earth's strength flowing back into you. Picture it as a green energy flowing up through the roots of the tree into the trunk and branches that is your body. Visualize its power flowing into you until you feel calm and centred. When you feel you have come to the end of the visualization, release the stone.

Stones for grounding

Black onyx: protection against negative energy, good for emotional stability; encourages connection to material goals and their achievement

Black tourmaline: grounding and protective, absorbs negativity

Haematite: banishes fuzziness and aids concentration, memory and self-discipline; self-healing

Jet: grounding, earth power; wards off nightmares and avoids ill-health

Obsidian: very powerful grounding crystal; dissolves anger and fear; snowflake obsidian has a softer effect, restores balance and clarity

Smoky quartz: lightly grounding and balancing, counteracts hyperactivity, fosters self-acceptance and awareness of divine protection

Psychic training

You may already have found that your magical interests have led to your getting "hunches" about doing, or not doing, certain things, or that hints and clues are found in dreams, or that you actually perceive future events clearly in meditations or during divination sessions. Gradually, these psychic impressions will become clearer and easier to interpret, especially if you are able to devote some time to learning which skills you already have, and which need to be rehearsed. There are many simple techniques that you can practise to train your psychic abilities, but it is important that you work at a level and pace that feels comfortable for you; too much progress too quickly could make you feel overwhelmed by your ability to pick up impressions from the otherworld.

The human mind can be trained to realize its full psychic potential.

Psychic Games

Some of the most valuable training techniques are psychic "games" which you can experiment and have fun with. It is worth trying some experiments in extra-sensory perception (ESP), psychokinesis (PK, affecting material objects by "mind power"), and expanding psychic awareness. You and your magical companions, or perhaps a slightly wider group of your friends and family, for example, can get together to try out skills such as telepathy (conveying information from one mind to another), precognition or clairvoyance (guessing which card, for example, will be turned up next), or retrocognition (listing the order of an already shuffled pack of cards).

If you have a pack of ordinary playing cards, you can begin some simple tests. Get someone to spread out the playing cards face down on a table and shuffle them very thoroughly, and then give you the whole deck, face down. You then take this pack and, picking the cards up one at a time, still face down, try to guess, imagine or see what colour each one is. Place each card in turn, still face down, on one of two heaps, representing black and red. If you get stuck with some cards, make another heap and go back to them at the end. When you have reached the end of the pack, turn over the heaps and see what has happened. You might be surprised how many you get right first go! Let a companion have a turn and see if they do better or worse.

Zener Cards

To test a psychic's powers of telepathy, a popular research tool used by parapsychologists is a pack of "zener cards". Designed by J.B. Rhine, a Harvard biologist, in the 1920s, each pack consists of 25 cards depicting five different symbols: a circle, a cross, a square, a five-pointed star and three wavy lines. Each symbol appears on five cards, and is boldly printed against a

Use packs of cards to work on your psychic skills. Innate powers of telepathy, precognition and retrocognition can all be improved on with practice and training.

white or plain-coloured background. In a typical experiment, the cards are shuffled and turned over one by one by a "sender", who then concentrates on the image for a minute or so while the "percipient" (the person who is trying to pick up the image telepathically) tries to identify each card by drawing or saying whichever image comes into his or her head. Sometimes the sender and the percipient are in separate buildings, and the test is repeated several times, with the deck shuffled each time, to reduce the possibility of a chance good result. If you come across zener cards you might like to try some experiments yourself; alternatively it would be relatively simple to make your own deck.

It is important to discuss your results together, as the images you receive telepathically might not always be identical to what was being transmitted.

Psychic Tarot

Another experiment, which may be more interesting to magicians, uses Tarot cards. There are layers of interpretation attached to every Tarot card, which may be contradictory, depending on which of the 500 or so Tarot decks you are using. In other words, your view of the cards may be linked to the symbolism of the card, or to your own or a more traditional interpretation.

Place a pack face down across the floor or a large table and stir the cards about. The experimenter then picks up a card and, without seeing the picture, tries to name it, or describe the feelings, symbols or meaning of the card to a partner. Then both of you look at the card and see if any of it fits. Often, because the experimenter gets immediate feedback, by seeing the card after they have guessed, they will get better, more accurate impressions. This "game" has the added advantage of helping you to form telepathic links with your partner, as well as possibly discovering deeper levels of meaning to the Tarot. You could also try this with runes.

Psychic experiments

Parapsychologists, working in laboratories with carefully selected subjects and using well-tested methods under strictly controlled conditions, have found that new subjects often score higher than those who have tried, and become bored with, card guessing, or attempts at bending metal. It has also been found that a relaxed frame of mind is a help to "remote viewing" (astral travel to the magician).

Taking Your Skills up a Level

Later on, you may be able to send each other messages at a distance. For instance, you could agree with a friend that at a certain time you will "send" them a thought form which they should try and "tune in" to. To begin with, think of something relatively straightforward, such as a colour, shape or number, or you could try a feeling, such as calm, upset, happy and so on. With practice, you might be able to make the information more complex. For instance, you could try sending a number and a suit of playing or Tarot cards that would include a message, derived from the interpretation of that card or cards.

Find out what sorts of information you can pass from mind to mind and use your imagination to invent experiments to try. Each will help awaken, strengthen and control your psychic faculties.

Picture Postcards

Start making a collection of picture postcards that contain clear images or graphic designs that you can use for telepathic experiments. The sender picks a card and tries to convey the illustration to the receiver in another room, who will attempt to draw or describe what they see.

When you are receiving telepathically, you need to be able to enter a relaxed and meditative state, allowing your mind to empty, so that the message can be clearly seen on the "blank screen" of your mind. Although it is not easy to draw exactly the same picture, receptive people should get some aspect of the design, or indicate the feeling of the sender's mind. For example, if the card showed yachts sailing on a calm sea, with birds flying above, the receiver might draw triangles and say it felt windy, or sunny, or that there was a feeling of swaying, etc. Sometimes the emotion of a picture of lovers, or the scent of a flower, or the speed of racing cars can be sent more easily than the actual shapes, colours or minor details of the design. Another technique is to allow the receiver to try to recognize the target card from a selection of the cards. Record your results and see how you improve.

Sensing Auras

An aura is an emanation of the subtle, non-physical energies that infuse and surround every living thing in creation. In magical thinking, this includes rocks and stones, as well as trees, plants, animals and human beings. An aura is like an invisible extension of the physical form and through psychic development it is possible to be able to see or to sense it. This ability can be used to "read" what is going on for a person on a mental, emotional and spiritual level, and for the purposes of healing and rebalancing energies.

The Three Layers of an Aura

Auras are a form of radiant energy that we can learn to detect. Many psychics see them as a halo of energy that has three distinct layers. These layers extend for about 30 cm (1 ft) from the human body, although the greater a person's spiritual vitality, the bigger their auric field. The inner etheric is easily visible to ordinary eyesight in a dimly lit room as a smoky band outlining the figure, and is seen best against naked flesh. Beyond that is a wider band of the astral health region, seen as faint-coloured filaments, such as you sometimes see around power lines on misty days. Outside that is an even fainter layer, the very fine threads of the emotional aura, which connects to all the people, places and objects with which you have any link.

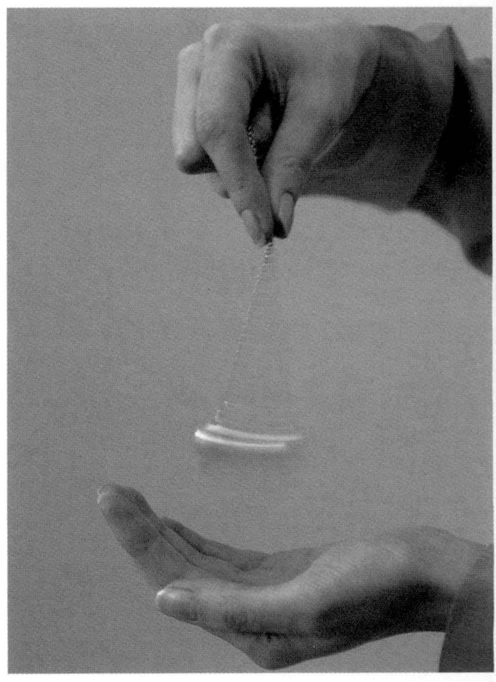

Before you use a pendulum to discover a person's aura, make sure you have established your yes and no responses.

A pendulum is a useful tool to help you sense the condition of a person's aura. You can ask specific questions, as with other kinds of dowsing.

Measuring an Aura

One of the easiest ways of discovering the extent of a person's aura is with a pendulum. Start about 10 m (30 ft) away from them and walk towards them, stopping every pace and testing by asking the question "Does the aura reach here?" and waiting for the "yes/no" response. It is also possible to use your hands to sense an aura. Approach the person very slowly with your hands stretched out, and notice any changes to your body sensations. Your hands may become warm or tingle, or you may "feel" their energy field as a springy "ball" that you can push up against. You will have to trust your intuition.

Seeing Auras

It is also useful to be able to see auras, and this is a skill that can be learned with patience. Ideally, you should have your subject standing in front of a plain, pale surface and ask them to sway slightly from side to side while you stand about 5 m (15 ft) away, looking at the body's outline. After a while, you will see a light colour that moves as they do. With practice over a number of sessions, you will start to be aware of layers of lighter or deeper tone surrounding them. This is usually a series of bands, starting close to their body with the etheric, which is a dense, pale, smoke-coloured layer a few centimetres wide. Beyond that, stretching some distance, are a number of bands of what you will come to see as varied shades, going all around their outline, and in front of them too. You can try half-closing your eyes so that you are seeing through your eyelashes – some people find this helps. The aura is constructed of rays of light, to get an idea of what it looks like, try squinting at a candle flame. You may well see a kind of radiating rainbow of light around the centre. This is what an aura looks like, and it is a matter of time and practice before you can identify the bands, and eventually the separate colours. Some of these are beyond normal vision and may be hard to name or identify.

Interpreting Auras

There are numerous books on interpreting the colours of auras, as to state of health, mood and so on, but remember that you are also looking through your own aura so the colours are a combination and may seem murky. You can see your own aura by standing naked in front of a mirror in a dimly lit room, and gazing softly at your reflection. The colours of the outer aura will be changing all the time, varying with emotion, hunger and temper, as well as our general state of health, and concentration on other people, which will brighten the filaments of auric material by which we are linked. Each individual's aura is different, and interpreting an aura's health is dependent upon the individual and the intuition of the viewer.

It may well be that it is along these delicate threads that the shared thoughts of telepathy flow; when you are psychometrizing an object (sensing its history), the impressions you receive are obtained from the same source.

Sensing Chakras

Within everyone's aura are the chakras, a series of seven energy centres that run right through us. The base, or 1st, chakra is red and centred in the sexual region. It rules raw emotion. Next, is an orange sphere in the belly (the 2nd chakra), dealing with absorption and elimination, both physically and psychically. Above that at the solar plexus is a golden yellow chakra (3rd), our Sun and self centre. In the chest is the emerald green heart chakra (4th), for love and harmony. At the throat is a brilliant blue flower of living light (5th chakra), our power of communication and speech. At the forehead is a violet purple chakra (6th), linking to our intelligence and wisdom. At the top of the head is a brilliant white chakra of light (7th), which connects us to the Creative Spirit, through which spiritual feelings flow in and out.

You can use a pendulum on a partner to detect the vitality of each of their chakras; you can also tune in using your hands, in a similar way, to detecting the auric field.

Psychometry

Literally meaning "soul measurement", psychometry involves holding a physical object, such as a ring, a sealed letter, or a piece of clothing, and attempting to "pick up" something of its history and the emotions of those who have handled it (by psychic means). This is because everything we touch is linked to us through our auric field; by tuning in to this, it is possible to "read" information that relates to an individual's life. One of the most renowned psychics of the twentieth century, Eileen Garrett (1893-1970), is reported to have used psychometry to trace the whereabouts of a missing man by holding a piece of his shirt and tuning in to her impressions.

Meditating on a candle flame can help to open your inner vision and make it easier for you to see auras.

Astral travel

The starry, or astral, plane is thought to be another layer of reality that is separate from the everyday world that we inhabit during our waking lives. Many people believe the astral plane is the realm of dreams, while the astral body, which includes your aura, is thought to be able to leave the physical body and visit other locations. Those who walk the paths of witchcraft and magic teach themselves consciously to enter the astral planes and bring back information or power. Although some dreams may be thought of as astral travel – particularly those that involve flying – being able to travel at will rather than by accident is a skill that can be learned through meditation and visualization. This is also known as astral projection.

It is possible to teach your mind to travel to other worlds, leaving your body behind.

Leaving the Body

Meditation is a doorway to the inner landscapes and guided meditation, creative visualization and pathworking all teach the astral traveller how to shift from the outer, mundane level of awareness to the inner, and return safely with a full awareness of what has been observed. This does take practice, however, and you are unlikely to be able to travel if you do not have a regular meditation practice. Before attempting to travel, you need to get comfortable with moving in and out of your body.

As you enter meditation, visualize yourself splitting into two: in your mind's eye, see the physical you that is sitting in meditation, and your astral or auric body as a shadow or outline, separating from your physical body, but connected to it with an "umbilical cord" of white light. You may start to feel floaty or light-headed (this is why it is important to be well-grounded before attempting this sort of work); you may even find yourself being able to look down on or at your physical body and having what is known as an "out of body" experience.

Learning From a Teacher

Out-of-body techniques are probably best learnt from someone who has a lot of experience of this work. Mastering the techniques can take years of practice and you have to have the passion to really want to do it. Some people don't like the feeling of loss of control that goes with out-of-body travel, so it is important to work within your own limits of what feels comfortable and safe for you.

Meditation is the doorway to astral travel. Burning incense will help you to achieve the mental state necessary for your journey.

Concentrating on the flame of a candle will help to focus your mind during meditation.

Flying witches

It is quite possible that the stereotype of a witch flying across the night sky on her broomstick actually came about as a result of reports of mind travel and out-of-body experiences. These in turn are linked with traditional shamanic practices such as shape-shifting and journeying between the worlds.

The inspiration for inner journeys can be provided by a magical companion, who can lead the traveller onwards, and then bring them safely back.

The Collective Unconscious

Influenced by Jungian depth psychology, some esotericists believe that the astral realms are not outside of us but lie deep within the collective unconscious, the primordial part of the mind that is universal and where archetypal themes and symbols reside. The astral plane, it is argued, is the realm of feelings and emotions and its forms reflect the beliefs of every human being who has ever lived. Hence it is a land of demons and angels, dragons and unicorns, and all the saints and sinners, heavens and hells, and gods and devils of myth and legend.

Making an Astral Journey

Like many of the other aspects of magic, you will need a quiet time and place. If you are intent on going into the astral levels you will also need a companion for basic guidance to share your visions with and help clarify their meaning.

1 Clear a physical and mental space, set up a basic circle and sphere of light around yourself and, having chosen a simple aim, say:
I wish to travel to the astral realms in order to discover….

2 Sit with your companion nearby. Your friend could speak a narrative leading you to the kind of place in which you imagine what you seek would exist. You have to find the landscape, which really already exists on the astral plane. Look on it as another continent or a different dimension of space. Acknowledge that it is real, and that, unlike some images you make, you can't change what you see.

3 Once you have seen the surroundings, which may be sufficient for one day, come back to normal awareness, report to your friend, and close your circle.

4 A second attempt will require a different exercise. Here you need to create your protective circle, but instead of setting off into the other dimension, begin to construct an image of your own body, perhaps dressed in the costume of the astral realm, standing before you, but facing away. In other words, see your own back in front of you. Work on this until you are really able to see it.

5 Once you have built your own figure, you need to transfer your awareness to it, by a kind of mental leap. This immediately puts many people back to themselves, but with gentle effort you can succeed. You then need to transfer to your "astral self" and insert that self into the inner surroundings so that you can meet your hero or Goddess. For this you may need help from your companion, who will describe the setting when you have indicated that you are in your astral body. What you will experience there is completely real but it has a different look or feel to "real life". With practice over a number of short sessions, most people find that they can do this if they don't force it. A few short sessions of half an hour are far better than a prolonged attempt lasting hours.

Bilocation

The ability to be in two places at the same time is known as "bilocation". Essentially a double of you (the astral body) can go out into the world and allow you to see what is going on while you remain going about your daily affairs. To do this, you enter a state of deep meditation and envision a filmy image of yourself leaving your body behind. Bilocation is a very advanced technique and usually takes many years of practice before it can be mastered.

DREAMWORLDS

To dream is to move beyond the bounds of everyday reality and to enter the dreamworlds. This is a place where anything can happen – a magical world of limitless possibilities, where the dreamer can fly, shape-shift, walk through solid objects or swim in the sun. And, especially while the dream is going on, it is every bit as real as the common reality that we all share in our day-to-day existence. Magical thinking recognizes the validity of these other worlds and even suggests that our everyday world could be the "dreamscape" of some other dimension of reality. Being able to work with dreams is an invaluable skill for workers of magic: it develops intuition, heightens sensitivity to otherworldly experiences, and increases self-awareness and personal power.

Dreamscapes have an otherworldly quality to them, with a special, magical atmosphere.

The Dreaming Tradition

Whether or not we can remember our dreams, dreaming is something that we all do every night. Through the ages, workers of magic have always valued dreams and taken them seriously. Dreams have been regarded as messages from the gods and used as oracles to predict the future. They have also been attributed with the power to solve problems, heal sickness and bring spiritual revelation, and shamans and priests, wise women and sages have all acted as dream interpreters.

In magic, a dream is often seen as a way for the spirit self to communicate with the physical body, relaying information in allegorical frames that relate to the dreamer's life and experiences. This has an analogy with modern depth psychology, where dreams are widely believed to contain messages from the unconscious mind; in this context, dreams can be used to work out personal problems as well as a tool for emotional and spiritual growth.

Prepare to Dream

Throughout the ancient world, "dream incubation" was widely practised at holy sites and shrines, many of them dedicated to the gods and goddesses of sleep and dreaming. This was an

Herbs, incense and oils for dreaming

Certain plants are conducive to relaxation, dreams and visions. You can use them fresh or dried, burn them as incense, or vaporize them as essential oils. You could also try making a dream pillow, using a mix of some of your favourite ones.

- Frankincense
- Sandalwood
- Agarwood (aloes)
- Dream herb (zacatechichi)
- Nutmeg
- Valerian
- Hops
- Passion flower

We can nurture the dreaming process through using herbs and oils that prepare body and mind for a restful night's sleep.

intensely ritualistic procedure designed to encourage an especially informative dream from the gods on a variety of issues – from everyday matters to omens and portents for the future. When you want to "incubate" a dream, it is important to put yourself in the right frame of mind before you go to sleep. This means using the evening as a time to relax and let the cares of the day float away as you reconnect with your inner self. Taking a leisurely bath with oils and/or herbs, burning incense, and practising meditation before going to sleep are all helpful.

Dream Recall

By their very nature, dreams are elusive and have an annoying habit of slipping away from the wakening mind very easily. Keeping a dream diary is one of the best ways to help with dream recall. Dedicate a special book or folder as your dream journal – you could use your Book of Shadows if you wish – and get into the habit of recording your dreams. Dreams can offer valuable insights into life situations, and keeping a record not only gives you material to work with, but sends a message to your subconscious mind that you are interested and wish to remember your dreams. Keep the book and a pen by your bed so that you can write the dreams down the moment you wake up, even if this is in the middle of the night. Don't worry about it making sense, and even if you can only remember a fragment, this can be enough to work with.

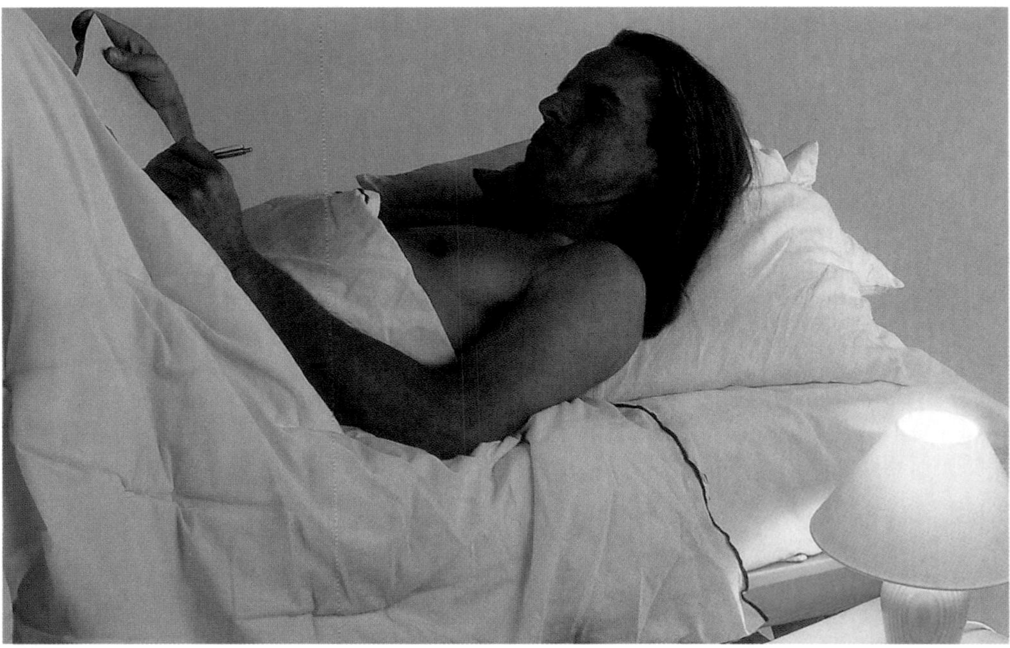

Record your dreams in a dream diary. You will need to write them down as soon as you wake up, even if that is in the middle of the night.

Dream catchers

The "dream catcher" charm is a traditional Native American Indian device for capturing good, wise dreams and for letting the bad ones pass through it and into the night. It has a single thread that is wound in a spiral from the outside to the centre, symbolizing the journey from the waking world to the world of dreams. The native Americans believe that their dreaming selves pass through the heart of the dream catcher and return with knowledge of the dreams of their true selves.

Making a dream catcher

Dream catchers are available ready-made but it is also possible to make your own. A dream catcher is a very personal thing and making one gives you plenty of scope to design it in a way that says something about you.

You will need

a thin bendy stick about 60 cm (2 ft) long
twine, such as fishing line, or strong cotton thread
coloured ribbon
knife
beads
feathers

1 Curl the stick into a circle and fasten it with twine wrapped around. Some people like to cover the whole of the wood in ribbon before they start, but it is up to you. Cut off any sharp ends of wood at the join and wrap some ribbon around it.

2 Tie one end of a length of twine on to any point on the circle and thread it across ¼ of the circle. Tie it onto the circle and cut off the long end.

3 Come back towards your starting point and tie another cross-twine across the circle. Repeat this four times until you have four lengths going around the circle.

4 From the centre of each of these tie one twine to each of the other three. This gives you a sort of "cat's cradle" effect. Experiment until you have a pleasing criss-cross of lines resembling a spider's web. An alternative way to do this is to use a single length of twine, but this might take some practice before you succeed.

5 Add a bead in the centre of the web to represent the spider.

6 Finish by decorating the dream catcher with some ribbons hanging from the bottom of the circle. Add some feathers and beads to these downward-hanging ribbons.

Learning to lucid dream

The most important key to learning how to generate lucid dreams is your level of motivation. The second is being adept at recalling your dreams, which comes through practice. However, the following techniques may also be used to encourage lucidity.

pre-sleep suggestion: as you drift into sleep, repeat a request or statement in your mind about becoming lucid in your dreams.

periodic questioning: develop a "critical-reflective attitude" to your state of consciousness while awake, asking yourself "could I be dreaming now?" through the day.

rehearse dreaming: sit down and pretend that you are dreaming. Use your imagination to create a dream.

if this were a dream: several times a day, stop and ask yourself "if this experience were a dream, what would it mean?"

meditation: practice your ability to meditate; people who regularly practise meditation seem to have more lucid dreams.

dream groups: it is possible to join up with other people who are interested in exploring their dreams. People with a regular forum in which to discuss their dreams tend to become regular lucid dreamers.

Interpreting Dreams

There are many dream dictionaries and interpretative guides to dreams, yet ultimately the best expert on your dreams is you. One way of unlocking the meaning of a dream is to decode its symbolism. Traditionally, certain symbols (such as an animal, a building, fire and so on) are associated with certain meanings, but it is probably best to ask yourself what a particular symbol means for you: dreaming of water, for instance, may mean quite different things to two different people. Another way to start to understand your dreams is to ask yourself how you feel when you first wake up: are you happy or sad, angry or fearful? Notice if this feeling is connected with your dream. You could also ask questions of whoever or whatever is in the dream and let that "part" speak to you.

Replaying Dreams

It is very useful to be able to replay your dream again later when you are relaxed and awake as you may gain fresh insights. You can also interact with dream characters and landscapes to try to find out more information; for instance, you could ask the characters and even the places involved: "Who are you? Why are you here? What are you telling me? Why am I here?" Go with the first answer that comes to mind but don't accept "No". A character may run away, or try to frighten you, but don't be intimidated, follow them – they will lead you to an answer.

One way of becoming more at home in your dreamworld is to replay your dreams when you are awake.

Changing Dreams

Because all worlds are dreamscapes, the ability to change or direct a dream means that we can decide how we would like events to turn out, rather than letting things "just happen" to us by chance. Usually, the dreams that we want to change are ones that cause fear, pain or anger, and by taking control over them in the dreamworld, we are affirming our strength here, in this physical world.

When changing a dream, don't try to force things to happen, just let your intuition flow and allow your creativity to

Consider every aspect of your dream, noticing figures, landscapes and any symbols.

If you dream of falling, and wake up before impact, revisit the dream and control its ending.

Your dreams are about you

Usually the main characters and events in a dream represent various aspects of yourself. For example, disturbing dreams – perhaps involving death or violence of some kind – are not necessarily portents that some harm is about to befall the characters involved. Rather, the injured parties represent aspects of yourself that are being harmed, perhaps by not being allowed their full expression in the waking world, and that harm has a detrimental influence on the whole. By questioning the characters in the dream you can determine what aspects of your personality are trying to communicate with you, such as the child-self or the male/female-self.

Many people believe that when you dream, essentially you are dreaming about one person – and that is you.

come to the fore. Remember, anything can happen in a dream, so don't restrict yourself to the logical constraints of everyday life.

Changing What Occurs

To change a dream, you will need to replay it, looking out for where you want to make the changes. For instance, say you have a dream in which you feel powerless, perhaps chasing someone who eludes you. A way of changing that type of dream is actually to catch the person you are pursuing. They may continue to escape when you re-enter the dream, but be persistent and persevere until you reach your goal.

Changing Your Response

In a similar way to changing the events, changing your response is another method of taking control. Fear dreams are often recurrent, and many feature being chased or stalked by a menacing presence. This can cause a great deal of anxiety and the dreamer may wake up short of breath and with a pounding heart. A way of taking control in this situation would be to transmute the reaction; instead of being tense and afraid in the dream, be light-hearted and happy. This will help dispel anxiety.

Extending a Dream

Most of us have experienced dreams that end prematurely when we wake, usually with a fearful start. A good way of changing this type of dream is to allow it to continue and see where it goes. Simply recall the dream and, at the point where you woke up, carry it on using your creative intuition. A typical situation in this type of dream is that the dreamer is falling, which can signify a leap into the unknown. The dream usually ends abruptly just before impact with the ground – but who knows what might happen if the dream were allowed to continue? Perhaps the ground might open up to allow safe passage, or maybe it would be soft and resilient. One way to find out is to give your creative intuition free rein and take that leap.

Lucid Dreaming

The term "lucid dreaming" is used to describe the state of being aware that you are dreaming whilst you are in the dream state. Lucid dreams seem to introduce us to that part of ourselves that creates our dreams. Consequently, learning how to recognize and generate such dreams has enormous magical potential – once we can direct our dreams at will, we are in touch with powerful forces for changing our lives in accordance with our wishes.

Journeying to other worlds

We all have the ability to journey to different worlds, and indeed do so when we dream. As we know from dreams, these otherworlds are places of limitless possibilities, where information is relayed in a format the traveller can relate to. Unlike dreams, however, the journey to another world is undertaken with conscious intent and with a specific goal in mind. You may like to light a candle and cast a magic circle around you before you begin.

When you are preparing for a journey you need to focus your attention before you begin.

Planning a Journey

When journeying to another realm, it is important to be open to whatever may happen and to anything you might meet. Trust your intuition, because what first comes to you is the right thing, whatever it may be. Just go with the flow and don't try to force anything. Remember that you have control over what you can accomplish in this otherworld that you travel to and don't be inhibited by fear. Be creative in circumventing problems and challenges that may arise.

As with physical travel in this world, if you prepare yourself properly before a journey, things will go more smoothly and it will be a more fruitful experience.

Preparing for a Journey

This simple ritual helps to prepare you for any kind of journey by centring you and focusing your attention on the journey you are about to undertake.

1 Gather your tools together (these may include musical equipment and an appropriate piece of music, incenses, oils or candles) and create a

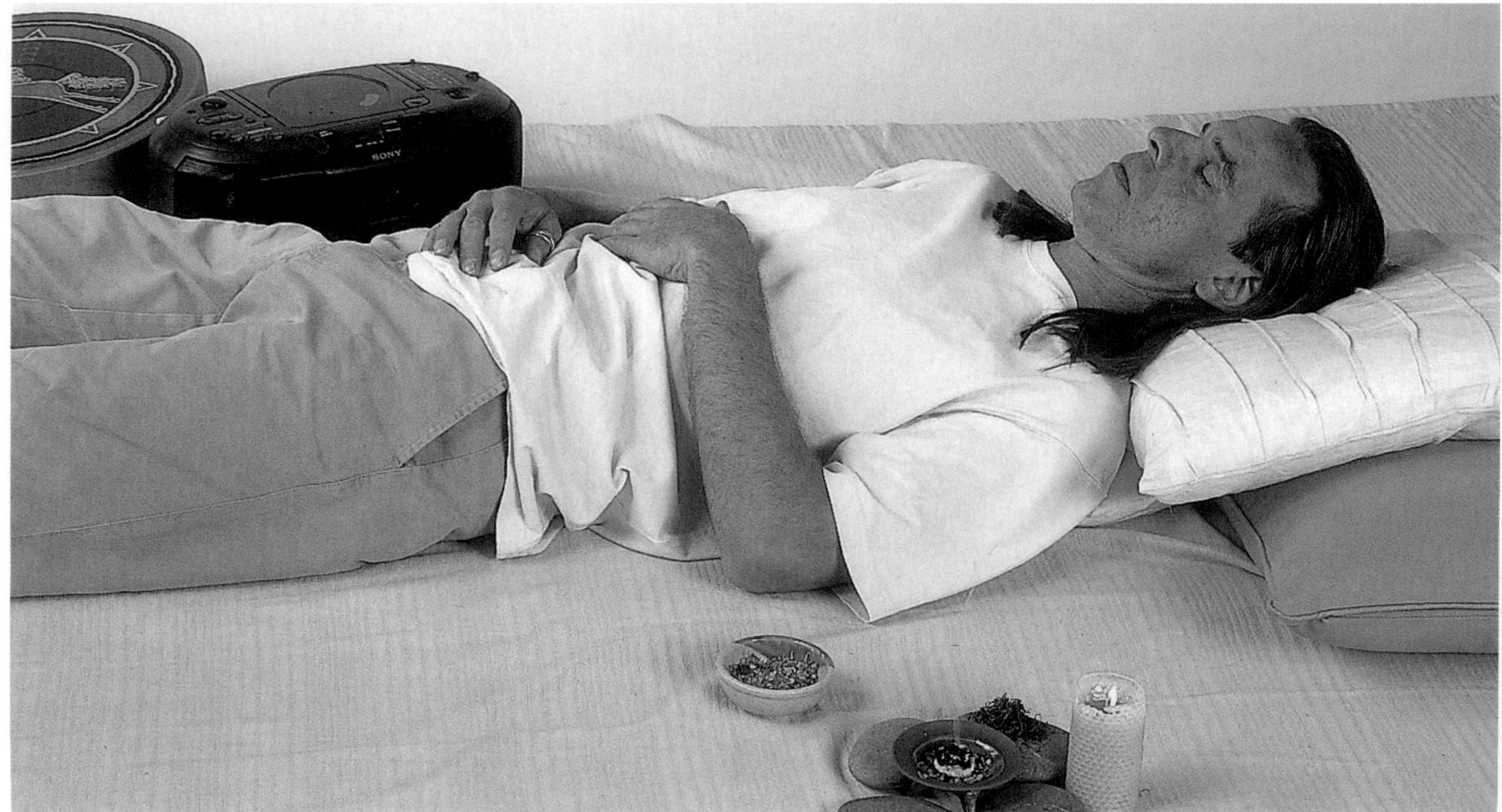

Before you begin your journey make sure you are comfortable and relaxed, and that you will not be disturbed.

comfortable place where you feel relaxed and safe from disturbance. Light a candle for inner illumination and contemplate it quietly for a while.

2 Smudge yourself, the tools and your surroundings. Make an offering to whichever spirits, gods or goddesses or angelic beings you are working with and voice your intent:
I call on (say the name) to assist me in this journey to (state reason of journey) and I make this offering in honour of you and in gratitude for your aid.

3 When you are ready, sit or lie comfortably and breathe deeply to get relaxed. Start the music if you are using it, and take some deep, regular breaths as your journey begins.

Journey to the Hall of the Gods

Here is an inner journey to a place that is peaceful, powerful and magical, and where it is easy to sink into an altered state of awareness to commune with the gods. Make sure you will not be disturbed for about half an hour and get into a meditative frame of mind. If possible, record the narrative on tape, pausing after every sentence to allow the images to build up, or get a friend to read it to you, or go through it a number of times until you can recall the various stages. Allow the images to become as real as possible. You are creating the pictures partly from memory or imagination, and partly because they are real in another realm or dimension.

1 Sit upright, close your eyes and concentrate on your breathing. Allow it to slow down and become deeper.

2 Begin to build up a picture of an elaborate doorway; see the frame and the details of the closed door. What is it made of? What does it feel like? Does it open? This is the door from your world to the realm of the gods. There may be a guardian who is there to ask who you are and why you wish to go through, or ask for a password or token. You will have to find the answers.

You might like to perform your dream journeys within a magic circle, so that you benefit from the protective energy field that no hostile or negative forces can penetrate.

3 After a few moments, as you continue to relax and make the experience deeper, you will find that the door can be opened. At first a great light seems to be shining through the doorway, and you stand on the threshold while your inner vision adjusts.

4 The light dims so that you can look into the place beyond, and what you see is a glorious hall, built of golden stone. Upon the walls are paintings or hangings picked out in bright colours. You step forward on to a paved floor covered in mosaics.

5 Everything you see is on a grand scale. The ceiling is high above but that too is painted and gilded, and everything is beautiful. To one side of the room there is a platform reached by several steps covered with marvellous brocade, and on the dais is a throne, carved and covered in gold. Upon it you start to make out a figure that is awe-inspiring but also approachable.

6 You move towards the steps and try to make out the face of the figure seated above you. This is the deity you have come to meet. Take as long as you need with them, and when you have had your audience, give thanks, even if the advice is not immediately clear, and act with respect.

7 Allow the image of the great hall to fade, so that you see again the door and threshold. The light dims and gently you return to your own place. Come back to normal awareness slowly, allowing yourself to recall every detail.

Shamanic Journeying

The ability to journey to otherworlds is a traditional shamanic practice. It is a very powerful way to gain insights into problems, to look for healing, to seek allies or just to relax. When you journey, you enter a different world. It is essentially one that you create and guide yourself through, although your conscious self relinquishes control to your spirit. Before starting a journey, make sure you are in a place where you feel safe and won't be disturbed.

The Drum

Traditionally, a drum is used in shamanic journeying and it is good to have someone drum for you, as a regular rhythm of around 200 beats per minute helps you achieve the focus needed for the opening of a gateway. It is good to build up the rhythm gradually to allow the traveller to become acclimatized.

At first it is best to journey for a set time of around five minutes. At the end of this period the drummer can initiate the return with a call-back signal – say, four one-second beats followed by some very rapid drumming. With experience, the drummer will be able to use their intuition to tell when the journey is complete. Making a drum tape for journeying can also be very useful, as you can record several sessions of various lengths and incorporate your own call-back signal.

Journey to Meet a Power Animal

A power animal is your own personal spirit ally which takes the form of an animal. Meeting a power animal is a useful journey to start with because the animal can accompany you on future adventures and give you guidance, wisdom and protection. How to do this is described in the section on Animal Totems. This is not a deep journey but it does expand your awareness, taking you to the edge of your sacred space, where it borders the realms of other spirits. The animal you find could be anything, and it may not be what you were expecting, but once you have found each other you should spend some time together on subsequent journeys. Be aware of the love it has for you. Remember, the greater the detail the more real it will seem. If it feels appropriate, transform yourself into the same animal and run, fly or swim. Above all, have some fun.

When you have returned from your journey, go over it in your mind or, better still, write it down to help fix the details. This will aid you in future travels and make it easier to contact the animal.

Entrances to the upperworld

The way into the upperworld could be:

- A gap in the sky which can be reached by flying or leaping
- A cave mouth high up a cliff that you need to scale
- A tall tree to climb
- A mountain that pierces a cloud
- A flight of stairs
- A ladder

The drum plays a very important part in Shamanic rituals. If you are working alone it is a good idea to make a drumming tape for your journeys.

Journeying to Otherworlds

Deeper journeys to otherworlds require going beyond your sacred space. The otherworlds that shamans journey to are many and varied and can encompass any number of features, because each is a construct of the shaman who enters it. Essentially though, otherworlds are confined to two realms and when you journey from your sacred space you can travel downwards to the underworld or upwards to the upperworld.

Entrances to the underworld

The way into the underworld could be through any of the following openings:

- A cave or crevice in the side of a rockface
- A recess or a knothole in a tree
- An animal's burrow in a bank
- A wormhole
- A well
- A doorway or gate
- A waterfall or stream

When you are journeying for another person, spend some time tuning in to your partner's mind.

The Underworld

Most shamanic journeys involve going to the underworld, which is not comparable with the hell of Christianity and other faiths, but represents the inner recesses of the traveller; you could also think of it as the deepest recesses of the unconscious mind. It is not a sinister place but a place of challenge and adventure. A shaman enters it to seek solutions and understanding. The challenges you might encounter are all manifestations of your own fears and problems. By confronting them and finding solutions in the underworld you are facing them within yourself and allowing your spirit to communicate the solutions to your conscious self. Because you are journeying deep within yourself, you are seeking an entrance that will lead downwards and in. Remember, to gain entry you can transform yourself to any size and shape required.

The Upperworld

Associated with the higher self or the soul, the upperworld is the place to go to for inspiration and communion with other spirits. Whereas the underworld is about confronting your inner fears, the upperworld is more concerned with seeking assistance from others, by meeting other spirits on an equal basis and sharing knowledge with them.

This realm is very light and tranquil, with a feeling of limitless space that stretches away forever. Because it is related to the higher self, it is reached by going upwards. As with a journey to the underworld, it is good to have some structure to follow to help maintain your focus. Because going upwards relates to the soul, a good focus to have is to connect with your higher self. This part of your being is calm and all-knowing. It is dissociated from the emotions that have such a strong influence on the physical, and can therefore give counsel with a dispassionate objectivity that will cut to the heart of a problem.

Journeying for Others

Sometimes a shaman may be required to journey to the upperworld or underworld on behalf of another, for purposes of healing or to seek the answer to a question. The principle is always the same: go with a specific aim in mind and be open to what befalls you on the way to your goal. The meaning of the tests and solutions might not be immediately apparent, but when you describe your experiences to your partner, they may understand the symbolism in ways that you did not.

Journeying on behalf of another person is mutually beneficial, and can form a close bond between the people involved. When you are doing this, take some time to develop a level of empathy with your partner by sitting quietly for ten minutes, holding hands and feeling each other's energy.

Inner guides

The occult arts have always recognized the reality of the unseen forces that may help and heal, instruct and guide. Magicians and witches do not usually call up the spirits of the dead, accepting, on the whole, that the immortal human spirit needs to rest and assess its past life before being brought back into incarnation. Although there are discarnate sources of knowledge that may be contacted through magical applications of some of the spiritualists' methods, magicians and witches generally prefer to use their own ways to receive information from hidden masters or inner guides.

The one-eyed god Odin, leader of the Wild Hunt, had a central role in Nordic mythology.

Meeting Inner Teachers

Magicians and witches may have the ability to talk to teachers of wisdom from the past, or their own ancestors, or the people who founded their magical tradition. This can be done by creating an inner journey to the place in which these wise beings would dwell, and going there to hear what they have to say. Throughout, the modern magic worker is in control and able to terminate the experience if necessary.

Inner Plane Adepti

Some schools of magic have named inner teachers who are known as the Inner Plane Adepti or Hidden Masters of Wisdom. These great instructors may once have been famous living people or they may be angels who have never lived on earth.

A well-established magical lodge will have one or more of these teachers, who are invited to witness the workings of the magical order and give guidance or instruction as necessary. If a group is fully aware of its Inner Plane Adept, they may see him or her during group meditations, or else one member of the group may have the skill to perceive this inner teacher and convey their words or philosophy to the other members. It requires a lot of faith and trust to enter a mind-to-mind contact with some unseen being, but those who are experienced in this method gain a great deal of genuine and original teaching material.

Egyptian temple pictures sometimes show deities and other celestial beings, as having wings. Here it is Isis who is shown as possessing angelic qualities.

Mythological Heroes

Legends and myths have given inspiration for guides and teachers to many traditions, in particular the Arthurian legends and Norse sagas. The Norse god Odin, leader of the Wild Hunt and giver of knowledge, is a complex figure who traded one of his eyes to drink in the underworld well of the wise god Mimir, and is therefore seen as a source of wisdom himself.

Angelic Beings

Among the other unseen beings who are often called on to help in magical work are the angels and archangels. They have many functions: as healers, teachers, protectors and illuminators of humanity.

Angels, whose name means "messenger" in Greek, are thought of as the active hands of the God or Goddess,

Angels appear in many different spiritual traditions, acting as intermediaries and guides between this world and the next.

the source of all, or the One. They have no free will and travel between Earth and Heaven, bringing news or offering assistance. Working with angels is very popular because they appear to be benevolent beings of light, and are found in many religious philosophies. Pictures from ancient Egyptian temples show winged goddesses who seem to have many of the qualities of angels, and Christians, Muslims, Jews and many other faiths have accounts of angels in their religious texts.

Many different kinds of angels are particularly important to followers of the Hebrew mystical system of the Cabbala. The central glyph of this philosophy is the Tree of Life, which has ten spheres of creation. These are commonly linked to the powers of the planets, but each sphere also has an angel who rules over its working in the Earth plane.

The planets and archangels

The Earth and seven "personal" planets are each associated with an angel, who rules over its working in the Earth plane.

Earth: Sandalphon
Moon: Gabriel
Mercury: Raphael
Venus: Anael
Sun: Michael
Mars: Zamael
Jupiter: Sachiel
Saturn: Cassiel

Meeting Angels

Angels may be called upon by lighting a candle, relaxing and asking them to appear, or they might offer help unasked, if you genuinely need their assistance. They don't always look like we imagine them to be, as they can be vast in size, and as subtle as auric light. Sometimes you see them as huge, delicate cloud formations like wings or feathers blown by the wind, and tipped with sunlight. They are always beautiful, and if you find yourself in their presence, it can be very moving and inspiring.

Meeting Your Higher Self

Your higher self resides in the upperworld, or starry realm. It is the wisest and purest part of yourself that wants only what is best for your highest spiritual purpose – which is not necessarily the same as what your "lower" or everyday self desires.

To meet your higher self, you will need to journey to the upperworld (see Journeying to Other Worlds earlier in this chapter). Once there, pause and take a moment to observe your surroundings. Your higher self, or soul self, might be right there or you might have to go in search of it. When you meet your higher self, greet it with love. Pose any questions you may have and receive the answers gratefully. They might not be what your mortal self wants to hear but they will be honest. When it is time to return, thank your higher self for the meeting and slowly come back. Make a record of the events in a journal, because the meaning may not be immediately apparent and you may wish to read through the account again at a later date.

A word of warning

It is wisest not to attempt trances or try to contact discarnate spirits unless you have a reputable teacher, or expert help is at hand. Some people who have taken part in séances, played at "raising ghosts" or light-heartedly dabbled with Ouija boards have scared themselves. A few have opened doors to psychic perceptions that they did not know how to close, or have attracted the attention of entities they could not control. If you are aspiring to master the skills of magic, always work in the power of light, act sensibly and treat all beings – be they angels, gods, ghosts or elementals – with respect.

EXPLORING PAST LIVES

Natural magic honours the cycles of nature and its eternal round of birth, growth, death and rebirth. In human terms this is mirrored by a belief in reincarnation, which holds that each soul lives through many lifetimes, gradually gaining skills and strengthening its power to evolve. An aspect of this divine spark is within everyone – it is immortal and does not die when our bodies do. We recognize this eternal factor within us and probably think of it as our "inner self". Just as plants grow, blossom, fruit and die, so the human being grows, learns, reproduces, dies and is born again.

Trees "die" in winter and are "reborn" in spring, symbolizing the soul's eternal round.

THE SOUL

Throughout our time on the Earth plane, our soul gains new experiences and becomes more complete. When we die, it rests in a state that might be thought of as "heaven". Here it is not "judged" or made to account for "sins" but assesses its own progress and sees dispassionately how it has done in life. If a certain part of its development has been overlooked, it will reincarnate in another physical form to learn the lessons it needs to learn. The soul continues to reincarnate until its lessons on Earth are complete, when it transcends the birth, death, rebirth cycle by becoming one with the cosmic unity or the One.

KARMA

The theory of karma is central to the idea of past lives. Karma is a Sanskrit term to denote the concept of action and reaction, similar to the idea in Western thought of reaping what you sow. This means that every action has a consequence, and even if we may appear to "get away with it" this time around, our actions can return to haunt us in a future incarnation. Some people think that the qualities we are born with are the results of either "good" or "bad" karma, or that misfortune could be the results of karmic debts being paid off. Others believe that it is possible to choose to come to Earth in imperfect bodies in order to learn hard lessons quickly, and so evolve spiritually. It is impossible to agree on a precise doctrine,

Once the cycle of rebirth is over, and the soul has learned all it needs to know, it transcends birth and death to become one with the cosmic unity.

Discovering past lives

One way of discovering past lives is through hypnotic regression. This is not something that you can do by yourself and should only be undertaken with expert guidance. However, an effective way of finding out about past lives by yourself is to develop an inner journey to the Hall of Records where you can locate your own personal Book of Lives and look in that to see who you have been. It also avoids the emotional impact of re-living the past, which can be associated with regression techniques.

1 Sit in meditation and visualize yourself entering an old building and climbing a staircase to a great library. This is the Hall of Records and in it there are a great number of books of all ages, sizes and types. Explore the place fully using all your senses.

2 Librarians are available who can help you find your own records; you just need to ask for their help. The volume of your lives will have your current name on it and it can be taken to a quiet corner to study.

3 Continue to relax and allow whatever symbol of this personal record that arises to do so, rather than making it have a particular form. It could be a book, a stone tablet, or even a computer screen – there is no right form.

4 When you are focused, look at your personal record and you are sure to find something of interest. It could be a family tree, written words in familiar or ancient languages, pictures, or an image that is more like a window, through which you can pass to explore your own past.

5 Take your time and enter into the experience as deeply as possible, while making a mental note of everything that you find. You may experience life from the outside, merely witnessing domestic events as an onlooker, or you may find yourself viewing some past incarnation. What you get, and how deeply you are affected, will depend on how much you can go with the process.

6 Write up your experience in your Book of Shadows or other journal. You could also add drawings and anything else you gain from research later on.

Use the smoke from a snuffed candle to draw you into the meditation, and light it again afterwards to ground yourself.

but the idea of karma and its balance of good and bad deeds makes a worthwhile lesson. It is hard to get to the bottom of a single event, as every life is affected by complex patterns of action and reaction and it is the soul that chooses the conditions into which it will be born each time. No other being directs the pattern of reincarnation.

Soulmates

It is possible that long-lasting relationships can continue from one life to the next. When people describe having a "soulmate", in the true sense of the word, they mean a lover with whom they have journeyed through many lives. This is because true love is eternal and its bonds outlive the grave.

Past-life Recall

If you are interested in exploring your own past lives, go about it sensibly, because it can be an unsettling experience. It is vital to have a reliable companion, plenty of time, and to make detailed records. Do not take everything you learn for granted without checking the facts – there are plenty of accurate historical accounts of most times and places, and the research can help confirm whether what you recall is valid and "real". However, even if it is just fantasy, your imagination may have something valid to show you about yourself.

A mirror spell to see who you have been

This will allow you to get a small glimpse of the past, on which you can work to gain more details.

1 Make a magical circle of protection and calmness by sprinkling blessed water around you. Become relaxed and focused.

2 At night, place a mirror on a stand and a single lit white candle on a table so that the light shines on your face. Also take a sheet of writing paper and a pen. Write clearly the following words, then carefully burn the writing in the candle flame:

I wish to see who I have been in a past life, at a time when all was going well. Reveal to me in this shining glass, I summon old "me" by this spell.

3 Just focus your vision on your eyes reflected in the mirror and after a while you may see the image change and become another face. It can seem a bit weird at first, but if you are patient and certain it is what you want, it will happen.

4 When your face returns to normal, say:
Thank you, me, whoever you seem, perhaps we will meet again in dream.

MAGICAL CORRESPONDENCES

Magic is a vast and ancient subject and tables of correspondences have always been an important part of the magic-worker's tool kit. They provide a useful at-a-glance guide to some of the main properties of the various magical "ingredients" that are used in spells, ceremonies, rituals and all other kinds of magic. Once you start looking, you will find that there are literally hundreds of tables available – both ancient and modern – that can all be used to help you with your magical journey.

What is given here is a selection of some of the most useful correspondence charts to get you started, but as you become more experienced you will find the confidence to develop your own charts based on your own magical knowledge. This final chapter contains correspondence charts on the symbolism of crystals, birds and animals, trees, plants and herbs, incense and essential oils as well as colour. It also contains tables of the elements, of planetary associations, and a guide to some of the main gods, angels and spirit beings in magical use today. Remember that such information is not intended as a substitute for in-depth knowledge, but as a quick reference tool to help you when selecting the appropriate ingredients for use in your magic.

The symbolism of crystals

Crystals are a powerful magical tool.

Amber	Good luck stone, draws out disease and clears negativity and depression
Agate	For inspiration from the spiritual realm
Amethyst	Peace, protection and spirituality; healing; release from addiction, help with meditation and peaceful sleep, eases transition between life and death
Angelite	Heals anger, restores harmony; helpful in telepathic communication, connecting with angels and spirits
Aquamarine	Helps in the expression of spiritual truths; aids dreaming to increase psychic power
Aventurine	Healing at all levels, dissolves blockages, balances the emotions; green aventurine attracts good fortune and increases perception; pink aventurine heals relationships
Azurite	Mental clarity and renewal, releases painful ideas from the subconscious; also known as "the stone of heaven", can help attunement to the psychic world
Beryl	Enhances psychic ability
Black onyx	Protects against negative energy, helps emotional stability, encourages connection with reality
Blue lace agate	Symbolizes health and long life, grounding, brings inspiration and facilitates self-expression
Calcite	Balances male and female energies; allays fears and stress, assists with astral travel; orange calcite is particularly useful for shock or trauma
Carnelian	Aids creative flow, grounds in the present, inspires confidence, courage and motivation
Celestite	To link with angels and spirit guides, a bright moontime crystal
Chrysocolla	Soothes and calms, eases fear and guilt, attracts luck
Chrysoprase	Emotionally uplifting, attracts abundance and success, spiritual energy
Citrine	Prevents nightmares, enhances self-esteem and responsible use of power, brings abundance and material wellbeing; a crystal of the sun
Clear quartz	Amplifies energy, spiritually and emotionally healing, aids meditation; a bright moontime crystal
Diamond	Symbolizes power, purity, strength, trust, commitment and love; instils wisdom and confidence
Emerald	Physically healing and protective; lends insight and security in love
Fluorite	Gathers together different energies and assists in focus and concentration; aids communication with higher self; yellow fluorite promotes self-confidence
Garnet	Stimulates energy, aids expression, strengthens love and friendship
Haematite	Aids concentration, reasoning, memory and self-discipline; healing and protective; grounding
Herkimer diamond	Releases energy blockages, helps with dream recall
Jade	Clarity, justice and wisdom; balances the emotions, promotes peaceful sleep; attracts prosperity
Jasper	Often referred to as a talisman; one of the most powerful healing stones
Jet	Calms the subtle bodies, clears a heavy head and helps lift depression, useful for clearing negativity; a dark moontime crystal
Kunzite	Redresses compulsive tendencies and restores balance; opens up the heart and connection to higher self
Kyanite	Balances emotional disturbances, promotes inner peace; helps intuition
Labradorite	Develops psychic ability
Lapis lazuli	Strengthens will, awareness, integrity in relationships; aids the release of emotional wounds
Malachite	Healing, absorbs negativity, stimulates creativity
Moonstone	Wishes, intuition and new beginnings; restores harmony in relationships, calms emotions and induces lucid dreaming; a bright moontime crystal
Moss agate	Connects with earth spirits, brings abundance and self-confidence
Obsidian	Protective and grounding, reduces escapism and dissolves anger and fear; snowflake obsidian has a softer effect, restores balance and clarity
Opal	Visionary, attracts inspiration and insight
Pearl	Enhances purity, clarity and grace; balances emotions, increases confidence in inner wisdom
Pyrites	Harnesses creative thinking and practicality
Red jasper	Connects with earth energy, emotionally calming
Rhodonite	Fosters patience, selflessness
Rose quartz	Heals emotional wounds, restores love
Ruby	Amplifies emotions, releases and dissolves anger, attracts loyalty, awakens passion and beauty
Sapphire	Symbolizes peace, gives protection and wisdom
Selenite	Mental focus, clarity and clairvoyance
Smoky quartz	Lightly grounding and balancing; fosters self-acceptance; absorbs negative vibrations
Sodalite	Calms troubled mind and emotions; promotes inner peace
Sugilite	Aids physical healing and purification of all body systems; strengthens will; aid to meditation
Tiger's eye	Creates order and harmony; attracts beauty
Topaz	Symbolizes light and warmth, heals and absorbs tension, attracts love and creativity
Tourmaline	Grounding, healing and protective, absorbs negativity and brings discernment and vitality
Turquoise	Healing and protection; blessing and partnership

The symbolism of birds and animals

Alligator/ crocodile	Guardian and fierce protector; stealth, ferocity; primal power
Antelope	Vision and foresight, speed and quick action; gentleness
Armadillo	Armour, boundaries and protection
Badger	Strength and perseverance; fighting for what you want, tenacity; prophesy and divination
Bat	Death and rebirth; initiation, transition, change
Bear	Receptive female energy, earth wisdom, introspection; lunar energies
Beaver	Industrious; flexibility and creativity
Blackbird	Gatekeeper
Bison (buffalo)	Wisdom of the elders; provider and protector; fertility, sexual vigour, power
Bull	Male sexual potency, strength; war
Cat	Independence, intuition; sacred to the Goddess, female medicine
Cow	Fertility and prosperity; motherhood, family life
Coyote	Childlike trust, innocence and playfulness; a trickster figure, mischievous and exposes pretensions in others
Crow/raven	Change; foresight and prediction; shape shifting; good and bad luck; all aspects of witchcraft and magic
Deer	Security and protection; male and female sexuality; keeper of wisdom, storyteller
Dog	Friendship, kindness, loyalty and protection, guardian of ancient secrets
Dolphin/porpoise	Understanding, wisdom; unconditional love; laughter, harmony and healing
Dove	Peace and love; marriage, spiritual harmony; purity and clear vision
Dragon	Mythical beast, symbol of good luck; energetic, fun-loving, confident
Duck	Love and harmony, domesticity, abundance; motherhood and children; new beginnings
Eagle	Divine and earthly power; freedom, fearlessness striving for higher goals; clarity, clairvoyance
Fish	Mystery, the depths of the subconscious, emotions; lunar magic
Fox	Trickery and guile, secrets; protection, family, maternal instincts
Frog	Cleansing, emotional healing; fertility; change and transformation
Goat	Relaxed and happy-go-lucky; ability to live in the present; creative, friendly; ambitious
Goose	Storytelling; protection, fertility; rebirth; links with the Great Mother
Hare	Quickness of thought; intuition, sensitivity, creativity; associated with the moon goddess, fertility

Hawk	The gift of foresight, perception, psychic powers; messenger from spirit world bringing knowledge and wisdom
Heron	Self-reliance
Horse	Freedom, swiftness, stamina and endurance; earthly and otherworldly power; strength and self-confidence
Jaguar (panther, leopard)	The gift of vision; prediction, prophesy and divination; intuition and psychic power
Lion	Strength, majesty; power and leadership
Lizard	Illusions, letting go; adaptability; change, transition
Magpie	Relationships
Moose (elk)	Strength and endurance; male and female sexuality; relationships
Monkey	Inquisitive, energetic, competitive; leadership; clever and sharp-witted
Mouse	Finely attuned sensitivity; messenger; abundance and fertility
Owl	Wisdom; understanding hidden truths; insight and telepathy; all forms of magic
Ox	Patience, kindness and responsibility; routine, order and discipline
Pig	Diplomacy, common sense; prone to greed
Pigeon	Messages
Rabbit	Fertility and love; fear and cowardice
Ram/sheep	Lust, fertility; action without forethought, youthful zest
Rat	Self-motivated, strong sense of self-preservation; cheerful, ability to bounce back
Robin	New beginnings; protection
Rooster	Flamboyant; a good communicator
Snake	Shedding of the old; transformation; philosophical, mysterious, shrewd, sensual; underworld guardian
Swan	Purity, serenity, peace; spirituality and dignity
Tiger	Rash, impulsive, dynamic; risk-taking, leadership
Turtle	Endurance; knowledge; Mother Earth, women
Wolf	Loyalty; freedom; independence; afterlife and rebirth; teacher
Woodpecker	Magic and prophecy; sacred cycles; rain, storms and thunder
Wren	Protection

The proud eagle symbolizes freedom and fearlessness

The wolf symbolizes loyalty and freedom.

The symbolism of trees, plants and herbs

Angelica	Burn dried leaves for protection and healing
Anise	Keeps away nightmares
Apple	For love and friendship; youth, beauty, innocence
Ash	The world tree; purification and cleansing
Basil	Gives protection, repels negativity, brings wealth
Bay	Guardian of the house, protects against illness; burn leaves to produce visions
Beech	Stability, flow of energy; protector of written wisdom, guardian of knowledge
Blessed thistle	Brings spiritual and financial blessing; fresh plant brings strengthening energy to a sickroom
Cabbage	Brings good luck
Carrot seed	Illuminating; use for visions and vision quests, journeying
Catnip	Encourages a psychic bond with cats; attracts luck and happiness
Chamomile	For meditation and relaxation; use in prosperity charms to attract money
Chickweed	For attracting love or maintaining a relationship
Chilli	Assures fidelity and love
Cinnamon	Aphrodisiac; draws money, protection and success
Clove	Banishes hostile or negative forces and helps to gain what is sought; use in spells to stop gossip
Clover	For love and fidelity
Coltsfoot	Brings love, wealth and peace
Comfrey	For safety when travelling
Cyclamen	For love and truth
Dandelion	Enhances dreams and prophetic power
Dogwood	Charm and finesse
Elm	Love, light and purification; death and rebirth;
Fennel	Protects from curses
Gardenia	For peace and healing
Garlic	For magical healing, protection and exorcism
Ginger	For success and empowerment
Grape	For fertility and garden magic, attracts money
Hawthorn	Marriage, fertility, happiness, protection of children; gateway to the otherworld
Hazel	Wisdom and fertility; used for wands, divining
Hibiscus	Attracts love, aids divination and dreams
Honeysuckle	Strengthens the memory, helps in letting go of the past
Holly	Strongest protective tree; dream magic, wisdom and courage; healing of subtle bodies
Hops	Improves health and induces sleep; goddess energy
Hyacinth	For love and protection

Clover is associated with love and fidelity.

Tobacco is a sacred herb in the Native American Indian tradition

Hyssop	Purification; dispel negativity
Jasmine	Induces lucid dreams; brings good fortune in love, friendship and wealth; raises self-esteem
Juniper	Calms and brings good health; berries ward off evil
Lavender	Purifying; brings peace and happiness, love; helps sweet dreams
Lemon	Attracts happiness, relieves stress
Lettuce	Induces sleep, assists in divination
Lily-of-the-valley	Brings peace, harmony and love
Lime	Increases energy, encourages loyalty
Lotus	Emblem of enlightenment, elevates and protects
Magnolia	Assures fidelity
Marigold	Enhances visions and dreams; renews energy
Mistletoe	For protection, love and visionary ability; hang on the bedpost for beautiful dreams
Mugwort	For clairvoyance, scrying and dream interpretation
Oak	Wisdom, strength and endurance; groves of oak trees associated with prophecy and divination;
Olive	Brings peace of mind and fidelity in love fruitfulness and security
Orange	Attracts peace, power and luck
Orris	Attracts love and romance
Passion flower	Fosters friendship, brings peace and understanding
Pennyroyal	Increases alertness, helps peace between partners
Pine	Grounding and cleansing, use for a fresh start; repels evil; cleansing and purifying
Rice	Attracts fertility and money
Rose	Blesses love, domestic peace, generosity and beauty
Rosemary	Protects the home, brings mental clarity and sharpens memory
Rowan	Protection against evil, enchantment and negative energies; development of psychic powers
Sage	Brings wisdom, fertility, healing and long life
Silver birch	New beginnings, healing; mysteries of the maiden
Strawberry	For love and luck
Sweet pea	For friendship and courage
Thyme	For courage and confidence
Tobacco	Introduces sacred spirit
Valerian	Brings love and harmony
Vervain	For inner strength and peace
Violet	Contentment and love
Willow	Love and regeneration; lunar and feminine rhythms; healing and to empower wishes
Yew	Immortality, transformation and inner wisdom

The symbolism of incense and essential oils

Acacia (gum arabic)	Protection; develops psychic awareness
Agarwood (aloes)	Protection, consecration; prosperity and success; connection with the upperworld
Amber	Love and healing
Benzoin	Aid to meditation; grounding, helps reconnect with inner self
Bergamot	Attracts success and prosperity; use in rituals of initiation
Camphor	Guardian of rebirth; assists in change and transformation; used in moon magic
Cajeput	Spiritual expansion and freedom
Cedar	Associated with magical power, vitality and immortality
Chamomile	Peace, tranquillity and emotional stability; aid to sleep and dreaming
Clary sage	Aphrodisiac; stimulates vivid dreams and encourages dream recall
Clove	Clears the mind and assists in past life recall
Copal	Protection, purification and banishing negativity; a fragrance of the gods and angels
Dragon's blood	Neutralizes negative energies; cleansing and protecting
Eucalyptus	Healing and purifying; use in space clearing
Frankincense	Calms and quietens the mind; an aid to meditation; use in rituals of initiation and rites of passage
Galbanum	Spells for endings and letting go; clears negativity
Geranium	Balancing and adjusting; assists with new projects
Helichrysum	Opens channel for healing, dreams and visions; spells for inspiration
Jasmin	Imagination
Juniper	Clearing negative energies
Lavender	Psychic balance; brings emotions under control
Lemon grass	Cleansing and purifying; releasing the past, forgiveness
Mandarin	Inspiration; aid to communication, useful for harmony with friends and family
Mimosa	Opens up channel of communication with higher self, angels and spirit beings
Melissa	Strengthens connection with cosmic energies; love, harmony and happiness

All kinds of incense can be bought in stick, cone or resin form.

The smoke of any incense will add the Air element to your ritual.

Musk	For love and sexual attraction
Myrrh	Helps connect with True Will, courage to follow the soul's path
Myrtle	For spiritual love and immortality of the soul
Neroli	For love and fertility; use in wedding ceremonies
Niaouli	Clearing negative thoughts, expanding consciousness
Nutmeg	Stimulating aphrodisiac; clairvoyance and psychic development
Olibanum	Similar to frankincense, but with a lighter, more delicate fragrance. An incense of the sun
Palmarosa	For letting go of the past and spiritual illumination
Patchouli	Relaxing aphrodisiac; grounding, helps connection with earth energies
Peppermint	For clarity and courage; increases perception and awareness in the dream state
Ravensara	For spontaneity and determination; deepens meditation
Rose	To honour the Goddess and strengthen a connection with all aspects of the feminine force
Rosewood	For space clearing
Sandalwood	Aphrodisiac (especially for men); comforts the dying and helps ease transition between the worlds; opens the gates to spirit guides
Storax	Ancient incense burning substance with long tradition of use in magic and sacred ceremony; calming and relaxing, helps the mind unburden
Tea tree	For space clearing and purification; a light in the darkness
Tobacco	Sacred to native Americans, usually used for making offerings
Vanilla	Aphrodisiac (especially for women); attracts love and romance
Vetivert	Protection against negative energies; for over sensitivity to psychic impressions
Ylang ylang	For love and sensuality

The symbolism of colours

Colour	Symbolism	Uses
Red	Blood, passion, the life essence, power, physical energy, courage, bringing change in difficult circumstances. Associated with Mars, battle, the element of fire, the south, projective energy	Use red for a lack of enthusiasm and interest in life, low energy; inability to turn dreams into reality, feelings of insecurity, fear or anxiety; sex magic
Pink	Love and kindness, reconciliation, peace and harmony, compassion, gentle emotions. Associated with family, children and friendship, receptive energy	Use pink to bolster yourself up; in any aggressive or threatening situation; visualizing with pink can calm an angry mood and reduce tension. Magic for peace, love and romance
Orange	Abundance, fertility, health, joy, attraction, luck, friendship. Marks the boundary between self and others. Associated with the sun, projective energy	Use orange for feelings of boredom and bleakness; difficulty to adapt to change and let go of the past; over-seriousness and unable to enjoy life's humour; energy blocks. Magic associated with fire element
Yellow	Communication, the intellect, learning, concentration, also movement, travel and change. Associated with Mercury, the element of air, the east, projective energy	Use yellow for confusion and indecision; vague fears and anxieties; nervous exhaustion; poor memory, inability to study or concentrate, tendency to suffer "winter blues". Magic associated with the air element, storytelling spells
Green	The heart and emotions, love, also nature, gardens and growth, money and prosperity, employment. Associated with the earth element	Use green for feelings of being trapped or restricted, a need to break rigid patterns, a need for new ideas; fear of the unknown; a new state of balance; negative emotions such as jealousy, envy and greed. Fertility magic, spells for children, earth spells
Turquoise	Confidence, inner strength, positive self-esteem; allows expression of wishes	Use turquoise for protection against negativity, low energy and lack of interest in life, lack of courage to strike out and risk being different
Blue	Wisdom, patience, possibility, the healing of the spirit, idealism, truth and justice. Associated with the moon, the element of water, the west, reflective energy	Use blue for calming agitated, excitable or chaotic states; clear communication; peace, detachment, solitude and rest. Goddess magic; magic for dreams, past lives, and any associated with water element
Purple	Royal and priestly, a link with the higher dimension, wisdom, inspiration, magic, religion and spiritual strength. Associated with Osiris, the Egyptian god who judges the dead	Use purple for reflection, contemplation and deep meditation; be inspired by the bluish purple of the night sky. Magic for psychic development and divination

Use everyday objects, such as beads, to add colour to your magic work.

The colour purple is ideal for magic to connect with higher powers.

Add colour-symbolism by burning the right coloured candle.

Incense can be used for its colour association, as well as its scent.

Violet	Temperance, spirituality, repentance, transition from life to death	Use violet for rebalancing subtle energies; speeding up healing process; using the imagination in practical ways; integrating new skills into daily life; removing obstacles. Magic to connect with higher powers
Magenta	Letting go, change and transition; moving to a higher plane	Use magenta to take time out for healing, self-repair. Magic for change and transformation
Brown	Earth and earth spirits, instinctive wisdom, the natural world. Practical and financial matters, the home, stability, old people, animals. A protective force	Use brown when there is a need to blend or fit in; for grounding especially when overtaken by impractical and unrealistic ideas. Animal magic
Grey	Compromise and adaptability, psychic protection and secrecy	Use grey to project a cool, detached attitude and emotional stability. Magic for protection
White	Divinity, potential, the life-force, energy, purity, innocence. Contains all other colours. Associated with the sun	Use white for new beginnings, clear vision and originality; space clearing on all levels. Magic for purification and spirituality
Black	Death and regeneration. Conclusions that lead to new beginnings, marking a boundary with the past, banishing and releasing negativity, shedding guilt and regret	Use black to project mystery and self-control; to foster silence and a restful emptiness. Magic for protection and banishing
Gold	Worldly achievement, wealth, long life and ambition, confidence and understanding. Associated with solar deities	Use gold to relax and enjoy life; banish self-doubt. Magic for health, stamina and good fortune
Silver	Dreams, visions, intuition, hidden potential; cosmic intelligence. Associated with the moon and lunar deities	Use silver for development of psychic abilities, divination. Goddess and dream magic

The symbolism of gods and angels

Agni	Hindu god of fire
Amaterasu	Shinto sun goddess
Anubis	Egyptian god of the underworld, depicted with a jackal's head
Aphrodite	Greek goddess of love and beauty; known as Venus to the Romans
Apollo	Greek god of the sun, medicine and music, patron of the Muses
Arianrhod	Celtic mother goddess and keeper of time and fate
Artemis	Greek goddess of the waxing moon, protector of women; known as Diana to the Romans
Athene	Greek goddess of war, wisdom and the arts; known as Minerva to the Romans
Uriel	Archangel, earth
Bast	Egyptian cat goddess of love and fertility
Brigid	Celtic triple goddess, fire deity and patron of the hearth, healing, prophecy and inspiration
Cassiel	Archangel who assists with overcoming obstacles
Ceridwen	Celtic goddess of wisdom and death; her cauldron contained the brew of inspiration
Cerunnos	The celtic horned god, like Pan he is a fertility god; god of the witches
Cybele	Phrygian dark moon goddess who governs nature, wild beasts and dark magic
Demeter	Greek goddess of the earth, corn and vegetation; represents abundance and unconditional love; known as Ceres to the Romans
Dhagda	Celtic father god
Dionysus	Greek god of wine and ecstasy; known as Bacchus to the Romans
Epona	Celtic horse-goddess of fertility, abundance and healing

The huntress goddess Artemis was known as Diana to the Romans.

Pan, half man half goat, is the Greek personification of the horned god.

Freya	Norse mother goddess of love, marriage and fertility
Gabriel	Archangel of the moon, associated with the west
Gaia	Primeval Greek earth deity, prophetess of Delphi, goddess of dreams
Ganesha	Elephant-headed Hindu god of wisdom and literature, son of Parvati and Shiva, patron of business
Hades	Greek god of the underworld; known as Pluto to the Romans
Anael	Archangel of divine love and harmony, beauty and the creative arts
Hathor	Egyptian sky-deity, goddess of love, joy and dance, usually represented as a cow
Hecate	Greek triple goddess, rules magic, sorcery, death and the underworld; associated with crossroads
Hermes	Greek messenger god; represents communication, transition and exchange; associated with magic, healing and thieves; known as Mercury to the Romans
Hestia	Greek goddess of the hearth and stability

Horus	Egyptian sun god, depicted with a falcon's head
Indra	Hindu god of war; associated with weather and fertility
Ishtar	Mesopotamian goddess of sexual love, fertility and war
Isis	Egyptian mother-goddess, wife of Osiris and mother of Horus; represents life, loyalty, fertility and magic
Ixchel	Mayan goddess of storms and protector of women in childbirth
Janus	Roman guardian of the entrance and god of transition
Jizo	Japanese protector of children and travellers
Kali	Destructive aspect of the Hindu mother goddess
Kuanyin	Chinese goddess of compassion
Kwannon	Japanese goddess of compassion
Lakshmi	Hindu goddess of abundance, wealth and harmony
Lugh	Celtic sky god, associated with skills and the arts
Luna	Roman goddess of the full moon
Maat	Egyptian goddess of truth, justice and order
Mars	Roman god of war, lover of Venus
Manjushri	Buddhist bodhisattva of wisdom
Michael	Archangel of the sun, associated with rulership, marriage, music
Minerva	Roman goddess of wisdom
Mithras	Roman god of light
Morrigan	Celtic goddess of battlefields and death
Nephthys	Sister of Isis, the Egyptian mother goddess, guardian of the dead Osiris
Neptune	Roman god of the sea; known as Poseidon to the Greeks
Odin	Norse sky-father god and Master of the Runes
Osiris	Egyptian god of vegetation and judge of the dead, brother and husband of Isis; symbolizes regenerative power of nature
Pan	Greek horned god of wild things, half man, half animal
Parvati	Hindu mother goddess, consort of Shiva
Persephne /Kore	Kore, Greek goddess of Spring was abducted by Hades and became Persephone, Queen of the underworld
Raphael	Archangel of the air element, associated with communication and business
Re	Egyptian sun god and creator
Sachiel	Archangel ruling justice and financial matters
Samael	Protective archangel, helps with matters that require courage or perseverance
Sekhmet	Egyptian goddess of destruction and healing, depicted with the head of a lioness
Selene	Greek goddess of the full moon
Shang Ti	Chinese supreme god
Shiva	Hindu creator god whose meditation sustains the world
Shu	Egyptian god of the air, creator of earth and sky

The majestic glory of archangels must be treated with the utmost respect.

Sif	Norse goddess of the grasslands, wife of Thor
Sophia	Greek goddess of divine knowledge and wisdom
Sul	Celtic goddess of healing
Sunna	Norse sun goddess
Surya	Hindu sun god
Tara	Tibetan goddess of wisdom and compassion
Thor	Norse god of thunder and industry, married to Sif
Thoth	Egyptian god of wisdom and the moon, scribe of Osiris
Tiamat	Mesopotamian creator goddess
Tsao-chun	Taoist kitchen god
Uriel	Archangel of high magic
Vesta	Roman goddess of the hearth
Vishnu	Hindu protector of the world
Zeus	Greek supreme god; known as Jupiter to the Romans

Table of the four elements

	Air	Fire	Water	Earth
Direction	East	South	West	North
Season	Spring	Summer	Autumn	Winter
Time of day	Dawn	Noon	Sunrise	Midnight
Moon phase	New	First quarter	Full	Dark
Planets	Sun, Mercury, Uranus	Mars, Pluto	Moon, Neptune, Venus	Earth, Saturn
Astrological signs	Gemini, Libra, Aquarius	Aries, Leo, Sagittarius	Cancer, Scorpio, Pisces	Taurus, Virgo, Capricorn
Magical tool	Dagger, athame, sword	Candles, lanterns, solar icons	Chalice, cauldron, mirror	Pentacle/stone, wand
Altar symbol	Incense	Lamp or candle	Chalice	Platter
Communion symbol	Scent	Heat	Wine/water	Bread/salt
Elemental symbol	▲	▲	▼	▼
Archangel	Raphael	Michael	Gabriel	Uriel
Polarity	Male positive	Male negative	Female negative	Female positive
Human sense	Hearing and smell	Sight	Taste	Touch
Art forms	Poetry/painting	Dance/drama	Music/song	Sculpture/embroidery
Creatures	Birds, bats, winged insects	Lizard, snake, lion, ram	Cat, frog, turtle, dolphin, whale, otter, seal, fish	Ox, dog, wolf, goat, stag
Elemental beings	Sylphs	Salamanders	Undines	Gnomes
Exhortation	To will	To dare	To know	To keep silent
Mythical beast	Winged horse	Dragon, phoenix	Sea serpent	Unicorn
Magical arts	Divinations	Ritual	Healing	Talismans
God forms	Sky/weather god	Sun/protector god	Moon/water goddess	Earth/underworld goddess
Meditation	Sky/clouds	Bonfires	The ocean/rivers	Fertile landscape
Colours	Yellow, blue, violet	Red and orange	Blue, turquoise, green	Russet, brown, black, olive-green, sometimes white
Instruments	Wind instruments/harp	Brass instruments	Strings/bells	Drums/percussion
Natural symbols	Feathers, incense smoke, fragrant flowers	Flame, lava	Shells, water, river plants, watercress	Fossils, stones, grains and seeds, salt, earth
Trees	Elder, eucalyptus	Oak, hawthorn	Willow, alder, ash	Cypress, pine
Herbs	Comfrey, lavender, mint	Basil, bay, garlic, hyssop, juniper, rosemary, rue	Chamomile, hops, lemon balm, orris, seaweeds, yarrow	Pennyroyal, lovage, sage
Incense	Sandalwood, lemon	Frankincense, cinnamon, basil	Jasmine, rose	Myrrh, patchouli
Minerals	Mercury, aventurine, topaz	Brass, gold, iron, fire opal, garnet, haematite, red jasper, sardonyx, flint, pearl, sapphire	Silver, copper, amethyst, aquamarine, turquoise, tourmaline, opal, jade, moonstone	Lead, emerald
Images and Themes	Mountain Tops, flying, sunrise,	Flames, Volcanoes, walking through fire,	Lakes/pools, living under water, setting sun,	Caves/rocks, growing organically, moon/stars/
Wisdom and knowledge	Sun at Noon	Healing and calm	night, Growth and life	

Fire element can be added with heat and flame.

Use smoke in your magic to add the Air element.

A bowl of water will bring the Water element.

Table of planets

Planet	Moon	Mars	Mercury	Jupiter	Venus	Saturn	Sun	Earth
Day	Monday	Tuesday	Wednesday	Thursday	Friday	Saturday	Sunday	Any
Metal	Silver	Iron	Quicksilver	Tin	Copper	Lead	Gold	Any
Colours	White, silver, blue	Red	Yellow	Royal blue, violet, purple	Green	Black	Gold/orange	All, but especially earth shades (browns, russets)
Gemstones	Moonstone. pearl	Garnet, ruby, bloodstone, haematite	Opal, beryl, agate, carnelian	Amethyst, lapis lazuli, aquamarine	Emerald, peridot, jade	Jet, onyx, obsidian	Diamond, amber, topaz	Agate
Number	9	5	8	4	7	3	6	10
Angel	Gabriel	Zamael	Raphael	Sachiel	Anael	Cassiel	Michael	Sandalphon
Deities	Artemis, Luna, Selene	Mars, Samael, Anath	Hermes, Mercury, Athena	Zeus, Jupiter, Juno	Aphrodite, Venus	Cronos, Saturn, Kali	Helios, Sol Apollo, Re	Gaia, Ceres
Trees	Aspen, willow, lemon, eucalyptus	Larch, hawthorn, dogwood	Ash, hazel	Almond, horse chestnut, oak	Apple, fig, magnolia, pear, elder, damson	Alder, beech, holly, elm, yew	Acacia, bay, birch, cedar, walnut, lime, orange, rowan, juniper	All
Plants and herbs	Jasmine, poppy, white lily, all aquatic plants	Anemone, tobacco, coriander, garlic	Impatiens, caraway, lavender, marjoram, dill	Honeysuckle, nutmeg, sage, star anise, cloves	Heather, hyacinth, rose, love-in-a-mist, iris, vervain, myrtle, yarrow	Ivy, evergreens, asafoetida	Mistletoe, marigold, bay laurel, benzoin gum, angelica, cinnamon, bay leaves	All
Incenses	Jasmine, sandalwood	Tobacco, pine	Mastic, lavender	Cedar, honeysuckle	Rose	Myrrh, cypress	Frankincense	Dittany of Crete patchouli
Magic for	Increasing intuition, psychic ability, fertility and all female issues	Improving strength, power and authority; banishing conflicts	All forms of travel and communication, including writing, teaching, speaking, learning, studying	Luck and prosperity; employment opportunities, travel, money, justice and wealth	Love, friendship, marriage, beauty and harmony creativity, artistic endeavours	Clearing obstacles and restrictions; patience	Good fortune in all areas of life; health, success and prosperity	Connecting with the Earth's mysteries, and the underworld

Saturn's influence in magic helps clear obstacles and remove restriction.

Use the moon's influence in magic to increase psychic ability and intuition.

Glossary

Adonai Hebrew name meaning Lord of Light.

Akashic Records Also known as the Book of Lives, a living archive helad on the astral planes, in which details of every life on earth, past, present and future, is detailed.

Altar A focal point for magical activity, symbolizing a gateway to the otherworld.

Amulet An object, often in the shape of an eye, worn to ward off harm.

Anael Angel of the planet Venus.

Angels Divine beings that act as messengers, protectors and guides.

Animism The belief that everything in the natural universe has a soul or vital essence.

Archetype A universal pattern, symbol or figure of primordial origins.

Astral planes the invisible, starry realms that are beyond space and time.

Astral travel Spiritual journeys, often during sleep, when the dreaming self leaves the physical body to visit the astral planes. Sometimes called "out-of-the-body experiences".

Athame (pronounced Ath-a-mey) A ritual dagger used by Wiccans.

Aura The energy patterns around living things, visible to witches and magicians.

Beltane Celtic May Day fertility festival to mark the beginning of summer.

Book of Shadows Originating in the Wiccan tradition, a personal record of spells, poems, rituals and other useful information collected by the magic worker.

Cabbala A form of Hebrew mysticism that uses the symbolism of the Tree of Life as a path to salvation. Also spelt Kabbalah and Qabalah.

Cassiel Angel of the planet Saturn

Ceremonial magician Male or female, of any religious tradition, a ceremonial magician's knowledge is more philosophical and intellectual than it is religious. The different, ancient traditions of the Western Mysteries are important.

Chakra Sanskrit for "wheel", one of seven energy centres running through the body.

Coven A group of 13 or fewer wiccans, led by a High Priestess and High Priest. Derives from the same word as "convent".

Deosil To move in a clockwise direction.

Devas A name for beings of the light.

Discarnate A spirit that does not inhabit a physical body (such as a ghost or angel) and so therefore not belonging to the earthly plane.

Divination The many arts of consulting the "divinity". reading Tarot cards, seeking water or consulting oracles such as the runes or the I Ching.

Dowsing From the old Cornish for "to seek", especially water or buried treasure, using a Y-shaped hazel dowsing wand or a pendulum.

Druid A follower of a spiritual tradition based on veneration of the Earth and nature as a deity.

Elementals Spirit beings associated with the four elements: sylphs (air), salamanders (fire), undines (water), gnomes (earth).

Ephemeris A list of tables of positions of the planets, the Sun and Moon, used by astrologers.

Equinox One of two fixed points of the year, spring and autumn, when day and night are of equal duration.

Esbats Times of lunar celebration.

Ether The invisible fifth "element" of spirit, from which we get the "etheric" body, the subtle or spirit body.

Gabriel (pronounced Gabr-I-el) Archangel of the moon, whose name means "the Strength of God".

Geomancy The study of earth energies.

Goddess The Great Mother and source of all life and its cycles of birth, growth, death and rebirth.

Golden mean This is a ratio between the lengths of the sides of a rectangle which produce regular patterns. It occurs in nature in spiral snail shells and flower petals.

Hall of records The place where the Akashic Records, or Books of Lives, are held.

Hedgewitch Magic worker who practises alone and according to their own style and belief system.

Hermetic mysteries Hermes was the Greek God of wisdom, based on the Egyptian god Thoth, who gave the understanding of magic to humankind.

Higher self Also known as god-self, the spiritual part of you that seeks to align you to your True Will.

Holy or holey stones These are stones, sometimes fossil sponges, which have natural holes right through them. For hundreds oahung by red wool or ribbon to bring luck.

Imbolc Celtic festival marking spring.

Inner plane adepti These are otherworldly teachers: some are discarnate wise people; others are angels.

Invocation Used at the beginning of magic work to call upon the aid of spirits, angels and other spiritual beings.

Journeying The ability to visit the otherworld through an altered state of awareness.

Karma A Sanskrit word for fate or balance. Every action accrues spiritual profit or loss, and through a series of reincarnated lives, the balance must be worked out.

Kokab Hebrew name for sphere of Mercury

Lammas Celtic festival of the harvest.

Levanah Hebrew name for the moon.

Lodge A group of magicians meet in a lodge, as do Freemasons. It is a term used for both the building or temple and the group itself.

Mabon In Welsh this means "son" or "boy" and is another name for the divine child born at midwinter.

Madim Hebrew name for the planet Mars.

Magic circle A sacred space "between the worlds" used in magic work.
Mantra Repetition of a sacred sound to induce an altered state of consciousness.
Medicine wheel Originating in the native American tradition, a framework for understanding and experiencing life based on the four compass directions and their symbolic correspondences.
Medicines Another word for spells where natural magic is used to attract, repel, maintain or balance energies.
Michael (pronounced Mik-I-el) Archangel of the sun, the leading angel, whose name means "Like unto God".
Mote Old English word meaning "may" or "might".
Mysteries Occult or secret knowledge that can only be gained through experience; novices are usually initiated into a particular mystery path, such as the Western Mysteries.
Nogah Hebrew name for the planet Venus.
Och Healing spirit of the sun
Otherworld The invisible spiritual world accessed by workers of magic.
Pagan One who follows a spiritual tradition that venerates the power of the Mother Goddess and the natural world.
Pentacle A five-sided shape (*penta* is Greek for five); as opposed to a pentagram, which has five points.
Psychometry To sense by touch the history of an object or information about its owner.
Raphael (pronounced Raph-I-el) Archangel of the planet Mercury, whose name means "Healer of God".
Rite of Abramelin This is a six-month-long magical retreat aimed at establishing communication with a Holy Guardian Angel.

Ritual An activity following certain set procedures designed to focus attention on the otherworld.
Sabbat Derived from "Sabbath", the holy day of the week, these are the eight important seasonal festivals of the wiccans.
Sachiel Angel of the planet Jupiter
Samhain Celtic festival, also known as Halloween.
Scry Derived from the French *descrier*, to proclaim, scrying means divining by crystal-gazing. A scrying glass is a crystal ball, or other reflective surface such as a mirror or pool of water.
Shabbathai Hebrew name for the planet Saturn.
Shaman Through trance, drumming and using herbs, one who shape-shifts and journeys to the otherworld ; most types of magic have their roots in some kind of shamanic tradition.
Shemesh Hebrew name for the sun.
Sidereal Star time, used by many astrologers as the time frame from which they calculate the positions of the planets and stars in a horoscope. It differs slightly from "clock" time.
Sigil A pictorial depiction of a name.
Smudging Cleansing, using the smoke of burning herbs, especially sage.
Solstice One of two fixed points of the year, marking midwinter and midsummer, when the sun's power is at its weakest and strongest respectively.
Talisman An object which draws on the power of astrology, often using archaic writing, to bring about a single specific purpose.
Telepathy The ability to communicate thought-forms using other than the known senses.
Thought-forms Subtle vibrational patterns produced by the mind that make up an atmosphere.
Totem A symbol or emblem adopted by a magic worker as an ally or helper.
Tree of Life A diagram consisting of 10 spheres connected by 22 paths showing the spiritual evolution of creation. It is central to the Cabbala and is used by many western magicians as a kind of road map, showing where planetary or angelic powers may be located.
True Will Your divine purpose, the reason you are here on earth; when you are aligned with your True Will, your magic will be much more effective.

Tzedek Hebrew name for the planet Jupiter.
Underworld The hidden or occult realm through which all souls must journey on their passage into death and rebirth.
Upperworld The heavenly realm; associated with the higher self and spiritual transformation.
Uriel (pronounced Ur-I-el) Archangel of the north and Earth, whose name means "Light of God".
Waning The moon's decrease in influence.
Waxing The moon's increase in influence.
Wicca A modern form of witchcraft that venerates nature, based on the teachings of Gerald Gardener. Wiccans are initiated into a coven, where they are led in their seasonal rituals by a High Priestess and High Priest.
Widdershins To move anti-clockwise (counter-clockwise).
Witch A person, male or female, who uses the powers of Nature to work magic for healing or guidance. Witches may use ritual and celebrate the passing seasons but they are not necessarily pagans.
Wyrd An Anglo-Saxon term for the magical web of life, where everything in the universe is believed to be interconnected along fine energy pathways. This belief is at the heart of natural magic.
Yule A pagan festival to celebrate the rebirth of the sun at the midwinter solstice. The word "yule" is derived from an old Norse word, written "Jul", meaning "wheel". The festival lasts for 12 days and nights and is accompanied by feasting, and the enactment of ritual.
Zamael Archangel of the planet Mars.
Zen A Buddhist tradition based on the idea that spiritual perfection (nirvana) is attained when all is reduced to nothing.

Index

Acknowledgements

The Publisher would like to thank the following picture libraries for the use of their images:
The Bridgeman Art Library pp: 14 top *Medicine Man with Sling and Medicine Bow*, engraving, American School (19th century); 14 bottom *Book of the Dead of the Scribe Ani*, papyrus; 15 *A Brahmin* by Bernard Picart; 16 top *Mystical conversation between Sufic sheikhs*, Indian School, 17th century; 16 bottom *A Pilgrim's encounter with the messenger of Necromancy*; 18 *Sir Galahad* by George Frederick Watts; 19 *Demeter Mourning for Persephone* by Evelyn de Morgan; 20 top *A Zulu Witchdoctor* English School, 20th century; 20 bottom *Medicine man*, photograph c1915; 21 *The Magic Circle* by John Waterhouse; 28 top *Lilith* by John Collier; 29 *Pan and Psyche* by Sir Edward Burne-Jones; 30 *Why Seek Ye the Living?* by Howard Pyle; 31 *Dancing Fairies* by Richard Doyle; 28 bottom *Diana and her Hand Maidens* by Fernand le Quesne; 108 *The Achievement by Sir Galahad* by Sir Edward Burne-Jones; 234 top *Odin* by Sir Edward Burne-Jones; 234 bottom *Ramesses IV* by Jean Francois Campollion; 235 *The Angel Gabriel* by Sir Edward Burne-Jones.

Corbis: p17.

The Fortean Picture Library: pp 18 top; 22; 23.

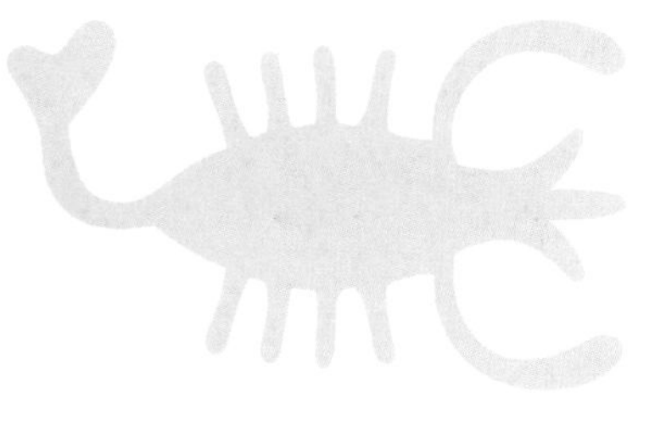

This edition is published by Hermes House

Hermes House is an imprint of Anness Publishing Ltd
Hermes House, 88–89 Blackfriars Road, London SE1 8HA
tel. 020 7401 2077; fax 020 7633 9499; info@anness.com

A CIP catalogue record for this book is available from the British Library.

Publisher: Joanna Lorenz
Editorial Director: Helen Sudell
Executive Editor: Joanne Rippin
Photographs: Michelle Garrett, Don Last, John Freeman
Designer: Anthony Cohen
Production Manager: Steve Lang
Editorial Reader: Penelope Goodare

Printed in China

1 3 5 7 9 10 8 6 4 2